Go Quickly and Tell

Go Quickly and Tell

RADIO MESSAGES FOR THE SECOND PART
OF THE FIFTEENTH LUTHERAN HOUR

By

Walter A. Maier, Ph. D., D. D., LL. D.
PROFESSOR OF OLD TESTAMENT INTERPRETATION
AND HISTORY, CONCORDIA THEOLOGICAL SEMINARY,
SAINT LOUIS, MISSOURI

CONCORDIA PUBLISHING HOUSE
Saint Louis, Missouri

Copyright 1950 by
Concordia Publishing House
Saint Louis, Missouri

MANUFACTURED IN
THE UNITED STATES OF AMERICA

To

OUR FRIENDS IN THE CLERGY AND LAITY
OF WESTERN NEW YORK STATE

"Ye also helping together by prayer for us, that for the gift bestowed upon us by the means of many persons thanks may be given by many on our behalf."
    II CORINTHIANS 1:11

FOREWORD

BY the uninterrupted progress with which our almighty God has blessed Bringing Christ to the Nations, the fifteenth season of our mission of the air has reached a new high level in all measurable aspects, particularly in the size of the broadcast, its reach, the response, and the measurable results. So that there will be no misunderstanding, we begin by giving God all glory and acknowledging His goodness as it has blessed every aspect of the broadcast. The Lutheran Hour truly is a miracle of modern missions, because from its very beginning it has been led by the Holy Spirit's guidance and accompanied by His enlightenment and indwelling. No one should read the remarkable record of the fifteenth season without praising the true and Triune God, from whom every blessing in this radio mission has come. It is with humble recognition of the Almighty that we present the foreword. A recent reviewer suggested that this preface might be omitted, since, he felt, everybody knows the remarkable spread of the broadcast. How we wish this were true! Few people in our country, outside the official Lutheran Hour family, have a true picture of the broadcast's reach and blessing. These pages are the only means we have at present for reporting the progress of our work, and we know from many letters that they are welcomed by readers at home and abroad.

The present volume, the twentieth presentation of Lutheran Hour messages, covers the second part of the fifteenth season (from February to May, 1948). During this period, letters came to us at our Saint Louis headquarters and at our branch offices from these more than one hundred different countries and territories (the asterisk indicating countries with stations broadcasting Bringing Christ to the Nations):

Admiralty Islands	Fiji Islands*	New Zealand
Alaska*	Finland	Nicaragua*
Algeria	France*	Nigeria
Angola*	Germany	Northern Rhodesia
Argentina*	Gibraltar	Norway
Austria*	Gold Coast of Africa	Nova Scotia
Australia*	Greece*	Orange Free State
Bahama Islands	Guatemala*	Palestine
Basutoland	Haiti*	Panama*
Bechuanaland	Hawaii*	Paraguay*
Belgian Congo*	Holland	Peru*
Belgium	Honduras*	Philippine Islands*
Bermuda*	Hungary	Poland
Bolivia*	Iceland	Portugal
Brazil*	India	Portuguese China*
British East Africa	Ireland	Puerto Rico*
British Guiana*	Italy	Scotland
British Honduras	Jamaica	Solomon Islands
British West Indies*	Japan	Southern Rhodesia
Canada*	Java	South West Africa
China*	Luxembourg*	Spanish Morocco*
Chile*	Madagascar*	Sweden
Colombia*	Malaya	Switzerland
Costa Rica*	Marshall Islands	Tanganyika
Cuba*	Martinique*	Tangiers*
Curacao	Mauritius Island	Tasmania*
Czechoslovakia	Mexico*	Transvaal
Denmark	Monaco*	Union of South Africa
Dominic. Republic*	Morocco	United States*
Dutch Guiana *	Mozambique*	Uruguay*
Ecuador*	Natal	Venezuela*
England	Netherlands	Virgin Islands
El Salvador*	Newfoundland	Wales
Ethiopia*	New Guinea	Yugoslavia

We do well to review some of the highlights of the fifteenth Lutheran Hour season.

To do so is to pay a tribute of overwhelming thanks to our almighty God, Giver of every good and perfect gift, and to our beautiful Savior, to whom each Lutheran Hour broad-

Foreward IX

cast is dedicated. To our Triune God, Father, Son, and Spirit, be all honor and glory!

1. During this fiscal year the Lutheran Hour received in financial support approximately $1,250,000.

2. During the fifteenth Lutheran Hour season we were privileged to add four new languages to our broadcasting schedule: Slovak and Polish, Chinese and Italian. Slovak programs are prepared in co-operation with the Slovak Lutheran Church by the Reverend J. J. Pelikan, Sr., of Chicago. Polish programs are prepared through the co-operation of the Reverend Emil Mach.

3. During the fifteenth Lutheran Hour season we established two new offices: for Africa in Johannesburg, South Africa; and for Central America in Guatemala City, Guatemala. To the managers of these two branch offices, Mr. G. J. McHarry and the Reverend Robert Gussick, we owe a vote of deep appreciation.

4. During the fifteenth Lutheran Hour season we added the following nine countries to our broadcasting schedule: Austria, Bermuda, Ethiopia, Greece, Luxembourg, Madagascar, Martinique, Portuguese China, and Spanish Morocco.

5. During the fifteenth Lutheran Hour season we added a total of 117 stations to our system.

6. During the fifteenth Lutheran Hour season our radio mission entered the field of television, as our first television programs went out over the air on New Year's Day and on Good Friday.

7. The fifteenth Lutheran Hour season made notable advances in the field of international short wave. Station KJE8 beamed the Gospel to the Far East, while WIUL-WRUW-WRUX reach Europe and Africa. We also experimented with more comprehensive short-wave broadcasting by means of high-power transmitters located in Manila, the Philippines.

8. The fifteenth Lutheran Hour season recorded notable advances in European broadcasting, using Radio Luxembourg, Radio Monte Carlo, Radio Dornbirn, Radio Innsbruck,

Radio Graz, and Radio Klagenfurt. In many ways Europe still holds a tremendous future for the work of our program.

9. The fifteenth Lutheran Hour, by God's grace, made forward strides in the Far East, in areas that were closed to us during the war. We broadcast over seven stations in the Philippines, as well as outlets in Shanghai, Chungking, Kunming, Hankow, Nanking, and Peiping, China.

10. The fifteenth Lutheran Hour season inaugurated the Lutheran Hour Bible Correspondence Course. This promises to become a mighty adjunct to the work of our radio mission. In the brief span of nine months after it was inaugurated, a total of 30,000 enrolled in this course of Christian instructions in the fundamentals of our faith.

11. The program of Lutheran Hour Easter Seals was introduced to offer another medium for Lutheran Hour support.

With God's continued blessing the Lutheran Hour will continue to march forward for Christ, to the glory of His name and the salvation of many preciously bought souls.

The fifteenth Lutheran Hour brought about 410,000 letters to our headquarters and branch offices. In Saint Louis a staff of almost a hundred workers, excluding many part-time helpers, assisted in answering this vast flow of mail.

We praise God especially that this miraculous increase was accompanied by inner blessings. Twenty-six centuries after Isaiah wrote God's promises by inspiration of the Holy Ghost, God's testimony to His own Word is still true: *"It shall accomplish that which I please, and it shall prosper in the thing whereto I sent it."*

CONTENTS

	PAGE
AMERICA, PRAY AS NEVER BEFORE!	1
Daniel 10:12	
THE GLORY LOOK	22
Saint Luke 9:28-36	
CHRIST, KEEP US FROM MONEY-MADNESS	43
Saint John 12:1-8	
IT IS GOD IN THE GARDEN	62
Saint John 18:4-9	
CHRIST — OR CRIME?	83
Saint Matthew 27:15-18, 20-22	
RENOUNCE SIN, RECEIVE THE SAVIOR!	103
Saint Luke 23:8-11	
PARDON FOR YOU AT THE CROSS	123
Saint Luke 23:39-43	
DARK DEATH AT CALVARY	144
Saint Luke 23:44-46	
DON'T FEAR DEATH! CHRIST LIVES!	165
Romans 6:5	

	PAGE
GOD SAYS, "HURRY!"	186
Saint Luke 24:12	
CHRIST, SET OUR HEARTS ON FIRE!	206
Saint Luke 24:32	
HEAVEN'S HAMMER AND SICKLE	227
Jeremiah 23:29; Revelation 14:16	
SEEK THE SAVIOR NOW!	250
Isaiah 55:6-7	
JESUS NEVER LEAVES US	272
Saint Luke 24:50-53	
CHRIST FOR UNHAPPY HOMES	293
1 Samuel 25:3, 32-33	
PENTECOST POWER FOR YOU	316
Acts 2:38-39	
GOD, TRUE AND TRIUNE	337
Saint Matthew 3:16-17	
CHRIST'S PEACE FOR YOU!	357
Saint John 14:27	
AIR-WAVE TESTIMONY	380

AMERICA, PRAY AS NEVER BEFORE!

"Fear not, Daniel; for from the first day that thou didst set thine heart to understand, and to chasten thyself before thy God, thy words were heard, and I am come for thy words."
                                         DANIEL 10:12

LOVING FATHER: At the beginning of a new month we praise Thee across this wide land and even beyond its borders for the mercy which did not cast us off in our transgressions, but sent Thy dear stainless Son, Jesus Christ, to become sin for us and by suffering the agony and death which were rightly ours, free us from the doom of hell. Endless thanks be to Jesus for His free, full, and finished salvation! Make this Gospel grace the dominant force in our lives, and let the imprint of Thy love on our souls lead us ever more frequently and faithfully to use the privilege and power of prayer! "Lord, teach us to pray," we say with the disciples, as we confess that too often we know not what we beg and even more frequently we have not because we ask not. Bring America down on its knees in repentance and true supplication! Send Thy Spirit to break our pride and fold our hands in humble petition to Thy grace! Guide the poor, the sick, the lowly, the hungry, the bereaved, the imprisoned, the heartbroken to carry all their sorrows to Jesus, to lay them and leave them at the foot of His cross! Lord, make us pray, pray humbly, pray trustfully, pray contritely, pray submissively, pray in Jesus' name! *Amen!*

JUST one hundred years ago this month Karl Marx wrote his *Communist Manifesto*, which was to become one of the most important documents in modern history. While Marx hated the Church and directly urged its destruction, claiming in his oft-repeated slander, "Religion is the opiate of the people," the narcotic which puts them to sleep, unaware of their misery, during the past century his followers far outstripped their master in attacking Christ's Gospel. Thus Nikolai Lenin cries out, "Religion is a clumsy sort of spiritual whisky." Again: "We must fight religion; that is the ABC of all materialism and consequently of Marxism." Once more: "A Marxist must be a materialist, that is to say, an enemy of religion!" Lenin's widow issues this even more sweeping call to battle: "The very root of religion must be . . . completely extracted." Listen to these threats by present-day disciples of Marx, announcing their determination to destroy Christianity: "All our cultural institutions from the school to the theater, from the Academy of Science to the village reading room must be considered by us . . . as means for curing the masses of this evil disease," religion. "Every idea of God . . . is the vilest infection." "All religions are one and the same poison, intoxicating and deadening the mind, the will, and the conscience; a fight to the death must be declared against them. Our task is not to reform, but to destroy all kinds of religion!"

Not only has the Communist hatred of the Church grown more intense in these one hundred years; it has also spread far beyond its first European confines. If you think that this assault on the faith is too far distant to concern us in America, let me read from a handbill circulated in Detroit — and I quote this from *The Congressional Record* — "Vote for Comrade ———! He has come out definitely against the Church, which has kept the people in darkness and ignorance for 1900 years. His slogan is, Close the churches. . . . Down with religion. . . . There is no God."

As shocking as has been the advance of Red atheism in the century since Marx issued his *Manifesto*, no reasonable doubt remains that for the future this fight against the faith will be even more fearful. The Bible warns that, as a sign of the approaching world end, unbelief, bold and blasphemous, will oppress believers on a wider scale than ever before. Thank God, however, Scripture also gives every follower of the Savior the means by which he can overcome all satanic enemies and put their boasting threats to naught. You, too, have a divine, unfailing source of power, guidance, protection, for every adversity in your own life. That supply of assured strength is provided in the treasure of prayer. As I call out today

AMERICA, PRAY AS NEVER BEFORE!

may the Holy Spirit teach you the nature and blessing of true petition from the lesson of our text (Daniel, chapter ten, verse twelve): *"Fear not, Daniel; for from the first day that thou didst set thine heart to understand, and to chasten thyself before thy God, thy words were heard, and I am come for thy words."*

I

PRAY FERVENTLY, AS DANIEL DID!

A great calamity had come upon God's people because they had forgotten the Lord. Jerusalem was destroyed, Judah laid waste, Israel's artisans and leaders brought into cruel Babylonian captivity. Those were barbaric times, you say, 2,400 years ago, when cities were devastated with such savagery and their people sent into exile. However, in our own civilized, cultured age the last war brought far heavier atrocities than Nebuchadnezzar's campaign against Jerusalem. In that conflict 18,000 civilians were taken from their homes and transplanted into a strange, pagan land; but in our last war far more than eighty times 18,000 were uprooted and deported to distant banishment. Even today, and the International Red Cross has again protested against this wholesale violation of International Law, millions of war prisoners, almost three years after the European struggle is over, are still kept in slavery, far from their families.

While God's people groaned in Babylonian slavery, the Lord had chosen for them a leader, a guide, a comforter — Daniel, one of the most challenging figures in the Old Testament. We note at the outset that Daniel was not a member of the clergy, but a layman. The New Testament calls him a "Prophet." We see, then, that laymen, too, can be and should be God's spokesmen. Our Christian creed asks that everyone, pastor or church member, who knows the record of the Redeemer's love, His sin-removing death, His life-giving resurrection, should personally proclaim this grace. Twentieth-century churches have not grown with the astonishing forward march which blessed the first century, although the first followers of our Lord were poor and persecuted, while today they have often become rich and enjoy powerful means for spreading the Gospel. In that early age every convert became a missionary; and with no theological seminaries and no sacred edifices, believers during those Apostolic days won victories for the Savior greater than this age has seen. The Holy Spirit put Daniel's undaunted devotion into your hearts and make you messengers of Heaven's mercy! What miracles the churches of Christ could record if their laity were all loyally active for the Lord! Men and women of God, how can you remain idle when you know that the world cannot be saved without Jesus and when you see His enemies working overtime to wipe out His Church?

Again, Daniel was of royal blood, a prince whose very name (Daniel means "God is my Judge") showed the faith he lived. A supreme need in human affairs today is governmental officials who love the Lord and walk in His ways. Most of our world is not led by faithful followers of the Savior. Therefore let America safeguard its Christian heritage! When our Continental Congress held its first session in Carpenter Hall, Philadelphia, 174 years ago, it began with prayer. Doctor Jacob Duche opened the meeting with a petition which started, "O Lord, our heavenly Father, high and mighty King of Kings, Lord of Lords . . . look down, we beseech Thee, upon those American states who have fled to Thee from the rod of the oppressor . . . to be henceforth dependent only upon Thee!" He continued to pray for peace and asked that "truth and justice, that religion and piety, prevail and flourish"; and he concluded, petitioning for the members of the first Continental Congress: "Preserve the health of their bodies . . . and crown them with everlasting glory in the world to come. All this we ask in the name and through the merits of Jesus Christ, Thy Son, our Savior. Amen." The task of creating a free America began with prayer in the name of our blessed Redeemer. If we maintain that trust in the Lord of love, we can steer a clear and and confident course for the future; but if we, misguided by our prosperity, become too proud to acknowledge Him, we will finally find ourselves too weak to avert disaster. This is the warning of the Almighty Himself: *"It shall be, if thou do at all forget the Lord thy God, and walk after other gods, and serve them, and worship them, I testify against you this day that ye shall surely perish."* The Holy Spirit give us God-fearing pilots at the helm of our ship of state and God-fearing citizens who will pray down guidance upon our leaders!

There were times in exiled Daniel's life when he was fearful for his people's fate, and our text is taken from a chapter which thus reveals a disquieted, distressed Prophet. What would become of his nation, its cities ruined and its independence gone, all because of unbelief and repeated uprising against God? What, he asked himself, would happen to those who clung to the faith of the fathers? Would they be crushed to pieces by mighty world powers? Would the Lord forget His people and let them perish in pagan lands?

Millions know the distress which shook Daniel's soul, for our age suffers from the same sins which punished Israel. We are told that the Almighty *"sent to them [Daniel's countrymen] His messengers . . . because He had compassion on His people . . . but they mocked the messengers of God, and despised His words, and misused His prophets, until the wrath of the Lord arose against His people, till there was no remedy."* Multitudes today, similarly sure that there is no remedy, are fiercely gripped by fear. Atomic scientists have been afraid of their own invention; some of them pleaded officially that their bombs should not be dropped on inhabited towns. Bacteriologists are terrorized by their own discoveries, because at their last international congress in Denmark they officially begged the governments never to sanction bombardment with germs. They know, as one of our congressmen declared, that there is a "secret biological warfare far more devastating than atomic bombs," and that this can "wipe out all forms of life in a large city." The common people all over the earth are horrified because many have seen millions of homes blasted to rubble and masses crazed by hunger. As I first rode through Berlin and saw house after house, block after block, district after district, in scarred ruins, with only the gaunt walls of gutted buildings still standing, I exclaimed, "What if this were Saint Louis, Chicago, Los Angeles, New York!" When we read that of 701 churches in London the Nazi raids left only 77 which were not wholly or partially destroyed, must we not ask, "Can this happen in Washington, Boston, Philadelphia, San Francisco?" Anyone who says that it cannot, is blind to fact.

Now what did Daniel do when gripped by this fear for his people and himself? Did he begin secretely to drill underground troops near the Tigris River marshes? No, he knew of a power stronger than military might. Did he send disguised messengers to the courts of neighboring heathen kings, asking their support? No, he remembered the rebuke of God's Word, *"Shouldest thou help the ungodly and love them that hate the Lord?"* Did he surrender to despair? No, he knelt in prayer and, although he was a man of frequent and earnest petitions to the Almighty, the verses preceding our text indicate that he besought the Lord as never before. For *"three full weeks"* he pleaded. During these twenty-one days, a period of soul lament, he pushed fancy food aside; he refused to drink wine; he neglected to anoint himself, paid no attention to his personal appearance, and secluded himself from public life.

We, too, will do well to follow Daniel in prayerful devotion to the Lord. Over a world threatened with heavier dangers than we have yet known, his example pleads with us: Pray, America! Pray as never before! Indeed, we can learn necessary lessons from Daniel's communion with the Lord, mentioned at least a dozen times in his short book. From these passages we see first that this mighty man of God humbled himself when he prayed. He was not ashamed to drop on his knees, even to fall on his face before the Almighty. There were years, too, when in many American homes the family took time at least once a day to bow before the heavenly Father as they united in household worship; but today kneeling is neglected. In a sense of pride which overlays much of the United States, people say: "We have never been defeated in war." "We have the greatest gold reserves in the world." "We have the best territory of all nations." "We have the most food, the finest homes, the costliest luxuries." These are blessings, and they all come from the Giver of *"every good gift and every perfect gift";* yet in misdirected self-applause many forget the Lord and think that they gave these pre-eminences to themselves. Therefore fewer people humble themselves before the Most High, and fewer homes kneel to implore His grace.

More than mere outward humility, however, prompted Daniel's prayer. He came before the Lord, as you and I should, a poor, helpless sinner. Instead of boasting, as the Pharisee did, that he was better than other men, the Prophet joined the publican, in effect pleading, *"God, be merciful to me a sinner!"* In the chapter before our text Daniel reveals, *"I was speaking and praying and confessing my sin and the sin of my people."* We, too, must learn this penitent pleading. God promises to forgive our transgressions and heal our land when we humble ourselves and approach His throne, not insolently demanding an answer, but repentantly deploring our unworthiness. Your petitions will never be granted unless they come from a contrite, sin-confessing heart.

Note also that Daniel did not make the mistake of praying only once and then, because the Almighty was not pleased to reply when and where he insisted, contemptuously casting communion with God aside! For three weeks he asked Heaven's guidance! Have you ever pleaded with the Lord that long? Too many people make prayer a "try-it-once-and-see-what-happens" experiment, whereas the New Testament, directing, *"Pray without ceasing,"* lays before us the duty of continuing with the Lord until He grants our requests.

Daniel prayed at all times, not only in hours of peril. His enemies noted that he fell on his knees three times a day, busy as he was; and even in his prosperity, after Nebuchadnezzar had made him one of the country's three presidents, he still took time to thank the Sovereign of his soul. Most people reserve prayer for moments of danger. What did the fifty-three passengers in the DC-4 airliner do when that plane turned upside down 8,000 feet above the earth? An official reports, "Everybody prayed fervently." When "The Bermuda Sky Queen" came down on the mid-Atlantic and for a while it seemed that all on board might find a watery grave, what did they do? A member of this radio audience who was on that ill-fated air transport wrote us, "They all prayed." In a recent railroad crash in Missouri, when a second section, running past red lights, rammed into the first, what did the victims pinned beneath the wreck do? Bystanders tell us that they kept on praying for help. Thank God for this privilege of enlisting His aid in accident and emergency, but do not insult the Almighty by reserving your request only for sudden danger! The Scriptural ideal is, *"Praying always with all prayer."*

Nor should you make the mistake of thinking that you can draw near the Lord only in churches. Rather learn from Daniel that you can raise your petitions wherever you are! He was 600 miles away from the ruins of the Temple where he had eagerly communed with his Creator; but in our text we find him bowed down on a river bank. Of course, you want to approach your heavenly Father both in His house, the church, and in your house, dedicated to Him; but learn to speak reverently with Him on your way to and from work, in employment and at leisure, with friends and alone! Take a walk on these bright winter days, and as you find yourself surrounded by uncounted miracles of His might, open your soul to the joy of praising the Almighty!

The Holy Spirit also help us be prayer-heroes as Daniel was! His personal enemies made Nebuchadnezzar issue an edict which would prevent the Prophet from petitioning the Most High; but with the courage you and I need he refused to stop. In full sight of his foes he knelt down at the open window so that all could see his loyalty to the Lord. This almost cost him his life; and it may cost you more than some of you are ready to pay to be known as one who prays. Do not drop your supplication because you think that this may be displeasing to men! It is said of Henry Clay that one night after he had sought refuge in a Kentucky home, the father of that family planned to omit the evening worship, thinking that this might displease his visitor; but when Clay learned of it, he showed the father his mistake and grate-

America, Pray as Never Before! 11

fully took part in the devotional exercise. Last Easter, in the Russian zone of Germany, authorities prohibited Lutheran pastors from using a prayer written especially for that glad festival. May the Almighty prevent anything like this in the United States; yet if this should occur, God give us men who will dare to be a Daniel and pray their own prayers!

Learn from the Prophet also that we must plead for others! Almost every time we read of Daniel's intercessions we note that he appeals also for his people. The Holy Spirit help us overcome selfishness in supplication! How the numberless needs of others plead for our petitions! Passing a hospital, you can ask Heaven to bless the patients and the doctors. Whenever you see a school, beg the Lord to guide the children! If your way takes you past a church, humbly beseech the sacred Enlightener that the Gospel of grace may there be preached and souls won for their Savior! As you ride past a penitentiary, intercede for the prisoners, requesting that they be brought to repentance and faith! At dinner, besides thanking the divine Provider for His gifts, raise your voice in behalf of the hungry and starving! Enjoying the warmth and comfort of your home, speak to the Lord for the deserted and shelterless! When you cash your pay check, mingle your praise with a petition to the Almighty for the poor and the destitute throughout the world! Can you imagine the bountiful blessings which would rain down from heaven on suffering, sorrowing mankind if those who know Christ would regularly approach Him in the interest of their fellow men? Pray for the President, the Congress, and those in authority! Pray for the peace and prosperity of our country and all nations! Pray, as Jesus did, even for enemies!

•

In Babylon Daniel saw men prostrate themselves before hundreds of idols. He beheld costly sacrifices made to Marduk, Ramman, Ishtar, and other false gods. None of that for him! He knew the one, true, and only God, and without condition or compromise he directed his prayers to Him. Today, however, many people think of God as unknown and unknowable. They call Him a mysterious, a secret Spirit and address Him, "Whoever and whatever Thou art," although the Lord has told us who He is and has clearly revealed Himself in His Word. When you pray, be sure that you address your petitions to the Triune God of the Bible! Otherwise, no matter how eloquent and emphatic you may be, your requests are as hopeless as those of India's heathen, who throw little mud balls at their idol and think that if they stick to the statue, their plea is heard.

According to our text, Daniel chastened himself before the Almighty! He did not try to dictate to the Lord at what time or place and in what manner his requests should be granted. He put himself under divine direction and prayed, as you and I should, *"Thy will be done."* God's way is always best. You may not understand this when long-cherished plans and hopes collapse before your eyes; but once the Holy Spirit leads you to give Jesus mastery over your life, your whole existence becomes part of a perfect pattern, in which the dark threads of sorrow and the bright texture of joy are woven together into a heavenly design which proves that *"all things work together for good to them that love God!"*

The last prayer lesson we learn from Daniel's devotional hours is first in importance. He was an Old Testament Prophet, but He foresaw Christ and proclaimed Him as *"the Son of Man,"* with His marvelous New Tes-

America, Pray as Never Before! 13

tament power and reign. Daniel believed in Jesus, the divine Deliverer, and his prayers bespoke that faith. In these crisis years we must realize that not every petition has the promise of answer, but only those spoken in faith focused on God's Son. If 500 years before Christ, Daniel pleaded with trust in his triumphant Redeemer, certainly we, who know more about Jesus from fulfilled Gospel records than this ancient Prophet could, should speak our prayers in the Savior's name. When you hear His pledges: *"Hitherto have ye asked nothing in My name; ask, and ye shall receive"; "If ye abide in Me, and My words abide in you, ye shall ask what ye will, and it shall be done unto you"; "Whatsoever ye shall ask in My name, that will I do,"* know that if your requests are to find acceptance, they must spring from a true faith in the divine Deliverer.

To find the fullness of this grace and promise, you must understand that none of us in ourselves has any right or reason to expect the Almighty and All-Holy One to hear our prayers. It is hard enough for loyal supporters to have a few moments with the busy President of the United States, and even harder to gain audience with one of the world's remaining monarchs. How, then, can we, who by thoughts, speech, and action have opposed the Lord of Lords, expect Him to grant our requests? Why should the Everlasting and All-Powerful bother with us who are mere clay and ashes? Yet in His endless, deathless love our heavenly Father planned a perfect way by which our appeals can come before Him. Because of our unforgiven sins we should be barred forever from His blessings. If our entreaties are to find acceptance, our transgressions must be wiped out. In only one way, a hard, costly way even for the Almighty, could our iniquities thus be removed and we be restored to His love. The Lord is too holy simply to overlook and forget our violations of His Law. Their punishment had to be paid, their charges canceled, their sentence served, their guilt taken away. Who could perform this superhuman, super-angelic task? None other than Jesus Christ, God's Son Himself! He alone could suffer in my stead and yours the penalty of the evil to which we must plead an unconditional "Guilty"; and, thank Heaven! He alone — and now we stand before the most magnificent of divine mercy — reconciled the willful, wicked world to His Father, when, nailed to Calvary's cross as the one, all-sufficient Atonement for the entire race of rebellious men, Jesus suffered and died, your Substitute and mine, as *"the Lamb of God, that taketh away the sin of the world."*

To make you absolutely sure that this saving grace is for you, I emphasize with the Spirit's help that the Bible does not proclaim, nor do we preach, merely a possible salvation, the hope that God sometime in the future may be reconciled to men; not a partisan salvation which holds that Christ died only for a few; not a partial salvation which claims that the Lord Jesus brought you some of the way closer to His Father and that you must bring yourselves the rest of the way; not a "perhaps" salvation which says that you may be saved but you can never be sure. Opposing all this, crystal-clear, unbreakable Scripture assures you of a complete redemption, with pardon offered every penitent sinner, even for crimson crimes, and with everything the holy God can demand for your deliverance fully paid by the blood which His Son shed for you.

Let me tell it to you again: No matter who you are

and what you are, Jesus died for you in full payment of the punishment for your guilt. Deny this, and you tear up the certificate of complete pardon and the promise of Paradise which the Almighty offers you. Believe it, bow in faith before Christ, confess your sins, trust His bleeding love, His reconciling death and you, who were a child of wrath, become a son of God, a joint heir of heaven. Thus preciously redeemed, you can bring before your heavenly Father, as children confidently approach their earthly parent, every need of soul and body, assured that because He loved you with the incomparable devotion which *"spared not His own Son, but delivered Him up for us all,"* He will hear your requests and answer them according to His might and mercy.

Here, then, is the Christ-charged prayer which our beloved country and each of us in the United States need with double necessity in these dangerous days. It may take worse and far wider opposition to the Church, the collapse of artificial prosperity, even organized persecution, to bring America on its knees in repentant reconsecrating prayer. For some of you sudden reverses, shocking sorrows, heavy assaults on your pride may have to precede your humbling yourselves before the Almighty. Yet, O renewing Spirit, give us whatever it takes to make this nation and its millions bow before Thee and in the Savior's name to pray as never before!

II

PRAY EFFECTIVELY, AS DANIEL DID!

When you thus follow Daniel's prayer in fervent faith, you will also plead effectively and receive Heaven's answer, as he did. Burdened for his people and himself, he had asked the Lord for an understanding of the future, and God not only replied, but with the love which leads Him to give His children more than they ask, also sent a divine messenger with personal reassurance. We, too, often request a mite, yet our Father enriches us with much. We request the iron and slag of the commonplace; mercifully He grants us the gold and silver of His mercy. We seek temporal blessings, and lo! His love provides eternal benedictions.

See how mightily the angel helped the terror-stricken Prophet! *"Fear not, Daniel!"* he begins, and continues, *"I am come for thy words,"* that is, "in answer to thy prayer." For twenty-one days Daniel had mournfully knelt before the Lord, and finally here comes the reassuring reply, *"Fear not."* Whatever the sorrows similarly besieging your heart may be, they, too, can be banished by the Almighty's answer to your prayer. Some of you are troubled because in this day of inflation, of a-dollar-a-pound butter, twenty-four-cents-a-quart milk, you cannot make ends meet. "Take it to the Lord in prayer!" In the biography of Dr. Henry Allan Ironside we read that once in Toronto his widowed mother had absolutely no food in the house, and that when her two boys came to the breakfast table, all she could offer them was water. Nevertheless, the mother insisted, "We will give thanks, boys," and she prayed, "Father, Thou hast promised in Thy Word, *'Bread shall be given him, his waters shall be sure.'* We have the water, and we thank Thee for it, and now we trust Thee for the bread or that which will take its place." Hardly had she finished, when the doorbell rang. There on the steps stood a man with a large bag. "Mrs. Ironside," he explained, "I feel very bad. We have been owing you for months for that dress you made for my wife. We've had no money to pay you, but just now we are harvesting our potatoes, and we wondered if you would take a bushel or two on account." Before long the trusting mother was frying potatoes for her sons, in direct, dramatic answer to her prayers. You can have the same assurance of Christ's providing love. Even more: you can help the foodless find a radiant reply to their pleas for food.

Others among you are fearful of your health. You face a serious operation. The doctor may say your sickness is incurable. Ask the heavenly Healer's help! Then you will have the comforting assurance that buoys up a young woman in an Ohio hospital. She has been in bed with tuberculosis for almost a year. Now the doctors are planning to collapse her lung. She writes: "On top of all this, my friend left me for another girl. It was almost more than I could take; yet it was nothing alongside what our Lord went through for us." Looking to that Savior, she had the assurance that the Almighty can heal her. If you, as a child of God, hear these words on a sickbed, remember that "nothing shall be impossible" for Jesus as your Redeemer and Ruler. Should healing be for your eternal good, the divine Physician will cure your illness; but if He wants you, His dearly beloved, for whom He laid down His life, with Him in heaven's indescribable glory and painless perfection, should you not thank Him for giving you that higher, happier answer?

Are you troubled by your sins? Guilt-stricken, do you seek pardon and peace for your soul? Over in Suva, in the Fiji Islands, a brother and two sisters were groping for the Light, and, as well as they could, they asked God for guidance. Marvelously He answered by leading them to our radio message and now they report: "Many persons came to our house last night to listen to your broadcast. No other sound could be heard, and no movements were noticed in the house during your message, which shows how eager the people are to hear the broadcast. I thank God that He has given me a place to hear the Word right in my own house. My brother, sister, and I have accepted Jesus Christ as our Savior, through hearing your broadcasts."

In the Jackson, Michigan, penitentiary a young man serving his sentence was upheld by his father's and mother's persistent prayers for his soul, and, wonderfully, our radio crusade brought the Savior into his cell. The pleading of his parents has been answered, for, the young prisoner writes, "I was once a thief, but, as the thief on the cross was saved, so am I now saved." Yes, as that penitent, crucified with Christ, received the promise of Paradise when he pleaded that Jesus remember him in His heavenly kingdom, so, sin-burdened, sin-stained, sin-cursed as you may be, if you likewise look to the Lord with even a glimmer of faith, your plea for forgiveness will be heard and, through cleansing by Calvary's blood, heaven will be yours.

Therefore, do not crush happiness from your heart by refusing to take all your troubles to the Lord in prayer! Why make your family life miserable when, if only you would unite with your dear ones in beseeching the Savior's guidance for your household, the Holy Spirit would help revive dying love, check selfishness, and promote self-sacrifice? Why continue to torment yourself with trouble when Christ urges you to confide in Him and promises, *"Come unto Me, all ye that labor and are heavy laden, and I will give you rest"*? God has to keep His Word by answering your prayers. True, He may not reply at once. In our text the angel tells Daniel, *"From the first day that thou didst set thine heart to understand . . . thy words were heard."* Though the Almighty thus heard the Prophet as soon as he began to pray, twenty-one days of intercession passed, before the answer came. It may take twenty-one years, even two or three times that long, before your petitions are granted; but you can be sure divine delays are disguised blessings, since Heaven's time is always the right time.

The angel not only brought Daniel the comforting message, *"Fear not"*; because he had asked to understand the divine design for the future, that request was also granted when the angel reveals to the light-seeking Prophet both the course of the perilous times ahead and the glorious victory of Christ's kingdom over the hostile powers of earth and hell. Praying Daniel thus receives the pledge of eternal triumph for all believers. However imposing the foes of the faith may be, they are not too strong to be defeated by divine intervention. The entire history of the Church, with its ten-thousand prayer-besought deliverances from disaster, proves the force of faithful, fervent petition. John Wengatz, missionary near the Quanza River in Africa, writes of a neighboring cannibal tribe, the Libolos, who planned to kill everyone in the mission. At the secret palaver the big chief announced: "When the next moon comes out of the sea and stands full straight over our heads, at the first cockcrowing in the early morning, then let every Libolo strike. . . . Every white man must go into the cooking pot and be eaten." The dread night came when the moon hung straight overhead, and what a time of horror it was, with the war cries, the beating of the tom-toms, and the frenzy of blood madness! After the mission schools were emptied, the children and many of the Christian natives sent into hiding, the missionaries themselves knelt in prayer for the three hours still remaining before daybreak. Then came the dawn, but somehow no man-eating hordes. For two weeks the missionaries prayed and fasted, and for two weeks the Libolos could not cross the river. Then word came that the 12,000 cannibals had begun fighting among themselves and were returning to their huts. The mission had been saved by prayer. A year and a half later three members of the Libolo tribe came to the station which they had previously planned to destroy; now their approach was in peace and for the purpose of securing a missionary for their own tribe. What brought about this change? Hundreds of native converts had prayed for many days and nights that the man-eaters would cease their cannibalism and come to Christ. If with the same devotion the believing world would intercede day and night for the foes of our faith, asking God to make atheist leaders cease their assaults on the Savior's Church and turn to Jesus, we could push away the danger of world war III, save hundreds of thousands of young lives, prevent the horror of atomic and bacteriological destruction.

However else you may be restricted in your work for the Kingdom, you can certainly pray. You may never be a preacher, a teacher, a leader, but you can plead for Christ's cause. Albrecht Duerer, master artist, had a young friend, Franz Knigstein, who sought to become a painter but lacked the necessary talent. In disappointment he folded his hands, asking God to keep him from despondency. Duerer, seeing his friend's arms lifted in prayer, called out, "Wait, Franz, hold that position!" Quickly the young artist sketched the hands thus reverently raised in supplication, exclaiming, "These hands may never paint pictures, but they can certainly help open men's hearts." This famous picture, "Praying Hands," should be a symbol and an assurance for you. Your hands may never know an artist's skill, a musician's touch, a designer's deftness, but you can certainly fold them in faithful prayer and thus help bring down the bounty of Heaven's blessings on your country, your fellow men, and yourself. Therefore pray, America, pray! Pray as never before! Pray in Jesus' name! Pray as Daniel did and receive the victory! O Spirit of God, teach us all to plead in this truth and through Jesus Christ, our Lord and Savior! *Amen!*

THE GLORY LOOK

"After these sayings, He took Peter and John and James and went up into a mountain to pray. And as He prayed, the fashion of His countenance was altered, and His raiment was white and glistering. And, behold, there talked with Him two men, which were Moses and Elias, who appeared in glory and spake of His decease, which He should accomplish at Jerusalem. But Peter and they that were with him were heavy with sleep; and when they were awake, they saw His glory, and the two men that stood with Him. And it came to pass, as they departed from Him, Peter said unto Jesus, Master, it is good for us to be here; and let us make three tabernacles, one for Thee and one for Moses and one for Elias, not knowing what he said. While he thus spake, there came a cloud and overshadowed them; and they feared as they entered into the cloud. And there came a voice out of the cloud, saying, This is My beloved Son: hear Him! And when the voice was past, Jesus was found alone." SAINT LUKE 9:28-36

LORD OF LIFE AND LOVE, OUR PRECIOUS, SELF-GIVING SAVIOR: Once in ancient days Thou wast marvelously transfigured on a mountain top before Thy disciples. Today we ask to see Thee, not in that glistening glory, nor in the radiance which outshines the sun; but we do plead that Thou wouldst show Thyself to us in Thy measureless mercy, as our God and King, our sin-removing Redeemer, and our death-destroying Deliverer. Reveal Thyself to us in the fullness of Thine atoning love, so that we may constantly praise Thee and serve Thee all our days. To this end may Thy Holy Spirit first convict each of us of our guilt, but then teach us that greater grace by which Thou, the Son of God, didst Thyself suffer the pain and penalty of all human transgressions, dying

The Glory Look 23

on Calvary's Cross the death which was the wages of sin! Help us all in faith this week to go up to Jerusalem with Thee and in deep devotion begin again to study the Lenten story of Thy self-sacrifice for our deliverance! Pour the comfort of Thy strengthening love on the afflicted and heartbroken! May Thy holy example encourage us to supply the hungry and starving in Europe! Guide the President, as all our Federal and State officials, to walk in Thy ways! Make our lives daily conform more closely to Thine, and thus, blessed Savior, transform us by Thy Truth. We ask all this because Thou hast promised to hear and help us. *Amen!*

For months people in the United States, especially the women, have been reading and speaking about "the new look," that is, the new styles of clothing and the new appearance these help produce. If only the masses in our country were as vitally concerned about the new life which the Holy Spirit gives those born again by faith in the Lord Jesus Christ, praise His saving name! In our mad materialism outward show, not inward faith, often counts. After services on a recent Sunday in Saint Louis a pastor met a young man and woman, strangers who, sweeping aside the question as to whether they wanted to join the church explained: "We are here, sir, because we plan to be married, and we are looking for the right-sized church, with a good center aisle. Well, yours meets the requirements, so we dropped by this morning to hear you. We think your voice and manner are great; so how about handling the wedding?" Not a word concerning the mutual prayers and pledges; instead, the interest centered in a showy wedding!

Similarly millions overemphasize the "new look." Every healthy-minded person approves of neat, attractive clothing; yet when women worship style and selfishly scheme to outdo others in fashions and finery; when they buy $10,000 mink coats, thousand-dollar gowns, hundred-dollar shoes, while across the ocean hungry hordes wear burlap bags as coats and wrap pieces of carpet around their feet as shoes, we must remind ourselves that undue devotion to dress is certainly not in the spirit of the Lord Jesus. He told His disciples, *"He that hath two coats, let him impart to him that hath none,"* and He instructed the Twelve sent to preach the kingdom of heaven, *"Neither have two coats apiece."* The clothing standards of our age completely contradict Christ's.

Our present-day pride and hypocrisy claim, "Clothes make the man"; and people are accepted or rejected on the basis of their wardrobe. Not long ago Alf' Landon, former candidate for the presidency of the United States, was barred from entering the Metropolitan Opera Club in New York because he wore a business suit instead of full dress. Mighty Americans, men like Abraham Lincoln, were they with us today, would similarly be banned from many elite social functions. How strengthening, by contrast, to know that the Almighty, who loves us all in Christ, does not insist on tails or tuxedos, but wants us to be clothed in our Redeemer's robe of righteousness and to say,
  Jesus' blood and righteousness
  My beauty are, my glorious dress.

Thank God, the Savior's mercy will welcome you in this country and abroad who, in greater number than ever before, write us pleading for warm, clean clothing, no matter how often worn and how outmoded in style!

Frequently we are deceived by outward appearance. A New York Negro clergyman rented a purple turban, affected a foreign accent, and invaded the Deep South, where, instead of suffering from class prejudices and Jim Crow laws, he was hailed as an Oriental dignitary, welcomed by civic, political, and social leaders. He rode in the white sections of segregated trains, he ate in restricted dining cars and otherwise forbidden restaurants, merely because his turban and his manners made many think he was an East Indian potentate. A police captain informed him confidentially, "If a Negro gives us any trouble, we just knock him down." Similarly, fashionable clothes may mislead many, but they cannot deceive God. To receive His blessing, you must truly become *"a new creature"* inwardly, with a new heart and a new spirit. Much more than expensive apparel is required to bring about this change. The costliest of all coats is the garment which immoral Catherine the Great gave her lover Prince Gregory Orlov. This cloak was made with a lining of pure gold, containing Catherine's deed to an estate of one million acres and 40,000 slaves. The coat itself was priced at 3,000,000 gold rubles, a present-day purchasing power of $30,000,000 — given, as Catherine officially declared, "for value received." Those who know of the lust and vice in her reign need not seek far for an explanation.

In contrast, how we thank the Lord today that by the promise of His sacred truth we can broadcast this assurance: With the Savior — and without money, fashion, and frills — you can have a truly new appearance, marvelous beyond your understanding, since the Almighty has reserved for every one of you in Christ a spiritual beauty marvelous beyond all earthly comparison. For the next moments forget the new look and give your attention to

THE GLORY LOOK

as this is described in our text, the record of the Transfiguration, contained in Saint Luke's ninth chapter, verses twenty-eight to thirty-six! Here we read: *"After these sayings, He took Peter and John and James and went up into a mountain to pray. And as He prayed, the fashion of His countenance was altered, and His raiment was white and glistering. And, behold, there talked with Him two men, which were Moses and Elias, who appeared in glory and spake of His decease, which He should accomplish at Jerusalem. But Peter and they that were with him were heavy with sleep; and when they were awake, they saw His glory, and the two men that stood with Him. And it came to pass, as they departed from Him, Peter said unto Jesus, Master, it is good for us to be here; and let us make three tabernacles; one for Thee and one for Moses and one for Elias, not knowing what he said. While he thus spake, there came a cloud and overshadowed them; and they feared as they entered into the cloud. And there came a voice out of the cloud, saying, This is My beloved Son: hear Him! And when the voice was past, Jesus was found alone."* May the Holy Spirit help you understand what this heavenly look is and how you can be assured of its radiance!

I

WHAT IS THIS GLORY LOOK?

This week brings us Lent, the forty days set aside by the ancient Church for the special study of our Savior's suffering and death. Lent is only a human institution; it is not mentioned in the Bible, and some of you write to protest against observing it. Why should it be wrong,

The Glory Look

as some of you claim in your letters, especially during these weeks before the anniversary of Christ's crucifixion, to meditate on the matchless mercy by which God's Son permitted Himself to be seized by scoffers, beaten by blasphemers, crucified with criminals, and killed by cruel-hearted men? If you who have forgotten how the inside of a church looks now suddenly find yourselves burdened by problems you cannot solve, I promise that if you will attend Lenten services to hear and believe the true story of your Redeemer's love, this closeness to the Crucified can mightily change your whole life. Besides, since Jesus Himself frequently emphasized the pain and purpose of His Passion, can we be wrong in observing a period of sacred study centered on the Savior's cross?

Immediately before the events in our text our Lord points to His impending torture and death. We read: *"From that time forth began Jesus to show unto His disciples how that He must go unto Jerusalem and suffer many things of the elders and chief priests and scribes, and be killed, and be raised again the third day."* Peter did not like this Lenten message, but when he cried out, *"This shall not be unto Thee,"* Christ turned to him and with one of the strongest, most startling rebukes in the entire New Testament told His impulsive disciple, *"Get thee behind Me, Satan; thou art an offense unto Me."* However, Jesus did more than rebuke. Before He went to Golgotha, He wanted to fortify His followers with a vision of His divine power which they could remember even in the depths of the loneliness and agony which were to come.

So He chose three of His companions, *"Peter and John and James,"* the same trio who were to see Him so close to death in Gethsemane that an angel had to strengthen Him; and with them He began the steep climb to one of Mount Hermon's heights. As the four ascended the mountainside in the purple haze of the late afternoon, one of the most attractive views in the Holy Land unfolded itself before them. With each step upward they beheld an ever wider panorama of Palestine's green garden land. However, it was not to enjoy scenery that the Savior led His disciples to these heights. He *"went up into"* this *"mountain to pray."* Busy as He was, with tasks ten thousand times more important than any work you do, God's Son always found time for prayer. To Him communion with His heavenly Father was a pleasure, a privilege, a powerful support. No single activity of our Lord is mentioned more frequently in the Gospels than His thankful, pleading petition with the Almighty. Let Jesus teach you how to pray! Make these personal meetings with your Creator a major concern in your life! If many of you would spend only half the time you waste through futile fears in humble pleading with God, you would be blessed with new joy and calm.

What did the three chosen disciples do while Jesus knelt on those mountain slopes? They slept. The same eyes which were to be closed by heavy slumber in the Garden of Gethsemane during the depths of Christ's agony were also shut here on Mount Hermon in the high point of Gospel glory. How, we ask ourselves, could these three associates of our Lord, privileged above all other human beings, slumber on both during their Master's humiliation and His glorification? Perhaps climbing the mountain had tired them. Perhaps it was evening now. Still we can hardly escape the conclusion that if the Savior Himself stayed awake to pray, certainly these three followers, with far greater need of pleading to the

The Glory Look 29

Almighty, should have kept Him company. Why single out this tired trio for criticism, when many who call themselves Christian slumber on today in fatal indifference toward the Kingdom's cause? Some of you are asleep in sinful security, though sacred Scripture asks you to wake up and realize that you are lost in your transgressions. You keep your eyes closed to the ruin that surrounds you and to the redemption God's Son offers you, or, dazed by desperate sorrows, you doze off, when you ought to rouse yourself to full radiance on your Redeemer's sustaining comfort. Wake up, America! the divine Word cries out in alarm. Wake up to the anti-God, anti-Bible, anti-truth forces multiplying in your midst! Wake up to the enemies from without who seek to destroy your liberties and blessings by wiping out your churches!

While Jesus prayed near His sleeping comrades, a mighty miracle occurred. Suddenly, as Matthew puts it, our Lord *"was transfigured,"* His entire appearance was transformed, and when Peter, John, and James awoke, they saw a Christ they had never before beheld. His face was divinely different. Gone were the signs of sorrow they had sometimes noted before. Gone was the imprint of fatigue and travel's toil. Our text tells us, *"The fashion of His countenance was altered"*; a parallel passage reports that *"His face did shine as the sun,"* with an unparalleled brightness. The Savior as God *"took upon Himself the form of a servant,"* now, as a servant, took upon Himself the likeness of God. Heavenly light shone round about Him, and His garments, no longer the common, travel-marked garb which Jesus usually wore, became *"glistering,"* *"white as the light,"* or as

Mark testifies, *"exceeding white as snow; so as no fuller on earth can white them."*

When the three fully awakened men became accustomed to the brightness of our Lord's transfigured glory, they also noticed, as the text records, *"Behold, there talked with Him two men, which were Moses and Elias."* The representatives of the Old Testament Law and the Old Covenant prophecy conversing with the radiant Redeemer! We know what the subject of that hallowed discussion was; for we read that they *"spake of His decease, which He should accomplish at Jerusalem."* You see, then, the greatest theme even for the saints in heaven is the Savior's crucifixion for our redemption. This atonement, which the two Old Testament leaders foresaw and foreknew, was their "theme in glory." How much more should we on earth "love to tell the story" of our divine Deliverer's death for our life! Yet too often our conversation, instead, dwells on trivialities and trash! Strengthening Spirit, make each of us determined to speak gratefully and convincingly of *"Jesus Christ, and Him Crucified,"* the most sacred subject even for saints and angels!

Although the disciples had never before seen Moses and Elijah, who lived long centuries before their time, they recognized them on Mount Hermon. This fact can bring blessed comfort to us in our bereavements. The question is often asked: "Will we know each other in heaven?" "Will we there be able to recognize those who were near and dear to us on earth?" God's Word never stops to give a direct answer, but Holy Scripture does not deny this truth. Rather does the Bible take it for granted, as it presents a long list of testimony pointing straight to the joy of a radiant celestial reunion. If the disciples on the Mount of Transfiguration, without any previous personal acquaintance, knew who Moses and Elijah were, then certainly in the Paradise to come, where our knowledge will be made perfect, we shall recognize those in the Lord whom we have loved on earth. Moses and Elijah appeared on Mount Hermon, as they were in heaven, in the same radiant, transfigured resurrection body which was theirs in eternity. Be assured, then, that the homeland above is not an abode of vague spirits who have lost their identity. The Savior mentions individual people who will be gathered before the throne; the Apostle Paul tells the Thessalonians that he will meet them in the new Jerusalem and rejoice over them; the Bible's last book identifies the saints in glory and the martyrs robed in white; our text represents Peter, James, and John, disciples with human limitations, as realizing who the two Old Testament leaders were, although they had died long centuries before. All this, together with Scripture's promise, *"Then shall I know even as also I am known,"* entitles you to believe that you will recognize not only your faith-filled husband or wife, your Christ-exalting parents or children, your God-fearing friends, but in heaven's fuller understanding, also many whom you never knew in this life, including mighty heroes of faith, writers of sacred Scripture, Prophets, Apostles, and above all, the Savior Himself.

There, in the ten thousand times ten thousand, all washed in the blood of the Lamb, the Lord will help me meet many of you to whom for fifteen seasons, through peace, war, and reconstruction, I have been privileged to preach Christ Crucified, *"the Way, the Truth, and the Life."* A few days ago I received a letter from Joe Rabbit, leader of an Athabascan Indian group who live in the wilds of northern Alberta, Canada. Far from a church, they receive God's Word through this broadcast, and every Sunday Joe Rabbit translates our words for a group of his red-skinned brothers and sisters. They want to hear more about Christ, so that they can grow in grace. We will probably never meet these Indians on earth; but the Holy Spirit sustaining them and me in the faith, we will greet each other in heaven. Lepers in the Philippine Islands who regularly gather to hear our messages; Negroes in South Africa who sit around their radios listening to our programs from Lourenco Marques; copper-skinned descendants of the Incas at the headwaters of the Amazon in Peru to whom missionaries translate our Spanish broadcast; natives in Shanghai and other parts of China who write us as a college girl there did: "I enjoy your radio Bible programs so very much that I became eager to write a letter to you after listening. I am Chinese, so I am very sorry not to know how to express my gratitude to you, but I shall tell my classmates also to listen to your broadcasts. They make me think about Christ, our Lord" — these, and uncounted groups and individuals from Alaska to Tierra del Fuego, from Tangier to Cape Town, through increasing areas of war-wrecked Europe, in Asia's teeming multitudes, and among masses on the islands of the sea who have heard this Gospel pledge, *"Believe on the Lord Jesus Christ, and thou shalt be saved"* — all these we will never meet here below, but God grant that at the Resurrection we can present those of you whom the broadcast has helped fortify with faith to the risen, ascended, and glorified Savior! The Bible assures us that in Heaven's perfect peace there is no regret; on the other hand, hell is full of remorse, and one of the heaviest pains in that endless

The Glory Look

punishment is the sorrow of having denied the divine Deliverer and thus being separated eternally from a believing husband or wife, a father or mother, a son or daughter, a brother or sister, who died in the Lord. You scoffers who in overbearing pride and self-righteousness have cast Christ aside and are still crucifying Him by unholy living, stop! Think what it means to be banished forever in hell from those whom you love here on earth! Picture to yourself, as nearly as you can, the frightful remorse which will shake your soul when, suffering the consequences of your unbelief, you yearn for only a glimpse of your dear ones who accepted the faith you spurned, and even this glance is denied you! Now, while the Holy Spirit, through this message, asks you to repent, to confess all your sins, and especially to declare Christ your Rescuer, your Redeemer, your Reconciler to the Father, get down on your knees, before the devil's agents push this desire from your heart, hear Jesus promise, *"Him that cometh to Me I will in no wise cast out,"* claim the forgiveness He purchased on the cross with His own blood, and declare, as God and His angels rejoice, "From this moment on I am Christ's, and by His grace on the Day of Judgment, as forever and thereafter, I, together with my loved ones, redeemed, reclaimed, and reassured of eternity, shall be part of *'the whole family in heaven.'*"

Almost exultingly our text reports of Moses and Elijah that they *"appeared in glory."* Both of these Old Testament leaders had long left the world. Moses was buried in an unmarked grave 1,400 years earlier, and Elijah was taken to heaven in a fiery chariot nine centuries before he was seen on Mount Hermon. Clearly we find evidence for two mighty truths: first, there is a life after death, and, second, there is a resurrection of the body in divine splendor. God's Word not only teaches that for the believer a new existence begins when he stops breathing, that the body *"is sown in corruption; it is raised in incorruption";* but this account of the transfiguration on Mount Hermon also mercifully guarantees us this glory. Both Christ's promise and the record of this transfiguration tell you burdened by recent bereavement to dry your tears and believe that because your loved ones died in the Lord they will also live again with Him in beauty and brilliance far beyond comparison with anything we now know. These patriarchs, Moses and Elijah, had been old when they left the earth. They, as other human beings, had been subject to disease, surrounded by the danger of accident; but here on the Mount of Transfiguration the eternal verity testifies that they *"appeared in glory,"* with all marks of weakness, each sign of old age removed, replaced by the radiance of dazzling brightness and heavenly perfection.

II

HOW CAN YOU GET THIS GLORY LOOK?

My fellow sinners and fellow redeemed, you, too, can be resurrected in this celestial beauty; you, too, can have the glory look, even if you never have the new fashion look. Your body may be disfigured by injury, marred and scarred by accident, lamed by paralysis, stained by sickness; your members may be removed or restricted by amputation; your sight or hearing may be impaired or destroyed by age; your mind may fail as your power of reason refuses to function; but if you are Christ's, then, though your body becomes motionless in death, though decay destroys your flesh and turns it back to the dust, you will nevertheless be raised in a glory incomparably more magnificent than the most attractive forms and features earth knows.

Even more, by faith we shall share our Lord's radiance in the resurrection. While we have no hope of being transfigured on any Mount Hermon here below, our Savior's Word gives us the double assurance, *"We shall be like Him,"* and again, *"We shall be also in the likeness of His resurrection."* Simply be with God in heavenly splendor would be such marvelous mercy that eternity would not be long enough worthily to proclaim this grace; but what can we say when in the Almighty's greatest gift we have not only the promise of being with Jesus, but also the sacred pledge that, cleansed by His blood, we shall be like Him and share His glory in heaven?

You need no light, as darkness drops its curtain over Mount Hermon, to behold once more the Son of God, the Salvation-Bringer, Moses, the lawgiver, and Elijah, the Prophet messenger; for the brilliance of their transfigured glory reveals them in their full radiance; but you do need the illumination of Holy Scripture to give you the guarantee that you, too, can have that same splendor. Take your Father at His Word! Believe this happy evidence on Mount Hermon! Banish all doubt! If plastic surgeons — God bless their efforts! — can rebuild facial features, eaten by cancer, disfigured by disaster, why question the Omnipotent's power at the resurrection to give you the glory look? If medical scientists can operate, as they did on a girl whose throat was so almost completely closed that for months parents and friends had to keep her awake day and night lest she fall into deep sleep and stop breathing; and if, with the metal throat which these specialists placed in her neck, this girl's new soprano voice could win a state-wide high school singing contest, why sould you question the Almighty's ability to give you a beautified voice in the heavenly hallelujah chorus and in wider wonder to fulfill His pledge, *"It is sown in dishonor; it is raised in glory"?* Instead of doubting, believe!

There on Mount Hermon the disciples not only saw this transfigured triumph; in the practical, powerful lessons God's Word teaches they also learned how that glory look could be theirs. Overcome by the magnificence of what he had beheld, impetuous Peter, seeing the two Old Testament leaders depart from Christ, cried out to Jesus, *"Master, it is good for us to be here; and let us make three tabernacles, one for Thee and one for Moses and one for Elias!"* There was nothing wrong in wishing for the Savior's continued presence, nothing amiss in desiring unbroken peace; yet our text rebukes Peter and says that he made the proposal for the three tabernacles *"not knowing what he said."* Our Lord paid no attention to his suggestion, for He knew that if He stayed on Mount Hermon, there could be no triumph of transfigured grace for you and me, no glory look, no resurrection to life. To remain on that pleasant elevation would have kept Jesus from the horrors of another hill, Calvary, where, as the Son of God, He was to be crucified for the sins of the world. Because He loved us with an unquenchable passion for our soul's salvation, nothing could detain our blessed Redeemer from the crucifixion which meant indescribable anguish for Him, but deliverance for a race of ruined men.

The disciples were thus to learn that service to God's Son means more than happy hours of fellowship with the faithful. They were to find that the climax of the Christian creed brought blood, agony, terror, death in its most hideous form. Have you understood this truth? Do you know that church membership means much more than congregational suppers, entertainments, theatricals, committee meetings, choir rehearsals? Do you realize that if you ally yourself with the Savior, you declare war on Satan? In this generation ten thousands of martyrs outside our own country have paid for their loyalty to the Lord with their lives. Do you honestly think the United States can indefinitely offer absolute freedom of religion and remain the world's greatest citadel of Christianity without suffering savage counterattacks by organized atheism? Why should our country continue to boast of this uninterrupted privilege, when masses within our borders refuse to appreciate it and others mobilize to oppose it? This is not the time for believers to build beautiful villas on mountainsides to which they can retreat from the assaults of a hate-filled age; but this is the urgent, challenging time to strengthen our faith under the impress of Jesus' statement, *"In the world ye shall have tribulation,"* and its echo in the Apostles' reminder, *"We must through much tribulation enter into the kingdom of heaven."*

Peter had not finished explaining his proposal when a triumphant climax capped the Transfiguration. We are told, *"While he thus spake, there came a cloud and overshadowed them* [the disciples]; *and they feared as they entered into the cloud."* The awe of the Almighty came upon them; terror overtook them, as suddenly and unexplainedly they felt themselves in the divine presence. Truly they were, for our text records, *"There came a voice out of the cloud, saying, This is My beloved Son."*

A high point in human history had come when the Father thus publicly proclaimed Jesus His own Son, adding, as Saint Matthew states, *"in whom I am well pleased,"* His dearly beloved, only-begotten, eternally perfect Son.

On Mount Hermon's holy ground, at this triumph of Christ's transfiguration, we meet the central fact of our faith which separates the Bible's creed from all others: Jesus is God's Son. How divinely strengthening that the Most High Himself gives us this assurance! National leaders may neglect this truth; world figures forget it; highly distinguished scholars doubt it; modernist preachers misinterpret it; red scoffers ridicule it; the super-intelligent ignore it; the quibblers question it; devils in hell seek to desroy it; but here it stands, the firm foundation of our faith: "Jesus Christ is the Son of God." You cannot remove the Rockies by shooting off firecrackers at the foot of their towering heights. You cannot blow the Atlantic Ocean dry by puffing with all your might against the waves; even less can all the Scripture-slashers in the world, with the hordes of hell behind them remove the slightest part of this divine guarantee: Jesus Christ is not only good and godly, but He is the good God Himself, the Son of the Almighty, together with Father and the Spirit, the one true and triune Lord. The voice of the Most High from the cloud over Mount Hermon declared this sacred verity; the Savior Himself restated it, and the Bible reverently repeats it. In only the three short letters of Saint John, which you can read altogether in fifteen minutes, this Sonship is mentioned twenty-three times.

Christians of America, hold fast to this first article of your faith! Fight for it! Defend it! Spread it! Above all, believe it yourselves! Know that Jesus, glorified by His transfiguration, is your God, with the power and might, the truth and triumph you can ever need! He is your God, with healing and health for the ailments of soul and body, with inner riches and spiritual wealth for the pain of poverty, with joy and gladness for each hour of sorrow, with heavenly comfort and consolation for every affliction, with light and life for the valley of earth's shadow of death itself. He is the unchanging God of yesterday, today, and tomorrow; the ever-present God for morning, noon, and night; your Prophet, Priest, and King; your Teacher, Friend, and Guide. If you have never before known this keystone in the arch of our Christian assurance, or, if having once believed it, you now restrict or reject it, may the Holy Spirit today so enlighten your soul that you join Peter in His victorious confession of faith, *"Thou art the Christ, the Son of the Living God!"*

However, add: "Thou art the crucified and risen Christ, the saving Son of the living God!" For Jesus is also the Lord of grace, compassion, mercy, and a hundred other human terms which we might enlist to describe His limitless love, but which, with the embellishment of men's speech, fall far short of describing His depthless devotion to you, lost as you were in your sins. Let this lesson sink deeply into our hearts today! It is not enough to say, "Jesus gave me pardon and peace. He took away my guilt. He delivered me from death." You must understand the frightful price He paid in granting you these blessings, the horror, agony, heartbreak He endured when, cursed, lashed, tormented, and tortured by fiendish enemies, He did what only God could do, serve the sentence your transgressions had imposed upon you, paid the penalties your punishment had heaped up, and, as your saving Substitute, died the death which through your unnumbered iniquities you deserved.

The most important truth you can ever hear is this message of your Savior's mercy: He died for you. If you believe it, you have God's promise of redemption and resurrection, His guarantee of the glory look, together with the unbreakable assurance that heaven is certainly yours by grace, through faith. If, however, despite the pleas and prayers raised in your behalf, you continue to reject your Redeemer, I must tell you the awful sentence which divine justice clearly and repeatedly outlines: you are headed, not for a prepared place in Paradise but for the gruesomeness of hell! May God have mercy on your soul and bring you by whatever drastic means of misery and suffering may be required, down on your knees before Jesus in repentance, but in reliance on His power to save to the uttermost.

Because *"there is none other name under heaven . . . whereby we must be saved,"* besides Christ's, the Father's voice on Mount Hermon's heights told the fear-filled disciples, *"Hear Him!"* A command, the most vital ever issued, yet stated in the most concise and compact language! Only two words, but what an unsearchable wealth of divine wisdom they contain! If the world today would *"hear Him"* instead of having international leaders ignore the Savior, our age would have Heaven's warrant that world war III could be pushed aside, that millions of our fellow men would not barely exist, cold, hungry, homeless, hunted and haunted by their fears and their foes, but know life's highest happiness. More pointedly, if you would *"hear Him,"* give yourself to Christ, serve Him as your Savior, peace, joy, blessing,

The Glory Look

such as you have never known previously, would take the place of sin, sorrow, despair. You cannot escape making a decision for or against God's Son. Either you will be saved with Him or damned without Him. Which will it be for you? Will you *"hear Him,"* or will you jeer Him?

One last, blessed truth in this record of the Transfiguration remains to be told. After God had majestically spoken, after Moses and Elijah had disappeared, Christ came to the awe-filled disciples, and when they now raised their eyes, behold, *"Jesus was found alone,"* or, as Saint Mark puts it, *"They saw no man any more, save Jesus only."* Take this saving, strengthening, *"Jesus only,"* as your life's motto! *"Jesus only"* — not your good works, good intentions, good resolutions — as the seal of your salvation! *"Jesus only"* for your victory over temptation, sin, and the enticement of the devil! *"Jesus only"* as the divine guarantee for the resurrection of the body and the glory look in the everlasting hereafter!

If you, too, see *"Jesus only,"* and that means wholly, truly, and continually, then, with the assurance that your sins have been washed away and that heaven is yours, you can have a foregleam of the glory look here on earth. Do you recall that when Moses spent forty days with the Almighty on Mount Sinai, his face shone when he returned to his people? Do you remember that when imprisoned Peter and John were haled before a council of their countrymen, these enemies recognized that the two disciples had been with Christ? The imprint of the Savior was still on their lives. If you are inclined to say, "All this is ancient history," then listen to this letter which came to me from a prisoner in one of our penitentiaries who is soon to face trial for his life. Having heard this broadcast, he was led by the Spirit to acclaim Christ the Redeemer. Now he writes me: "You say that *'joy shall be in heaven over one sinner that repenteth,'* but I almost feel sure that this cannot surpass the joy in my heart at once again being brought to my knees and feeling God's healing power both in body and soul. No longer do I need the medical attention I had required the past years. My painful headaches have left me. At night I no longer roll and toss my head, racked with pain. I now enjoy quiet, restful sleep and am putting on the weight that I had been losing steadily. Nobody around here can understand the change that has come over me." In prison, perhaps in the shadow of the electric chair, this man, who has come to His Savior, is beginning to receive the glory look.

You, too, can have that blessing when you also say, *"Jesus only!"* Therefore, my brothers and sisters, don't hang your heads in fear and failure, but lift them up to the crucified Savior! Don't let the sin of your soul speak through angry, envious, lustful glances, but behold the beautiful Savior and have His radiance reflected in the peace and happiness which shines from your eyes! Don't go through life grimly and God-forsakenly, but, as your Lord walked resolutely to Jerusalem, where, He knew, He would be sentenced to the cross, prepare to follow Him, and with the joy of your salvation expressed on a Christ-enlightened countenance, and in a Christ-blessed life, start to reflect the glory look even now! God help you thus to reflect your redemption until in the heavenly transfiguration, through Jesus, you shall be like Jesus! *Amen!*

CHRIST, KEEP US FROM MONEY-MADNESS!

"Then Jesus, six days before the Passover, came to Bethany, where Lazarus was which had been dead, whom He raised from the dead. There they made Him a supper, and Martha served; but Lazarus was one of them that sat at the table with Him. Then took Mary a pound of ointment of spikenard, very costly, and anointed the feet of Jesus, and wiped His feet with her hair; and the house was filled with the odor of the ointment. Then saith one of His disciples, Judas Iscariot, Simon's son, which should betray Him, Why was not this ointment sold for three hundred pence and given to the poor? This he said, not that he cared for the poor, but because he was a thief, and had the bag, and bare what was put therein. Then said Jesus, Let her alone; against the day of My burying hath she kept this. For the poor always ye have with you; but Me ye have not always."
SAINT JOHN 12:1-8

PRECIOUS, SELF-SACRIFICING SAVIOR: What can we give Thee, who on Calvary's cross didst give Thyself for us? What return can we make for Thy redeeming love when, dying for our transgressions, Thou, as our Substitute, didst earn for us all the gift of heaven's glory? The most we can offer will be far too puny and paltry. Help us, therefore, by Thy Holy Spirit, to acclaim Thee our divine Deliverer from death and give ourselves to Thee, dedicating the best that we have to Thy service! Particularly would we present Thee, as our sincere thankoffering, our contrite souls, cleansed by Thine atoning blood. Come to us, precious Jesus, abide with us, and help us daily show forth Thy praises, since Thou hast called us out of the darkness of self-deceit into the marvelous light of Thine unfailing grace! Draw many to Thee through Thy glad Gospel invitation! Comfort the afflicted! Cheer the sick! Open our hearts to help feed the hungry and provide shelter for the homeless! Above all, strengthen us to accompany Thee on the pathway of Thy suffering for our salvation, so that through the Lenten mercy we may realize fully the height and depth of Thine atoning compassion and thankfully live for Thee and with Thee. *Amen!*

SIX years ago *The Saturday Review of Literature* printed this story, the source of which the author said she had never been able to learn: In the Middle Ages a renowned artist was commissioned to paint the life of Christ on the walls of a cathedral in Sicily. For long years he toiled at this task, which was to be his greatest work. At last the mural was almost completed; for, search as diligently as he would, the creator of the work had been unable to find models either for the Christ Child or for Judas Iscariot, and he had to leave their figures unfinished. Then, suddenly, in the slums of his city he met a twelve-year-old boy, with the face and features he required for the youthful Savior. The lad lived with him during the many sittings, and finally this part of the mural was completed. However, the quest of a model for Judas, the betrayer, was still unsuccessful. People from far and near, hearing of the painter's perplexity, urged those with evil, leering countenances to volunteer their services; but the master, now aged, found no one who depicted Judas in the way he envisioned the traitor. Then, one afternoon, in an inn near the cathedral, a ragged, wretched figure lurched into the room and tumbled to the floor, pleading: "Wine! Wine!" Hurrying to help him, the artist found the face he had sought many years — a criminal's countenance, engraved, it seemed, by every vice known to man. Here, at last, was his Judas Iscariot. It required only the promise of food, shelter, and clothing to induce this human wreck to pose as the treacherous arch traitor. In the studio, with each succeeding day the artist noted a stronger dismay in the eyes of his model. He inquired: "My son, what troubles you? I would like to help you." The man of sin and misery sobbed violently, but after he had composed himself sufficiently to speak, he looked pleadingly at the painter and asked: "Don't you remember me? I was the model for your Christ Child years ago."

While no one can name this story's author, each one of us should learn from it the factual lesson: Even those who can serve as models of the Master may fall so low that they play the role of traitorous Judas.

May we personally heed this warning in an age when for masses gold takes the place of God, and cash crowds out Christ! Today, as the United States, with greater resources, larger income, heavier profits than ever before, still investigates cases of war-profiteering, even after public figures have been found guilty of graft, the greed for gold is so close to most of us that we should fervently pray:

CHRIST, KEEP US FROM MONEY-MADNESS!

Tear the avarice of Judas from our hearts and strengthen us with Mary's spirit of self-sacrifice as we study the words of our text (the first eight verses of Saint John's twelfth chapter): *"Then Jesus, six days before the Passover, came to Bethany, where Lazarus was which had been dead, whom He raised from the dead. There they made Him a supper, and Martha served; but Lazarus was one of them that sat at the table with Him. Then took Mary a pound of ointment of spikenard, very costly, and anointed the feet of Jesus, and wiped His feet with her hair; and the house was filled with odor of the ointment. Then saith one of His disciples, Judas Iscariot, Simon's son, which should betray Him, Why was not this ointment sold for three hundred pence and given to the poor? This he said, not that he cared for the poor, but because he was a thief, and had the bag, and bare what was put therein. Then said Jesus, Let her alone; against the day of My burying hath she kept this. For the poor always ye have with you; but Me ye have not always."*

I

KEEP US FROM THE JEALOUS GREED OF JUDAS!

It was the Friday before Good Friday, and our Lord had openly come into Bethany, the lovely town outside Jerusalem. His stay in the village created wide public interest, since we are told, *"Much people . . . knew that He was there."* We also read that the chief priests and Pharisees *"had given a commandment that, if any man knew where He was, he should show it, that they might take Him."* These leaders wanted Christ killed before He came to the Temple with the Passover pilgrims. "You never can tell," they said to themselves, "what may happen if He speaks to the crowds." So they issued the order directing anyone who might see Jesus, immediately to reveal His whereabouts. Usually men thus hunted by hatred hide away; but not our blessed Redeemer! With the courage which the Holy Spirit will give every believer for any future persecution, the Son of God never thought of concealing Himself, but openly faced His foes. Besides, *"His hour was not yet come."*

Christ, Keep Us from Money-Madness! 47

Why, we in America pause to ask, did the men in high positions plot to slay the Savior? What evil did He do? Did He undermine His government, betray His country, blaspheme God, ridicule religion? Was He a criminal, a warmonger, a murderer? Did He exploit His people, cheat them, rob them? Did He try to crush the masses and rule as a tyrant? Simply to ask these questions is to answer them with a clear-cut denial. Even those who do not regard Him as their Lord and Savior often pay Him lavish tribute. Albert Einstein, front-rank, world-famous scientist, does not know definitely that there is a God, yet he answered a newspaper reporter's question, "Do you accept the historical existence of Jesus?" with these words: "Unquestionably; no one can read the Gospels without feeling the unusual presence of Jesus. I am enthralled by the luminous figure of the Nazarene. . . . No man can deny the fact that Jesus existed, nor that His sayings are beautiful."

Christ loved His fellow men, He prayed for those who persecuted Him, and pleaded on the cross for those who crucified Him. Constantly He showed His hearers the Almighty and the wonders of His mercy; everywhere He went He helped the sick and the sorrowing. Still His enemies killed Him. Why? One definite reason for this hatred and lusting after His blood was this: If the Son of God were permitted to continue His Gospel of mercy and love, He would drive the money-changers from the Temple, cut down their incomes, weaken their support, and finally put them out of office. It would cost them too much if they let Him live.

The Bethany of our text was one of the few places which befriended our Lord. Indeed, we have no record of any locality where He was more warmly greeted than in this small town on the Mount of Olives. Which village in the United States, do you suppose, corresponds to ancient Bethany as being the most devoted to God's Son? We cannot tell; but we are sure that you who love Jesus should strive to make yours a Christ-centered community. I ask you plainly: Are you believers praying, working, giving to make the place in which you live a citadel of the Savior? Don't close your eyes to the fact that throughout America evil forces are working day and night to build strongholds of Satan! Get busy and *"fight the good fight of faith!"*

Here at Bethany our Lord was the guest of a person otherwise unknown in Scripture, Simon the Leper. Was he a man whom Christ had cured of leprosy and who wanted to show his appreciation, or a person of means who could give this large dinner? Again, we do not know who Simon the Leper was, but the Almighty does, and on that great Day of His Judgment this Simon, diseased outcast though he probably was at one time, now, saved by the faith which led him to open his dwelling to Jesus, will be welcomed into the heavenly home with the greeting, *"Well done, thou good and faithful servant!"* — If the Savior were with us today, would you put your house at His disposal and invite Him to dine with you? Thank God, many of you would! Yet I pray for others among you who say, "Of course, we would want the blessed Redeemer with us," but who contradict this by refusing to make and take time for Him now. If almost two of every three households in America do not think enough of our Lord to invoke His presence at their meals, and an even smaller proportion conducts regular home worship, how can we reasonably suppose that if Christ were to knock at our door we would, like Simon, urge

Him to stay and invite a large company to dine with Him? The most vital task before you fathers and mothers in this radio mission, after you yourself have come all the way to God's Son, is to make your home His dwelling place. The Holy Spirit grant you the strength to begin today with family prayer and Scripture reading. The enlightening Comforter give you young folks, eagerly looking forward to your wedding day, the holy determination to start and maintain your married life with Him who is the Savior of your soul!

Our text reminds us that Bethany was the place *"where Lazarus was which had been dead, whom He [Jesus] raised from the dead,"* and it continues to record that *"Lazarus was one of them that sat at the table with Him."* Russian doctors claim — experts on this side of the Atlantic flatly deny it — to have resurrected the dead, although these scientists are forced to admit that in many cases their patients died soon afterward. Yet as proof of Christ's divine power you find Lazarus, months after his return from death, here at the table with His divine Deliverer. Indeed, Lazarus was so much alive that the leaders of our Lord's enemies sought to kill him. The old gangster tactics of removing the evidence!

It seems that the whole town of Bethany, and many from near-by places, thronged out to Simon's house, not only to catch a glimpse of Christ, but, as John explains, to *"see Lazarus also."* Well might a large crowd gather to behold both the Master and His living miracle; here was patent proof that Jesus was God. Only the Almighty can bring the dead back to life. It is now revealed that a mysterious swami, a Hindu "holy" man who claimed the power to revive the departed, was flown to New Delhi where Gandhi, champion of India's freedom, lay dead eight hours. For a long time the swami labored over the corpse, chanting weird prayers and incantations. While anxious friends stood by, he stroked the soles of the Mahatma's feet, trying to transmit his own life impulse to the rigid body. When this failed, the Hindu healer prepared a medicinal paste, prescribed by ancient secret formula, to put into Gandhi's throat, but the friends of the deceased leader stopped him. They knew that his efforts were useless. Yet Jesus can never fail. He Himself tells us in unbreakable truth, *"I am the Ressurrection and the Life,"* and pledges those who trust Him as Savior, that for them He will perform a miracle far greater than the resurrection of Lazarus a few days after his death: Christ will take their bodies, long decayed, disintegrated, pulverized, and recreate them into heavenly radiance and glorious perfection.

Here at Simon's house in Bethany we meet two women who have a personal message to you mothers and daughters. The first is presented in the words, *"They made Him a supper; and Martha served."* This Martha, many of you will remember, was Lazarus' sister; and when some time before Jesus visited their home, she had complained that her sister, Mary, left the task of preparing the meal to her and instead of helping sat at the Master's feet to hear His instructions. Now, however, Martha has learned her lesson. She, too, knows *"one thing is needful,"* God's Word. In that new faith she happily serves her Savior and at the same time gives American women a high, challenging ideal. In an age when a wife divorced nine times receives wide newspaper publicity; when women in public life, far away from the kitchen and domestic duties, become the focus of attention, some of you mothers may feel that the world about you has little thought for you who try to live in the Lord, keep your family healthy, happy, clean, and take care of your home. Whatever men may think, take heart in the truth that the Most High Himself has given His verdict! If you want to know whom the Almighty selects as the most eminent of all women, read the last chapter of the Book of Proverbs where it describes the wife and mother who *"looketh well to the ways of her household."* To her God says, *"Thou excellest them all."* The Holy Spirit give the United States Christ-minded, consecrated women instead of the small, selfish, sophisticated, sin-loving type lined up before the bar of cheap taverns or preening themselves in the highest-priced places of amusement!

It is Martha's sister, Mary, with whom our text is especially concerned. She, too, attended this meal, bringing with her *"a pound of ointment of spikenard, very costly,"* kept in *"an alabaster box,"* as both Matthew and Mark inform us. This was a precious perfume-like ointment worth *"three hundred pence,"* a prize possession for any woman. No name is given to the sweet-smelling substance in Mary's carved-stone container; it has remained for our age to call perfume, another of God's gifts, by names which indicate sin, sensual allurement, temptation, and transgression. Mary's ointment cost about forty-five dollars a pound in modern money, but our stores advertise "the most expensive perfume in the world" at forty-five dollars an ounce; and the choicest attar of roses (it takes an acre of rosebushes to make only ten ounces) sells for $100 an ounce. A private tutor of millionaires' children reports that he asked a small group of these youngsters to name the three greatest needs of life, hoping, of course, that they could see through the haze of luxury to mention food, clothing, and shelter. The first lad to raise his hand answered: "I know. Perfume!" After a few moments' instruction he readily admitted that food was more essential, but he added, "I still think Mother could do without food better than without perfume." Some women unquestionably devote themselves more to cosmetics than to Christ. Isaiah has a word of warning for them. Read it in his third chapter, the twenty-fourth verse!

Now, while Mary prized that alabaster box highly — and God's children should enjoy beautiful things — she thought more of her Savior. There at Simon's supper she took the *"ointment of spikenard, very costly,"* as Saint Matthew's somewhat fuller account relates, *"poured it on His head,"* and, as our text continues, *"anointed the feet of Jesus, and wiped His feet with her hair."* Such anointing was the customary courtesy extended to guests in that hot, dry climate. Yet Mary's action surprised and displeased even the disciples, for when *"the house was filled with the odor of the ointment,"* Judas Iscariot, and our Scripture labels him in advance as the one *"which should betray Him,"* protests, *"Why was not this ointment sold for three hundred pence"* (he had the whole thing figured out) *"and given to the poor?"*

If at first you may be inclined to agree with Judas, read on in our text and find the charge, *"This he said, not that he cared for the poor; but because he was a thief, and had the bag, and bare what was put therein."* A pious hypocrite, he was guilty of greed and dishonesty. Those are the same sins to which an inordinate love of money can lend us. Look at Judas! Was he an underprivileged Galilean like the other followers of the Savior? No! He came from self-respecting Judea, the only one from

Christ, Keep Us from Money-Madness! 53

our Lord's country. Was he a hard-pressed fisherman like most of his associates? No! Someone has well called him "the only gentleman in the Twelve." Was he simple-minded, inexperienced, easily mislead? No! His comrades thought so much of his ability that they entrusted him with their common treasury. In a certain sense he was the disciple among the dozen from whom the most loyalty could be expected; yet he was guilty of the basest possible betrayal. Why? Because he let the love of gold push from his heart the love of God. He worshiped money, slaved for it, sold his soul for it, took his own life for it, and went to hell for it.

The same money-madness which cursed Judea blights many in our day of gilded prosperity. Why has crime marched on in these past years, with more burglaries and robberies, more cheating and swindling, more youthful violations of God's commandment *"Thou shalt not steal!"* than in any previous period? Is the reason for this ruin not to be found in the cruel covetousness which makes gold its god? Last week, when food prices tumbled on the stock market, the farmers in our country lost more than $200,000,000, and owners of farm products additional hundreds of millions. At the same time others profited by their loss! Congress has been asked to appoint an investigating board to find out just who gained and why. Every day drunken masses in the United States are sold more drink and made more dangerous; every day the purity of teen-agers is viciously attacked in the sale of printed, pictured immorality; every day commercialized vice takes its tribute of millions of dollars throughout the land; every day illegal operations, dishonest divorces, and the willful neglect of children demand the payment of staggering sums. Why? Because sin-stunted minds think more of silver than they do of souls. What is the cause of the frequent family troubles? Experts tell us that most domestic strife centers about money. Why have some of you been robbed of the joy you once had in Jesus as you become cold, unsympathetic, self-centered? Be honest and admit that you, too, have made gain, either by fair or foul means, the one, all-consuming goal in your life! Confess that gradually you have come to serve cash — not Christ!

Before your heart becomes altogether hardened and you cut yourself off from the Savior's repeated appeals, recall what happened to Judas! Immediately after our Lord rebuked him in Simon's house, he hurried, enraged, to the high priest and completed the details of the devilish deal by which he would receive thirty pieces of silver (about $16.50 in our money), not for the poor, but for himself, the pay for betraying his Redeemer. In his money-madness he lost even those paltry shekels; for later, in despair, he brought them back to the Temple and threw them, clattering, on the floor to rid himself of their bloody curse. He lost his good name as a disciple of Jesus; he lost his life, ending as a suicide; he lost his soul in hell, spurning Christ, whose all-embracing love would have pardoned even his betrayal, if only he had repentantly returned to redeeming grace!

Do not make the same money-mad mistake! Bring all your sins of greed and gold-worship contritely to the Son of God and the Savior of your soul! Confess your guilt, but trusting Him who showed the highest measure of His mercy to a thief crucified with Him at Calvary, accept His pledge of pardon!

Then ask the Holy Spirit's sustaining strength to help you restore whatever you have taken dishonestly, to make

Christ, Keep Us from Money-Madness! 55

good any loss you have caused others! Recently the newspapers told of an Ohio village in which a freight train hit a trailer truck and scattered its contents around the wreckage. Spectators from far and near somehow felt they were entitled to take as much as they could for themselves. When the mayor of the village and its two pastors saw practically the entire cargo carried away, they put large boxes in various public places and asked the people to deposit whatever they had taken from the wreck. To the credit of this Ohio community, the boxes had hardly appeared on its streets when a procession of people began to fill them.

Suppose throughout the country government officials and clergymen would unite as the mayor and pastors of that village did, appeal to the conscience of our citizens, asking the return of illegally gotten goods; and suppose the people of the United States would react with the same response given by those Ohio folks — can you not see millions of boxes from coast to coast filled with money sinfully gained? Fifty years ago today the battleship *Maine* was blown up in Havana Harbor, and if all the dishonest money made during the wars in the half century since that disaster could be stored; if we could undo the graft and corruption which increase when greedy men selfishly seek their own profit while their fellowmen unselfishly lay down their lives, we would have not only a better and cleaner country, but also a stronger and more richly blessed nation. Twenty-five years ago this week the United States Senate received its second resolution to outlaw international conflict. It failed, and we will never show any progress in banishing bloodshed until we remove the possibility of wartime profiteering.

What our power-crazed world needs above all else

today; what the money-minded, spiritually blinded in our own land must have for their soul-happiness and the guarantee of grace; what you and I really require if we are to be blessed with rest for our souls and the reassurance of our redemption, is personal reliance on the Lord Jesus Christ as our merciful Savior, and with this, the Holy Spirit's rebirth into a new life, which replaces the grasp of greed with the spirit of self-sacrifice and service.

II

GIVE US THE SELF-SACRIFICING LOVE OF MARY!

Praise the Almighty and All-Merciful that you, too, can have this compassionate Redeemer and through faith in Him avoid the craze of money-madness! Learn this from Mary's record in our text! She was moved by faith, whereas Judas had been prompted by jealously and greed. She worshiped Jesus. This is the third time the Gospels picture her on her knees before the Son of God. She knew how to humble herself before her Lord.

Our Savior told the disciples who joined in Judas' objection, *"Let her alone; against the day of My burying hath she kept this,"* or, as Matthew states, *"In that she hath poured this ointment on My body she did it for My burial."* Repeatedly Christ had spoken of His atoning death, but more and more forcefully, we can see from Scripture, as the day of His betrayal and arrest drew near. Here in Bethany, a short week before His crucifixion Mary believed that tragic but triumphant truth: The Master would die as her Redeemer to remove her guilt; and the broken alabaster box was proof of her gratitude for that limitless love.

Do you have this trust? Is your conviction that Jesus

died on the cross as your Deliverer a true, living, victorious, heart-and-soul faith? Are you personally so completely convicted of your own rebellion against Heaven that you feel lost and condemned in your sins? Are you convinced that neither you nor any other human being can rescue you from ruin; that the most you can do, the highest amount you can pay, the severest penance you can perform, will never move you even an inch closer to God? If you are, then your grief-gripped, repentant soul can triumph over doubt, despair, and the devil, by coming to Jesus, confessing all your sins, and acclaiming Him your Savior, who was tortured for your transgressions and crucified for your crimes. Do you believe, even though you can never fully understand nor measure this unspeakable mercy, that complete forgiveness of your evil, peace with your Lord, the new birth and the new life, the joy of salvation, the victory over death, the radiance of the resurrection, and the hallowed blessing of heaven are all yours, yours fully, yours surely, yours eternally, simply by trusting faith in the Son of God's cross-crowned compassion, His self-sacrifice for your redemption?

If you can truly say, "Yes, by divine grace I have that faith," then, reborn as a new creature in Christ, you will not be satisfied until you have laid at His feet the gifts of your love. On the other hand, if you turn away from your eternal Deliverer, whom these Lenten weeks picture in His atoning agony; if up to this time, year after year, you have rejected or repulsed the only Redeemer you can ever have, then may the Holy Spirit now use the winged words of this appeal to reach you, and finally, at last, break down the barriers of unbelief, bring you, guilt-burdened but mercy-seeking, to Him who in His own words came *"to call . . . sinners to repentance"!* Then you, too, will be able to defeat the devil of money-madness.

See how completely Mary experienced this triumph! That spikenard ointment cost much; yet the best she had was not too good for her divine Deliverer. Overcome by the realization that the Son of God would lay down His life for her, she was ready to surrender everything to Christ. Indeed, according to Saint Mark's record, our Savior says, *"She hath done what she could."* Mary was a maximum giver; *"she hath done what she could."*

Do the people of the United States, the wealthiest of nations, follow her example? No! Tabulation of income-tax returns shows that our countrymen are giving only one third of the 15 per cent of their income which the Government permits them to deduct for church work. A cheerful 15 per cent given to our heavenly Father and to suffering mankind, instead of a skimpy, less-than-5-per-cent contribution, would bring us remarkable blessing and could help solve some of our most complicated problems. Despite the highest profits, salaries, and incomes this country has ever known, our people are contributing proportionately less to church and charities than they did in the lean depression period fifteen years ago. The war did not bring America closer to God, despite the sacrifice of almost one third of a million of our young men. If we do not increase and expand the Kingdom's work in our own country and then bring the message of the Cross across the oceans into the very center of present day unbelief, we will have to pay a hundredfold in money and lives for that stinginess. A dollar now offered for the spread of Christ's peace can prevent the expenditure in years ahead of one thousand dollars for defense against atheist aggression.

Are you showing Mary's devotion by contributing what you can? Some among you have been exceptionally blessed by the Almighty: you have outstanding talent, exceptional brain power, a fine voice, good health, and you could be maximum givers by consecrating yourselves to the Lord's work in an age when war-racked nations and sin-poisoned people plead as never before for the saving Gospel, by using your divinely bestowed endowments and helping bring the Word of truth to them. The Holy Spirit wants many of you young folks in high school and college to become messengers of the Savior's mercy, missionaries of salvation, teachers of His love, at home and abroad. He needs some of you doctors and nurses entirely and directly in the service of His sweet charity. He asks you laymen and laywomen to consider prayerfully the various fields open to you in the Church's expanding activities. First of all, however, in the spirit of Lenten love, He wants you to make a soul pilgrimage to Calvary, to forget everything else in the world as you behold the cross and there, kneeling before Him, the Son of God, crucified for you, realize that He sentenced Himself, His own holy body, His own matchless mind, His own sinless soul into the death of all deaths for you! Then, the Holy Spirit sustaining you, cry out, "Jesus gave what He could, everything, for me. May I be strengthened to give what I can, my life, to Him!"

When Jesus, defending Mary, told Judas, *"The poor always ye have with you,"* he did not, as some people erroneously conclude, encourage us to neglect the sorrowful and suffering. While Mary's exceptional gift was the anointing for His self-sacrificial death, His followers could always show that they loved men in their misery better than money by sharing their blessings with famished and destitute mankind. In fulfillment of Christ's truth, and in contradiction of godless visionaries who long ago promised that poverty would be banished from the earth, we today have the poor with us, probably to a greater extent than ever before, especially in war-ravaged Europe and Asia. In the merciful Redeemer's love, let us help them! While the Savior said, *"The poor always ye have with you,"* He added these meaningful words, *"But Me ye have not always."* How true this prediction proved for those gathered in Simon's house at Bethany! Soon our Lord would leave these friends, never to return to them, and after His resurrection and by His ascension He would depart even from His disciples. How true, likewise, for some of you unbelievers, that you will not always have the saving Son of God with you! He never promised that He will plead with sinners endlessly, and, after they have rejected Him a thousand times, come to them on their deathbeds, to save them in the eleventh hour. Likewise Jesus never pledged you that, no matter how viciously you sin, nor how brazenly you blaspheme Him, He will be at your side constantly until your last breath. Be warned: You can drive the merciful Son of God away by steady, rebellious unbelief! You can keep on crucifying the Savior anew; you can continue to cry out in your godless homes, *"His blood be on us and on our children!"* and never have a chance to repent. You can die in your sins, without receiving Christ as your Redeemer.

Today our heavenly Father wants me to speak these words right into your hearts: *"Seek ye the Lord while He may be found!"* Stop resisting the Spirit! Come to

Christ, Keep Us from Money-Madness! 61

Christ today while His arms are stretched out to the whole world, but in this moment of mercy as you hear His plea, extended particularly to you with the guarantee that whatever your past has been or your future may be, *"the blood of Jesus Christ, His* [God's] *Son, cleanseth us from all sin."*

Because Mary believed, and the broken alabaster box gave proof of her love, the Savior concluded His remarks at Bethany, according to Saint Matthew's Gospel, with this emphatic assurance, *"Verily I say unto you, Wheresoever this Gospel shall be preached in the whole world, there shall also this, that this woman hath done, be told for a memorial of her."* That prophecy has again been fulfilled by this message, as it is broadcast in a half dozen languages and in forty-two countries outside the United States, and heard in more than one hundred nations, as transmitted through the world's largest program. The money-madness of Judas is condemned by all right-thinking men, but Mary's loving sacrifice will be perpetually and universally acknowledged as the memorial of trusting faith.

In His matchless mercy the Lord has an even more marvelous promise for you who this day acclaim Him as your Redeemer. While you will be saved from the sin of greed, as from every other transgression, men may never hear of you; but by Christ's sacred truth you will have a memorial in heaven, the place Jesus Himself prepared for you, and there angels, not only men, will rejoice with you. You who have still not pledged the Savior your allegiance, remember His words of warning, *"But Me ye have not always,"* and come to Him for rescue and redemption now, while you can! *Amen!*

IT IS GOD IN THE GARDEN

"Jesus, therefore, knowing all things that should come upon Him, went forth and said unto them, Whom seek ye? They answered Him, Jesus of Nazareth. Jesus saith unto them, I am He. And Judas also, which betrayed Him, stood with them. As soon, then, as He had said unto them, I am He, they went backward and fell to the ground. Then asked He them again, Whom seek ye? And they said, Jesus of Nazareth. Jesus answered, I have told you that I am He; if therefore ye seek Me, let these go their way."

SAINT JOHN 18:4-9

GOD OF OUR FATHERS: With grateful hearts we praise Thee for the love which gave us Christian leaders, like Washington, the father of our country, and for the gracious gift of freedom our people enjoy. Continue to bless us with God-fearing statesmen who, guided by Thy Word, will spurn every compromise with atheism and personally, as well as politically, promote the righteousness which alone exalts a nation! Impart Thy benediction to the preaching and broadcasting of the pure Gospel, that men everywhere, convicted of their sins, may be drawn to Thy Son, acclaim Him their God, their Savior, their unfailing Friend in every need, and trusting in His divine power, dedicate themselves wholly to Him! Make those of us who know our precious Redeemer more Christlike every day! Help us reflect His love by testifying to His saving grace, providing for the poor, feeding the hungry, visiting the sick and the imprisoned! Keep us from pride, self-righteousness, hypocrisy, and make our faith the humble, contrite trust which looks only to the Cross for guarantee of our salvation! Gracious God, we believe Thy Son's promise: "Whatsoever ye shall ask the Father in My name, He will give it to you." Hear our petition, then, and enrich us with a wide outpouring of Thy Spirit, since we pray in Jesus' name! *Amen!*

It is God in the Garden 63

ON April 23, 1891, in the city of Philadelphia, a book of only twenty-four hand-written pages was purchased at public auction. Records no longer show the price paid; but, had it been sold for its weight in gold or diamonds, this would not outweigh the value of the lessons which these two dozen pages teach our country. The tiny volume mentions no hidden treasure, no secret formulas, no quick roads to wealth; rather its title, *The Daily Sacrifice,* and its contents show that it is a prayer book, with petitions planned for the morning and the evening of each day in the week. Listen to only a few of its contrite pleadings: "Pardon, I beseech Thee, my sins, remove them from my presence, as far as the East is from the West, and accept . . . me for the merits of Thy Son Jesus Christ!" "Remit my transgressions . . . and cover them all with the absolute obedience of Thy dear Son . . . Jesus Christ, offered upon the cross for me!" "O blessed Father, let Thy Son's blood wash me from all impurities . . . that I may know my sins are forgiven by His death and passion!" "I humbly beseech Thee to be merciful to me in the free pardon of my sins, for the sake of Thy dear Son, my only Savior, Jesus Christ, who came not to call the righteous, but sinners to repentance."

Who wrote these reverent prayers, expressing a deep consciousness of sin, yet even more, a victorious faith in the mercy of God's Son, voicing a fervent supplication for family, friends, Church, and State? Were these petitions laboriously penned by an aged servant of the Lord? Were they the pleas of a missionary, the intercessions of a humble scientist, the devotions of a reverent author? No! These were the prayers of George Washington, America's most illustrious leader, the anniversary of whose birth our country observes today.

Written when the defender of our liberties was twenty years old, in the prime of youth, the age in which too many young people now find no time for personal communion with their heavenly Father and show too little regard for the Savior, these prayers teach pointed lessons. They direct us, 200 years later, to spurn atheist advances which would remove God as the Author of our blessings, just as they strengthen us who love the Lord never to be ashamed of the Savior's name. Today many leaders speak publicly of "God," "Providence," "the Deity"; but except in the two extremes, profanity and worship, how seldom do we hear the name *"which is above every name,"* Jesus Christ? Washington was so completely dedicated to his Redeemer that he wrote the Marquis de Lafayette: "I am not ashamed to call myself a Christian, and I earnestly try to be one." In a memorial address, commemorating the first President's death, General Lee declared, "Washington, the savior of his country, did not disdain to acknowledge and adore his great Savior." The United States experienced its mightiest benedictions when its leaders most reverently exalted the Lord Jesus, and, conversely, our heaviest hardships came upon us when we opposed and neglected the Gospel of His grace.

The climax in Washington's struggle for our liberty came just 170 years ago this winter, when our cause seemed hopelessly lost. Many of our troops perished in below-zero weather at Valley Forge; others, half-starved and only thinly clad, were being urged to desert. In comfort and warmth at Philadelphia, Americans, enemies of Christ, attacked Washington, trying to undermine his leadership. Now, where did our country's father find strength to carry on? His officers noted that once every day, often after their staff meetings, Washington would

It is God in the Garden

walk into a secluded, near-by woods — but for what purpose none of them knew. Then one day pro-British Isaac Potts, a millowner and minister, passing through that grove, heard a solemn, pleading voice, and stopped. Peering through the thickets, he saw Washington, commander-in-chief of our revolutionary forces, kneeling in earnest prayers, tears streaming down his cheeks. Reverently Isaac Potts listened to the end of the intercession, and then, as Washington arose, he quickly returned to his home, no longer a Tory, but pledged to the American cause; for, he wrote, "If there is anyone on this earth to whom the Lord will listen, it is to George Washington. . . . Under such a commander there can be no doubt of our eventually establishing our independence, and that God in His providence has willed it so."

Today, as we envision Washington, the Christian patriot, kneeling in prayer at Valley Forge, our thoughts in this second Lenten devotion center on Washington's Savior when in another crisis, the heaviest in all history, He, the world's Redeemer, also knelt on the ground to begin with prayer His suffering for the atonement of our sins. We invite you to behold Jesus in Gethsemane and to believe

IT IS GOD IN THE GARDEN

This is the sacred truth taught by our text (Saint John's eighteenth chapter, verses four to nine) which tells us: *"Jesus, therefore, knowing all things that should come upon Him, went forth and said unto them, Whom seek ye? They answered Him, Jesus of Nazareth. Jesus saith unto them, I am He. And Judas also, which betrayed Him, stood with them. As soon, then, as He had said unto them, I am He, they went backward and fell to the*

*ground. Then asked He them again, Whom seek ye?
And they said, Jesus of Nazareth. Jesus answered, I
have told you that I am He; if therefore ye seek Me, let
these go their way."*

I

SEE HIM AS YOUR ALL-KNOWING GOD!

As in spirit we enter Gethsemane with our Lord, there in the Passover moonlight to behold the Garden's hushed beauty, we remind ourselves that, as Jesus frequently sought out this attractive spot on the slopes of Olivet, so His followers are entitled to choose the beautiful. Many people have the mistaken idea that Christians must prefer the plain, the monotonous, the severe, the drab, and the ugly; but the entire Bible protests against this. Our Father made the world His marvelous masterpiece, filled with scenes of exquisite loveliness; and even after man's sin had disfigured the earth, it still is adorned with unnumbered scenic wonders which Heaven wants us to enjoy. If you have a pretty home with attractive grounds, thank God for these endowments and devote them to His glory, as Christ hallowed Gethsemane! Indeed, if you yourself are pleasing in features or personality, praise your Maker for this gift of His grace, and let your consecrated life radiate a spiritual charm! Noted painters and sculptors, talented musicians and singers, outstanding poets and authors, have been humble followers of the Savior, who employed their creative artistry to produce beauty in marble and on canvas or through sound, song, and words. The earth's magnificence is for you who love the Lord. Use it to His honor, but don't abuse it in serving sin!

It was not the scenic attraction which frequently drew Jesus to Gethsemane and again brought Him there on the

It is God in the Garden

last night of His life. He resorted to its shaded recesses, alone and far from the noisy city, to speak with His heavenly Father in earnest, intimate petition. To our blessed Redeemer prayer was a high privilege, a divine power, and an unfailing promise; and as the silver moonlight of spring gleamed on the Garden, during the final hours before His arrest, we find Him engaged in supplication such as the world has never otherwise seen.

Christ's most ardent followers have likewise dedicated their last moments to sacred communion with the Father. In Africa, Livingstone died praying on his knees. A century before, the tireless Moravian George Schmidt, driven back to Europe from the South African mission field by colonists' hatred, was likewise found dead on his knees, his spirit having departed while he pleaded for his poor Hottentots. Will you have the comfort of prayer in your last hours? You can hardly expect to be blessed by this confidence when the end approaches if now, in health and strength, you refuse to commune with your God. Sudden accident, a long coma and unconsciousness, may prevent you from beseeching the Almighty when you need Him most.

How all-important, then, that now, while you can, you follow the fourfold lesson of fervent and effectual prayer Christ teaches here in Gethsemane! First: beseech your heavenly Father earnestly, as you see Jesus on His knees, and headlong on His face, appealing with an intense fervor while bloody sweat covers His countenance and an angel from heaven has to strengthen Him! Then, ask repeatedly, as three times you hear the silence of night broken by the Savior's *"O My Father, . . . let this cup pass from Me!"* Bow submissively before the Almighty, as your Redeemer's resigned obedience pleads, *"Never-*

theless not My will, but Thine, be done!" Above all, pray in His saving name! Believe assuredly that because of the battle He fought and won in the Garden, because of the life He laid down at the cross and took up again at the open grave, you can fully trust His pledge, *"Whatsoever ye shall ask the Father in My name, He will give it you."* Then you will pray triumphantly, and, as the crucifixion gave way to the resurrection, so your requests will be answered by divine replies.

Saint John passes by these early events marking the Savior's agonized prayer, since the purpose of his book is not to restate what the other Evangelists record, but to supplement Matthew, Mark, and Luke with material not found in their writings. Especially, however, would John emphasize that Christ in the Garden, despite His anguish, is God in the Garden. Toward the end of his Gospel, John declares that his chapters *"are written that ye might believe that Jesus is the Christ, the Son of God."* Of the four New Testament accounts of Gethsemane, John's is the more directly concerned with showing us the Redeemer's divine power and with emphasizing that the grief-gripped Sufferer is our God, with heavenly might and glory.

Therefore, the Fourth Gospel starts this eighteenth chapter by mentioning the murderous mob which stormed up Olivet's heights to capture our Lord. John tells us of the high priests' henchmen and followers, the Pharisees, the Roman legionaries, altogether at least several hundred persons, we may believe, who suddenly crashed into the Garden, intent on seizing a single, solitary Prisoner. Look at this mob of soldiers and civilians, the Jewish opponents and Roman conquerors, groups which otherwise hated each other, now united in a common cause, the determination to put Christ out of the way! When the F.B.I surrounds a gangster's hideout, it uses a dozen or two agents, at the most, to make the capture; but rushing into Gethsemane, breaking its shadows by streaking glares of light, turning its silence into a riotous rumble, are several hundred murder-bent men armed *"with lanterns and torches and weapons," "with swords and with staves."*

Here John brings his first proof that the suffering Savior is God. He describes our Lord, no longer agonized, but composed, and as *"knowing all things that should come upon Him."* Truly Jesus knew just where, when, and what He would suffer. Only the All-Wise could have such foreknowledge. Abraham Lincoln did not recognize in advance that Booth would assassinate him in Ford's Theater. Mohandas Gandhi was unable to foretell the date of his death or the name of his killer. Could he have done so, he might still be alive. Yet the Redeemer of our souls knew from the very beginning the exact time and the most minute details of His crucifixion; and He could have side-stepped Gethsemane's grief to do away with Calvary's death torture. He could have; but He did not, for He loved us so boundlessly that deliberately, compassionately, He took upon Himself the most crushing of all cruelties and went the way of the cross in order that we might go the way to the crown.

How utterly weak and helpless men of themselves are as they seek to learn the future! What a sorry mess the so-called best minds of the nations have made of our age! With two global conflicts in the past, and the threat of a third, all-out, atomic annihilation not far ahead, scientific thought has completely failed in guaranteeing security and happiness for tomorrow! In California a professional man, beset by the fear that one of his three children might be run over and killed by an automobile, changed his plans to buy a home in Pasadena, which he regarded as too crowded, therefore too dangerous, and instead purchased twelve acres on a mountain. To make this remote place absolutely safe for his family, the father had "Slow Down" warning signs posted at each turn of the road leading to his estate. Before building the house, he himself fenced in a play-yard, so situated that no automobile could get within fifty feet of it. He erected his home, then his garage, so arranged that only his car could be driven up to it. The construction finished, he could find only one hazard; he had to back out of his garage, and he feared that in some way he might unknowingly run over one of the children. At once he drew plans for a turn-around, which would do away with backing in and out; and he was planning to pour the concrete for this final safety measure, when, as he backed his car from the garage, his eighteen-month-old son broke from his sister's grasp, ran into the path of the auto, and was killed instantly.

No matter how secure you feel yourself, however confidently you rely on your money (hundreds of millions were lost in recent stock-market crashes); however assuredly you build your hopes on good health (accidents demand a greater toll of our people than the bloody battles of the war took); however surely you look forward to a long life (did you read of the Pennsylvania pastor who, pleading with his congregation to prepare themselves to meet God, suddenly slumped over himself and died in the pulpit?); however trustfully you follow men's roseate forecast for the future (and remember, only four short years ago Nazi leaders were loudly claiming

It is God in the Garden

victory! Recall, too, that while the whole world was promised full freedom of speech and religion, freedom from want and fear, in shattering reality the Christian faith is opposed and persecuted today; multiplied millions on the face of the earth, their consciences tyrannized, dare not speak their mind; world hunger and want are wider than mankind has ever previously known, and the fear of global disaster rises as a haunting specter to terrorize the peace-loving); whatever happy picture fortune-tellers may draw for the years ahead, push these faulty guesses aside! You need Heaven's guarantee of grace; and here, thank God! in Christ, is this divine certainty.

Look to Him who in the one Gospel of Saint John at least fourteen times proves Himself the all-knowing God by showing His foreknowledge of the future! Say to Him, "Thou knowest *'the way I take,'*" commit yourself to the loving care which led Him to die on the cross for you; pray trustfully,

> Take Thou my hands and lead me
> O'er life's rough way,

and as your God He will truly guide you on every step you take.

Many of you need this perfect love of the Lord Jesus particularly now, because heavy calamities have struck. Near the seminary in Saint Louis a few nights ago a house caught fire, and six children burned to death. A few days later in Utica, New York, when flames swept their two-story frame house, eleven members of one family perished. Sudden accident may have brought bereavement to your home, and you feel that you can go no further. Your letters show that some of you are saddened by divorce or by unfaithfulness on the part of your life's mate, by the disrespect or disobedience of your children. A score of other sorrows, loss of health or limb, pain of sickness or surgery, reduced income or deceased earning power, may loom close to you; but in the Son of God's precious name I can give you, the believers who crown Christ Savior and Sovereign of everything you are and have, this radiant assurance: Just as surely as Gethsemane, Gabbatha, and Golgotha were planned by His self-sacrificing love as the merciful means for your redemption, so, clinging to your Redeemer, you are guaranteed that your burdens and problems, sorrows and sufferings, have all been foreseen by Him as disguised blessings, the deep evidence of His undying devotion, which enables you to exult, *"Whom the Lord loveth He chasteneth."* The Savior's leading may take you over rough paths; but never doubt, Christ's way is always the right way, the sure way, the only way to your eternal happiness! Nothing you may suffer is unknown to Him; for He, as your great and good Lord, paying the total penalty for your transgressions, enduring far more than you will ever be asked to bear, measures from His own experience every agony which can afflict you; and He has promised that your burden will never break you.

Therefore, trust Him, your God! Raise your hearts joyfully to Jesus, even when it seems that there can be no help and hope for you! Rely on Him so completely that you recognize His redeeming love in your reverses, His purifying power in your pains, His sustaining strength in your sorrows! Over in Germany it was my privilege to meet one of the most distinguished New Testament scholars, Dr. Gerhardt Kittel,* who is held in semicustody

---

* Dr. Gerhardt Kittel died in the Lord, July 11, 1948.

It is God in the Garden

at Beuron in the French Zone. With unforgettable emphasis this internationally recognized authority on the Greek language told me that the terrors of war and subsequent imprisonment, the bleak and blank future, had made him build his hopes on divine grace more constantly and completely than ever before. In each of his frequent letters since that memorable visit he has never failed to express his joy in the all-knowing Savior. Why, then, should you, in a free, victorious, wealthy country, unhindered in your activities, live on, downcast, disheartened, and desperate, when, once in trusting faith you keep Jesus as your omniscient Guide, the Lord of love is at your side every moment? Here, my fellow redeemed, in the Christ who sees and knows you, your God in Gethsemane, is Heaven's help, hope, and happiness for you. The Holy Spirit grant that you will receive Him as your Redeemer and revere Him as your God!

II

SEE HIM AS YOUR ALMIGHTY GOD!

Saint John's second proof that our Savior is the Lord of Lords is given us when our text continues, *"Jesus . . . went forth and said unto them, Whom seek ye? They answered Him, Jesus of Nazareth. Jesus saith unto them, I am He. . . . As soon, then, as He had said unto them, I am He, they went backward and fell to the ground."* We do not understand why the armed band of His enemies did not seize Christ immediately after Judas placed the traitor's kiss on His brow, nor why the Temple troops did not know Him. Perhaps the flare and smoke of their torches blurred their vision; perhaps the leaders had never personally seen Him; perhaps — and I submit this as another explanation — these man hunters were half drunken, inflamed for their loathsome task by liquor, just as in our day killers prepare for crime with a double dose of whisky.

At any rate, the mob did not recognize Christ, and how easily He could have escaped! Yet — eternal praise for His limitless grace! — Jesus cherished you too much for that. He loved you in your sins more than His own life in its perfection. Therefore, to prevent these armed fanatics from seizing someone else by mistake, our Lord, calm and undisturbed amid the clamor surrounding Him, tells the leaders, *"I am He."* Hardly had He thus identified Himself when, as our Scripture reports, *"They went backward and fell to the ground."* Bible students have long debated as to whether for a few short moments our Savior took the divine form which He assumed on the Mount of Transfiguration; but nothing in our text indicates this. Rather does the record lead us to believe that the words He, as God Almighty, spoke threw His would-be murderers into retreat and then cast them sprawling on the garden ground.

Only the Almighty's words can thus paralyze armed forces. Scientists claim to have produced a whistling sound beyond the range of our hearing which can sometimes make men dizzy; but no leader of experts will ever be able to repeat this miracle, by which a voice, without amplification or machinery, hurls helpless men on their backs. Science is not God; but Jesus is.

The Savior's word could have kept His enemies prostrate, and another word could have battered down His foes — Annas, Caiaphas, Herod, Pilate, the misled mob, the calloused Roman legionaries — every one of them. Here, again, however, the Son of God shows you the all-

It is God in the Garden 75

enduring mercy which is beyond human comparison. Believe it, trust it, thank Heaven for it today: the Lord of love permitted those prostrate foes to arise again because, in His consuming passion for your soul, He was determined to die for you, as He pushed aside every possibility of escape from Calvary's cruelty and crime!

Jesus was not afraid of His enemies there in the Garden, for He knew that everyone who would repent of that monstrous evil and come to Him in true faith would be saved eternally, just as He could foresee that all who kept on hating Him would be struck down by three other words of His judgment, *"Depart from Me!"* Tradition and history combine to tell us that Christ's hardened persecutors were violently destroyed. Annas and Caiaphas lost their high priesthood; Herod died in anguish; Pilate ended as a suicide. Similarly the royal fiends of the first Christian century, their hands and souls stained with martyrs' blood, disappeared in hideous horror. Nero, banished from the throne, took his own life; Domitian was assassinated by his servants; Hadrian ended with intense physical and mental agony; Decius drowned in a marsh, and his body was never recovered; Valerian was captured and skinned alive; Diocletian became insane; Maximianus died of strangulation. Finally Jesus always wins, and His enemies always lose. *"Be not deceived; God is not mocked,"* the errorless Word proclaims throughout this age of blasphemy. Every agent of atheism, no matter how proud and mighty, will be hurled to defeat. The regiments of Red ruin which today sneer: "There is no God." "Religion is the opiate of the people." "We will strike God from the skies." "The churches must be destroyed" — these and other literally translated slogans of spiritual sabotage and slaughter repeatedly re-echo in our day — will die as whispers when the Lord speaks in His wrath.

How overwhelmingly important, then, for you still at enmity with the Savior to understand that if you persist in rejecting your Redeemer, you, too, will be hurled, not to the ground for a few moments, but into hell forever! What sustaining strength, on the other hand, to have the assurance that when your life is *"hid with Christ,"* He will repulse every foe of your faith and will help you make His divine Word your sure defense! Martin Luther, surveying a world of wickedness, but above and beyond that beholding his "Mighty Fortress," sang triumphantly, "Though devils all the world should fill . . . one little word can fell them." Believe this power of Christ's Word for peace and joy and strength! Are you young folks besieged by the forces of sinful desire, and do you yearn for the resistance to overcome them? Trusting Christ and His Word, you can challenge every agent of evil with the Savior's own *"Get thee behind Me, Satan!"* and thus triumph over temptation! Do you middle-aged folks want peace to replace trouble in your homes, new love instead of lost love? Put sacred Scripture to work in your family circle, and by the Holy Spirit's indwelling, this truth, *"which is able to build you up,"* will cast down selfishness and stubbornness in your household, to make way for Him who says, *"Peace I leave with you, My peace I give unto you."* Are you older folks, approaching the end of your pilgrimage, eager to have a sure hope of heaven on a foundation so firm that *"the gates of hell shall not prevail against it?"* Go back to Jesus, your Lord, in the Garden, hear Him say, *"I am He,"* or, as the the original Greek has it, *"I am,"* part of God's Old Testament name, *"I am that I am,"* and,

It is God in the Garden

pointing to the Crucified, say, "He is my God and my Savior!" Then the foes of your faith will vanish, and you will have the guarantee of glory which neither men nor devils can destroy.

III

SEE HIM AS YOUR ALL-LOVING GOD!

Besides showing us Christ in Gethsemane as our all-knowing, all-powerful God, John also pictures Him in climax as our all-loving Lord. When His heavily armed enemies, helpless before His might, regained their feet, Jesus again asked them, *"Whom seek ye?"*; and when dazed by their sudden defeat, they answer, *"Jesus of Nazareth,"* our Lord tells them pointedly, *"I have told you that I am He."* What magnificent heroism, and what startling proof of His voluntary suffering in this twofold *"I am He!"* How true Christ's declaration to His disciples, *"No man taketh it* [My life] *from Me, but I lay it down of Myself."*

However, the height of divine love in the garden is seen when the Son of God directs the man hunters surrounding Him, *"If therefore ye seek Me, let these go their way."* He was ready to suffer the pain and shame of the cross, but He wanted His followers freed. The command *"Let these go"* has since that night in Gethsemane become His mandate of mercy for us. After we, too, pledge Him our allegiance, recognizing and revering Him as our all-sufficient Savior, He protects our souls as He shielded the disciples' bodies in the Garden, since He surrendered Himself to liberate His loved ones. That substitution, *"the Just for the unjust,"* the Redeemer for the ruined, is Scripture's summit truth. When the infallible Word tells us, first, *"with His stripes we are healed*"; second, "*He died for all*"; third, He was "*made a curse for us*"; fourth, He "*suffered for* [our] *sins*"; fifth, He "*laid down His life for us*"; sixth, He "*washed us from our sins in His blood*"; seventh, He reconciled us "*in the body of His flesh through death*"; eighth, He purchased us "*with His own blood*"; ninth, He "*was once offered to bear the sins of many*"; tenth, He "*gave Himself for our sins*"; eleventh, He "*died for the ungodly*"; twelfth, He "*died for our sins*" — Holy Writ thus in a dozen different passages, chosen from a dozen different books, invites us to "*behold the Lamb of God, which taketh away the sin of the world*," these multiple messages of mercy guarantee us that today, too, with the same grace He showed in the Garden, Jesus stands between us and our souls' enemies to repeat this reassurance of redemption, "*Let these go!*"

If your conscience insistently recalls the guilt of sins with such crushing force that you begin to doubt whether Heaven's compassion is meant for you, and you feel you have fallen too low to be restored; if the devil tries to convince you that your transgressions are too terrifying to be forgiven; if the dread thought of meeting death and its judgment pursues you, then, with Satanic foes mobilized to tear the guarantee of the Savior's deliverance from your soul, believe the Gethsemane grace, "*Let these go,*" and the Calvary compassion that guilt is washed away by His blood and the penalty of your iniquities fully and forever paid by His redeeming death on the cross!

Only God could direct, "*Let these go,*" and give Himself to secure our eternal freedom from sin, death, and damnation. Brave men can lay down their lives for their fellow men. Recently President Truman awarded the

It is God in the Garden

Medal of Merit to Dr. Claude Barlow, who in Egypt twice permitted himself to be infected with the dread Bilharzia disease, a bladder malady caused by parasites. Three years ago Christmas Dr. Barlow's condition became grave, but he refused all treatment, preferring to serve science as a host to the Bilharzia parasite. His robust health shattered, he continued to search for the cure. Even the high award, the Medal of Merit, cannot express fully our gratitude for self-sacrifice such as this; but Jesus' atoning love was immeasurably greater. Dr. Barlow suffered in the effort to find a cure for one disease of the body, but Jesus gave Himself to heal all the sicknesses of the soul which, if unremoved, bring everlasting death.

The Post Office Department will issue a commemorative stamp featuring the heroism of four Army chaplains aboard the ill-fated troop transport *Dorchester*, torpedoed in icy Arctic waters during the war. Because there were not enough life preservers for the troops, these four chaplains removed their own, gave them to four G. I.'s, and drowned when the ship sank. Postage-stamp recognition and Congressional award cannot do justice to the *"greater love"* which these heroes showed. Their deliberate choice of drowning stands out in contrast to the greed for gold which made many seek huge, personal profit in warfare. Yet indescribably more merciful was our Lord's choice of the cross and His death of shame! Each of the four self-sacrificing chaplains saved the life of one man — a friend, but by His eternally planned atonement, our Savior offers the teeming millions of mankind, His enemies, eternal life with Him in heaven.

He had to be divine, you see, for only God could

thus remove the ruin from a sin-cursed race; and by the eternal Word of truth, He is God, together with His Father and with His Spirit, the one true God. Triumphing over the man-made idols of our selfish age, He is your God, your saving and sustaining God, your loving and living God, your eternal and atoning God.

Thirteen years ago Joseph Majczek, found guilty of murdering a Chicago policeman, was sentenced to ninety-nine years' imprisonment. Recently when his innocence was established, Governor Green granted him pardon, and the Illinois legislature awarded him $24,000 in payment for the twelve years he had spent in the penitentiary. What can you give Christ, when you know that He, the sinless Savior, was wounded for your transgressions, and crucified for your crimes? Loan sharks in Missouri now collect up to 1,200 per cent interest on a few hundred dollars' loan. How much could Jesus demand in repayment for His redemption? Yet no money can remove that indebtedness; and, far more than silver or gold, the merciful Redeemer wants you, your soul sin-cleansed, your heart faith-hallowed, your spirit sanctified, your body transformed into His living temple.

Therefore, no question which any person can ask you approaches in importance these ten words: Do you believe that Christ is your God and Savior? George Washington had the victorious faith which unhesitatingly and uncompromisingly answered "Yes," and it brought him power, guidance, blessing, and finally heaven. If today you make Jesus your Redeemer, then from this Sunday on He will be with you through sunshine and sorrow, health and sickness, gain and loss, life and death. You, too, will have Christ's assurance chiseled on Washington's granite tomb at Mount Vernon, *"I am the Res-*

It is God in the Garden

urrection and the Life." In His holy name, the only saving name, the one everlasting name, I plead with you, "Be reconciled to your heavenly Father through repentant trust in His Son, your Savior!"

If you already have pledged Him your allegiance, stand up for Him as your God! Defend this divine truth with all your might, because it is widely and wickedly assailed! From the beginning of the Church, men have hated to bow before Christ as their Lord. Sixteen hundred years ago politicians began to play with the fundamental facts of our faith, and in their unbelief to comit the sin of which many are guilty, denying Jesus' deity. In that apostasy the Holy Spirit had chosen a champion of His truth, a young man, Athanasius. In the year 325, at an immense gathering of believers, called the First General Council of the Christian Church, in Nicea, Asia Minor, a creed was adopted which now bears his name. It expresses faith in Jesus, who is called "the only-begotten Son of God, begotten of His Father before all worlds, God of God, Light of Light, Very God of Very God." This loyalty to the Savior made the mobilized forces of unbelief seek to destroy Athanasius; but when he was told by Emperor Constantine, "The whole world is against you," he answered courageously, "Then Athanasius is against the world." Five times leaders who would have made Christ a mere man forced him into exile. Six times the reigning emperor planned to kill him, demanding that those who found him deliver him. Nevertheless people shielded him, and not a single person was base enough to reveal his whereabouts. Then, twenty-one years after the Nicene Creed had been adopted, truth, as it always must, triumphed. Athanasius came back to his church at Alexandria in the greatest victory that place had ever seen. People marched to meet him a hundred miles outside the city, and the festive celebration which marked his return excelled even the most imposing procession of military triumph Egypt had previously known.

If, in the smaller circles of your influence, with the same devotion and fearlessness you also proclaim and defend the Christ of the Garden and the Christ of the cross, as "God of God, Light of Light, Very God of Very God," you, too, will meet the opposition of hatred. In the end, however, as Athanasius did, you will win, for *"this is the victory that overcometh the world, even our faith."* Then, in the Almighty's time and by His grace, you will march in a procession incomparably more radiant and resplendent even than the triumphal advance of Athanasius. You will come to the eternal throne, where Christ, no longer tortured and crucified, but victorious and glorified, will be revealed in heavenly majesty as your almighty Ruler and Redeemer. Bow before Him now in spirit, and acclaim Him *"My Lord and my God!" "Fight the good fight of faith,"* continue in the faith, and die in the faith! Then, all praise to Him who *"loved us"* and *"gave Himself for us,"* you will live forever, no longer merely believing, but in reality seeing your blessed Savior as your gracious God. The Holy Spirit bring all of us together for that glory! *Amen!*

CHRIST -- OR CRIME?

"Now, at that feast the governor was wont to release unto the people a prisoner whom they would. And they had then a notable prisoner, called Barabbas. Therefore, when they were gathered together, Pilate said unto them, Whom will ye that I release unto you? Barabbas, or Jesus, which is called Christ? For he knew that for envy they had delivered Him. . . . But the chief priests and elders persuaded the multitude that they should ask Barabbas, and destroy Jesus. The governor answered and said unto them, Whether of the twain will ye that I release unto you? They said, Barabbas. Pilate saith unto them, What shall I do, then, with Jesus, which is called Christ? They all say unto him, Let Him be crucified." SAINT MATTHEW 27:15-18, 20-22

SACRED SPIRIT OF TRUTH AND LIGHT: At the close of the extra day which Thy grace has added to this year, we praise Thee for the merciful guidance by which Thou didst rescue us from the ruin of eternal death and damnation by bringing us to faith in Christ's saving Gospel. What blessed assurance we have in Jesus, whose blood has cleansed us from all guilt, whose suffering and dying delivers us from the horrors of hell, guarantees the glories of heaven! Humbly, but earnestly we beseech Thee to call many sinners to repentance and to reliance on the finished salvation our blessed Redeemer purchased with His life on Calvary's cross! Make the extra day in this leap year the spiritual birthday for masses, who contritely confess Christ their Savior! We ask, not for recognition, applause, earthly esteem, but we do beg Thee, O sanctifying Spirit, for many souls drawn to their divine Redeemer, reborn by Thy might. Help millions now hear the supreme question: "What shall I do, then, with Jesus?" and answer by giving themselves to the saving Son of God! Without Thee we cannot call Jesus Lord; therefore come to us now, Holy Spirit! Take full possession of our hearts and minds! We ask it in our only Savior's blessed name. *Amen!*

IN Paris, before the World Wars, the Emberts were a wealthy, prominent family. Elise Embert, the charming daughter, devoted to the Lord, was planning to marry a handsome suitor, popular in Parisian social circles. He feigned interest in her devotion to Christ, but on the night before the wedding, at a large prenuptial party, he revealed his hatred of Scripture. Taking some younger guests off to a corner, he entertained them at first with sly, and later open attacks on the Bible and the Christian creed — "old women's faith," he called it. Elise Embert, the bride-to-be, happened to overhear him and quietly begged him to stop, insisting she could not endure such mockery. He waived away her objections with the smiling rebuke, "My clever little bride is surely not involved in such silly things." Then, turning from her, he began anew to ridicule religion, this time in blasphemous earnest. He had not spoken long, however, when Elise approached him again to announce: "Whoever does not hold God and His Word sacred will not hold the marriage tie sacred. Whoever does not love God will not truly love his wife. From this moment on I am no longer yours." The stunned bridegroom protested that he had merely been joking, insisted that he did revere the Almighty; but his insincerity was too apparent. Elise Embert stood by her decision, preferring to remain unmarried and keep Christ, rather than be bound in lifelong wedlock to a scoffer.

Not so dramatically, perhaps, but nevertheless certainly every one of you must make a choice between the

Christ — or Crime?

Savior and sin. The Lenten question, *"What shall I do, then, with Jesus"* is the one issue which confronts all of you — rich or poor, healthy or sick, learned or unschooled, high or low, American or foreigner, white or black, red or yellow. You can avoid a thousand decisions, but you can never completely side-step this choice between God and godlessness. Therefore, in our third Lenten study, proceeding to our Lord's trial in Pilate's palace, I remind you that you, too, must choose either

CHRIST — OR CRIME

May the Holy Spirit help you decide for Jesus, as you hear the record of our text (Saint Matthew, chapter twenty-seven, verses fifteen to eighteen, and twenty to twenty-two): *"Now, at that feast the governor was wont to release unto the people a prisoner whom they would. And they had then a notable prisoner, called Barabbas. Therefore, when they were gathered together, Pilate said unto them, Whom will ye that I release unto you? Barabbas, or Jesus, which is called Christ? For he knew that for envy they had delivered Him. . . . . But the chief priests and elders persuaded the multitude that they should ask Barabbas, and destroy Jesus. The governor answered and said unto them, Whether of the twain will ye that I release unto you? They said, Barabbas. Pilate saith unto them, What shall I do, then, with Jesus, which is called Christ? They all say unto him, Let Him be crucified."*

I

THE TRAGEDY OF CHOOSING CRIME

After the council of our Savior's countrymen had found Him guilty, *"worthy of death"* — and they gave this verdict because Jesus had told the truth, declaring that

He was *"the Christ, the Son of the living God"!* — the high priests' henchmen dragged Christ, early on Good Friday morning, to the palace of Pontius Pilate, the Roman governor, whose approval of the sentence was required. What a shocking spectacle: leaders intent on spilling innocent blood, hurrying to secure official permission for His murder! God strengthen us to keep Church and State completely separate in our country, and rebuke all who would wield the sword against any creed!

This must be said to Pilate's credit: first, he regarded Jesus as innocent; for the various Gospel accounts tell us five times that the Roman governor declined in effect, *"I find in Him no fault at all."* Second, he understood Jesus had been brought before him, not because He was a dangerous criminal who deserved death, but because the Temple higher-ups were jealous of His power, hated Him for personal reasons, and wanted Him removed. Our text clearly states, *"He* [Pilate] *knew that for envy they had delivered Him."* Third, Pilate tried to dissuade these bloodthirsty destroyers in half a dozen different ways. Of course, he was weak, vacillating; had he been a real man, the best principles of his paganism would have induced him to set Christ free immediately and unconditionally. Despite his weakness, Pilate was not so bad and brutal as many of our time. Pierre van Paassen tells of an interview in Paris with Marshall Lyautey, controller of French colonies and North Africa empire builder. In the conversation Van Paassen asked the French leader for his estimate of Pontius Pilate as a colonial administrator. "Bah!" snapped Marshall Lyautey, "He was too lax. He let Jesus' teaching spread too far." When Van Paassen countered by asking, "What would you have done, Marshall Lyautey, if you had been Pilate?" Unhesitatingly the French warlord replied, "I would have settled the whole matter early and easily by putting Jesus in front of a firing squad when He was up north in Galilee." Modern unbelief, you see, is worse than ancient hatred of Christ. Nero and his successors murdered martyrs by the thousands, but present-day Red atheism has killed them the ten thousands. The Roman Diocletian ruined scores of churches; but listen to this terrifying Communist toll in Russia: 88,000 religious buildings destroyed or closed, 18,000,000 acres of church property confiscated! Watch, work, and pray to prevent enemies of God from securing control of our country!

One of the ways by which Pilate hoped to free Jesus was inducing the crowd to request a Passover pardon for Him. As at Christmas time President Truman set a number of conscientious objectors free, and as on other holidays governors similarly pronounce amnesty, so, we read, *"at that feast the governor was wont to release unto the people a prisoner whom they would."* Shirking his own responsibility and seeking to shift the burden of decision from himself to others, Pilate concluded that if he gave the mob its choice of the prisoner to be freed, they would be moved to demand the release of the Galilean, especially when they had to select either Him, innocent as He was, or a condemned, grossly guilty criminal.

In Jerusalem just at this time *"they had . . . a . . . prisoner, called Barabbas."* The little we know definitely of him may be summarized in these brief notes: Barabbas was a *"notable"* prisoner, that is, a notorious lawbreaker, popular, perhaps, with the perverted mob. His name meant "son of a father"; but what man would want a son like this, a rebel, a robber, a murderer? This criminal, representing the very opposite of Jesus — guilt instead of innocence, violence in place of virtue, murder rather than mercy — Pilate had selected in his plan to acquit the Savior, for we read, *"When they were gathered together, Pilate said unto them, Whom will ye that I release unto you? Barabbas, or Jesus, which is called Christ?"*

Not the slightest doubt remains that if the crowd had been left to itself, without being poisoned by prejudice and blinded by brutal bigotry, it would have set our Lord free. Behold these two prisoners side by side! The One, wrongfully accused of rebellion, and the other, grossly guilty of this crime! Jesus, whom even false witnesses and perjured testimony have not been able to convict of a single misdeed, since, in Scripture's summary, He *"went about doing good"*; and Barabbas, convicted as a rebel, a robber, a murderer! You need not be a believer to recognize the difference between the two men is as between heaven and hell.

Hardly had Pilate made this proposal and put the choice squarely before the mob, when the leaders, checking any rising sympathy, lined up the crowd for the most damnable decision men have ever made. We can hardly believe our eyes when the text reports, *"The chief priests and elders persuaded the multitude that they should ask Barabbas, and destroy Jesus."* Keep clearly in mind that those milling before the palace were not Jerusalem's ruffians and riffraff, gangsters and gunmen! No, the masterminds in this murder plot were *"the chief priests and elders."* The leaders in Church and State, officials who were to show truth, justice, honor, here use tactics that would make the underworld blush! Impatient for their reply, Pilate repeats his question, *"Whether of the twain will ye that I release unto you?"* and now hear this record of ruin, this fatal decision, which was to bring death and destruction, this terrifying tragedy in three words, *"They said, Barabbas"!* In the choice between the Savior and sin, God and godlessness, they deliberately decided for crime and against Christ.

We could not understand this verdict, had not men, since that day, continued their rejection of the Redeemer and their selection of sordid evil. We see this in the world about us. We face a choice between peace and war; but vain, godless leaders described by Scripture in these words, *"Destruction and misery are in their ways, and the way of peace have they not known; there is no fear of God before their eyes,"* choose bloodshed for personal or national profit. In this enlightened generation one hundred million human beings are captured, wounded, or killed. The Almighty filled the earth with plenty of food for everyone, but confronted by the Christ-or-Barabbas choice, the greedy select selfishness, and tens of millions now hover on the very edge of starvation. Our Lord asks us to show mercy. *"Love your enemies,"* His directive reads; but Barabbas-like brutality directs world figures to use force and forget kindness. Too often cruelty wins over compassion. According to expert estimate 4,800,000 displaced persons, civilians driven into Germany from their homes in Eastern Europe, not only lost all their property, but died miserable deaths.

For rebuilding this war-ruined world, men can either adopt the clear blueprints outlined in sacred Scripture, which start with spiritual reconstruction, or they can follow the designs of disaster which dishonor the Most High, deny His existence, deal in unspeakable cruelty.

Yet — God have mercy on us for Jesus' sake! — blind leaders of the blind willfully and boastfully rebel against our heavenly Father, persecute His children, and bring millions the closest approach to hell this earth knows.

Who can foretell the severe punishment divine wrath may visit on our age for this widest of all revolts against the Lord of Lords? The last issue of the *United Nations World* magazine describes a new gas, which the Nazis made during the war. First this produced blindness, cramps, and convulsions in those who inhaled it; then it made its victims insane, maniacs with murderous urges. Even without this gas, however, our best scientific minds are often occupied with a driving desire to find new means for killing greater masses of mankind. If infidel leaders continue their mad revolt against the Lord, He may let them use their hellish forces against each other, as the horrors of atomic, cosmic, chemical, bacterial destruction turn large areas of the earth, entire nations, into wilderness. After the first atomic bomb exploded in the New Mexico desert near Los Alamos, investigators found that its heat had melted the sand into green glass. Recently archaeologists, digging in the cradle land of the human race, the Euphrates Valley, discovered underneath the layers of the various ages a stratum of fused green glass, the same material, they say, which atomic explosion produced. Some have asked, "Did mankind once before have the atomic secret and use it to destroy itself?" This hardly seems possible; but one truth is certain, fulfilling, as it does, Jesus' promises concerning the beginning of the world's end: We in this age, farther from the Almighty than our forefathers were, when we should be closer, may experience the crushing curse of bowing to Barabbas rather than clinging to Christ, as global tribulation sweeps down upon a God-forsaking generation.

We note the same fatal folly in our own country. Sin is selected, and Christ is rejected by ungrateful, unbelieving millions. The United States is at the crossroads, where one path, obedience to God's Word, is marked by the promise of His blessing, and the other, disobedience to His truth, is cursed by His wrath. *"Thou shalt not kill,"* Heaven declares. Pushing Christ aside in favor of crime, more than 13,000 people in our country each year, 36 each day, commit murder or manslaughter. *"Thou shalt not steal,"* the Lord commands, but again, preferring Barabbas to honesty, godless men in these United States, every twenty-four hours on the average, commit 172 robberies, 981 burglaries, and 2,580 miscellaneous thefts, more than a million and a third of such crimes annually. Every day during 1946, 630 automobiles were stolen, an amount which is half of the total production of a large company. *"Thou shalt not commit adultery,"* the Holy Law demands. Confronted with the choice between the beauty of pure love and Barabbas-like impurity of lust, which do our people prefer? A New York newspaper maintains that at least 500,000 G. I. babies were deserted by their fathers in various parts of the world, principally in the war areas from London to Tokyo. Half a million half-American, forsaken children, many of them living in disgrace and semistarvation!

Much more alarming, however, is the tragedy that in their choice between Christ and crime, masses throughout the United States in the "we-want-Barabbas" spirit are rejecting faith and promoting unbelief. Why do more people attend the theaters and motion pictures each week than the churches on Sunday? Why does the United States spend more for liquor than it does for the education of its children? Why do our cities count more taverns than churches? Why on typical Sundays are more than three people in this country outside the church for every one inside? Because the devotion to the spirit of Barabbas is increasing, while the devotion to the Lord is decreasing.

If a prophet of the Most High had stood before the mob at Pilate's palace and told them that by preferring crime to Christ they were signing their own national execution orders, he would have been laughed to scorn, perhaps stoned to death, as others before him had paid for such warning with their life. Yet the cry, *"Release unto us Barabbas!"* truly meant, "Give us destruction, slavery, ruin!" Before another generation had passed, the Temple, where the arch plotters met to discuss their plans for the crucifixion, was so completely devastated that not one stone was left upon another. Jerusalem, which had rejected its Savior, was rejected by Him and utterly ruined after a siege filled with cannibalism, fiendish cruelty, and unspeakable bestiality. The curse which the crowd at the governor's palace invoked on itself, *"His blood be on us and on our children!"* became a grim, ghastly reality as the Roman conquerors nailed the cruel crucifiers and their children to crosses until no more wood remained for further crucifixions.

May the United States be warned while there is still time! — Or is it too late? Have we gone too far in our forgetfulness of Heaven's mercy? Robert Ley, the high Nazi suicide at Nuremberg, left a farewell note in which he confessed: "I am torturing myself to find the reason for the downfall [of the German people], and this is the result of my contemplation: We have forsaken God, and therefore we are forsaken by God. We have put our human will in the place of His godly grace!" The Almighty keep us from this self-destruction and make us realize that when His Word warns us, *"The nation and kingdom that will not serve Thee shall perish,"* neither our size, wealth, power, nor brains, can keep us from catastrophe if we continue in growing degree to choose crime rather than Christ.

What is your choice? Do you select sin and reject your Redeemer? Be open and honest, realizing that the All-Knowing One sees even the hidden thoughts of the heart! Answer truthfully: Are you Barabbas-minded or Christ-minded? Husband, are you true to your wife, or, tired of her who helped you succeed, are you running around with another woman? Are you planning unholy divorce? Wife, are you guarding your wedding vows and, forsaking all others, keeping yourself only for your husband, or are you secretly unfaithful? Married couples, do you appreciate or despise God's gift of parenthood? Young people, dreaming of wedded happiness, do you follow the example of Elise Embert, who, as I mentioned at the beginning, refused to marry a scoffer, declaring, "Whoever does not love God will not truly love his wife"? Are you ready to start a home without Jesus' companionship, when Scripture warns you, *"Except the Lord build the house, they labor in vain that build it"?* Do you believe the Bible when it promises that purity brings Heaven's blessing, or do you bend your knees before the Barabbas of lust, declaring that you will enjoy life to the fullest, come what may? In a dozen disastrous ways, in matters of marriage, home life, and personal purity, some of you select the spirit of Barabbas and deliberately reject your Savior's love.

Even worse, too many of you prefer the anti-Christs of unbelief to the Prince of eternal pardon. You are urged to stop serving sin and begin to bow before God's Son as your Rescuer from everlasting ruin; yet repeatedly, until this moment, you have bellowed for Barabbas and consigned Christ to the cross. Again and again you have been asked to join the church; a believing wife has wept for you, prayed for you, and pleaded with you that you give yourself to Jesus; many times a pastor has visited you, inviting you to join a truth-exalting, Bible-preaching congregation; but you have preferred taverns to the temples of the Almighty; you have insisted on making Sunday sports-day instead of the Lord's day; your attendance at God's house is restricted to church suppers, with never a thought of worshiping in church services. You do not want God to tell you what to do, the Bible to curb your passions, Christ to give you pardon and peace; and as you plan the Barabbas-like spirit of rebellion over the humble surrender and service to the Savior, you are letting loose on your soul an avalanche of eternal agonies. Your willful rejection of Jesus not only darkens the last days of a devoted mother, whose eyes are red with tears on your account; you are not only bringing misery into a household which, were you to make it united in allegiance to the Lord, could be the happiest place on earth; your preference of crime to Christ not only leads others astray; but — listen carefully and get this straight: as your unbelief casts a ballot for Barabbas, you sign your own death warrant and sentence yourself to everlasting hell!

You may be uncertain about most facts of the future,

Christ — or Crime?

but the Bible's unbreakable truth leaves you in no doubt whatever concerning your destiny in the hereafter, if you continue to spurn your Redeemer. He Himself made this unmistakably clear when He warned, *"Whosoever shall deny Me before men, him will I also deny before My Father which is in heaven."* You may not know what will happen to you tomorrow, but you can be sure of what will happen when life ends, if you die in unbelief; for again the Son of God Himself declares in the seven most tragic and terrifying words in our language, *"He that believeth not shall be damned."* You may not know where you will be next week or next year; but if you live and die in boasting, Barabbas-like blasphemy, I can tell you on the basis of God's Word where you will be in the next life. In hell, in such horror that if you would only realize its agony, you would cry out in soul anguish, *"What must I do to be saved?"* and devote day and night to the search for deliverance!

The enraged mob's first reply, *"Release unto us Barabbas!"* did not settle the case for Pilate. He still thought that the sight of Jesus, beaten, bruised, and bleeding, would awaken even in the cold hearts of His accusers a sigh of sympathy, a feeling close to compassion; He still imagined that one last appeal might silence their bestial cry for the Savior's blood. Even this Roman official, who could order a hundred people cut down in cold blood without flicking an eyelash, did not know how deeply degenerate, how much worse than wild animals, godless men may become. So when he voiced his last, indirect, half-hearted plea for our Lord, *"What shall I do, then, with Jesus, which is called Christ?"* his cruel, pagan mind was hardly prepared for the raucous reply, the cruelest cry of all history, *"Let Him be crucified!"*

II

THE BLESSING OF CHOOSING CHRIST

Nineteen hundred long years have passed since that heartless crowd condemned Christ to death and consigned itself to ruin. Nineteen hundred years of startling scientific and cultural progress; yet the human heart is still the same source of vileness; each of us must ask and answer Pilate's *"What shall I do, then, with Jesus?"*

Before you try to reply or turn your radio off with a smug, indifferent "Well, *they* nailed Him to the Cross, didn't they? So what have I to do with it?" let me tell you: we helped kill God's Son. Our transgressions doomed Him to His death. Not one man, Judas, sent the Savior to Calvary; we all did, when our sins, as heavy hammer blows, pushed the nails through His quivering flesh. Not one city, Jerusalem, spilled His sacred blood on Golgotha's gloomy heights; the crimes of London, New York, Paris, Berlin, Los Angeles, Moscow, Chicago, Rome, Miami, yes, the evils of Happy Haven, Sleepy Hollow, Paradise Crossroads, Eden Valley, those of the largest metropolis or the smallest settlement — all combined to crucify Him. Not one nation, His own countrymen, scourged and tortured Him; the Germans and the Japanese, the British and the French, the Italians and the Russians, and just as certainly, we in these United States and you in Canada — all forced the crown of thorns on His whitened brow, made the lash cut more deeply into His bleeding back, and pushed the spearhead into His side. Not one age, the years of our Lord's life on earth, should be charged with the sole guilt in that most merciless miscarriage of justice, the choice of Barabbas and his brutal crime, the rejection of your Redeemer; indeed, our generation, after centuries of startling testimony to the

Savior's power and pardon, counts more unbelievers than that first century knew.

I have been trying to tell you, with the Spirit's help, that you with your sins, as I with mine, brought Calvary's unspeakable soul-and-body cruelties to Christ. Yet by the mystery and mercy of His self-giving love, so high, so wide, so deep, and especially so undeserved, that we cannot begin to measure its magnificence, Jesus, who gave Barabbas bodily freedom, gave us, in God's sight just as guilty as that Jerusalem thief and murderer, eternal soul freedom. He took our sins, their guilt, their curse, upon Himself, suffered their full pain and penalty, torture of body, agony of soul, and desolation of death, so that, reconciled with our Father above, we could be reassured of Heaven's glory. Scripture sums it all up in this clear, terse truth, *"While we were yet sinners, Christ died for us";* and in the plain, personal application this means that you are a sinner and that Christ died for you.

Now that you have heard what you did to the Savior and what the Savior in His marvelous mercy did for you, you are squarely, unavoidably before Pilate's question, *"What shall I do then with Jesus?"* Don't think for a moment that you can side-step this issue! You must answer; and you will answer, if not before, then surely after it will be too late for repentance and reliance on His redeeming love. One world power can veto the verdict of another, but no human vote can set aside God's decree, *"We must all appear before the judgment seat of Christ."*

Don't say that you are too young to make a decision or that you want to live many more years, and then perhaps in old age or eleventh-hour repentance give yourself to your Savior! The Almighty refuses to have people dictate the time when finally they condescend to receive

His grace. Neither say that you are too old to change, that you have spent all your years without bothering about religion, and, if you do say it yourself, that you have gotten along quite well! How about those fear-filled moments when you think of the grave, when an inner voice sternly warns you that you must face your God, when, despite your boasted independence, you begin to wonder what will happen to you, if the Bible is right when it says there is a heaven and a hell, that you must face the Lord whom you have cast aside?

The Holy Spirit help you realize your responsibility and make you understand that once you see your Redeemer as I have been privileged to portray Him to you, you must decide what you want, faith in Christ or allegiance to the sordid sin symbolized by Barabbas! There is no middle ground, no neutrality. Our Lord clearly stated the absolute either — or when He said, *"He that is not with Me is against Me."* You either glorify Him or crucify Him; you cannot always ignore Him.

Which will it be for you, the Christ of God or the crimes against God? Which should it be, once you begin to measure the unsearchable riches of your Savior's grace and realize that He freely and fully offers you everything you need for earth and heaven; that He loved you with a devotion which makes human affection fade away in comparison? Believe this triumphant truth: Jesus never fails! For weeks a Saint Louis hospital patient hovered between life and death. The best that medical science could offer had been procured for her help. She was treated with more than $150 worth of penicillin a week and was given forty-five blood transfusions. This, however, could not cure her, and she died. When we are fatally afflicted with the most dread disease of all, the ravages of sin's ruin, and we look to the divine Redeemer of our souls, we have the victorious assurance that His blood has already cleansed us and that with the Holy Spirit's renewing power transfused throughout our being we have no more guilt in God's sight, but are new creatures, blessed by the guarantee after death we shall live eternally in glorious resurrection bodies with Christ, for Christ, like Christ.

Therefore, in His name and for your soul's salvation, I ask you — and try to think that this supremely vital question is directed personally to you, as if your heavenly Father were face to face with you in this moment! — What will you do with Jesus? I have prayed that many of you who have spurned Him, hastened from Him, tried to hide from Him, will now come to Him with all your sins, not excusing, disguising, belittling any of them, but admitting your guilt and realizing the awful weight of woe they laid on the stainless Savior. If never before in your cold, calloused life you have found time to study the shocking curse of crime against God, may you now behold Christ crucified for you, and cry out, "Oh, what fearful punishment, what crushing agonies my iniquities heaped up, since I could be saved from them only by the indescribable anguish and death of God's Son!

What will you do with Jesus? Heaven help you, repentant and relying on His mercies, bow before Him as your Lord, believing His promises that as your Redeemer and Substitute He transferred all your transgressions to Himself, paid their full penalty with the price of His precious blood, and made you a child of God, saved by grace, with absolute certainty of your salvation.

What will you do with Jesus? Show your loving faith by trusting Him! Dark clouds streak the international horizon as leaders plead to prepare for the possibilities of another war, and hopelessness reigns in many high places. Over in London the common people tell this story: A policeman, standing on a bridge over the Thames River, saw a disheveled man jump up on the railing in an attempt to hurl himself into the water. Before he could make the fatal plunge, the officer took his arm, persuaded him to come down, led him to a bench, and said, "Let's talk things over." "What shall we talk about?" the would-be suicide asked, to which the officer replied, "The future." For a long time they were engaged in serious discussion; but finally both the rescued suicide and the policeman jumped into the river and drowned. They had both found the future too frightful. Masses throughout the world have no real hope for the years ahead, and the best human arguments can give them none. Yet when you, facing fiery personal tribulations, not to mention the terrifying threats of world warfare, look to Christ as your great and glorious God, you will have the permanent peace He promised by His pledge, *"Neither shall any man pluck them out of My hand."*

What will you do with Jesus? Make Him yours and be comforted by His assurances of divine consolation! He guarantees all His followers, *"Your sorrow shall be turned into joy."* Blessed by His constant companionship, you should not live dark, drab, discouraged lives, but rejoice in His salvation. The love which led Him to die for you should teach you that whatever He, your Savior, may send you, comes from His wisdom and mercy, designed to fortify your faith and reinforce your reliance on His love. How marvelous are the means He uses to purify His Church and beautify our individual lives! Thirteen short years ago Mussolini unleashed savage slaughter on the helpless Abyssinians. In this willful, premeditated attack his Italian troops broke every international law regulating warfare. They sprayed the dread mustard gas on open cities, bombed groups of women and children, even poisoning the wells of drinking water. Together with this, they ruthlessly expelled missionaries, destroyed churches, made believers face the firing line. Then came our victory with Italy's defeat in World War II. After the missionaries returned, they found that the persecution had purified the believers; and since their work has been resumed, unprecedented numbers of Abyssinians — 40,000 in one mission alone — have been brought to Jesus and baptized. A similar revival of the true faith can mark Germany; but we are assured, beyond all question of doubt, that when you crown Christ the Savior of your soul, you will rejoice in your salvation because you know that "Whatever God ordains is good," that the setbacks to earthly success you suffer are really advancements for your spiritual growth; your money losses, faith's gains; and the sicknesses which may befall you, inner healings of your mind. *"I can do all things through Christ which strengtheneth me,"* Saint Paul exults; and this is no exaggeration. You, too, fighting *"the good fight of faith,"* can rise from turmoil to triumph and change your pains for praise.

What will you do with Jesus? When you know Him, love Him, trust Him, live for Him, spread His spirit of mercy! This is a time of hunger for millions in the Old World. Our Lord fed the famished, and so should you. In His name again we invite you to join the hundreds in this mission of the air who are helping to keep families alive across the sea. In your own community provide for the destitute, comfort the sick, visit the imprisoned, befriend the widows and orphans; and such obedience to Christ will bring you new and unknown joy.

What will you do with Jesus? May the Holy Spirit strengthen many of you, especially you gifted young men and women who truly love Him, to testify to His Gospel and proclaim His name abroad! We ask the Holy Spirit to show all of you how blessed it is to accept the priceless privileges of lifetime service to the Savior. When the remains of Livingstone were brought back to England, a prosperous, well-dressed man stopped before the casket, and with tears of regret declared, "I emphasized the wrong world." Livingstone, his friend, had lived for heaven, always was intent on helping his fellow men secure a place there; but this wealthy mourner had existed for this earth and now by contrast found his life empty and vain. My fellow redeemed, there are two worlds, not one, and your greatest concern should be to have the promise of the life to come, which is yours, only but surely, through Christ.

This twenty-ninth of February is the first and last time for most of you that the extra day of leap year is the Lord's Day. Who knows, perhaps the Holy Spirit has added these additional twenty-four hours for your sake, to give you one more opportunity to accept the invitation for pardon here and Paradise hereafter. For the seventh and final time today I ask you, "What will you do with Jesus?" Your heavenly Father Himself is awaiting your reply. Your eternity may depend upon it. For your soul's sake, and for your Savior's, join me in this promise of perpetual loyalty: Oh, Christ, my Ruler and gracious Redeemer, I will love Thee, I will adore Thee, I will cling to Thee, through death, into everlasting life. So help me, almighty God! *Amen!*

RENOUNCE SIN, RECEIVE THE SAVIOR!

"When Herod saw Jesus, he was exceeding glad; for he was desirous to see Him of a long season because he had heard many things of Him; and he hoped to have seen some miracle done by Him. Then he questioned with Him in many words; but He answered him nothing. And the chief priests and scribes stood and vehemently accused Him. And Herod with his men of war set him at naught, and mocked Him, and arrayed Him in a gorgeous robe, and sent Him again to Pilate." SAINT LUKE 23:8-11

PURIFYING SPIRIT OF GOD: Create a clean heart in us today, and make us wholly new creatures in Christ! We confess without excuse that we live under the grasp and greed of evil; that without Jesus we are hopelessly, helplessly lost in our transgressions. We know, too, that just as little as a corpse can raise its arm, so we, dead in trespasses and sin, can do nothing to change our lives. That divine renovation must come from Thee. Therefore we praise Thee, together with the Father and the Son, that in the endless mercy of divine compassion our Savior came to us in the flesh, took our iniquities from us, assumed their full guilt and punishment, died on the cross in our stead, paying our complete penalty and thus giving us the guarantee of glory in heaven. Oh, bring that triumphant trust into many sorrowing souls! Fill us all with a deep sense of repentance, but with an even stronger reliance on our blessed Redeemer! Shed the comfort, strength, and courage of a firm faith into every afflicted, sin-sorrowed, grief-broken heart, and by the constant, world-wide preaching of His Gospel let Jesus Christ be mightily magnified as our only, all-sufficient, ever-glorious, never-failing Deliverer! We plead in His saving name. *Amen!*

Not long ago the inquiring reporter of a Chicago newspaper asked a group of college students this question: "Would you have two wives if the law permitted?" Only one replied, "No!" explaining, "I don't believe a man can find true love for more than one wife." The rest responded with an enthusiastic, "Yes!" Listen to their reasons! One said, "The two wives could take turns keeping house and accompanying me. There would always be one to stay with the children." Another stated, "It would be fine if a man could have two wives so that they could divide the work. They would have more freedom and would be able to help support the family." A third answered, "If I could find the sweet, simple type, I would be content with as many as possible." A fourth declared, "I'd have two or three or more. In fact, I favor a community comprising all of the privileges and none of the drawbacks of marriage."

These are not simply the opinions of careless students. No, Scripture's high and holy ideal: husband and wife united in lifelong union of love, to be separated only by death, this absolutely basic requirement for home happiness and national prosperity, is held up for systematic ridicule on some of our campuses. At the same university where these questions regarding two wives were asked, the student paper contained so much objectionable material that the editor, a young woman, resigned under fire. We must keep the morals of our college youth straight and clean. If the leaders of our country's tomorrow renounce the Biblical principles of purity, God help the United States.

Although God's Word clearly prohibits more than one wife when it directs, *"Therefore shall a man . . . cleave unto his wife"* (not "to his wives," and how can a man cleave to one if he has two?), yet in sordid practice, millions of American men are not satisfied with one wife but, setting the Almighty aside, make marriage vows, shake them off, take new vows, break them in what has well been called "successive polygamy." The University of Indiana studies state — and what a shocking indictment they present! — that about one half of the married men in our country have at one time or another been unfaithful to their marital vows. In this debauch lies devastating danger for our nation. Some scientists predict that a way will be discovered to counteract atomic destruction; but history knows no preventive for a country's collapse, once the marriage standards, set by divine truth, are cast aside. Let lust replace love, sensuality crowd out sincerity of devotion, and our glory is gone. We have not enough money power, brain power, man power, production power, to overcome this treacherous evil. When people forget decency, they forget God; when they disregard marriage morality, they disregard the Almighty. If they leave the Lord, they will leave their wives. Irreligion and impurity go hand in hand.

Our Lenten text shows this fatal connection between unbelief and unchastity, when it tells us how a man who, having exchanged his wife, failed in a great crisis. This record taken from the story of our Savior's suffering pleads with us:

RENOUNCE SIN, RECEIVE THE SAVIOR!

May we all heed the Scripture chosen for the fourth Passiontide meditation, the words of Saint Luke, chapter twenty-three, verses eight to eleven: *"When Herod saw Jesus, he was exceeding glad; for he was desirous to see Him of a long season because he had heard many things of Him; and he hoped to have seen some miracle done by Him. Then he questioned with Him in many words; but He answered him nothing. And the chief priests and scribes stood and vehemently accused Him. And Herod with his men of war set Him at naught, and mocked Him, and arrayed Him in a gorgeous robe, and sent Him again to Pilate."*

I

TOO MANY, LIKE HEROD, SERVE SIN, TO THEIR ETERNAL SORROW

As we review the trial of our Lord, we see that Pilate repeatedly tried to shift to others the responsibility concerning Christ. He wanted the chief priests and elders to give the verdict; he asked the common people to decide. He urged Jesus to settle the case. Like some of you, He did not realize that once you have seen God's Son, listened to His words of grace and truth, you yourself must either accept or reject Him as your Redeemer. How many of you, following Pilate, are ready to sidestep the Savior or let others welcome Him! You husbands are often content to have your religion in your wife's name. It is all right with you if she attends church, but you don't want to be bothered. Let the children enroll in Sunday school, just so they do not ask you to go! Regular church attendance may have been in place for your godly parents, but, you say, times have changed now; besides, you have other plans for the Lord's Day. Yet just as the Roman governor finally had to give his own verdict, so you who have heard that He is the Son of God and the Savior of the world, must choose between receiving or repelling Him. Delay as long as you may, resist the Holy Spirit's appeal as repeatedly as you wish, your time of decision is inevitably

Renounce Sin, Receive the Savior! 107

approaching. Claim as fully as you will that you have a free, open mind in religious issues, you cannot escape Christ. You may avoid giving a formal verdict, but your whole life, without Jesus and against Him, is the proof of your unbelief; and some day, when it is too late for repentance and faith, you will have to admit your opposition to saving truth, since it is written, *"We must all appear before the judgment seat of Christ."* God help you escape the sentence of eternal guilt by confessing His Son your Redeemer now!

One of the methods by which Pilate sought to shift his responsibility is told us in these words: *"When Pilate heard of Galilee, he asked whether the Man [Jesus] were a Galilean. And as soon as he knew that He belonged unto Herod's jurisdiction, he sent Him to Herod, who himself also was at Jerusalem at that time."* Our Savior was quickly led to Herod, after He had been dragged from one court to another. Within less than ten hours' time He had faced Annas, the high priest, then Caiaphas and the council of his countrymen, then this same group a second time, then Pilate, and now Herod. Again, within only two hours after this hearing, He was on His way to Calvary to be nailed to the cross. Contrast with such haste the delays which our courts grant! After a long-drawn-out trial, Archibald Herron was found guilty of first-degree murder and sentenced to the electric chair. He entered the New Jersey penitentiary in 1908, but his lawyers secured postponements and kept on filing claims until 1923, when the judge who presided over the original trial died; and under the New Jersey law only he could set the date of execution. So forty years after the jury gave the death sentence, this prisoner is still alive.

When Christ was led into Herod's presence, the

Galilean governor was confronted by one of the greatest opportunities any man can ever have, the privilege of pronouncing the stainless Savior innocent and of securing His release. Before we see what Herod did, let us learn more of the man thus asked to show justice to Jesus!

First, he was the son of Herod the Great, though why this ruler is called "great" is as much a mystery as why the same title is given Alexander, who died in drunken stupor, to Peter, who ruthlessly ruled over Russia, "without scruple, without even a memory of kindness, or conscience, or morals," to Catherine, in the same country, who counted her lovers by the dozen and crushed the masses, or to Frederick, the scoffer, who offered to sell his seat in heaven for a Prussian coin. Only the really humble are great in God's sight. True, Herod the Great built the massive Temple in Jerusalem which bore his name; but this immense outlay could not buy his way into heaven, for he was a cruel and crafty politician. Like many in our times, he did not hesitate to shed innocent blood. When we meet him in the opening pages of the New Testament, he appears as a lying hypocrite, who deceives the Wise Men in search of Christ, and as the fiend who ordered all Bethlehem children under two years killed. When he disappears from history, some of his subjects, captured for this purpose, were to be murdered in the Jericho arena, the moment the news of his death arrived. This was the only way he knew to create weeping and lamentation. Fortunately this massacre was averted.

What kind of son can you expect of a father like this? The Herod of our text, called Antipas, inherited the violence, the pride, the evil, that cursed his parent into hell. If some of you American fathers write me that you are satisfied with your unbelief and want to continue in your sin, not even God Almigthy will force you to accept Jesus. If you insist on ruining yourselves, you can, though I pray the Holy Spirit that somehow He will smash your pride and crush you into the misery which helps you turn to Him. Yet how about your children? Are you ready to be responsible for their damnation? Before the throne of eternity, do you want your own flesh and blood to rise up and accuse you, charging: "Father, you kept me from my Savior. I followed you on earth, and now I am following you into hell"? As Christ Himself indicated, it would be far better for you that a millstone were hanged about your neck and you *"were drowned in the depth of the sea."* If you do not want to be cursed in eternity for leading your own family into ruin, learn the love which the Lord Jesus showed for you, accept it, and teach it to your children! Then you will not only be saved yourselves, but your sons and daughters will rise up and call you *"blessed."*

The Herod of our text showed the evil he had inherited from his father, there where public sin often begins — in the home. He married an Arabian princess; but his family life evidently was too tame for his passions, and before long he began a secret, sordid affair with his own brother Philip's wife. Here, then, was royalty in scarlet sin, just as kings and princes throughout the centuries have boasted that they were their own law. This is not a weakness only of ancient monarchs; for if you have read the story of Aga Khan, the East Indian potentate, who last year was paid his weight, 243½ pounds, in diamonds, you will know that although he is worshiped as a god, he also has exchanged wives. Incidentally, he likes liquor, too; but since his religion prohibits him from drinking wine, he has promoted the legend that the moment wine touches his lips, it turns into water. How remarkable that none of his subjects suggests that he save himself the trouble of performing a miracle and start out with water!

This Indian glass trickery is as dishonest and hypocritical as the letters some of you men write me mentioning a "higher" and "holier" love, which makes you want to divorce your wife and live in "spiritual union" with a "soul mate." Most of those who violate God's ordinance requiring a man to *"cleave unto his wife"* never bother about such subterfuges. They are simply tired of their helpmates, who may have lost their beauty in slaving and sacrificing themselves for their husbands. They are attracted by younger, prettier — and craftier women. They live but once, they say, and they want to enjoy life; but they deceive themselves! No one who has ever boasted of deserting his wife has met with anything but reverse and rebuke by the Lord. See what happened to Herod! His wife left him and hurried back to her father in Arabia; and Herodias, his own brother's wife, moved into Herod's palace — without the formality of a divorce.

Don't think for a moment that these revolts against marriage are limited to royalty. Leaders in democracies throughout the world, enchanted by dream of power and position, have frequently disregarded their marriage ties. Disclosures revealing the secret lives of prominent politicians in France and Germany show us married men in high places who kept other women; and lest you think that lust is limited in its geography, let me remind you, as I ask the Almighty and All-Merciful to forgive us, that we in the United States are not better in this respect

Renounce Sin, Receive the Savior! 111

than most nations; that we are worse than some, with our heavy divorce rate, our wide marital unfaithfulness, our increasing illegitimacy. In many best-selling books and plays of the stage the complete disregard of marriage vows is portrayed as smart and sophisticated. The Holy Spirit bring America back to the Biblical ideal, husband and wife joined in marriage, for their lifetime, with death alone to part them!

Herod's choosing Herodias was not only the sin of unfaithfulness, but because of their close relation, it was incest. How vile those ancient rulers were, you say; but their shocking transgressions are multiplied in our own times. Some of you in this radio mission, your consciences aroused, have written to confess the same or an even worse sin. People like to glorify human nature, but how wild and wanton, how brutal and bestial it can become! When I learned in Europe what happened to hundreds of thousands of women there, little girls of eight and grandmothers of eighty, I realized as never before the truth of Scripture's indictment, *"The heart is deceitful above all things, and desperately wicked."*

Soon after Herod's real wife left him, her father declared war on him. To you, too, the trampling of God's marriage standards, the killing of love, can produce discontent, strife, and even bloodshed. Sin-blinded victims of their own vice like to believe that by following the lure of their lusts, they will learn how to live fully, when in reality they only create conflict for themselves or for others. Perhaps God has put you before your radio on this Lenten Sunday so that at this time, when you are devising designs for divorce or planning evil adventure, the Holy Spirit will lead me to speak the warning which can save you from that disaster. If the devil now tempts you to leave your husband or wife, to run away from your family, stop! You can never find happiness by discarding the divine Word. The last page of the Bible tells us that the impure are barred from heaven's gates; and even on earth the sins of the flesh reap a harrowing harvest in hardship and horror. Before it is too late and your evil plans become destructive actions, bringing manifold miseries on your family, ask the Almighty for the strength to tear the foul and filthy desires from your heart, to repent, and to return to those who love you!

Herod's incest moved him to murder. He had been curious to see John the Baptist; and when that wilderness preacher, with the courage every minister of Christ should have, spoke to the Galilean governor, instead of ignoring his sinful relations with Herodias, he declared pointedly, *"It is not lawful for thee to have her."* How much stronger America would be if all its preachers were filled with the same loyalty to the Lord. Then Herod ordered John thrown into prison, for his interest in the prophet stopped when that rugged messenger of righteousness unsparingly denounced Herod's sins, just as today people applaud a preacher until he uncovers the evil they have nurtured. Then they are through with him.

Sometime later, at his birthday celebration, with the drunkenness and sensuality which marked those royal banquets, Herod offered his guests an exciting form of entertainment, an oriental dance by Salome, the daughter of lewd Herodias. It must have been a licentious exhibition, since it drove Herod, in drunken debauch, to promise Salome anything she might ask, even to half of his kingdom. What fools women can make of weak men! Here Herodias stepped in — she had probably planned it that way — directing her daughter to demand the head of John the Baptist; and Herod, unwilling to break his promise, had the greatest human preacher of that age beheaded. If the devil or wicked men have misled you to promise something which dishonors God, harms your neighbor or yourself, do not keep your word! Never, under any circumstances, fulfill a sinful pledge!

As you thus see how sensual, selfish women made a murderer of Herod and a martyr of John, you young folks, looking forward to a joy-filled marriage, should realize how all-important it is to have as your life partner one who loves the Lord and is happy to make Christ the Head of your home. No matter what wealth and pleasing personality a young man may have; regardless of how beautiful and brilliant a young woman may be, if they sneer at the Savior, banish every thought of marriage with them! You will be a hundred times happier if you remain single, than if you pledge yourself for life to an enemy of Jesus.

As you picture hellish Herodias gloating over the gory head of John the Baptist, you also see the extremes to which strong drink and the sensual dance can lead. When the Church warns its young people against these two evils, it is often branded as old-fashioned and narrow. But ask the matrons at homes for fallen girls, and you will learn that in most cases the tavern and the public dance hall combined to produce these young women's ruin. A New Jersey high school arranged a Valentine dance a few weeks ago. A fifteen-year-old student, who in the afternoon had been writing a class essay on "The Ideal Mother," wanted to attend, but her parents objected. After a long dispute the girl struck her mother on the head with a beer bottle and killed her.

With John the Baptist beheaded, Herod doubtless

concluded that this wilderness preacher would disturb his peace no more; but evil men are superstitious, and when he first heard of Christ, he exclaimed, *"This is John the Baptist; He is risen from the dead!"* He believed in ghosts, good-luck charms, and similar frauds. Most people who do not know the true God are superstitious. During the war a Japanese sniper, shot down from a sixty-five-foot palm tree on New Guinea, was found to have a gold Buddha charm around his neck, three good-luck rings on each hand, a good-fortune amulet around his wrist, twenty-two antidanger tickets in his helmet band, antimalaria and antisnake charms taped to his leg, and in his pocket fourteen magic formulas promising him protection against American bullets. He could also have carried an assortment of four-leaf clovers, wishbones, and horseshoes, still he would have been shot down. Superstition is such a serious drag on progress in Japan that the government has appointed a large committee to investigate the losses it causes. We could well profit by legislation outlawing frauds in the United States, where, experts tells us, 10,000,000 Americans carry a rabbit's foot and people spend $125,000,000 every year on fortunetelling, while the sale of dream books, horoscopes, lucky charms, spiritist-séance literature becomes big business. If you support superstition in any form, stop it at once! It is all fraud and falsehood. When you know God in Christ, you have Heaven's own assurance that the Lord loves you, and that because He sent His Son to save your soul, He will also give His angels charge over you and keep you under His constant protection. With Jesus, you need no amulets. The Nazi swastika was an Indian good-luck sign, but does anyone seriously claim that it brought happiness?

You can understand, then, that with Herod living in lust and rebellion against the Almighty, guilty of murder, enslaved by superstition and unbelief, his rule of Galilee was marred by his lust and greed. Long before the Savior was brought to Him on Good Friday morning, Jesus had denounced him, calling Herod a *"fox,"* that is, a ruler with the craftiness, the deceitful, evil scheming, pictured by this animal. Some have accused Christ of preaching politics, mixing Church and State, as He voiced this rebuke, just as they would silence a preacher of God's Word today who cries out in protest against the public, open sin and unbelief in high places. Yet if you love America, pray the Holy Spirit for men in our country's pulpits who, without any partisan bias and purely on the basis of Scripture, will speak out unsparingly against those who abuse their political offices for the advancement of atheism or in the pursuit of selfish profit! In this year of grace there are many foxlike officials in control of world affairs, men who say one thing and mean another, who write — and I am quoting the Communist leader Nikolai Lenin: "We must be ready for any and every sacrifice, and even, if necessary, to practice trickery, to employ cunning and to resort to illegal methods, sometimes even to overlook or conceal the truth." Just as the Savior would never compromise with Herod, so we who love the Lord must reject such ruinous tactics.

This, then, was the Herod before whom Christ was led early on Good Friday morning — a mean, murderous man, sitting in judgment on God's Son, just as in our own time scoffers want to place themselves in control of believers. It may seem strange to us that, as our text declares, *"when Herod saw Jesus, he was exceeding glad"*; but lest you think this gladness was the eager joy of faith, read on to learn that Herod *"was desirous to see Him of a long season because he had heard many things of Him; and he hoped to have seen some miracle done by Him."* He was filled, not with compassion for Christ, but with curiosity, the kind that makes people crowd churches where misguided men fondle snakes. One tradition has it that the walls of the room in which Herod met our Lord were adorned with paintings of grapes and that Herod asked Him to turn these into real fruit. Whatever the Galilean governor may have wanted, the Savior would not grant it. He could have secured favor by producing a spectacular miracle; but Christ refused to serve as a court magician. Therefore we read the record: Herod *"questioned with Him in many words; but He answered him nothing."* In one of the saddest spectacles recorded by the New Testament, the Royal Redeemer, of whom the Old Testament Prophets foretold, *"Grace is poured into Thy lips,"* kept those lips tightly sealed.

Why? Because Herod was merely curious, not contrite, pleasure-bent, but not penitent. While no sincere seeker after light was ever spurned by the Savior, and while He has never permitted an earnest prayer for pardon to remain unanswered, here was a man who did not realize that he needed the Redeemer, and who, instead of beseeching Christ to forgive his sins, kept on with foolish questions and demands for miracles. Because Jesus was come to call sinners to repentance, not to entertain royalty and amuse the self-righteous, Scripture summarizes, *"He answered him nothing."* Only a few feet separated our Lord from Herod; but in spirit they were as far apart as heaven is from hell.

Finally, as it always must, proud indifference kept the governor of Galilee, who was losing patience with the silent Prisoner, from setting Christ free. While, as Saint Luke recalls, *"The chief priests and scribes stood and vehemently accused Him . . . Herod with his men of war set Him [our Lord] at naught, and mocked Him, and arrayed Him in a gorgeous robe, and sent Him again to Pilate."* What a shocking spectacle: the civil and religious leaders ridiculing the Son of God! It is true that Herod himself did not find any guilt in Him. He was merely amused at Him. He thought the strange Galilean a harmless dreamer. Accept Him as Savior and Sovereign, as Christ, the Son of the living God? Never! Similarly many of you are ready to say that it was wrong to crucify Jesus, that He was innocent of every charge hurled against Him; but you stop there. Like Herod, you want to continue in your sin. You are unwilling to repent and to renounce your service to lust. Like Herod, too, you are ready to make sport of the suffering Redeemer, to blaspheme His holy name; and as the Galilean governor had Christ arrayed *"in a gorgeous robe,"* to mock the claim that Jesus was King, and then sent Him back to Pilate, so you are ready to caricature our Lord and, refusing to accept Him, pass the decision on to others.

However, also like Herod, you will pay heavily for your unbelief. Later he went to Rome in search of promotion and more power; but then God stepped in and called a sudden halt to his ambitions. At the court of Caesar he was accused on various counts, deposed of office, and banished. Had he defended Christ and come to the faith, he would have been honored by all succeeding generations; but because he failed in the greatest opportunity any person can have, men brand him as a colossal failure. The Almighty, whose voice is higher than history's, has rejected him in eternity.

II
MAY YOU, UNLIKE HEROD, SERVE CHRIST — TO YOUR ETERNAL JOY!

To avoid that everlasting disaster, learn the personal lessons which Herod pushed aside! Realize the ruin of sin! If you are guilty of the immorality and vice that cursed Herod, come before your heavenly Father now, in earnest repentance! Confess the evil with which your soul is stained, and without stopping to find an excuse or give explanation, bow before the Lord to admit that your thoughts, your desires, your words, your repeated actions, have violated every part of His purity laws; that you have deserved to suffer His avenging wrath, that you are doubly guilty for helping to lead others to sin and shame! Don't be satisfied merely with admitting that personal impurity is wrong because of its deceit and falsehood, its sordid consequences to yourself and others! A thousand times worse even than this, it is an insult to the Holy God. By Scripture's verdict, *"The soul that sinneth, it shall die,"* your transgression is rebellion against the Almighty, which, if not removed, brings endless ruin. Learn to regard the iniquities of the flesh as screaming offenses against Heaven, and when tempted, ask the Holy Spirit for power to protest with Joseph, *"How, then, can I do this great wickedness and sin against God?" "Be sure,"* too, *"your sin will find you out!"* The Almighty sees all, knows all, and remembers all. Scientists have now made a calculator machine 250 times more efficient than the one they presented to Harvard University four years ago. This can keep 500,000,000 figures listed and ready for further use; but without this immense machine, which fills a large room, the eternal Judge will list the 500 billion times 500 trillion times

500 quadrillion and more transgressions of humanity for the final reckoning, unless — and I pray the Holy Spirit this is true of you! — your faith has firmly grasped Christ, and with Him, the knowledge that all your sins are washed away forever.

This brings us to the second lesson we must learn, by contrast, from Herod. What a ghastly mistake he made when *"he hoped to have seen some miracle done by"* Jesus. Here was the mightiest Wonder of the ages directly before him, and still he looks for some magician's trick. Don't be guilty of the same folly! Humbly believe that Christ the Almighty gives you the most magnificent miracle even His divine power can offer! Think of the Savior's miraculous nature, His being both God and Man; His miraculous love, longing and seeking for you, despite all your iniquities; His miraculous self-sacrifice, permitting Himself to be nailed to Calvary's cross, there loading the guilt, the punishment, the curse of all your transgressions on to Himself, suffering in His own body, but to an incomparably greater extent in His own mind and soul, the rejection, damnation, and death they demanded! Then, in crowning climax, think of His miraculous mercy, by which He offers you, no matter how men may bar you from human privileges because of your race or color, the full forgiveness of your sins, even these crimson crimes of the flesh; the free, priceless pardon that you could never purchase, were the wealth of the whole world yours; the firm and final assurance that your sins are washed away forever, beyond recall, once you look to the Crucified and say, "He was wounded for my transgressions, He was bruised for my iniquities, because He is and always will be my personal Redeemer." Think once more of His miraculous majesty as He raises the decayed remains of His beloved into new radiant bodies, like unto His own resurrection form! Think of the magnificent, miraculous privileges of heaven in the celestial places He Himself has prepared for those who die in the faith! Think of the miraculous companionship and help His Word gives believers when He promises, *"Lo, I am with you alway, even unto the end of the world!"* Sum up the glorious riches of His mercy, might, majesty — and the Holy Spirit lead you to say, not "Let me see signs and wonders!" but "My faith has seen the mightiest of miracles, Jesus, the Son of God, my Savior, killed on the cross for me, but resurrected, ascended, and eternally triumphant for me and every penitent sinner!"

The Lord help you come all the way to Christ, renouncing sin and receiving Him as your Redeemer! Then you will not ask Herod's foolish questions, which remained unanswered, but, trusting the crucified and risen Mediator's power to *"save . . . to the uttermost,"* you will approach your eternal Deliverer just as you are, seeking the solution to the problem which may confront and confuse you. Drawing close to Him who says, *"Come unto Me, all ye that labor and are heavy laden,"* you can ask Jesus, "Lord, wilt Thou receive me despite my many and frightful sins?" and find rest in His reassurance, *"Him that cometh to Me I will in no wise cast out."* You can say to Him, "Lord, why must I still suffer?" and He will reply, *"What I do thou knowest not now; but thou shalt know hereafter,"* namely, in Heaven's higher knowledge, when you will realize that your afflictions have been part of a divine plan designed for the deepening of your faith, the strengthening of your reliance on your Redeemer, and the guarantee of a glorious eternity. Bowing before the beautiful, bountiful Savior, you can ask Him, "Lord, how will I face the future with the difficulties which assail me and the hatred crowded into our cruel world?" Your heart will be strengthened as Jesus, whose Word is truth, turns your fright into fortitude by His pledge, *"Fear thou not, for I am with thee; be not dismayed, for I am thy God; I will strengthen thee; yea, I will help thee; yea, I will uphold thee with the right hand of My righteousness."* The Christ who sternly refused to answer impenitent, sin-enslaved Herod will never refrain from replying to every penitent sinner. The newspapers report that the twenty-four doctors in a California city refused to answer a call to the bedside of a seventy-six-year-old man, suffering from a heart attack. The fire chief, who came with a Pulmotor squad, reported, "We argued and fought with the doctors over the phone; we told them that the patient might be revived if a physican could attend him, but they all refused. Some said they were too busy; some said they were sick; some said they had to operate in the morning." Before daybreak the patient died. Because we know doctors who are disciples, we feel that this report may be mistaken; but we can give you Scripture's own guarantee that Jesus will always hear and answer every penitent, believing prayer. He promises — and *"heaven and earth shall pass away"* before this pledge is broken: *"If ye abide in Me and My words abide in you, ye shall ask what ye will, and it shall be done unto you."*

It is the purpose of this radio crusade, Bringing Christ to the Nations, to tell men all over the world, "Renounce sin; receive the Savior!" Hitherto we have sent out the Gospel grace — and we want to know nothing *"among you save Jesus Christ, and Him Crucified!* — in English, Spanish, Portuguese, French, Arabic,

Afrikaans, Polish. Today, in the steady march of progress with which God has blessed our efforts — all credit, all honor, all glory to Him only! — we bring you the happy news that this Sunday marks the beginning of our broadcasts in the Slovak language, timed by God Almighty to comfort the people of Czechoslovakia in this hour of their dire need. Pray for these Slovak messages and for the other foreign-language programs we are now preparing! If on the first Pentecost the Holy Spirit led the disciples to proclaim the saving grace in sixteen different tongues, surely He will help us use at least as many, and doubtless more languages in our radio mission.

It is our great assurance to know, not only that we use more than 1,000 stations in broadcasting in forty-three countries, but also that the Holy Spirit blesses our messages by calling many souls to Christ. Herod would not be justified in asking for a miracle if he could read our mail; he would see divine power and blessing in every day's letters. Can you imagine our joy when only a few days ago our new missionary in Shanghai, China, wrote me the *Foo Yin*, literally the happiness sound, the good news, that he is instructing for Baptism three women and a government highway engineer who came to him as a direct result of our broadcasting in that city?

Yet while we thank God for many conversions in distant places, we plead that you, much closer to us in our country and across its borders, give yourself to your Savior. Beloved, we want you with us — and far more important — Jesus wants you with Him! The Holy Spirit grant that as you have again heard of Christ's love, you, too, will renounce sin, receive the Redeemer, and live forever by that faith! *Amen!*

PARDON FOR YOU AT THE CROSS

"One of the malefactors which were hanged railed on Him, saying, If Thou be Christ, save Thyself and us. But the other, answering, rebuked him, saying, Dost not thou fear God, seeing thou art in the same condemnation? And we indeed justly; for we receive the due reward of our deeds; but this Man hath done nothing amiss. And he said unto Jesus, Lord, remember me when Thou comest into Thy kingdom. And Jesus said unto him, Verily, I say unto thee, Today shalt thou be with Me in Paradise." SAINT LUKE 23:39-43

JESUS, SAVIOR AND SOVEREIGN OF OUR SOULS: For us Thou wast nailed to the accursed tree at Calvary, there to suffer in serving the sentence of our guilt. For us Thou wast crucified between two criminals, being reckoned with transgressors as a transgressor. For us who contritely accept this grace Thou wilt repeat the promise spoken to the penitent thief and assure us that, enthroned in Thy heavenly kingdom, Thou wilt remember us and bring us to Thee. Humbly we praise Thee, precious Savior, that in Thy dying love, tortured by the pain and penalty of all our scarlet, shrieking sins, Thou didst show a repentant robber and every contrite believer the full, free, and final salvation purchased with Thy blood. Draw many to that saving trust this day, and let them lay hold of the comfort Thy love offers the afflicted! Keep the conscience-stricken from falling into the delusion that their iniquities are too heavy and heinous to be removed even by Thine atoning crucifixion! In these dark, heavy days bless the President, the Congress, and all in authority! Rebuke Communist atheism and its blasphemous assaults on Thy Gospel! Strengthen us to show our faith also by supplying the needs of war's victims, sick and hungry as millions of them are! Each day make us more like Thee, and in Thy good time bring us all to our prepared place in Paradise, ever to be with Thee. *Amen!*

WHAT will give you peace and blessing? Not fame, power, money! Newspaper readers should have realized this last Monday, when on the pages of their dailies they found the tragic story of an Indiana author. He was a young man, only thirty-three years old; and his first novel, the work of seven years, had become an immediate success. It was high among the best sellers, the Book-of-the-Month selection, and the winner in a motion-picture contest, which paid more than an eighth of a million dollars for screen rights. Here was a man who apparently had everything; yet, with literary critics acclaiming him, he went out into his garage, locked the door, turned on the motor, and killed himself by carbon-monoxide poisoning. Why? He had everything, I repeat — except Christ. His book, which reviewers throughout the country have praised in lavish terms, not only revels in profanity and sins of sex, but is also crowded with sacrilege and blasphemy. The author denies the resurrection. He claims that Jesus was merely a misguided man. He calls the Easter record a crude myth, harmful to every truly religious feeling. He ridicules the miracles, speaks sarcastically of the Virgin Birth, has no room for the Atonement, charges that the Gospel records are untrustworthy, based on falsehood and superstition.

If this suicide exemplifies the fatal folly of fighting Christ, then today, by strengthening contrast, let me tell you of another man, who found peace and blessing in contrite faith! He was a penniless pauper, an outcast, a despised, condemned criminal. Life held no opportunity nor promise for him; for when we meet him in the pages of the New Testament, he is crucified with our Lord on one of Calvary's three crosses, He is — most of you know him — the penitent thief, the dying criminal to whom the Savior gives the promise of Paradise. He, more than anyone else in the pages of Scripture or in the annals of history, shows Jesus' boundless mercy and the blessedness of trusting Him as Deliverer.

Wherever, whenever, and in whatever language this broadcast sends out the record of redemption, may we always be given the power to proclaim the guarantee of saving grace which Jesus Himself gave the malefactor crucified at His side, the Gospel comfort and courage we offer you today! Standing in spirit on Calvary's crest, we tell you, no matter how scarlet and crimson your sins may be, however hard-pressed and overburdened you are, that there is

PARDON FOR YOU AT THE CROSS

We give you this assurance in Jesus' name and by the warrant of His unbreakable Word; for here in our text (the Gospel of Saint Luke, chapter twenty-three, verses thirty-nine to forty-three) is this most remarkable record of redemption even Scripture contains; here is the pledge of Paradise for you. This passage of pardon and promise reads: *"One of the malefactors which were hanged railed on Him, saying, If Thou be Christ, save Thyself and us. But the other, answering, rebuked him, saying, Dost not thou fear God, seeing thou art in the same condemnation? And we indeed justly; for we receive the due reward of our deeds; but this Man hath done nothing amiss. And he said unto Jesus, Lord, remember me when Thou comest into Thy kingdom. And Jesus said unto him, Verily, I say unto thee, Today shalt thou be with Me in Paradise."*

I

TO FIND IT, FOLLOW THE DYING THIEF'S FAITH!

It was not accidental that Jesus Christ, the Son of God and the Savior of the world, was one of three crucified on Calvary on that black Friday morning. Seven hundred and fifty years before, Isaiah foresaw that He would be *"numbered with the transgressors,"* and Saint Mark stops to tell us that this prediction was fulfilled when *"with Him they crucify two thieves, the one on His right hand and the other on His left."* How sure and certain are the utterances of God's Word, and how frail and faulty, by contrast, men's guesses! When Sir Isaac Newton, called the "prince of scientists," just as he was a prince of Bible students, read Daniel's prophecy that in the New Testament era men would hurry over the face of the earth, he believed it and ventured to declare that the time was coming when men would travel at the rate of fifty miles an hour. The French skeptic, Voltaire, hearing this forecast, declared sarcastically: "Now look at the mighty mind of Newton, who discovered gravitation! When he began to study the book called the Bible, it seems that in order to credit its fabulous nonsense he believed that the knowledge of mankind will be so increased that we shall be able to travel fifty miles an hour. The poor old simpleton!" Today, with airplanes reaching a speed of more than 700 miles an hour, we see how conservative the claim of Newton, the Christian, was, and how absurd the objection of the infidel Voltaire.

The late H. G. Wells, British writer, called "the champion of scientists," predicted that not before the year 1950 or perhaps 2000 would an airplane fly across the Atlantic, yet soon after he made this prophecy, Lindbergh spanned the ocean. Wells likewise foretold that gas would be the decisive weapon in World War II, and that its use would hinder the development of the tank; in reality, however, gas was not used to any extent worth mentioning, while tanks were made larger and more powerful than ever before. Wells also asserted that the first world conflict would be the last. When the gathering clouds of the second global struggle emphasized his error, he confidently declared that it would be impossible to keep the Japanese from landing on our Pacific coast.

If now, instead of such faulty guesswork, you want absolute assurance, a firmly grounded guarantee for the future, turn to God's Word! It is always true; it never fails, and particularly in its fulfilled predictions can you find proof of its perfect guidance. John Willmot, who became the Earl of Rochester, was one of the most licentious noblemen at the court of Charles II. Suddenly he was laid low by a fatal disease; but as in many instances which you, too, know, this sickness paved the way for his soul health. It gave him time, as your illnesses give you opportunity, to read Heaven's truth. A Greek translation of the Old Testament came into his hands, and by divine direction he was led to Isaiah's fifty-third chapter with its preview of Christ's suffering and its eleven statements proclaiming His atonement for our sins. How could Isaiah draw this marvelous picture, and who was this suffering servant of God? As Willmot lay on his sickbed, he pondered this question day after day, until by the Spirit's leading he came to the conclusion that the Scripture he had ridiculed must be divine because only the Almighty could thus foretell, long centuries in advance, the details of Christ's suffering at Calvary. Fulfilled prophecy thus led the Earl of Rochester to Jesus in what has well been called one of the most genuine examples "of real repentance on earth." If you have ridiculed Scripture, don't wait for a sickness to turn your thoughts to God! Take time now, study the Word *"which is able to build you up"!* See this clear demonstration of sacred power in the true prediction of the Old Testament, and declare that the Bible, unlike any other book, is divine, errorless, and powerful!

What contrast we behold when we see the sinless Savior crucified with two criminals — the Holy One flanked by two robbers! How this difference increases when we read in our text, *"One of the malefactors which were hanged railed on Him, saying, If Thou be Christ, save Thyself and us!"* That damnable, sarcastic *"if"!* The blaspheming thief had heard it from the high priests and the rulers of the people there on Calvary's crest, for they taunted, *"Let Him save Himself, if He be Christ!"* He had heard the soldiers mock Jesus, sneering, *"If Thou be the King . . . save Thyself!"* That soul-destroying *"if"* has persisted until our day. Here is a world faced with the possibility of devastation far worse than anything we have yet known, as scientists, one after another, describe the coming atomic, bacterial, chemical, and cosmic annihilation in pictures of darkening horror; and there in Christ's Gospel, the message of His sin-atoning death and life-restoring resurrection, is the one, only, and last hope of saving the world from this catastrophe. Yet unbelievers continue to sneer, *"If* Jesus is God; *if* He ever lived. . . ." They go even far beyond these sarcastic infidels at Golgotha and declare that the whole story of our Lord's life is a fairy tale and a lie. Such unbelief, particularly in high places, can bring hideous ruin on our age. If you want to build the best defense the United States can ever have, strengthen your own faith in God's Son, and help bring the Savior to others!

At first both crucified criminals joined in ridiculing Christ; but one of them stopped, and as he continued to behold our Savior, he started to see Him in another light. Soon it dawned on him that the Sufferer on the central cross was not guilty of the charges which had led to His crucifixion; and convinced that Jesus was innocent, he rebuked the other malefactor and said, *"Dost not thou fear God, seeing thou art in the same condemnation? And we indeed justly; for we receive the due reward of our deeds; but this Man hath done nothing amiss."* The dying thief's is thus the only voice raised at Calvary, before Jesus' death, to proclaim His innocence. If, in the milling mob at that place of murder, there were those who had seen our Lord's miracles and experienced His love, they now kept their lips sealed in silence against the planned injustice which murdered the Messiah. The scribes, the Pharisees, the high priests, better than anyone else, knew that Jesus was innocent, since their bribery had not been able to produce one false witness whose perjured testimony stood; yet they let the Savior die without a word of protest against the brutal miscarriage of justice. Even the disciples who returned to Golgotha were so cowed by fright that they witnessed this most hideous of all crimes without crying out, "He is altogether innocent." It took a dying outcast to defend Christ and to say, *"This Man hath done nothing amiss."*

Learn from this example, you who call yourselves our Lord's followers, to stand up and speak up for God's Son! Many of you ought to be ashamed of yourselves for keeping sinful silence when the precious name is profaned or loathingly ridiculed by atheists. Why don't you rebuke the enemies of Jesus and go on record as championing His innocence? Recently in New York State a baby was born without a mouth. Spiritually some of you are lipless and tongueless, for you have never contradicted unbelief, never defended the Gospel of grace. Surgeons are operating on that child to give it a mouth; and we pray that the Surgeon of souls, the Holy Spirit, who has promised to hear you when you cry out for Christ, may remove every impediment which keeps you from witnessing fearlessly for Him.

It took a long time, often days, for a man to die in the agony of crucifixion; and during those torturous, pain-racked hours the dying thief had time to behold our Lord at close range and to hear the statement of wondrous love which the Son of God spoke from His central cross. Before long he does more than declare Christ innocent; he goes all the way to acclaim Jesus His Ruler and Redeemer. What a personal, powerful appeal you skeptics, infidels, and atheists should find here! Most of you have never taken the time honestly and earnestly to study the Savior's words and works. Without ever having read the Bible, you condemn it; without once having carefully beheld Jesus, you reject Him. Listen to these shocking lines from a letter written us by a Columbus mother: "I have two children. Do I want them to cast their innocent eyes upon the sadistic picture of a man nailed to a cross and dripping in blood? No!"

Study the writings of the brazen foes of the faith, and you will find that, delighting to trample the sacred truths, they have made glaring errors. Julian Huxley, archenemy of the Almighty, wrote an essay in which he claimed that Samson killed an ox and found honey in its carcass, although our Sunday school children know he slew a lion. Dr. Maude Royden, foe of the faith once given, wrote in the book, *Sex and Common Sense,* that in the second chapter of the Bible God made woman the servant of man. You will never find this in Genesis 2. An American unbeliever spoke of Lazarus' refusing to give the rich man a cup of cold water in hell. Had he known his Bible, he would have realized that this was Abraham, not Lazarus. Two members of the House of Commons in Great Britain, hearing a Scripture passage, asserted that it came from the *Arabian Nights.* In many other ways which I could cite, men have misquoted Holy Writ and misquoted Jesus, because they knew neither the inspired Word nor the Incarnate Word.

On the other hand, when skeptics have come face to face with their Savior, the Spirit has often led them to renounce their denial. Orville Gardner, trainer of prize fighters, associate of New York City's underworld characters, was a thoroughly hardened, selfish, and merciless unbeliever, so crafty and cruel that he was called "Awful" Gardner. One night after his young son died, the father was in a Bowery saloon, when the sweltering heat drove him outside for a breath of fresh air. As he looked up to the starlit heavens, he asked himself, "Where is my little boy tonight?" In a flash his own conscience answered, "Wherever he is, you will never see him again unless you change your life." Moved by the Spirit, "Awful" Gardner hurried from the saloon, never to return. He went to his God-fearing mother, and together they spent the night in the study of Christ's promises and in prayer. Then "Awful" Gardner beheld Jesus in the light of saving faith, accepted Him as his Redeemer, and from that moment dedicated his energies to spreading the Gospel. Gardner, no longer "awful" but "awe-filled" by the Savior's love, preached to the inmates of Sing Sing, and through his ministry one convict became a convert who was to wield a mighty influence in helping save souls. He was a young Irishman, Jerry McAuley, who founded the mission that bears his name and to which literally thousands, through the Holy Spirit, owe their closeness to Christ.

My plea to you still far from heaven, and that means close to hell, asks you to make time to meet God's Son in His Word. Do not rely on the mistaken claims of poison-minded men! Do not allow yourself to be swayed by the errors of a highly publicized skeptic who has never read the Bible! Study the Word! Meet Jesus yourself, personally, as did the dying criminal! Then — and I pray the Lord for this blessing — the Holy Enlightener can lead you, too, from the darkness of sin into the dazzling brightness of your salvation.

How strikingly the dying thief showed his true trust! Note, first of all, his real, sin-confessing repentance. He does not lie, as many criminals do today, who claim they are innocent, when the Almighty knows and their own conscience tells them they are guilty. He does not excuse himself or blame anyone else. No; he tells the other crucified malefactor, *"We receive the due reward of our deeds."* No hypocrisy, no glossing over the crime, no shifting the guilt, no plea for removal of the death sentence! Instead, he publicly, unreservedly confesses his transgression.

May the Spirit bring you the same conviction! You

may never have committed highway robbery, but hundreds of other crimes stain your soul: sins against God, sins against your fellow men, sins against yourselves; sins of thoughts, words, and action; sins of idolatry, doubt and unbelief; sins of covetousness, envy, and greed; sins of lust, impurity, and fleshly desires; sins of dishonesty, falsehood, and hatred. If you want peace for your mind, calm for your conscience, freedom from the dread of death and the fear of hell, believe today that you must get right with God, baring your heart to Him, acknowledging that you have broken His holy Law repeatedly, admitting that you deserve His wrath and the punishment He has decreed for opposing His will! If you truly value your immortal soul and seek deliverance from eternal death, confess your guilt without excuse! No matter how men may glorify iniquity today and spend billions as they serve *"the lust of the flesh and the lust of the eyes and the pride of life"*; no matter how smart it may seem to violate God's Code of Holiness, and how completely many of the high and mighty disregard divine warning; if you want to escape the horrors of damnation, follow the example of the penitent thief on the cross, and admit your own sinfulness.

It is high time, past time, indeed, for a national day of humiliation and repentance in these United States. No one with the average quota of common sense can pick up a newspaper today without realizing we have come upon critical times. Reporters are warning us that aggression abroad has produced a mightier menace than that which we faced in Hitlerism. The advance of Red Atheism has called forth constant cries of alarm. What shall we do? Merely follow political programs, adopt this preparedness measure or that? My countrymen,

I plead with you: Help America humble itself before the Almighty and confess its sins! He has promised His grace to those who contritely admit their misdeeds; but He threatens punishment to those who in puffed-up pride spurn His mercy. A penitent nation can save itself untold sorrow and immeasurable misery. If you love this blessed land, help assure God's guidance by admitting your own transgressions and by supporting the battle against sin on every front!

With his repentance the crucified thief combined prayer. He spoke only nine words to Christ, *"Lord, remember me when Thou comest into Thy kingdom!"* but they were a plea to Jesus. One of the reasons many of you lead beaten, broken lives, filled with darkness and despair, is this: you spurn the strengthening, building power of true intercession. God offers you the resources of His almighty guidance in answer to your petition; but in ignorance, doubt, or utter disbelief, you refuse to exercise this privilege. Correct your soul-destroying mistake today! Get down on your knees and plead to God in Jesus' name, relying on His blood-bought redemption of your soul, and you will learn, as the penitent at Calvary did, what a privilege it is to carry everything to Him in trusting prayer! Speak to your heavenly Father every morning as soon as you arise, and every evening, before you are too sleepy! Give Him thanks for His protecting love! Pray at mealtime, as you picture the millions of perpetually hungry throughout the world! Pray at work and at play, in joy and in sorrow, in happiness, in danger, in life, and, as at Golgotha, in death! If you thus fulfill the Apostle's ideal, *"Praying always with all prayer,"* you will find a new victory of strength, conviction, and divine assurance.

In these overshadowed days intercede for the President and Congress, remembering that your petitions are much more necessary than your criticism! Pray for the enemies of our faith, asking that they may be restrained and converted! Pray for peace, assured that if millions in America would ask the Almighty in His mercy for Jesus' sake to avert the terrors of a third world war, He, with whom *"nothing shall be impossible,"* could check the warmongers and give our bleeding world surcease from further suicidal conflict.

How many marvelous lessons we find also in the content of the penitent's prayer! Plainly he asks that Christ remember him and bring him to heaven. We pray that the desire to be with Jesus after death is your constant, consuming desire. Yet how many — may God have mercy on them! — actually think that heaven is only a fairy-tale fiction? Recently one of you sent me this verse from a Valentine:

> "Heaven's really quite a wondrous place,
> At least so I've been told.
> It has shining stairs and pearly gates
> And streets all paved with gold.
> And I swear by all the angels
> When my earthly span is through,
> I don't wanna go to heaven,
> I just wanna be with you."

What moronic minds to insult the Lord by writing or sending such blasphemous lines! How even more tragic that masses, ruined by Red ridicule, cry out, "We want our pie now, not by and by, when we die, up in the sky!" If you do not want to go to heaven, you will go to hell!

Be sure, as you pray for heaven, that you plead in the true faith, as the crucified malefactor did! His nine words, *"Lord, remember me when Thou comest into*

Thy kingdom," contain everything that you need to know to be saved forever, so plain, so simple, so direct is our faith. This dying criminal, who probably never before had seen Jesus, now in his last moments recognizes more of the real, saving truth than many who have misspent years in studying Christ's life with the purpose of making Him a mere man among men. Even though his senses were beginning to fail him, this dying criminal shows that he recognizes, if only vaguely and dimly, that the Sufferer on the central cross is far more than a human being, that He is the *"Lord,"* the eternal Ruler, who even after death would be restored to His *"kingdom."*

Is the Crucified Lord of Lords to you? Is He the Sovereign of your soul? A mortal Messiah cannot help you, but a divine Mediator who can say, *"All power is given unto Me in heaven and in earth,"* a Christ who is your God, can deliver your soul from destruction and save your body in any danger. Therefore it is this Savior whom our broadcast seeks to proclaim throughout the world, but especially into your heart, the Lord whom Scripture calls God, whom believers and sinless angels worship as God, who by His mighty miracles proves Himself God, who, despite petty attacks by sinful men, is and always will be the true and eternal God, with all the wisdom, the power, counsel, and help you need.

To the dying thief Jesus was not only God, He was also the divine Guide to heaven. The prayer *"Lord, remember me when Thou comest into Thy Kingdom"* expresses the conviction, hazily but surely, that the Son of God will remember those who trust Him and bring them to His realm. On the cross of shame this criminal found the crown of grace; and at grim Golgotha, above this modern talk of Christ's self-sacrifices, His heroism, His martyrdom, His silent suffering of injustice, you, too, should see earth's and Heaven's highest truth revealed, namely, that our Savior, and He alone, is the Way to heaven, the Guarantee of glory. More clearly than the eyes of that dying thief could see and his failing mind could realize, we, who have the truth of the entire New Testament to strengthen us, can know in clear, unmistakable faith that there is pardon for us at the cross. The Son of God there suffers not the punishment of His own sins, for He had none, as even heathen Pilate had to admit; but in the mystery of God's love He, crucified for our crimes, endured the unspeakable anguish of body and soul we should have suffered, as He paid the penalty of our transgressions and died the total terror and torture of all human deaths, in our stead, to satisfy divine justice, clean our crime-cursed souls with His blood, and restore us to God, freed from the frightfulness of hell, assured even here on earth of never-ending blessedness in eternity.

Do you know Christ in this saving truth? Do you pray, "*'Lord, remember me'* now that Thou hast come into Thy kingdom?" In His sacred, saving name I plead, break down any barrier which keeps you from His mercy! Show the penitent's faith, pray his prayer, and heaven is yours.

II

TO BE SURE OF IT, BELIEVE THE CRUCIFIED SAVIOR'S GRACE!

Is this your faith? If it is, Jesus will offer you the same blessed assurance He gave that repentant robber. One might think that, weighted down by the guilt of all men, crushed in His soul by the crimes which mankind had committed and still would commit as century followed century, our Lord would have no ear for a solitary sufferer; but the Savior is the Good Shepherd, who leaves *"the ninety and nine"* and goes *"after that which is lost, until He find it."* I have read of men who have gone to their death almost unconscious of their surroundings, with never a glance nor a word for anyone; but not our Lord! In the deep terror of His torture, His wondrous mercy appeals, *"Father, forgive them; for they know not what they do";* and when a single soul begs for remembrance, not reward, His love, triumphing over the turmoil in His soul, answers a penitent outcast's plea. You, likewise, have Heaven's own guarantee that Jesus will hear you, one of billions in a world of suffering and woe. Did you read in the newspapers recently that a sailor on board the S. S. *Santa Clara* was accidentally hurled into the Carribean Sea without anyone on the ship knowing it until his absence was discovered at the roll call? Then the captain ordered the vessel turned around in an attempt to find the man on the trackless waters. There was but one chance in a thousand that the missing sailor could keep himself afloat. Yet, swimming as best he could, the poor man prayed continually, and under divine direction the seemingly impossible happened. Three hours later he was found and rescued. Won't you believe, then, that the same God who directed this ship back twenty-five miles to a lone sailor struggling against the waves, the same Lord who in His last hours found and saved the soul of that penitent thief, will surely answer your prayers, find you and deliver you from all dangers confronting your soul? Trust Christ's promise, *"Whatsoever ye shall ask in My name, that will I do,"* and receive one of the most powerful proofs of answered prayer in this deathless cry at Calvary, *"Verily, I say unto thee, Today shalt thou be with Me in Paradise."*

What universal, all-inclusive grace in this promise of Paradise, Heaven's highest love for a vile criminal in his last moments! These words tell us that the Savior, who was laying down His life for the redemption of a fallen race, is ready to welcome the worst sinner, the blackest criminal, the most vicious blasphemer, the most treacherous transgressor. Beloved, God wants you to believe that you cannot fall too frequently, sin too grievously, break His Law too repeatedly to be forgiven, if only you come to Him in contrite sorrow but with firm faith in Christ's power to save.

It was not accidental that the first convert at Calvary was no respectable, applauded citizen of Jerusalem from the highest level of human society, but a condemned criminal, a guilty murderer, an outcast, from the lowest depths of degradation. The Holy Spirit wanted to convince you that *"though your sins be as scarlet . . . though they be red like crimson,"* they still cannot be too deeply stained to become dazzling and spotless as the newly driven snow. Almost every day we receive letters insisting, "My sins are too grievous to be forgiven." Why do you who write in such despair place yourselves above the Almighty, when His own holy, unbreakable Word gives you this guarantee: *"The blood of Jesus Christ, His Son, cleanseth us from* ALL *sin"?* Remember, when the Lord says *"all,"* He means *"all"!* Again, letters come to our desk saying that, although you love Jesus, you fear you have committed the unpardonable sin. Stop letting the devil have his way, and, instead, trust your Redeemer's own promise that *"whosoever believeth on Him should not perish, but have everlasting life."*

Christ's power to save to the uttermost, rescuing even the deeply ruined, has not been lost. The same blessed Redeemer who promised Paradise to the penitent thief still shows His grace to many caught in crime. From a New York State penitentiary a prisoner writes us: "Every Sunday I hear your program asking the country to awaken and accept Jesus as its only Savior. I am in jail but, thank God, walls cannot keep a man from accepting the Lord as his Savior. Now that I have accepted Christ, I recognize and reject sin." A Wisconsin prisoner who killed his own wife heard our broadcast mention the penitent thief's rescue and wrote, asking if this promise held for him. We assured him it did and sent a pastor to give him the comfort and guidance of God's Word. After a thorough course of instruction this murderer, sentenced for life, was baptized. A prisoner in a Connecticut penitentiary, charged with murder and soon to go on trial, tuned in our message, and — praised be the Holy Spirit's power! — he was brought all the way to his Savior. He now says that, should the jury sentence him to the electric chair, he will go bravely, and with the peace of Jesus in his heart. Not only does our Lord's truth bless his own life, but love for his Redeemer has also led him to testify, especially during the one-hour recreation period, to two other men charged with first-degree murder. One of these prisoners tells us he is eager to hear more of the Christ who promised the penitent thief pardon and Paradise.

This message of Golgotha's compassion also proclaims Jesus' free mercy, the truth that the deliverance from sin and death is entirely His work and none of our own; that we are saved purely by grace, not by good works. The Holy Spirit chose as the first convert at Calvary a man whose helplessness was to convince us that we can and should do nothing whatever to earn the salvation which the Crucified completely purchased for us with His blood. That dying thief could not go to the Temple, for his feet were nailed to the cross. He could not bend his knees in humility before the Almighty, for he was rigidly affixed to that bloody post. He could not fold his hands, raise his right hand in an oath of allegiance, nor sign a pledge, for his arms were riveted to the beam. He could perform no rituals nor ceremonies; he could pay no money nor render any service. He could not even be baptized, and yet he was saved. Some of you ask, "Must I be baptized to be assured of heaven?" Christ's own words give the answer that under all normal conditions *"He that believeth and is baptized shall be saved."* You should be baptized; you need it, but the same Lord here assures us that if, under rare conditions like those on Good Friday, but only then, there is no possibility for Baptism, in His love He will still receive those who personally accept Him as their Redeemer. Here is the double promise of both Testaments: *"Whosoever shall call on the name of the Lord shall be saved."* With your salvation finished and free, you need only believe, only welcome the wondrous Savior into your soul, only trust the repeated pledge of His Word, *"By grace are ye saved, through faith."* Come, then, and receive for yourself full pardon as the free gift of divine mercy!

Christ's answer to the penitent's prayer also shows us His firm salvation. Each of these words is packed with promise guaranteeing Heaven's grace. *"Verily"* (this gives His promise the force of an oath), *"I"* (the Son of God and Savior of the world) *"say unto thee"*

(I give this holy promise to you, condemned criminal that you are), *"Today"* (before this Friday ends, immediately following your death; not after long periods of purging and preparation) *"shalt thou be with Me"* (the Savior of your soul) *"in Paradise"* (heaven's endless glory).

That was Jesus' promise to the penitent, and that will also be your assurance, whoever you are, whatever your past has been or your future may be, if you confess Christ, remain faithful to Him, and when your last hour comes, pray in spirit, if not in words, *"'Lord, remember me' in Thy kingdom of glory!"* I am not giving you mere wishful thinking, nor offering you a "perhaps" pardon, a possible or even a probable redemption; because I speak to you in the name of our Lord Jesus, I declare Heaven's eternal truth when I say there is pardon for you at the Cross.

Christ's deathless words, *"Verily, I say unto thee Today shalt thou be with Me in Paradise,"* reveal to us final salvation and give us strength when death draws near. The crucified criminal had lived in sin and unbelief all his days, until in his last moments, having seen his Savior, he was led by the Holy Spirit to faith. No matter how old you are or how close to the grave you may be, the same blessed Deliverer is rich in mercy to you, if only now, as you hear the invitation of His grace, you open your hearts to receive Him. It is never too late for you to welcome the cleansing Son of God, but it is never safe to rely on an eleventh-hour repentance, to live as you please and plan on a deathbed conversion. You may not have that chance. Death can come suddenly, and after a swift moment, life may be over for you. A few days ago one of the nation's foremost sales executives addressed a group of men in a Montgomery, Alabama, church. His theme was "The Eighteen Points of Business Success." In the course of his remarks he spoke in would-be humor of heaven, Saint Peter, the pearly gates, Moses, and others in the world to come. After he had finished, he was greeted by thunderous applause, and many of the guests came forward to congratulate him. Suddenly, while he clasped the hand of a friend, he collapsed, and a few moments later, unconscious, he passed into eternity.

Do not make a joke of heaven, but seek for it, strive for it, prepare for it, in the only way you can — by a penitent, trusting faith in Jesus' self-sacrifice for the redemption of your soul! Get right with God! Acclaim Christ your Savior and Deliverer! Say to Him now — and the Holy Spirit grant that all of you, in this country, beyond international boundary lines, on the high seas, and by the penetration of the short wave throughout the world, will join us in this prayer — "Lord, remember me, now that Thou dost rule in Thy kingdom!" Then, listen closely to the guarantee of grace with which the Son of God answers you, and believe it with your whole heart, *"'Verily, I say unto thee,'* forever *'thou shalt be with Me in Paradise!'"* The Holy Spirit help you find this pardon and peace at the Cross today! *Amen!*

DARK DEATH AT CALVARY

"It was about the sixth hour, and there was a darkness over all the earth until the ninth hour. And the sun was darkened, and the veil of the Temple was rent in the midst. And when Jesus had cried with a loud voice, He said, Father, into Thy hands I commend My spirit; and having said thus, He gave up the ghost." SAINT LUKE 23:44-46

CHRIST, OUR CRUCIFIED AND ATONING SAVIOR: Today, long centuries ago, Thou didst triumphantly enter Jerusalem amid the acclaim of chanting, cheering multitudes. Yet five days later in the same city Thou wast nailed to the cross of agony and shame. Forgive us, we beseech Thee, our glaring lack of steadfastness, the ease and speed with which our loyalty changes to desertion! Come into our hearts, and as we hear the message of Thy dark death at Calvary, may many be turned permanently from sin to salvation, from ruin to redemption! Make us understand that it was for us Thou didst suffer, bleed, die in anguish too frightful to be measured! Show us that without Thee we are headed for hell, but that with Thee, as we sorrow for our sins, yet truly trust Thine atoning self-sacrifice, we are eternally redeemed and rescued for heaven. Call those who have fallen from the faith back to Thy grace! Rebuke and restrain the increasing power of godless Communism! Draw its leaders to Thee in real repentance over their rebellion against Thy Gospel! Keep another world conflict from us, and although we have not deserved it, give us peace in our country, and especially in our souls through the mercy that led Thee to die for us at gory Golgotha! O Saving Son of God, everlasting praise and endless glory be Thine for the mercy and might of Thy self-giving love! *Amen!*

Dark Death at Calvary

WHETHER you realized it or not, when you arose this morning, you began a week which commemorates the seven most sacred days in history, those marking the last events in Christ's earthly life: His arrest, His crucifixion, His death at Calvary. Although Jesus lived in this world for more than thirty-three years, Saint Luke devotes one fourth of his chapters; Saint Matthew, two sevenths; Saint Mark, three eighths; and Saint John almost one half, to record this final week in our wondrous Savior's earthly ministry. Eleven chapters for thirty-three years, but nine chapters for this one week — so all-important is the Son of God's death at Golgotha!

Of what concern are these days to the United States? Despite special religious services and Good Friday observances, which receive increasing attention even in business circles, ten millions of Americans will keep their distance from any kind of church. During the very hours when men, aging centuries ago, thrust the crown of thorns on Christ's head, smashed their fists in His face, lashed His back bloody, and nailed Him to the cross, masses in this country who have not taken the time to understand the supreme price His love paid for them, will live on, sin on, sneer on, and curse themselves further into hell as they reject the only Rescuer they can ever have. *"Is it nothing to you, all ye that pass by?"* the Crucified asks each of you in the milling mobs which heedlessly hurry from His cross. Hear your dying Deliverer's compassionate cry and receive Him as your Redeemer! Then, by the Holy Spirit's power this week can become the most blessed in your entire life, because it has brought you from sin to your Savior. God grant it!

How deeply does the story of the atoning Christ touch your soul? Have you heard the story of grim Golgotha so often that you take it for granted or that its effect has become dulled? I often wonder how people can sit in full sight of Niagara Falls and turn their eyes from its majestic beauty to read so-called comic strips. Probably they have seen the crashing cataract so often that it has lost its attraction. With far sadder neglect, many churchgoers to whom our Lord has been revealed as the one and last Hope of a perishing world and as their only Savior are not gripped in their souls by the Good Friday record of redemption. Familiarity, together with worldliness, has bred, if not contempt, then neglect. Bishop Warner, returned to America from India, declared that he could never preach the message of the Cross there without having native men and women break into tears; but here in the United States, he continued, he was grieved to see that many could hear the account of Christ's dying in their stead and remain stolid, sometimes bored by Calvary's matchless mercy. If you have grown lukewarm or even cold toward the crucified Redeemer, may the Holy Spirit use this mission to fill your eyes with tears of repentance and to warm your heart with the fire of a truly fervent faith!

Christians of our country need to pray, *"O Lord, revive Thy work!"* The war, which brought misery to multiplied millions abroad, ruin to ten thousand churches, not only left our sanctuaries unscathed, but brought religious groups within our borders unparalleled prosperity. "Our churches are growing rich and richer," denominational leaders recently reported. "Never before have we paid off so many church mortgages as we have during the last years." As you hear these words, think of John's warning to the congregation in Laodicea, *"Thou sayest, I am rich, and increased with goods, and have need of nothing; and knowest not that thou art wretched, and miserable, and poor, and blind, and naked!"* The call in this critical hour is not for financially strong, but spiritually strong churches, rich in the crucified Savior's grace. The supreme need for your soul is humble, trusting faith in the love Jesus showed for you, especially when He finished the work of your redemption.

Let us unite our hearts in prayer, then, to ask the Holy Spirit's blessing as we focus our attention this Palm Sunday on the

DARK DEATH AT CALVARY!

May all now hearing this message understand and apply to themselves the lessons of personal warning and strengthening power contained in our Holy Week text (the Gospel of Saint Luke, chapter twenty-three, verses forty-four to forty-six): *"It was about the sixth hour, and there was a darkness over all the earth until the ninth hour. And the sun was darkened, and the veil of the Temple was rent in the midst. And when Jesus had cried with a loud voice, He said, Father, into Thy hands I commend My spirit: and having said thus, He gave up the ghost."*

I

THE CRIME OF THE CRUCIFIXION BROUGHT DARKNESS

It was nine o'clock on Good Friday morning when the murderers at Calvary committed the most devilish crime in human annals, when they nailed Jesus to the cross; and it was three o'clock on that afternoon when the Son of God, having completed the task of His deliverance, sank into death. These six hours on the cross may be divided into two parts, the three in the morning and the three in the afternoon, two markedly different sections of our Savior's suffering. The Gospel writers give us a somewhat detailed account of that tragedy, from nine until noon, there atop the Hill of the Skull. Not a word bemoaning His own agony escapes our Lord's lips during that time; instead, as our dying High Priest and Intercessor, He pleads for others. Hear Him, as in the first of His seven sacred utterances He prays, *"Father forgive them; for they know not what they do"*; and ask the Almighty to destroy your pride, selfishness, hatred, and give you a measure of such magnificent mercy! If only men today could be turned from mass destruction to mass devotion, from atomic annihilation to Christ's atoning compassion! Be sure of this: Not before human hearts are changed from loathing to love by faith in the Crucified can there be any real hope of checking war's horror! From Brighton, England, a tailor who eagerly listens to our broadcast writes that because of high prices and low income, people there bring him their coats to be reversed. He says, "Many a time when I am turning a garment inside out I am struck by the amount of dirt that accumulates in the hidden corners." Similarly, if we could peer beneath the surface into souls, we would see a stored accumulation of foulness and filth. We would understand why there can be no real peace until the minds of those controling international policies are changed. That British tailor removes the hidden dirt, remakes the garment, he says, as new, and declares, "Would it not be nice to get all the dirt out of our hearts and then find ourselves bright and clean?" Thank God, through the Crucified you can be remade "bright and clean," with pride, envy, strife banished! Look up

Dark Death at Calvary

to the Cross this day and hear Scripture promise, *"If any man be in Christ,"* this crucified, agonized, dying Savior, *"he is a new creature!"* Is your soul heavy with hatred? Is your family life filled with quarrel and selfishness? Do you cherish grudges and refuse to forgive? Does your temper flare up and anger harden your spirit? Do spite and jealousy prompt your actions? Are you quickly offended and easily hurt? Do you criticize others with loveless harshness? Stand again at Calvary, listen as Jesus pleads for those who had hammered the nails of death through His hands and feet, and then, as you fall on your knees to ask your heavenly Father's forgiveness, beseech the Holy Spirit to fulfill the Old Testament pledge, *"A new heart . . . will I give you."*

During the morning hours at Golgotha Jesus directs, *"Behold thy mother," "Woman, behold thy son,"* as compassionately He asks John to provide for Mary. By cruel, cutting contrast today we read of a seventeen-year-old Missouri girl charged with shooting both father and mother, of multiplied murders in the home, of aged parents forsaken by their children. Has your household lost its happiness? Then call all the members of your family together in this moment, and let me earnestly ask all of you, parents and children, to dedicate your dwelling place to the crucified Christ! Faith in Him will enable you to rebuild broken marriages, restore dying love, remove the cause of conflict.

Once again on Good Friday morning our Lord spoke. The third of His wondrous words from the cross was to tell the penitent crucified with Him, *"Verily, I say unto thee, Today shalt thou be with Me in Paradise."* Cling to this limitless love, which is ready to receive even a criminal without any payment of money or any performance of good works! Believe without question that the Savior is dying to pay the full penalty of your sins, and freely, but surely, to grant you complete forgiveness also of the vilest transgression! John Bunyan, author of *Pilgrim's Progress,* was long tortured by the thought that he was guilty of the unforgivable sin against the Holy Spirit. When he prayed, filthy thoughts clogged his mind; he felt that the devil was tempting him to curse Christ; and he spent years in the soul slavery which urged him to commit suicide. How completely he could have spared himself this anguish if only he had fully trusted God's promise, *"Though your sins be as scarlet, they shall be as white as snow; though they be red like crimson, they shall be as wool"!* Some of you are burdened by the same sorrow. You write me that when you pray, sing hymns, read the Bible, nasty, even blasphemous words unwillingly enter your mind, and you feel that you have been rejected by the Almighty. In Jesus' name I tell you: banish that thought from your mind! Stop limiting your Redeemer's mercy! As long as you love Jesus, all such transgressions are forgiven. Whenever these evil thoughts enter your mind, pray: "Precious Savior, thou knowest that I love Thee as my divine Deliverer, and Thou knowest that I hate these sinful impulses. Therefore forgive me, strengthen me, and help me overcome this evil!" With such faith you can triumph over your trouble, remembering that God's Son promised Paradise to a penitent criminal who only a few hours before had reviled Him.

It is noon now, and suddenly the scene at Calvary changes. No longer do we find the milling mob, the high priests and the Pharisees hurling their hellish taunts against the innocent Son of God. The voice of vicious

Dark Death at Calvary

sneering is stilled; the taunting ridicule is hushed, for a miracle has occurred: at high noon, when the sun's light should be the brightest, it fails. As our text recalls, *"It was about the sixth hour, and there was a darkness."* This was not simply a few hours of heavy, cloudy weather, since we are told, *"The sun was darkened."* It was not an eclipse, for a study of the heavenly bodies rules this out, since no total eclipse lasts three hours, and this darkness continued *"until the ninth hour"* or three o'clock in the afternoon. It was not merely a local lightlessness at Calvary, in Jerusalem, throughout Palestine; we are assured, *"There was a darkness over all the earth,"* and pagan writers record that at this time in distant domains the sun suddenly lost its brilliance.

Here, then, in the Savior's last hours was a mighty miracle. The sun, 329,000 times larger than our globe; the sun with a temperature of at least 10,000 degrees Fahrenheit; the sun from which issue flames thirty times greater than the diameter of this globe; this giant luminary is to God only as a flashlight is to man. In a moment, at Good Friday's high noon, the Lord suddenly cuts off its illumination. How all-powerful He is, and how completely we depend on His help!

What, we ask, was the purpose of this darkening? It has always seemed to me that the earth was to be enshrouded in blackness in order that our Savior's intense suffering should be somewhat shielded from the gaze of curious, prying eyes. None of us can realize the depthless anguish of a crucifixion. Usually the victim was handed a cup of wine mixed with a powerful narcotic to deaden the pain. Often the cruelty was too much even for the executioners, cold and calloused killers though they were, and frequently the Roman soldiers gave the condemned prisoner a blow under the armpits which hastened the end. So terrifying was the ordeal of expiring on the cross that often, as Cicero tells us, men sentenced to die offered large sums as bribes for the privilege of being strangled or otherwise nearly killed before they were nailed to the post and the beam. Sometimes, in strange mercy, the criminal was first executed and then affixed to the cross.

We remind you, by contrast, that nothing was done to ease Christ's suffering. He refused to drink the stupefying wine offered Him, probably by compassionate women, for He wanted to feel the full death anguish. And what ghastly torment the cross brought! It meant suffering a dozen different pains, devilishly designed to make the victim endure all possible torture short of finding welcomed relief in unconsciousness. The burden of the suspended body made the slightest movement a wrenching violence; the lacerated muscles ached unspeakably; the cut, crushed veins throbbed in mounting agony; the four nail wounds, in hands and feet, festered with fierce pangs of fire. Gradually gangrene set in; the blood became poisoned; the torment of tetanus began; high fever raced through the body; burning thirst produced utter dryness. Altogether crucifixion was one of the most brutal, barbaric forms of capital punishment men have ever devised. We can understand, then, why proud Rome decreed that under no circumstances could one of its citizens, whatever his crime, be nailed to a cross; and we can thank God that Constantine, Christian ruler of the Roman Empire, speedily abolished crucifixion. No wonder that Jesus, fever-racked and deathly dry, cried out, "*I thirst.*" No wonder, too, that the Al-

Dark Death at Calvary

mighty mercifully kept the sunlight from revealing the full extent of this fatal suffering.

A far deeper agony was to be shielded partially by this darkness at Calvary. Immeasurably worse than the physical pains of the crucifixion was the torment of soul and body which your sins and mine there heaped on the atoning Savior. If you never knew this before, give these words your closest attention now; and even if you have heard this truth from the days of your earliest remembrance, I still ask you to listen carefully: Jesus Christ, the Son of God, here on Golgotha bears in His own body, soul, and mind the total punishment, the entire and eternal damnation of every man, every woman, every child who lived and died in the past of human history, who now have their being, or who will yet live on this globe as long as it exists.

Have you ever taken the time to measure, as closely as you can, the misery which follows a single sin or curses a single sinner? If you could read the records of remorse which people write me, lashed by their conscience when the specters of a solitary crime in the distant past returns to haunt them; if you could survey the wreck and ruin of families, cities, nations, which one man has produced by his revolt against the Almighty, you would begin to understand the fearful consequences of the transgressions in only one life. I say "begin," for all the sorrows that the violation of Heaven's Law produce on earth: strife, grief, hatred, diseased bodies, muddled minds, broken hearts, are only passing gestures when compared with the everlasting agonies in hell, so frightful that Scripture itself can hardly find human terms to describe the horror of damnation. Now add to this punishment of one sin and the suffering of one unforgiven sinner, the total penalty of all transgressions, the curse, the physical and spiritual anguish which rests on the many billions of mankind in its aggregate, and then realize on this first day of Holy Week, as your eyes are trained to the central cross, that Jesus endured all this, nothing less, when He became *"The Lamb of God, which taketh away the sin of the world."* Picturing the force of the divine wrath which there struck the crucified Christ as He gave His life, a Sin Offering for all men of all ages, you can understand why the Almighty enshrouded Calvary in blackness and kept men from witnessing the whole writhing, torturing terror which helped break the suffering Savior's heart. His depthless anguish was too awful for human eyes fully to witness. Just as Moses on Sinai was not permitted to see the Almighty in His entire glory, so sinners at Calvary were not allowed to behold the complete grief of His Son, which made Him scream in soul terror far worse than any physical pain, *"My God, My God, why hast Thou forsaken Me?"*

Despite this death darkness, you can behold enough of the Savior's anguish to know that He was made to suffer the doom of the damned, because of your own repeated rebellion against heaven. In the intensely personal warning that Holy Week would send into your heart, you should realize that your sins against God the Father, against His saving Son, against the Holy Spirit, your sins against your neighbor, your own family and yourself, your sins against knowledge and conscience, your sins of hands, heart, and lips — all these helped nail the stainless Savior to those blood-reddened timbers. If you have never been lashed by sorrow over your iniquities, but instead have lived on brazenly breaking the Almighty's Law, then, to help rescue your soul from hell, I beg you in this dying Deliverer's name to hear and believe that your transgressions helped hammer the nails through His hands and feet. If before this Holy Week you have never understood your relation to the pain-racked Redeemer, then let me speak plainly when I charge you, as myself, with helping to kill the Lord of life, and indict you and, once more, myself, for first-degree murder of the merciful Mediator. If you have never fallen on your knees to confess your transgressions, may you now, contemplating Christ crucified for you, cast yourself down before your heavenly Father and cry out: "Oh, what a crushing burden my sins are, since they could be removed only by this self-sacrifice of Thy Son at Calvary! Oh, what a curse my crimes pressed on my soul, since I could be freed from their hellish penalty only by the cleansing blood which Jesus shed for me on the tree of shame and scorn!"

If despite your Savior's self-giving love you turn from His death agonies and continue to plot further plans of lust, to continue your hidden sins, your secret affairs, your concealed vices, your open defiance of divine Truth, stop and ask God, if necessary by shattering rebuke and crushing reverses, to shake you into your senses, to make you see yourself as you are, guilty, condemned, lost in the rebellion against God which riveted your Redeemer to Calvary's cross!

The gloom that engulfed Golgotha on the noon of Good Friday was also evidence of divine wrath and of the judgment to come. Throughout Scripture, darkness is the sign of the Almighty's anger. Never before had the sun thus been covered for hours; the crucifying of the innocent Christ was the supercrime of all ages. Never again, as long as the world stands, will the sun be thus robbed of its brilliance — never, until Christ returns on the Last Day to hold His final judgment. Then, as He Himself assured us, when the earth hastens to its end, *"shall the sun be darkened, and the moon shall not give her light."* Does anyone acquainted with international trends and the signs of the final days predicted in Scripture doubt that we are hastening on to *"the end of all things"?* Before this darkness again covers the earth, the Bible foretells, war, as *"rumors of war,"* will multiply; and no other age has heard more *"rumors of war,"* just as no previous generation has faced more savage slaughter than our own. Before this complete darkness encircles our globe, *"famines and pestilences"* are to sweep over the nations, as now epidemics demand the lives of thousands abroad every day. Before such blackness reappears to cover the continents at the end of the world, we are assured by prophetic Scripture, unbelief will control vast areas, and persecution of believers will rage. Look at a map, and you will see that most of Europe, Asia, and Africa is under the sway of blasphemous unbelief. Review the events of the last years, and you must agree that Red atheism is constantly spreading more widely over the face of the earth. Stalin, who controls more territory than any other man on earth today, recently repeated to the youth of his country his rejection of all religion. A Communist authority declares: "The campaign of the godless is financed by the Soviet government, and the campaign includes many antireligious films, posters, newspapers, and magazines."

Last Wednesday our President felt constrained to appear before a joint session of the Congress and to declare in outspoken terms that the U. S. S. R., champion of atheism, has not only refused to co-operate in working for peace, but "has actually sought to prevent it." He charged that the Red regime "has ignored and violated its promises," besides destroying "the independence of a whole series of nations in Eastern and Southern Europe." The President then asked Congress for billions of dollars, for the conscription of our youth, and for the re-establishment of draft laws—requests, he declared, vitally necessary for meeting this threat to our liberties. Today I am asking for your prayer that this menace may vanish and war be avoided; but I warn you that the spiritual dangers of this widest away-from-God movement in history are greater than the military threat. The worst is yet to come. Should a period of severe financial readjustment set in, the agents of atheism will have a Russian holiday here in these United States. They will not stop short of starting our first religious persecution. If it is time for our country to act on the political front, it is high time for our churches to plan an all-out program of prayer to counteract this evil and help prevent war.

Thus the darkness which enshrouded the world for three hours on the first Good Friday is paralleled by the blackness of blasphemy which has engulfed our globe for the three postwar years, the hatred, tyranny, and brutality otherwise unequaled in human annals. Too many millions of our fellow men have been killed in conflict which could have been avoided; too many hundreds of billions of dollars have been paid for purposes of bloodshed and for personal profit; too many myriads of sins against the Almighty, the cursing of His holy name, the rejection of His redeeming Son, have been committed to give mankind the enjoyment of smooth prosperity.

"Be not deceived; God is not mocked." He will demand punishment for every unforgiven violation of His Law, national and individual. Nor will the United States escape unscathed. There are more infidels in any large city of our country today than there were scoffers at Calvary, more Christ deniers in a dozen metropolitan centers within our borders than in Jerusalem when it was sacked and looted. We have more unchurched people within our borders than Germany had when under Hitler it was bombed into ruin and defeat. We will pay for this. As you see the darkness encircling the cross engross the globe, and Heaven's wrath overtake those who rebel against the Redeemer, realize that howling, hideous punishment can descend on us in the United States collectively and individually, unless we heed the Holy Week appeal for repentance, for contrite confession of all our sins, and a new dedication to God's Son crucified for our crimes!

II

THE COMPASSION OF THE CRUCIFIXION DISPELS DARKNESS

The Four Gospels devote little space to those afternoon hours when black night beset Golgotha. Saint Luke records only the three verses of our text, but he does tell us, *"The veil of the Temple was rent in the midst."* This, too, was a divine miracle. Do not think of the veil as a thin, gauzelike curtain! It was thirty feet wide, twice as high, closely woven, as thick as the palm of the hand, and so heavy that, according to tradition, it took 300 priests to raise it. No accident could have ripped that curtain *"from the top to the bottom."* Divine strength was required; and truly God desecrated His own Temple, because its leaders had desecrated His faith as they plotted to destroy His Son.

This was the first phase in the devastation of the proud Temple; the last came fewer than forty years later, when Roman invaders set fire to the sanctuary, battered down its walls, and in fulfillment of Christ's prediction left *"not . . . one stone upon another."* What a warning for our age, which has witnessed more damaged and destroyed churches than any previous generation! Had present-day world powers remained with the Lord, instead of deserting Him, those sanctuaries might have been spared. No matter how large and imposing are the churches we build, however costly the material and attractive the architecture, if they contradict Scripture or condemn the Savior, they are doomed. To prevent our churches from becoming blackened, broken ruins like those today etched against the skies of war-wrecked Europe, let American Christendom rededicate itself to the message of Holy Week, God's love for all men as shown by Christ's self-sacrifice on the cross!

The Temple curtain hung over the Holy of Holies, the most sacred spot of the sanctuary. No one but the High Priest was permitted to enter that hallowed chamber, and then only after he had been purified and sanctified. Even he could step into it on just one day of the year, the solemn festival of the Atonement. Now, however, the veil torn, anyone could behold the Holy of Holies. It had fulfilled its purpose. The Old Testament was finished, and the New Testament in Jesus' blood was begun. The single Sin Offering at Calvary had done away with all Temple sacrifices. Through the merciful Savior's atonement all those who believed had free access to the real Holy of Holies, the heavenly throne. There remained no more hidden mysteries of the faith to which a restricted few had access; for by His suffering and death God's Son had perpetually opened the gates of heaven, even for condemned criminals like the penitent thief crucified at His side.

The twenty-second Psalm, prophetic of Calvary's suffering, indicates that the hours on the cross seemed to drag on in long duration as their agony constantly increased. Gradually, the ninth hour, three o'clock in mid-afternoon, approached; then Jesus, *"knowing that all things were now accomplished,"* cried out, *"It is finished,"* the word in Greek written on ancient receipts, meaning "The payment is finished" in the same sense as our modern "Paid in full." What heavenly assurance for every contrite sinner! Jesus suffered the total death sentence for our deliverance. He completed every part of our atonement. He left nothing required for our redemption unsaid, unearned, undone. Do you believe and trust His finished salvation? Once when Beethoven, old and stone-deaf, was conducting an orchestra which, for the first time, played one of his master compositions, the musicians finished their scores and stopped; but Beethoven, who could not hear a sound, stayed on the podium continuing to direct. The symphony was concluded, but he did not realize it. Some of you, who have not fully believed Christ's *"It is finished,"* make a far more serious mistake. You think you must keep on trying to earn what the Savior has already acquired for you. You feel you must continue working for the salvation which He purchased with His blood and which He freely offers you by His grace. May the Holy Spirit indelibly impress on your soul the fact that by His death God's Son forever finished your redemption!

Dark Death at Calvary

Finally, as the pain and punishment of our sins broke our Lord's heart, He spoke His last words from the cross, not in a wavering, dying whisper, but in a vibrating voice of triumph. We are told, *"When Jesus had cried with a loud voice, He said, Father, into Thy hands I commend My spirit; and having said thus, He gave up the ghost."* Will your last words likewise be addressed to God in prayer? Will they be verses of Scripture, as was Jesus' last utterance? Will your farewell to life commend you into the almighty hands of your heavenly Father, as your crucified Redeemer entrusted His soul? To be sure of this blessing, come to the atoning Savior, and cling to Him forever! In Germany, before the war, a young man suffering from aggravated cancer of the tongue had been wheeled into the operating room. A renowned surgeon bent over to tell him: "My friend, if you want to say anything, you have the opportunity now; but I must warn you; your words will be the last you will ever utter. Think carefully, therefore, before you speak!" For a few moments the patient lay silent in serious thought while medical students, assembled to witness the surgery, bent forward to hear his final utterance. When the young man broke the silence, one could have seen tears in some eyes as in a loud, clear tone he cried, "Thank God! Jesus Christ!" Every believer's voice, though paralyzed by disease or death here on earth, will be restored to perfection in eternity, there always to praise our Lord's redeeming love.

When the Son of God died — I pray the Holy Spirit that by this time each of you will say, "He died for me" — the gloom at Golgotha suddenly vanished, when at that ninth hour on Good Friday the sun again gave forth its light. Gradually the mob left the skull-shaped hill, no longer jeering and jibing, but silent in strange sorrow, striking their breasts in grief. Only a few of the Savior's followers remained with the military guard.

Although none realized it, the light which now dispelled the darkness was a token of eternal triumph, for by His death Christ gave every penitent, believing sinner the brightness of salvation instead of the black despair of damnation. He guaranteed to all the brilliance and beauty of His sustaining love for every lightless moment of weakness, persecution, affliction, and sorrow. He assured them that by faith in the power of His shed blood and His sin-destroying death they could have the gleam of eternal glory in heaven.

Fellow redeemed, is your life overcast by the gloom of grief? Is your home heavily shadowed by sorrow and sin? Is your soul deeply darkened by denial of Jesus and doubt of His atoning love? I plead with you: make your peace with God here at the Cross, through His Son, who *"is our Peace."* Write us without delay that you want *"the Light of the world"* to dispel dark death from your soul! Let us send you ministers of His mercy who will show you the radiance of His redemption! Then, and I promise you by the power of the blood shed on Calvary's cross: If you believe that the Lord of love was crucified for you, all will be light, all will be bright, all will be right for you forever.

I cannot close this Palm Sunday message without an appeal to you who once acclaimed your Redeemer, but now accuse Him, just as in the first Holy Week the first day's warm reception of Jesus changed to the sixth day's cold rejection of His mercy. How can you spurn Him to whom you once sang your hallelujahs and waved the palm branches of faith? How, having once tasted the

Dark Death at Calvary

Savior's full, free forgivenesss, can you disregard His love and send your soul to hell? The suffering Son of God pardoned Peter who denied Him. He would have forgiven even a penitent Judas who betrayed Him. His blood was shed at Calvary for you, the false and fickle, who forget Him. Oh, come back to Him now! Return to His redeeming compassion, strengthened by His guarantee of grace, *"Him that cometh to Me I will in no wise cast out."*

The Holy Spirit grant that all of you, the faithful and the faithless, will join with us as in spirit we kneel at the Cross, behold the Rescuer of the race dying in fearful torture, and pray this ancient litany of loving trust:

"O Christ, Thou Lamb of God that takest away the sin of the world, have mercy upon us!

"O Christ, Thou Lamb of God that takest away the sin of the world, have mercy upon us!

"O Christ, Thou Lamb of God, that takest away the sin of the world, grant us Thy peace!" *Amen!*

DON'T FEAR DEATH! CHRIST LIVES!

"We shall be also in the likeness of His resurrection."
ROMANS 6:5

CHRIST, OUR RADIANTLY RISEN REDEEMER: Everlasting praise, endless glory, eternal honor be Thine for breaking the bonds of death and on the first Easter triumphantly leaving Thy tomb! Thankfully we bow at Thy empty sepulcher to exalt Thee, Thou Lord of life, for keeping Thy resurrection promise, proving Thyself our God with dominion over death, showing us that Thy Good Friday self-sacrifice to atone for the sins of the world was accepted and that Thou dost reign triumphantly to hear and help us in our need. Use the Easter message mightily in leading many to Thee, Thou Conquerer of the grave, and in convincing the bereaved and brokenhearted that by faith in Thine Easter mercies, "earth hath no sorrow that heaven cannot heal"! Help us believe fully that because Thou art now forever enthroned as Lord of Lords, all who are Thine shall defeat decay and in radiantly resurrected bodies rise from the dust, ever to be with Thee and their loved ones who depart in faith! Help us spread the Easter evangel into many darkened hearts and homes, both in our country and abroad! Preserve us all — whatever the earthly cost may be — for the eternal Easter with Thee! Because Thou livest, we, too, shall live! "Thanks be to God, which giveth us the victory through Thee," "our Lord Jesus Christ!" Hallelujah! Hallelujah! *Amen!*

Don't Fear Death! Christ Lives!

God grant you a joy-filled, peace-crowned Easter through faith in our resurrected, everliving Savior Jesus Christ! Saint John tells us that *"it was yet dark"* when Mary Magdalene, the first witness of our Lord's triumph over death, came to the empty sepulcher; and it is still dark in this war-mad world, where sinister, secret forces, led by men who never risk their lives in battle, are planning to embroil the nations in a third world conflict, which would count its victims by the millions. Pray God Almighty for help to frustrate their plans! Repeat the Psalmist's plea, *"Scatter Thou the people that delight in war!"*

It is still dark for myriads across the seas whose lives have been crushed by robbery and rape, the ravishes of hunger and the ruin of hatred — the 300,000 pitifully helpless people massacred in the Punjab of India because of their religion — the multitudes in Central Europe often fatally undernourished.

It is still dark for uncounted millions who live under the sway of godless Communism, which officially opposes Christ and in consequence robs men of their liberties and threatens world peace. Pray the Lord of Lords, who makes *"wars to cease,"* to break this tyranny of terror!

It may be dark in your home and heart this Easter because you are overclouded by sickness and sadness, broken health, and broken happiness. In one of earth's most haunting sorrows, a recent or an approaching bereavement may fill your soul with the fear of death. Continually some of you write me that your joy is gone because you cringe at the thought of life's end and the gruesomeness of the grave. You telephone and telegraph to request help in defeating this gloom.

How I thank my God, then, that on this happy Easter

Day, marking the mightiest victory of the ages, I can invite you to stand in spirit before Christ's open sepulcher and tell you:

DON'T FEAR DEATH! CHRIST LIVES!

We find this assurance in our Easter text (Romans, chapter six, verse five), the divine promise, *"We shall be also in the likeness of His resurrection."*

I

CHRIST'S EASTER VICTORY GUARANTEES
OUR RESURRECTION

You must be positively sure that no one but Jesus can reveal the true facts of the life to come. Spiritism, which claims to communicate with departed souls, is a falsehood and a fraud. Twenty-two years ago Harry Houdini and his wife made a pact. They gave each other sealed envelopes containing a secret message, and the one who died first was to try to send that statement from the grave. Mr. Houdini left this life in 1926, and thereafter on each anniversary of his death his wife sat alone in a dark room, illuminated only by a candle burning before his picture. After seventeen years' effort she stopped trying to contact her husband. "Nothing ever happened," she told reporters, explaining that spiritism, its table knocking, bell ringing, and ghostly voices are "not only phonies, they are fakes." Houdini could free himself from handcuffs, shackles, and tightly bound ropes, but he could not come back from the cemetery. The jail in Oklahoma City is called "escapeproof"; however, only recently a one-armed prisoner, crippled with arthritis, hobbling on crutches, successfully made a break

Don't Fear Death! Christ Lives!

for his freedom. Yet none of you will ever escape the grip of the grave until Christ's resurrection trumpet sounds. Do not listen to mediums who claim that they can establish contact with your loved ones long asleep in the family plot! Not only do they lie, they can also mislead you into misery. A Kentucky woman writes me to confess: "Last May I laid my daughter to rest, and since that time I am not myself any more. I am sorry to say, I have indulged in spiritualism for comfort and found none. The way becomes darker than dark. I have suffered and made myself and every one around me miserable." Keep away from séances and so-called consultation with the dead! They can destroy your soul.

Nor can money and carefully laid plans bring men back from the grave. Years ago John P. Bowman, having acquired a fortune in the leather business, built a gabled mansion at Cuttingsville, Vermont, where he retired. The new home was dedicated in a lavish housewarming celebration, but within three months Mrs. Bowman and two daughters died of a contagious disease. One day, five years later, Bowman summoned his servants and, standing beneath the stained-glass window of the grand staircase, told them: "I'll soon be leaving, but I'll be back. I promise that I will come back . . . and I have never broken my word." Then he retired to his room, and within an hour he died. When his will was opened, it was found that he left $50,000 in a trust fund to pay for the upkeep of the mansion until he returned. For sixty-two years the custodian of his estate has been awaiting his arrival. Every evening a special hot meal is prepared for Bowman, but he has never appeared; and this year the winter was so severe and the cost of fuel so high that the sprawling estate was closed until spring.

While dead men do not leave the grave, Easter testifies that God's Son on the third day after His crucifixion did keep His promise and was victoriously restored to new life. Without argument or debate our text speaks of *"His resurrection,"* the climax truth of the entire New Testament. So that none of you will misunderstand this term, *"resurrection,"* let me say that it means just this: sometime after midnight and before daybreak of the first Easter day *"the angel of the Lord descended from heaven, and . . . rolled back the stone from the door"* of the rock-hewn grave into which the body of Jesus had been placed after His death on Good Friday. At the same time Christ, without decay or decomposition, regained His life and in a marvelous, radiant body left that sepulcher, never to return.

In this day of increasing skepticism many, of course, do not hesitate to reject the Easter record. Throughout America unbelievers outside the churches and — the Lord forgive them! — inside, just as mounting myriads of atheists in Europe, try to explain away this miracle, simply because they do not understand it. How, then, do they account for the opened grave? None of the Savior's enemies, the scribes or the Pharisees, dared deny that the sepulcher was empty! The whole city of Jerusalem could see that it had been opened and that the body was gone. One of infidelity's greatest problems has always been to say what happened to the sealed grave. Those who crucified Christ were so stunned by His resurrection that, according to Saint Matthew, the chief priests *"gave large money unto the soldiers, saying, Say ye, His disciples came by night and stole Him away while we slept."* Would military men publish that they fell asleep at the post, thus inviting severe punishment, even death itself? Besides, why would they be foolish enough to pretend to know what happened when they slept?

Other teachers of international reputation claim that the women went to the wrong grave. Can anyone actually believe that with the precautions taken to prevent the resurrection, the guards would have watched the wrong sepulcher? Would all the disciples have gone to the wrong grave? Could the angel have been in error when he declared: *"He is not here; for He is risen, as He said. Come, see the place where the Lord lay"*? No reason whatever exists for even assuming that there was another burial place in Joseph's garden.

You can see, then, in these claims and in the more absurd theory that our Lord did not die on the cross, but actually was alive when buried, how truly the hatred of the Gospel makes fools of men. Despite their learning, the explanation and excuses scoffers use in rejecting the Resurrection present far more serious difficulties than does the truth itself. Whenever infidels claim to know more than the Almighty and protest that the statements of His Word are impossible, the explanations they substitute are rank nonsense. Thus, despite the system, design, and order in the world, they contradict Scripture's claims that the Almighty made this globe, and actually insist that the universe came into existence by mere accident; that man is not the divine masterpiece, but the haphazard descendant of apelike creatures. They brand the miracles mentioned in the Bible as impossible, yet propose the most unreasonable of substitutes. At the wedding in Cana our Lord did not change water into wine, they assert; instead He secretly brought the wine with Him and later produced it as part of a practical party joke. Jesus did not feed the five thousand, they object, insisting that it happened this way: A boy who had bread and fish for his own lunch unselfishly shared it with a few friends. When others in the crowd saw this generosity, they became ashamed of themselves, and one after another brought out their hidden food. Again, Christ did not walk on the water, Bible critics maintain, but on the shore. In the fog (which they invent) it only seemed He was striding on the depths of the Galilean Sea. True, we cannot understand the mightiest of God's miracles, the resurrection of His Son, but we can and should believe it, while no intelligent person can and will trust the absurd counterclaims of unbelief.

In the face of Red atheist ridicule at home and abroad, which prints the vilest of cartoons blaspheming the Resurrection, and in spite of the tragedy that throughout our own country sophisticates smile amusedly at the Easter story, I tell you, our Lord's victory over the grave is a firm fact, more certainly proved than any occurrence in the political history of that age. Christ's resurrection was predicted in ancient prophecy. Can you name another event in the life of Emperor Augustus foreseen and foretold long centuries in advance? So sure was the Savior's triumph at the sepulcher that He Himself repeatedly announced His conquest of the grave, as eleven passages in the Gospels testify. Can you produce one sentence from the writing of Julius Caesar to show that he knew what would happen to him? He was so unaware of the immediate future that on the very morning of his death, although warned of an assassination plot, he neglected to heed it, and blindly went to his end. Yet five eyewitnesses who actually saw the risen Redeemer, Matthew, Mark, John, Peter, Paul, have left us their personal account of Jesus' return to life. Try to produce five

Don't Fear Death! Christ Lives! 171

eyewitnesses to any other event in Greek or Roman history during the first century! You can ransack the libraries of our oldest and largest museums, but you will not find a single occurrence in that age recorded by five different men who actually saw it.

During Christ's lifetime the exiled poet Ovid died in a city on the Danube. No scholar of whom I know has expressed any doubt that he died there in the year 18, although only a handful of people, at the most, would have witnessed his death. Why, then, should we question Jesus' resurrection when people saw Him in Judea and in Galilee, on a mountain and at the lakeside, in homes and on the highway, at worktime and mealtime, alone and in groups of 500, by day and by night? The Apostles' writings are filled with passages like our text, which speak of *"His resurrection"* as an assured, unquestioned truth. Which part of the New Testament, do you suppose, was most frequently cited by writers in the Early Church? The fifteenth chapter of First Corinthians, with this supreme truth: *"Christ died for our sins according to the Scriptures; and . . . He rose again the third day according to the Scriptures"*!

Here, then, is fact, not fiction; firm record, not fairy tale. Yet a famous teacher at one of our universities does not hesitate to compare our Lord's emerging from the grave at Easter with Santa Claus's coming down the chimney at Christmas, thus making the mightiest truth in history appear as a childish myth. God have mercy on the United States if our young folks follow such falsity! Mighty minds, far from classifying the Easter triumph with the Santa Claus story, have reverently bowed before the risen Savior to affirm their personal reliance on His resurrection. If you think that only juvenile minds can accept the Easter evangel, let me cite these men who have believed every syllable of its truth: Charles Kendall Adams, president of the University of Wisconsin; James Burrill Angell, president of the University of Michigan; John Merle Coulter, president of Lake Forest University; Timothy Dwight, president of Yale; Merrill Gates, president of Amherst College; Mark Hopkins, president of Williams College; David Hill, president of the University of Rochester; William Johnston, president of Tulane University; Richard Jones, president of Alabama University; Nathan Lord, president of Dartmouth; Seth Low, president of Columbia; George MacLean, chancellor of the University of Nebraska; Henry Morton, president of Stevens College of Technology; Josiah Quincy, president of Harvard; Henry Wade Rogers, president of Northwestern. These and many more, all college or university presidents, have bowed before the revealed glory of the open grave and joined in the faith which prompted Cyrus Northrop, president of the University of Minnesota, to declare: "Jesus rose from the dead, as He said He would rise, and as we are told He did. I feel as Paul did, *'If Christ be not risen, then is our preaching vain, and your faith is also vain.' 'But now is Christ risen from the dead, and become the firstfruits of them that slept.'* . . . This, that, and the other may change or perish, but Christ remains the same yesterday, today, and forever, the divine Savior of the world." Why should you doubt this truth if college presidents have thus endorsed it? For pardon, peace, and power believe, "*Now is Christ risen from the dead,*" and join the members of the true Church in all ages and in all denominations to declare, "The third day He rose again from the dead."

Don't Fear Death! Christ Lives!

What glorious assurance our Lord's resurrection gives! It proves that He is indeed the Son of God, the Almighty Himself; for no mortal man has ever been able to come forth from the grave. Only the Lord of Lords could truly say of His own life, *"I have power to lay it down, and I have power to take it again."* Only God could give Himself into death for the sins of men and on the third day return in a radiant existence. You see, then, how all-important it is that the Church today kneels before the victoriously risen Redeemer and calls Him, as Thomas did, *"My Lord and my God."* A merely human Christ can never deliver you from death nor help you when you launch into eternity.

The Easter verity is the seal of approval on Christ's teaching, for it shows that He spoke the truth and kept His word. What man can give us unfailing assurance for the heavy problems before us? In October, 1929, the President of the United States declared: "The fundamental business of the country . . . is on a sound and prosperous basis," but within one short year the national income had dropped from $85,000,000,000 to $37,000,000,000; one of every four farms had been sold for taxes; 3,000,000 workers were unemployed. In 1933 this number had grown to 15,000,000. Five thousand banks were closed. Again, in 1929, soon after a Yale professor and financial expert had said that the price of stocks had reached "what looks like a permanently high plateau," American investors lost $50,000,000,000 in stock-market crashes. Remember this for the months and years ahead: no matter how insistently leaders may claim that our prosperity will continue, they can be entirely mistaken! America must pay for its unbelief, its ingratitude, its forgetfulness of the Almighty. Only divine mercy can save us from facing money shortages, unemployment, political disaster, and the woes of atomic war. Only a repentant, reverent, God-fearing nation can enjoy the promise of divine blessing. If Jesus kept His word in rising from the grave, He will also keep His word in rising up to rebuke those who oppose Him.

Christ's resurrection testifies that His self-sacrifice for the sins of the world has been fully accepted. Had He remained in the tomb, had His body moldered in a Palestinian grave, His death on the cross would have meant no more for us than the murder of any other martyr. No man can save you from your sins, even by giving his life. All the memorial stones on earth, were they merged together into a mighty monument, would not induce the Almighty to forgive a single sin. Only God could fully atone for your transgressions, and only God could break the grip of the grave as Jesus did to prove Himself your Lord. If Good Friday, with the voice of final victory, *"It is finished,"* assures you that everything required for your release from ruin has been completed forever, then Easter gives you the divine guarantee: death is defeated, sin is vanquished, hell is overcome, Christ has conquered, God has accepted the sacrifice of His own Son for the guilt of the whole world.

Standing in spirit before the open tomb, you are blessed with the assurance that your Savior lives. Men tried to kill Him in the first century, just as they seek to assassinate Him in our twentieth; but He triumphs in indestructible glory. Despite Red atheism abroad and scarlet denial at home, He lives. Despite unfaithfulness in the pulpit and hypocrisy in the pews, He lives.

Praise His eternal love, He lives to support His own in every need. Believers in the tornado-swept areas of

Illinois learned this a few days ago. At Bunker Hill our pastor and his wife had just finished their morning devotions when the roar of the wind made them run to the door to see if any damage had been done. Hardly had they stepped outside when a fierce blast struck them and carried them thirty feet through the air. After they came to their senses, they looked up to see the church and the steeple falling on them. Helpless, they could only try to roll away from that frightful menace. In a few seconds the beams and timbers of the broken house of God crashed to the ground, yet Pastor Waechter and his wife were not crushed. The living Savior Himself kept the wreckage one foot — twelve short inches — away. Because Christ lives, He will give His angels charge over you and protect you, according to His high purpose, on all your ways.

He lives to give courage and comfort to those staggering on under life's heavy burdens. Unbelievers who think Him dead drive themselves on in despair, curse themselves with steady sorrow, or, even worse, try the suicide's cowardly escape. Yet you, God's children, trusting the Savior's promise, *"I will come again* [after My crucifixion] *and receive you,"* know the truth of His promise, *"Lo, I am with you alway, even unto the end of the world,"* and can truly exult,

> He lives to silence all my fears,
> He lives to wipe away my tears;
> He lives to calm my troubled heart,
> He lives all blessings to impart.

He was resurrected to rule in heavenly power and to answer your prayers. Hundreds of millions of human beings bow down before dead idols of wood, stone, lifeless metal, or worship the false gods of their own fictitious belief; but you who are Christ's know that he has ascended to the throne of His majesty, there to receive the requests of His loved ones and to reply with reassuring aid. Unless you are convinced that Scripture is true, when four times in the Four Gospels it records the Easter miracle, you are wasting your time in bending your knees, folding your hands, and reciting your needs. Because Jesus lives, believe that He can, will, must hear all true petitions!

One marvelous, majestic benediction of our Savior's Easter victory remains. He rose again so that we could defeat death through Him. This is the guarantee written in our text, *"We shall be also in the likeness of His resurrection."* This is also the pledge of many glorious passages in which Christ Himself promises, *"Because I live, ye shall live also." "I am the Resurrection and the Life: he that believeth in Me, though he were dead, yet shall he live,"* and again: *"The dead shall hear the voice of the Son of God; and they that hear shall live."*

This, then, is the climax compassion which Joseph's opened tomb offers you and all believers. Death is not your final destiny. Decay is not your permanent portion. The grave will lose its grip on you. As the Son of God came forth from His sepulcher, so you can live again, live eternally, live gloriously with Christ. You shall arise because He arose.

Only Jesus can give you this marvelous mercy, for only He defeated death by defeating sin, which sentences us to the grave. Plainly God's Word proclaims, *"The wages of sin is death."* Despite the pretty poetry about the next life, the pictures of reviving spring, butterflies emerging from cocoons, the fanciful beliefs which people in every age have held concerning the world to come:

the one real assurance of our resurrection is granted us by faith in the Savior, who gave Himself as the ever-valid Sacrifice for your guilt and mine, yes, for the total transgressions of the race. Because He shed His crimson blood on the cross of pain and shame and then died the agonies of His atoning death, He has destroyed the power of evil, broken the tyranny of the grave, freed you from the curse of hell. Believe that the Son of God suffered the full penalty of your iniquities, and you are freed forever from eternal damnation! You will die, of course, because of the sins which have sown the doom of decay in your body, but your soul, cleansed by the atoning blood, will continue beyond the grave, to be reunited with your resurrected body on Judgment Day.

Do not think of this new existence as a vague, shadowy condition in which your spirit somehow survives. Scripture definitely teaches a restoration of the body, and our text assures us, *"We shall be also in the likeness of His resurrection,"* our Lord's bodily, visible, marvelous resurrection. Take comfort in this pledge, you who have dear ones in unknown and unmarked graves over the earth's expanse! If they trusted in the living Redeemer, then, though they are buried beneath the sands of Africa's deserts, though the frost of Arctic regions quilt their graves with thick ice, though they lie entombed in the ships sunken at Pearl harbor, though they were bombed to pieces or in air disasters crushed on distant mountainsides, at the call of the resurrection trumpet on the Last Day they shall come forth. Granite tombs, tons of earth, oceans of water cannot prevent them. *"The dead in Christ shall rise."*

Do not join the unbelievers who object: "This is impossible; it is only wishful thinking, childish imagination. When a man dies, he dies like a horse, a dog, an elephant, every kind of animal. His last breath brings the end"! I ask you the same question which Paul pointedly put to King Agrippa, *"Why should it be thought a thing incredible with you, that God should raise the dead?"* Why cannot the Lord, who made man at the beginning of human history, remake him at the end? Our newspapers tell us that Russian scientists in Siberia discovered the bodies of a boy and a girl, buried there two thousand years ago, almost perfectly preserved by the ice and the intense cold. Why, then, cannot the Almighty guard our lives and by His omnipotence restore our bodies? Insurance specialists tell us that a century and a half ago the average life span in this country was thirty-five years. Today, thanks to the efforts of medical scientists, the average reaches sixty-five years. Of tomorrow, experts declare: "Our studies indicate that within the course of the next decade or two it should be possible to extend the average length of life for the population of the United States to, at least, seventy years." If man, whose puny powers can hardly be compared with God's omnipotence, thus increases the span of our existence, who will say that the almighty Creator cannot restore life and increase its duration to eternity? If a small, plain acorn sown in the ground decays and disappears as it produces the first tiny stem which years later becomes a mighty, majestic oak tree, ten thousand times larger than the original acorn, have we any reason to doubt that the Most High can take our human bodies which are sown in corruption and, after they have decayed, bring them forth myriads of times more marvelous than they were here on earth?

Yet gross unbelief brazenly denies this. The editor

of a large Midwestern paper, who had never confessed Christ his Savior, wrote shortly before his death: "My hope is to go to bed at night, after a hard day's work, and never awaken. That would be absolute triumph." That would be absolute defeat, we declare. In order to show his scorn of Scriptural teaching that the dead shall arise again, dying Frederick the Great ordered that his body be buried in his garden beside his dogs. Scoffers go to two extremes. They embalm and thus seek to preserve the dead (witness the feverish efforts to keep the corpses of Red atheist leaders in Europe!) because they fear that when the body is gone, everything is gone. Or they leave orders that their remains are to be cremated and their ashes scattered thinly over land and sea. They do this, of course, because they fear death and the judgment which their conscience tells them they must face. How cowardly scoffers have cringed before the approaching end, and how loudly have their teeth chattered when their last hour comes! Hobbes, the British infidel, was so horrified by the specter of the grave that he kept a lamp burning in his room each night; and whenever he awoke to find that it had gone out, he was overcome by terror. He always shunned the discussion of death.

Sometimes those closer to the Lord are gripped by a similar horror concerning the hereafter. A circus magnate, who in his last words asked for the box-office receipts at the Madison Square Garden performance of his three-ring entertainment, sternly forbade the mention of death in his presence. Only a few days ago a long-distance telephone call came from a listener in Texas, an earnest man of God who declared he had no financial difficulties, no family troubles, no other distressing problems, yet was beset by an incessant fear of death. Why should a believer be tormented by the thought of the greatest good which the Almighty can bestow upon him — his salvation? Why should he be tortured by the dread of leaving this world with its sin and sorrow, when Easter testifies assuredly that *"the sufferings of this present time are not worthy to be compared with the glory which shall be revealed in us"*? Why should we not welcome the end, knowing that it is only the prelude to heaven, where, with our new, celestial bodies, we shall be like our resurrected Redeemer?

II

CHRIST'S EASTER VICTORY GUARANTEES OUR GLORIOUS RESURRECTION

Why, we continue to ask, should anyone want to remain indefinitely on this earth and grow older, weaker, slower, duller, when, through faith in the Savior's Easter triumph, we can enjoy *"the likeness of His resurrection,"* know the radiance of the Apostle's promise, *"The Lord Jesus Christ . . . shall change our vile body, that it may be fashioned like unto His glorious body,"* and find the five wondrous words *"We shall be like Him"* fulfilled in us?

To picture the magnificence of this pledge we must study our Lord's resurrection body, and, as far as we humbly can, begin to understand *"the glory which shall be revealed in us."* When Columbus discovered America, he saw only a few of the small West Indies Islands. He never surveyed the vast hemisphere with its northern and southern continents. He never knew the mighty Mississippi, the Great Lakes, the titanic Rockies. He could not imagine the majestic Niagara, the Grand Canyon

Yellowstone's marvels, the Pacific's broad expanse. So it is with us when, in our human limitations, we speak of the heavenly realm in which Jesus has prepared a personal place for those who love Him as their Savior, or when we try to describe the radiance of the after-death body which will be ours through faith. All that we can do is believe the sacred promises of Scripture and, as far as our limitations permit, peer into the splendor they reveal. Therefore we thank the Almighty for these seven sacred facts the Bible teaches us concerning Christ's resurrection and ours:

First, the same body which was nailed to the cross and which after six hours of never-equaled agony at Golgotha was laid into the grave was restored to life on the first Easter. Similarly our present bodies will be revived. This truth entitles us to conclude that in our Father's house we shall recognize God's children whom we loved on earth, just as we, in turn, will be greeted by fellow believers.

In the second place, these bodies will be glorified with a radiance and brightness we cannot explain. Perhaps the Transfiguration of our Lord shows vaguely how our physical frames will be wondrously transformed. At that miracle on the mountain we are told of Christ that *"His face did shine as the sun";* and believers are promised that they shall *"shine forth as the sun in the kingdom of their Father."*

Again, our resurrection bodies, like the risen Redeemer's, will be perfect, for the promise reads, *"It is sown in dishonor; it is raised in glory."* Gone forever are the signs of sin, the marks of misery, the stigma of sickness. Our faces will lose the furrows of worry and age; the scars of hard toil will be removed from our hands;

the imprint of illness will disappear from our bodies, which shall be transformed into blemishless perfection. What encouragement and comfort for you who languish on sickbeds or in hospitals to know that in fulfillment of our text, *"We shall be also in the likeness of His resurrection,"* your mortal frame will not be racked by arthritis, twisted by deformity, disfigured by disease or accident, deformed by war's cruelty! No more crippled limbs or amputated members; no more sightless eyes or failing senses; no more disordered minds or distressed souls; nothing but beauty, glory, splendor, to an extent which our imperfect perception cannot grasp!

In the fourth place, Scripture assures us, we shall be resurrected with bodies of heavenly might. The Apostle testifies, *"It is sown in weakness, it is raised in power."* Vanished forever will be the weariness which burdens many of you. Now we confess to our sorrow that *"the spirit indeed is willing, but the flesh is weak."* Then our strength will never be exhausted; we shall not be overcome by fatigue and have to drag our aching bodies through repeated agonies. Instead, ours will be a new joy, a celestial strength and zest. Recall, if you can, a beautiful spring day with reawakening nature throbbing about you, a day on which you feel yourself to be in perfect health, eager, alert, ready for achievement — and then believe that life at its best fails by far to approach the heavenly existence!

Again, the living Christ's resurrected body was not limited by time or space. His marvelous passing through locked doors; His sudden appearing and just as sudden disappearing; His power mysteriously to transport Himself from one place to another, all testify to this fact. How sustaining, then, this promise, *"We shall be also in the likeness of His resurrection,"* is for you, the bedridden for twenty, thirty, forty years or more, unable to leave your sickrooms to worship God in His house or to enjoy nature's beauties of nature! Take heart! The time is coming for you faithful to Jesus, when all these hardships will be supplanted by glorious power.

Our new bodies will be celestial, for Saint Paul writes, *"As we have borne the image of the earthy, we shall also bear the image of the heavenly."* In the next life our powers of understanding will overtower the world's highest standards. With fuller knowledge we shall grasp the mysteries of faith and the marvels of Heaven's providential direction concealed from us here below. Now our senses are limited, but there we may see ten thousand new colors and hear ten thousand new sounds. Sin and sorrow will disappear. Our minds will be attuned to holiness. Our eyes will constantly behold Jesus. Our transformed voices will sing His praises in vibrant tones too glorious for earth, since we shall be God's children, and with Christ our Savior, Christ our Brother, *"we shall be like Him."*

Finally, in the seventh sacred truth, our resurrected bodies will be eternal. Intoned at the burial service of believers is the divine pledge, *"It is sown in corruption; it is raised in incorruption."* Be assured, therefore, that with the risen Redeemer there is no decay nor death, while with every moment in this world we hasten to the grave.

Why, then, should the Savior's own fear the end? If only we could realize the full radiance of the resurrection, we would welcome death and yearn for its blessing. No wonder, Saint Paul, who was given a glimpse of the hereafter, tells us that it *"is far better"* to depart and *"to be with Christ"* than to remain on the earth!

Today the Easter evangel cries out to you: Don't fear death; your Redeemer lives, and through faith you shall live with Him in heavenly glory. Adoniram Judson, missionary to Burma, who died at sea, could exult, "I go with the gladness of a boy bounding away from school, I feel so strong in Christ"; and when his wife, Ann Judson, was taken fatally ill, she cried out, "Oh, the happy day will soon come when we shall meet . . . to part no more in our heavenly Father's house!"

Do you husbands and wives have this joy in Jesus? Or have you so long neglected your Redeemer that you can understand the feelings of David Strauss, German skeptic and scoffer who, after devoting his energies to the blasphemous purpose of disproving the Bible, had to confess in his last hours: "My philosophy leaves me utterly forlorn. I feel like one caught in the merciless jaws of an automatic machine, not knowing at what time one of those great hammers will crush me." If you feel likewise, then, this Easter, the time of decision in the Early Church, has come especially for you, to plead that on this blessed day, when your Savior *"brought life and immortality to light,"* you, too, overcome the sentence of sin and live anew in the Lord, because you accept Him in personal, penitent faith as your Deliverer from death!

With this triumphant trust you have the assurance of an eternal Easter glory. Fifteen hundred years ago large, well-equipped Saxon forces, invading England, attacked a small band of poorly armed Britons who, despite their handicaps, won the battle. Why? Led by Bishop Germanus, they marched toward their enemies singing "Hallelujah!" and because they were gathered in a narrow mountain pass, these hallelujahs, multiplied by repeated echoes, sounded like the battle cry of a mighty army. Panic seized the Saxons, and they fled. If today, confronted as you are by foes of your faith and powerful enemies of your soul, you cry out in trusting thanks: "Hallelujah! Praise God, Christ is risen!" Heaven's power will multiply that paean of praise until it helps defeat your fear of death.

As our Easter greeting to you we call out to you: "Hallellujah! Christ is risen!" The Holy Spirit help the echo of your faith reply: "He is risen, indeed!" With the Easter assurance, you, conquering the fear of death, will meet before the throne of our risen Lord — pray the Father that everyone of us will be there! — to sing in far loftier and sweeter strains: "Hallelujah! We are risen!" God give us this eternal Easter for our resurrected Redeemer's sake! *Amen!*

GOD SAYS, "HURRY!"

"Go quickly and tell His disciples that He is risen from the dead. . . . And they departed quickly from the sepulcher with fear and great joy, and did run to bring His disciples word." SAINT MATTHEW 28:7-8
"Then arose Peter and ran unto the sepulcher."
SAINT LUKE 24:12

PURIFYING SPIRIT OF GOD: Awaken us from the sleep of indifference, and arouse us to the danger of delay both in accepting the living Christ as our Redeemer and in bringing the message of His atoning death to others! Show us that for our beloved country, as for ourselves, the time for repentance and return to Thy mercies is short! Break the bloody plans of those who seek to hurl the nations into another world war and put to naught the evil designs which atheist Communism plots against Thy Church! Speed the success of our efforts in Bringing Christ to the Nations and so bless the messages of Gospel grace that we may reach many still without Jesus and lead them to their Lord, who Himself bore their sins in His own body on the cross and then rose from the dead for their justification! Sustain the sick and hungry, guide the blind and helpless, comfort the widows and orphans! As we give Thee our heartfelt thanks for Thy might and Thy mercy, we pray Thee: Help us work while it is day and before the night comes when Thy judgment descends on us! More than all else, we ask that Thou wouldst keep us in the faith and life which look only to Christ, our all-sufficient Savior! We plead humbly but confidently in His name. *Amen!*

God Says, "Hurry!"

LET me begin by expressing to you our heartfelt thanks for the interest you have shown in this broadcast, Bringing Christ to the Nations. I am happy to tell you, leaving out entirely returns at our foreign offices, that during the past three weeks our Saint Louis headquarters alone received almost 100,000 letters. Thank God for the largest response we have ever enjoyed! Thank you for the prayers and interest which show that there are tens of millions to whom *"the Gospel . . . is the power of God unto salvation,"* vast multitudes who have not bowed their knees before the Baals of modern unbelief!

This mail comes from more than a hundred different countries on the six continents. A staff of one hundred workers, besides a night shift, handles these huge mounds of letters written in many languages by listeners on the highest and lowest levels of human society, by widely known scholars and the plain people who otherwise write infrequently, by State governors and doomed men in State penitentiaries, by eager, active young people and lonely older folks like an Illinois teacher who laments: "This earth is full of suffering for me. I have no relatives to care for me. After thirty-eight years of teaching I am tossed out on the world which knows no mercy. Pray that God will take me out of my suffering!" These letters describe the sorrows of a thousand forms of agony, but, thank the Almighty God, they express the joy of many more thousands whom the broadcast with the Spirit's blessing has helped find their Savior, recalled to Jesus, or strengthened in faith.

This avalanche of mail should be convincing testimony to radio's power in extending Christ's kingdom. The words which we speak are carried around the whole world by short wave in only one-seventh of a second. A few days ago we aired another Lutheran Hour television program here in Saint Louis. Thirty-four congregations in Missouri and Illinois gathered to receive the telecast. It would have taken a circuit rider more than a month to bring the Gospel to these various audiences which saw and heard the televised message of redemption; yet we reached them in one night.

Thank the Lord for this speed! We must hurry to spread the message of full and free forgiveness in Jesus. Extreme haste is required in relaying the report of the risen Redeemer to the world's ends. If we are to help rescue this generation for Christ and from chaos, for God's benediction and from men's bacterial bombardment; if we want to avoid the atomic destruction of a third world war, we must use a new acceleration in spreading the salvation message. We must walk more swiftly than ever before.

This appeal for haste in heralding the living Savior's peace and pardon becomes evident in the Four Gospels after the resurrection. From this Easter evangel I have chosen the two passages of our text, first the words of Saint Matthew (chapter twenty-eight, verses seven and eight): *"Go quickly and tell His disciples that He is risen from the dead. . . . And they departed quickly from the sepulcher with fear and great joy, and did run to bring His disciples word,"* and then the record from Saint Luke (chapter twenty-four, verse twelve): *"Then arose Peter and ran unto the sepulcher."* These Scripture passages cry out to us:

GOD SAYS, "HURRY!"

Hurry for Christ, you who know His saving love! Hurry to Christ, you who are living without Him!

I
HURRY FOR CHRIST!

It is not without deep meaning that the earliest witness of our Savior's resurrection was a woman, Mary Magdalene. This was a recognition of woman's new and high importance in God's kingdom. Under the horrors of heathendom, mothers and daughters are often cruelly mistreated as slaves of lust, beaten and heartbroken by the brutality of their own husbands or fathers. Now, however, under Christ's sacred standard, with all believers on the same spiritual level, womankind was to reach its loftiest heights.

Again, the fact that Mary heard the resurrection record before all others may be regarded both as a token of blessing (she had been among the last at the blood-stained cross, and, her faithfulness rewarded, she was to be first at the empty grave) and as an indication of the prominent part consecrated women were to play in building the Church. While Shintoism, Taoism, Mohammedanism, Hinduism, and all the other "isms" of the pagan world crush the weaker sex down to dark, sordid depths, the New Testament, which exults, *"In Christ . . . there is neither male nor female,"* has given them the widest possible opportunity to help spread the Gospel. Thank the Lord, many consecrated sisters in the faith have accepted this privilege!

Especially, however, is this record of a woman as the first to behold the Easter miracle a pointed challenge asking you mothers and daughters to show the same devotion to the crucified Savior which moved Mary early on Easter morning. Since that day the records prove that when women truly love Jesus and actively support His cause, the churches prosper and show marked spiritual progress; but when women become worldly-minded, forget God, neglect their home, sacrifice their purity, both the churches and the government seriously suffer. The Holy Spirit give us Christ-minded women, we ask, when we survey, on the one hand, the opportunities confronting the Lord's kingdom in this fear-filled world, and on the other hand, the shocking spectacle presented by many modern women! Every day thousands line up before tavern bars to degrade themselves and their sex. Every week our courts are crowded by mothers charged with the neglect of their own children, or petitioning long-plotted, groundless divorce. Every night masses of wives are out on evil adventure, deserting or deceiving their husbands. One of the shocking signs of our country's moral weakness in this hour when our standards should be highest is the fact that in a typical American district, not the vicinity of Hollywood, California, Reno, Nevada, nor Miami Beach, Florida, but Hillsdale County, Michigan, the number of divorces has increased tenfold in less than fifty years, and that last year this county recorded one divorce for every two marriages. Unless you Christian citizens get to work and call a legal halt to this debauch, we will witness in these God-blessed United States not a nation-wide rate of one divorce for every two weddings, but one home broken for every new home established. That will mean the end of our country.

Nor is it simply accident that of all those who followed Jesus, Mary Magdalene should be the first to receive the report of the resurrection. She had long served the Lord, and God did not forget her faithfulness, just as He does not overlook the long years which some of you have devoted to the Savior. He may not remember you with the reward of earthly prosperity; but He can give you privileges which money cannot buy, the calm of peace, the joy of reconciliation with your heavenly Father, the strength of trusting faith.

As a most terrifying affliction, Mary had been possessed of seven devils; but the Son of God had cleansed her, and for this she wanted to thank Him, though she thought He was dead. He can help you, too, even when the most serious and hopeless disease lays you low. If you are seriously sick, of course, He does not want you to push prescriptions aside and refuse to call a doctor. Some years ago two American missionaries, among others, arrived at Sierra Leone, Africa, without medicine and without language books. Their belief in faith healing and the gift of tongues made them think physicians and language teachers unnecessary. Soon after landing, however, they were attacked by a malignant fever, and, refusing all medical aid, they died. Do not make the same mistake! Do not dictate to Christ the way in which He must heal you!

In how many hidden dangers He has rescued you! How often He has turned unseen perils from your path! How frequently He has kept the shadow of death from descending on you! When the Savior has helped, then praise Him, as Mary Magdalene tried to show her gratitude. How many times have you sincerely said "Thank you!" to Jesus for His boundless blessings?

Can you imagine the joy which must have surged through Mary's heart when, according to Saint Matthew's shortened account, sobbing in unrelieved sorrow over the death of her departed Deliverer, as she prepared to anoint His corpse, she heard the angel proclaim this first message of the Easter triumph, *"Fear not ye;*

for I know that ye seek Jesus, which was crucified. He is not here; for He is risen, as He said. Come, see the place where the Lord lay!" The day that had begun with gloom now suddenly burst into brilliance. The Master had kept His Word. He had not ended in failure. He had proved Himself God. He had overcome death. He was alive to heal and help men's souls.

Before Mary could fully grasp the marvelous mercy and might of the resurrection, the angel directed her and the women with her, *"Go quickly and tell His disciples that He is risen from the dead."* This is the first of the Easter passages which mention speed; but seven others speak of hurrying. You see, the angel, expressing God's will knew that the report of the Savior's return was such marvelous mercy that it should not be delayed. The joyous news that Christ had burst death's bonds after the crushing cruelties of the cross had to be brought the disciples immediately. They were cowering behind locked doors, fearful for their lives, gripped by gloom, dazed and desperate over the crime at Calvary; they needed the reassurance of the resurrection at once. Therefore the angel's command, *"Go quickly!"*

Mary and the women with her, models for us in their instantaneous response, did not stop to deny the resurrection, as some Bible critics have spent large portions of their lives trying to discredit the Easter record. They did not linger to debate this miracle, to ask why or how or when Jesus arose, removed the burial garments, and broke the sealed sepulcher. They believed and obeyed; for we are told, *"They departed quickly from the sepulcher with fear and great joy."*

Today we can travel with far greater speed than Mary knew, but usually men do not hasten with the *"fear and great joy"* which moved those early pilgrims to the grave. They were filled with awe of the resurrection, which proved the Crucified their God, their Savior, their ever-living Friend; and whereas a few moments before they had been oppressed by sadness and their faces moistened with tears, now the knowledge that Jesus lived filled them with jubilant rejoicing. Thus quickly, for you, too, my burdened friends, can Christ keep His promise, *"Your sorrow shall be turned into joy."* Indeed, never have men known a reason for rapture and a cause for gladness as mighty and majestic as the angel's assurance, *"He is not here; for He is risen."* This shows that no matter how bitter and brutal and bloody the battle of your life may be, the Destroyer of death lives to put foes of your faith to flight, to comfort you in affliction, strengthen you in weakness, fortify you against temptation, provide for all needs, protect you in every danger, and deliver you from evil. Raise your hearts in rejoicing, then, my afflicted followers of the Lord! Because the Son of God lives, the eternal victory over sorrow and suffering, loneliness and loss, darkness and disease, death and damnation, horror and hell, is yours personally, yours certainly, yours eternally, once you are His in humble, contrite faith.

Our text adds that the women *"did run to bring His disciples word."* How could they walk when they had such a wondrous message to deliver? And how can we tarry, when we have the mercy and might of a risen Redeemer, an everliving Lord, a death-conquering God, for a dying world? Indeed, much more urgently than Mary we are commanded, *"Go quickly and tell . . . that He is risen from the dead."* Today there are more souls on earth without the inner comfort of Christ's Gospel than on that first Easter day. The number of those who live in territories where the report of the resurrection has never once been preached far exceeds the 144,000,000 who populate the United States. Do you understand why the Lord says, "Hurry!" when great masses are not touched by any missionary work whatever? Unless we *"go quickly and tell,"* hundreds of millions for whom the Savior shed His blood and rose again to seal His redemption will die in utter ignorance of their salvation.

Again God tells us, "Hurry!" because the forces of atheistic Communism are speeding their conquest. Proportionately, organized godlessness is growing much more rapidly than Christianity. As high an authority as the President of the United States felt impelled to warn our people that the U. S. S. R., whose former leader declared, "Our propaganda includes necessarily propaganda for atheism," is taking control of one nation after another in Europe and Asia. Thirty-two years ago self-confessed atheists did not control any country; but today they absolutely direct affairs in 22 per cent of the earth's habitable surface. Thirty-two years ago you could find only a few hundred men who would openly admit that they were Communists; today more than 20,000,000 are registered as members of their party, officially pledged to close the churches. If any doubt still lingers in your mind that the movement as we see it spreading over Europe, strengthening its forces in China, Japan, Korea, the Far East, and gaining new, influential recruits in America every day, is anti-God, anti-Bible, anti-Christ, then listen to these selections from the so-called Communist Ten Commandments given to the militant youth for its battle against the churches:

"1. Never forget that the clergy are the bitterest foes of the Communist State!

"2. Try to win your friends over to Communism and remember that our leader, Stalin, is Head of the Godless . . . all over the world!

"3. Prevail upon your friends to avoid contacts with the clergy! . . .

"5. See to it that atheist publications are widely distributed among the people!

"6. A good Communist must also be a militant atheist. He must know how to use his weapons and be experienced in the art of war.

"7. Wherever you can, fight religious elements and forestall any influence they might bring to bear upon your comrade! . . .

"9. Support the godless movement with money which is needed particularly for our propaganda abroad, since under present circumstances it can only be carried on underground!

"10. If you are not a convinced godless, you cannot be a good Communist. . . . Atheism is indissolubly tied in with Communism. . . ."

No matter how this present-day tyranny disguises itself, conceals its real motives, and covers its true purposes, it is completely dedicated to fulfill the satanic slogan, "Down with religion!"

Again God says, "Hurry!" because of the screaming superannihilation which may soon confront us. The menace of another war has made scientists and leaders, including some who oppose Christianity, cry out in warning that only a few years remain before the greatest disaster which ever struck the world may become a reality. Even the titles of the books they write: *The End of Our Times, There Will be No Time, While Time Remains,* show how keenly some authorities realize with Scripture that *"the time is short."*

"Time is short," declares the Federation of American Atomic Scientists' report, as, unconsciously perhaps, but nevertheless exactly, it quotes this passage. "The sands of time are running out," a London newspaper asserts. "We have a very short time to put our house in order," Dr. John A. Simpson, chairman of the Executive Committee of Atomic Scientists of Chicago, testifies before a Senate committee. So seemingly certain is this impending catastrophe that Dr. Harold C. Urey, a leader in atomic research, calls it "the most dangerous situation that humanity has ever faced in all history."

Some foresee and foretell even the date of this disaster. A news commentator broadcasts, "We have twenty years left." A Sunday newspaper headline announces, "We Have Ten Years Left." What do the experts say? Dr. Albert Einstein claims that only nine years remain before the crisis comes, when, this first-line scientist holds, our enemies will have the atomic bomb. Leland Stowe, student of international affairs, says the storm will break in 1953. This cuts our period of peaceful existence down to five short years before, as one expert puts it, "The cities of men on earth can perish." Dr. Robert Hutchins, president of the University of Chicago, sets the date even earlier, at 1952, giving us only four years before this devilish devastation can break, in which 40,000,000 of our countrymen, as some scientists assert, will be burned to death in the first twenty-four hours of atomic bombardment.

God Says, "Hurry!"

Now, nobody but God knows whether these dates are correct; but do not think that these men are alarmists trying to scare you out of your wits; that all this is but an ugly dream; that men with sense talk differently! Some time ago President Truman appointed an Air Policy Commission, all experts, who devoted months to their investigation, consulting leaders in the armed forces, the business world, and scientific circles. In their report, one of the most depressing documents ever printed in the United States, the year 1952 stands out as the international deadline. Listen to the warning by America's foremost specialists: "It would be an unreasonable risk . . . to assume that other nations will not have atomic weapons in quantity by the end of 1952." This commission recommends a gigantic increase in our defenses to be completed in 1952, and for emphasis the report repeats, "We must start now on this program and complete it by the end of 1952." This droning re-emphasis of 1952 reminds us, if the experts are correct, that less than four full years remain before we may be overtaken by devastation, the horror of which will make the catastrophes at Hiroshima and Nagasaki seem insignificant and dwarf Dresden's disaster, where 250,000 civilians were killed in air-raids. Less than four years left before American cities and towns can be attacked by robot planes, loaded with bombs which can burn our cities to the ground, sending clouds of atomic destruction over our farm lands, massacring our people by the millions, and destroying many of those who survive by bacterial warfare which spreads the germ of botulism (food poisoning), psittacosis (parrot disease), tularemia (rabbit fever), besides pneumonia, meningitis, typhoid fever, and other common killers! Less than four years before a war can break in which, as one of our leading scientists predicts, "Most people may die from weapons that make no sounds, give no warning, destroy no forts, or ships, or cities, but can wipe out human beings by the millions!" Less than four years before a global struggle may begin which will feature a new superpoison so strong that a single ounce can kill 180,000,000!

Is there nothing, you ask, which can prevent this mowing down of the masses? Will the nations not be sane enough to refrain from suicidal struggle? Will they not agree to abandon this devilish destruction? No! The human heart is so brutal and hate-filled that it deliberately seeks the worst and widest means of massacre; and when politicians are lured by lust for power, all their signed, sealed covenants become scraps of paper. The President's own Air Policy Commission reported, "Even the most optimistic view of the record of the United Nations does not assure us that the United Nations will develop in time the necessary authority to prevent another great war." It should be clear to those who previously placed no reliance on religion that our only hope and our last hope for preventing the most hideous holocaust the world has ever seen is in Jesus — bless His holy name!

We who bow before Him know that only He, but surely He, can turn the mortal mind from hatred to compassion, from lust to love. Only He can make us new creatures in Christ; only He can fulfill the promise, "*A new heart . . . will I give you.*" Only through Him, the Prince of Peace, can men find joy instead of jealousy, beauty rather than bloodshed, grace and peace in place of grief and punishment.

Therefore God says: "Hurry! *'Go quickly and tell!'*" If 1952 is the deadline year when every large nation will have a huge supply of atomic bombs, more devastating than those which leveled the Japanese cities with the ground, then we still have almost four years for prayer and repentance. On Good Friday in the House of Representatives a member from Illinois urged his colleagues to go to their respective houses of worship on that day and plead for divine guidance. He reminded the House that when our country's Constitution was framed, the statesmen charged with the work frequently felt the necessity of taking time out "to pray that they might do the right thing, at the right time." Thank the Almighty for men in political leadership who recognize the fact that they need Heaven's help, and who ask it in humble, heartfelt appeal! However, the situation is so critical that we need such earnest petition not only on Good Friday but every day. Pray, America! Pray!

With prayer we must have repentance. This country must get right with God. Nineveh, center of Assyrian iniquity, was rescued from ruin when for forty days its people repented in sackcloth and ashes. Certainly the Almighty, who *"maketh wars to cease unto the end of the earth . . . breaketh the bow, and cutteth the spear in sunder . . . burneth the chariot in the fire,"* can spare the United States the burning devastation of atomic attacks if during these years ahead our people will really repent, individually as nationally, confessing all the sins which divine righteousness has charged against us.

Let us not postpone our national Day of Repentance until treacherous attack actually rains ruin from the skies! It was too late for Sodom and Gomorrah to repent when fire and brimstone fell from heaven, and it may be too late for us to fall on our knees when the new rockets, released 7,000 miles away by a push button, drop their deadly cargo within our borders. Therefore the Holy Spirit tells the churches: "Hurry! *'Go quickly and tell'* America the message of mercy and might, the promise of pardon and peace in the crucified but victoriously risen Redeemer!"

Regrettably many of this country's church members are slumbering on, utterly indifferent to Scripture's teaching, *"The time is short." "It is high time to awake out of sleep."* A religious leader, a liberal, too, writes: "I must acknowledge that I get a much more sobering impression of the lost estate of man and of the doom that threatens his institutions from the pages of *The New Yorker* than I do from most of my church contacts. I would like to see churches and church organizations spend less time celebrating the time they have been going one hundred, two hundred, five hundred years, and more on the prospect that they have only ten, twenty, or fifty years to go." With 1952, the deadline that our own military and scientific experts have set, is there still time for church members so to center their energies on card parties, chicken dinners, and entertainments that they have no energy left for spreading the Gospel?

Remember, those to whom God's angel first said, "Hurry! *'Go quickly and tell!'* " were not trained preachers, but untrained women! These humble disciples who *"departed quickly . . . and did run"* were Galileans without the advantage of college or divinity-school training. If the twentieth-century church, with its wealth and advantages, is to perpetuate the victory of the first-century believers, it must have the loyal, unselfish service of laymen, trained to make the Savior's mercies known. Without a testifying membership, the churches will work at only a low-per-cent efficiency; but supported by an intelligent, active, and aggressive laity, the cause of the Kingdom can successfully overcome atheism's startling advances. American laymen, this is your hour to arise in defense of Christ's Church, and if you will publicly testify to the Son of God, you can greatly help your country meet this crisis. Preachers in America, this is the time for the quickest and widest-possible spread of the good news proclaiming divine grace in Jesus. You are the keymen for preserving our national safety. Help our churches employ every suitable modern invention to speed the Gospel of the risen Christ! Use the radio, one of Heaven's mightiest gifts, for expediting the message of salvation! See to it that your churches establish their own television stations, which in sound and picture bring the guarantee of the Redeemer's mercy also to many millions now without the faith! Preach the Bible, preach repentance, preach redemption in Jesus; with all your heart, soul, mind, preach the Cross, the open grave, the open heaven, and the victory will be ours.

II

HURRY TO CHRIST!

However, God's appeal, "Hurry!" is directed especially to those among you who do not yet know His Son, who have never confessed Him your Savior, nor learned to know the height and depth of His holy love for you.

Saint Mark records that the angel instructed Mary and the women early on Easter morning, *"Tell His disciples* AND PETER." Simon Peter, therefore, was the first man individually named to receive the resurrection message. What marvelous grace! This disciple had most loudly proclaimed his loyalty to the Lord Jesus; but with the exception of Judas He had most shamefully denied Him. Three times Peter had declared his unwavering allegiance, assuring the Master, *"Though I should die with Thee, yet will I not deny Thee";* but three times he had grievously rejected his Redeemer. Yet Peter had repented with tears, and Christ, the living Lord of love, wanted His contrite follower with Him.

Today, too, Jesus is calling you, the once faithful, but now through unbelief, blasphemy, godless life, and willful sinning denying your Savior. The same Son of God, ready to forgive Peter, who cursed as he lied, *"I know Him not,"* eagerly pleads for your repentance and return. What wondrous love that Christ sends this message to you as He directs us, *" 'Go quickly and tell'* My faithless follower: In Me there is pardon for your sins and peace for your soul!" Every other founder of a religion was a mere man, without the divine power required to save you, but Jesus — hear it, believe it, cherish it! — is your God. All the authors of so-called new faiths cannot bring your soul a small sixteenth of an inch closer to the Almighty. In reality they can only tear you farther from your salvation. Yet Christ, the true Savior, the only Savior, took away all your transgressions, transferred them to Himself, cleansed you from their curse, and gave you His resurrection as a divine guarantee of eternal glory. Mohammed, Buddha, Zoroaster, Confucius, these and other inventors of creeds which contradict Scripture, died, were buried, and moldered in their graves. Though our Lord made His life a payment for your guilt, His body did not decay, but He arose again, as the Easter victory testifies. He lives, more certainly than you and

I live, as the eternal Ransom for every sin and for every sinner, your own personal Deliverer. He is your heavenly Friend, who wants to comfort you in the sorrows that are driving some of you to the depths of despair. A few days ago this letter came from a Virgin Islands listener: "I am in a leper colony now for twenty-eight years. God has been gracious to me in Christ all these years, and I know that He is the same today. Sometimes when I hear your broadcast, tears roll down my cheeks. You may ask, Why? Your messages make me consider how good God is to me, and I know that my afflictions, though they seem severe, are often mercy-sent. Please excuse my writing. I have lost some of my fingers, and I am trying to do my best." A leper, twenty-eight years in isolation, her fingers dropping off, thanks the Lord for His goodness in Christ! Still some of you, without the Savior, are ready to surrender to despair when even slight sorrow overtakes you.

Jesus lives as your cheering Companion, who goes with you, once you are His in faith, even into the valley of death's shadow. An American Air Force lieutenant wrote his parents these lines in the last letter before he was lost in action: "I go without a fear, trusting in my Lord Jesus Christ. If I am taken, do not mourn, for I will be with my Savior, waiting for you in heaven!"

Our blessed Redeemer lives to give you divine assurance of peace and joy. Shortly before his death Marcus Wright, historian and soldier, declared: "Whatever pleasures there may be in sporting life, in political life, in military life, I have tried them all, and until I was forty-nine years old, I never knew what peace meant. Rest and true joy were unknown; whereas for twenty-two years, since my conversion to God, my peace has been like a river."

Do you want this pardon, this joy, this glorious guarantee of a prepared place in Paradise with Jesus? Then follow Peter! After he heard the glad news of the Resurrection and received Christ's personal message — what did he do? Our text records, *"Then arose Peter and* RAN *unto the sepulcher."* He could not hurry to the grave quickly enough, and hastened with all his might to find the living Lord, whom he had denied as his dying Savior.

Now that I have told you how Christ died for you and rose again to seal the assurance of His salvation in your soul, will not you, too, speed your way to Him this day? Delay is always dangerous, sometimes fatal. More of our countrymen are killed in accidents than were cut down on the battlefields of World War II. Those who figure on an eleventh-hour repentance often die at nine-fifteen; some, long before this. Almost a hundred lives are daily crushed out in automobile crashes on our highways. How many victims of this traffic toll realized when they began the day of their fatal accident that they would never end it? What positive assurance have you that you will ever hear another personal appeal urging you to receive Jesus as your living Redeemer? Before this broadcast is aired again, almost 27,000 people in the United States will have died. No life insurance on earth can guarantee that you will not be one of them.

Are you ready to meet your God? Not without Christ and the assurance that your sins have been washed away in His blood! When your last hour comes, self-confidence, reliance on money, trust in your own intelligence, your own ability, will vanish. *The London Daily Mail* of February 1, 1924, prints this popular account, current in Russia at the time of Lenin's death: "The once all-powerful dictator" [who blasphemously wrote "Long live atheism!"] "spent his last days of activity crawling on all fours like a beast around the room in his carefully guarded retreat at Gorky, apologizing to the furniture for his misdeeds, the memory of which remained amid the ruins of his mind." He had money, might, and military power, but without Jesus he was mad.

To be rescued from such ruin, give yourself to the Savior this Sunday, not next; today, not tomorrow; this very hour, not late after midnight; now, right in your own home or your hotel, in automobiles, speeding trains, or swift airplanes, in sickrooms, or hospitals, in public institutions or prisons! Wherever you are and whoever you are, the Son of God can be yours from this moment on. You yourself can approach the Redeemer, who has promised, *"Him that cometh to Me I will in no wise cast out,"* and believing that your loving and living Savior has forever atoned for all your sins, you can be wholly His, without any intermediary to plead your cause.

Today again we have offered you Jesus' light, love, and life eternal. We are not asking you to think it over and sometime later to let us know what you will do about it; but we do plead: Welcome the Savior into your heart now! Make haste to the living Lord! Run, as Peter did, to your risen Redeemer! Come quickly to the conquering Christ and be blessed forever! God says "Hurry!" The Holy Spirit grant that you will speedily seize your salvation through repentance and faith in your divine Deliverer! *Amen!*

CHRIST, SET OUR HEARTS ON FIRE!

"They said one to another, Did not our heart burn within us while He talked with us by the way and while He opened to us the Scriptures?" SAINT LUKE 24:32

GOD, OUR FATHER IN CHRIST: As we praise Thee for the beauties of spring and the marvels of reawakened nature, we also ask that Thy Spirit create us anew by faith in the Lord Jesus! What a wondrous Savior He is, to offer His own body and soul on the cross in payment of our sins and then to rise from the grave to assure us of our resurrection! Yet how cold and calloused we often are when we hear the record of His reconciling grace! How easily we permit our own selfishness, our own personal, petty desires, to crowd the love of Christ from our hearts! Therefore we plead for new zeal in confessing our ever-blessed Redeemer before men. As once on the Emmaus road the hearts of two disciples burned within them when the living Lord opened sacred Scriptures to them, so may the enlightening Spirit stir our souls into flame when Jesus walks with us and talks with us in His Word! Bless the preaching of the Gospel and the study of Thy compassion all over the world! Use every message of the Cross by Thine almighty power, in drawing many to their divine Deliverer, in comforting the sick and bereaved, in sustaining the forsaken and desperate, especially in reviving the flames of dying faith! Hear us, Father, for we come before Thee in Christ, Thy Son, our Savior! *Amen!*

Christ, Set Our Hearts on Fire!

LAST Tuesday at Court Square in the heart of Memphis, an unusual monument was unveiled — the first of its kind in the world. It was not the statue of a war hero, a Tennessee statesman, or a fairy-tale figure — but an outdoor reading stand with an open Bible. Memphis businessmen felt that in critical times like these God's Word should be publicly displayed, its comfort and guidance constantly offered everyone. So at that central, prominent place they erected this marble Bible case where, all day, and with special illumination all night, peace-robbed, sin-sorrowed, light-seeking souls can find their heavenly Father's pledge of hope and help.

Every larger community in the United States should follow Memphis. Such Scripture-stands will do more than bring Holy Writ to the masses; they will stand as memorials to the faith which made our country great in the past and which alone can grant us assurance for the future with its staggering perils.

God give us in the United States a larger love for His Word during these critical days, when Bible bonfires flare in a dozen different countries under atheist control, as puny men proudly boast that they have cast the Almighty aside! Senator Wiley of Wisconsin told me last week: "On a recent trans-Atlantic trip, at a deck party on the *Queen Elizabeth,* I was introduced to Soviet Deputy Foreign Minister Vishinsky, who was on his way to a meeting of the United Nations. I took his hand, looked him straight in the eye, and said: 'Mr. Vishinsky, every night I pray God that Great Britain, America, Russia, and the other nations of the earth will have a sincere desire for peace.' To this Mr. Vishinsky answered, through his interpreter, 'I don't pray.'" Only a few days ago cable dispatches from Europe revealed another campaign to stamp out religious influences in Communist-controlled countries. This new anti-God offensive is directed especially against the clergy in small towns and villages, who are "struggling against the Kremlin's atheist tendencies." The Central Committee of the Young Communists' League calls for an "intensified battle" against all religion. While the blasphemy of Communism in the U. S. S. R. does not hesitate to erect a huge statue of Judas Iscariot, the suicide betrayer of our Lord Jesus Christ, let us in the U. S. A. publicly exalt the Bible and openly express our loyalty to the Savior!

Time was when our leaders gladly acknowledged God's Word their guide. To cite only one example, the founders of Rhode Island stated in their compact: "We ... submit our persons, lives, and estates unto our Lord Jesus Christ, the King of Kings and the Lord of Lords, and to all those perfect and absolute laws of His, given us in His holy Word of truth."

Today a different spirit reigns. No longer do our Presidents publicly exalt the Redeemer's name in their proclamations. No longer do our State Governors tell their people, as Governor Rice asked the citizens of Massachusetts, to praise God "for the redemption of the world by our Lord and Savior Jesus Christ," and "for His Holy Word." No longer does the Congress request the observance of national humiliation, as the Civil War Senate in 1863 instructed President Lincoln to set aside a day for fasting and repentance, as their resolution stated, "Deploring the national offenses which have provoked His [Almighty God's] righteous judgment; yet encouraged in this day of trouble by the assurance of His Word, to seek Him for succor according to His appointed way, through Jesus Christ." Confronted by the possibility of a struggle which in a single hour can destroy more lives than were lost by both sides in the entire Civil War, the people of the United States dare not continue their neglect of God and their opposition to His Gospel of grace in Christ. The churches must help rebuild the Bible-based faith of the fathers.

Whatever this nation does, or whatever anyone else does, you should be close to Jesus in His Word. If you are saddened by suffering, distressed by difficulties, harassed by hardships of soul and body; if, worse, you are indifferent, lukewarm, or even cold toward the compassionate Savior; if the flame of a once fervent faith has died down in your soul, join us in the plea,

CHRIST, SET OUR HEARTS ON FIRE!

Resurrected Redeemer, grant us that burning love for Thee and Thy Word, with which Thou didst once strengthen Thy two disciples, of whom our text (the Gospel of Saint Luke, chapter twenty-four, verse thirty-two) reports: *"They said one to another, Did not our heart burn within us while He talked with us by the way and while He opened to us the Scriptures?"*

I

CHRIST'S WORD WARMED HIS DISCIPLES' COLD HEARTS

It was Easter afternoon, and two followers of our Lord were hurrying from Jerusalem to the little village of Emmaus, eight miles distant. One of these travelers is called Cleophas, but we know nothing of his earlier or later life; the other remains unnamed. Again we see that the Savior shows His love particularly to those whom the world often passes unnoticed. Our faith gives no preference to caste or class, color or condition, for Jesus came to *"call . . . sinners to repentance,"* whoever and whatever they may be.

Had you met these disciples on the Emmaus road, you would have seen distress clearly written on their faces; and could you have overheard their conversation, you would have understood the cause of their grief. They had been in Jerusalem at least since Good Friday; perhaps they had been among those who *"stood afar off"* during the Savior's cruel crucifixion. Three days had elapsed. They were sure He had not risen from the sepulcher, and they wanted to get away from the royal city, where the Temple, the high priest's palace, the Roman governor's residence, the streets on which their martyred Master had staggered under His cross, the skull-shaped hill outside the city walls, all told them in their unbelief that Christ, crucified at Calvary, had failed; that He had not kept His word; that He was not the Son of God resurrected from the tomb, but a man like other men, defeated by death.

So they made the mistake of leaving the other disciples. Had they remained with the small band of believers, by this time they would have heard from Peter's lips the certain, strengthening account of the Lord's resurrection. Many of you have paid a similar penalty for forsaking God's house. Because something happened to displease you — and for what trivial excuses do people absent themselves from church! — you shun the services and cut yourself off from God's Word. If you are one of the millions in our country who once were enrolled in the army of the Lord but now are outside the Church, come back now, during this Easter season! When death approached Henry Drummond, Glasgow University scientist, only forty-six years old, he found that his unbelief offered him no hope whatever. So he told Sir William Dawson, noted scientist and devoted follower of our Lord: "I am going back to the Bible and believe it as I once did. I can no longer live in this uncertainty." He returned to Christ, his Savior, and in His redeeming death and resurrection he found *"the peace ... which passeth all understanding."* Today I ask you not to wait until a siege of sickness helps draw you to Jesus, but to overcome your pride and resume church attendance immediately. With new joy in his heart a Racine, Wisconsin, listener writes: "I have returned to Church after twenty-five years away from it. I was a drunkard, but no more. I heard your broadcast, grabbed a Bible, and called on my heavenly Father for the aid I received. It will be hard to make up for the years I wasted, but with the faith God has given me the past year, I will succeed." We will be glad to show you the way back to your Redeemer. You can never be happy without the Savior whom you once confessed.

Those two downhearted disciples were disturbed by imaginary sorrow. They were mourning a dead leader, when in reality the Son of God was alive. Similarly most of your fears and worries are groundless. According to an eminent specialist, healthy people are often unnecessarily worried that they have heart disease. Even more disastrously many of you doubt Jesus' divine promises and refuse to find help in the living Christ.

The grief-stricken men were walking along, discouraged and desperate, when suddenly, in the open country, they met a mysterious Stranger. A few hours later, again in a way they could not explain, He was to disappear before their eyes. In His glorious resurrection body our Lord was not restricted by limitations of time, travel, distance. Thank God, then, for the promise, *"We shall be like Him,"* the guarantee that our celestial form will have the same marvelous power! May this comfort sustain you believers who have been shut in sickrooms for long, weary years, unable even once to worship in the Savior's sanctuary! The time is coming, through faith in the resurrected Christ, who, as Scripture promises, *"shall change our vile body that it may be fashioned like unto His glorious body,"* when in eternal radiance, all human weaknesses gone, you will be forever blessed by the new perfection Jesus here showed.

The disciples did not recognize their Lord. Saint Mark tells us that *"He appeared in another form,"* and Saint Luke reports that *"their eyes were holden."* Perhaps it would have been too much for their heavy hearts if suddenly they were to find their risen Redeemer beside them. Before you criticize these Emmaus-road wanderers too harshly, let me remind you how often you, too, have failed to recognize your divine Deliverer and to heed His Word! He has come to you in your deep bereavement, yet you have pushed Him aside to charge Him with cruelty in calling a loved one home. Jesus has drawn close to some of you husbands and wives, pleading that you keep your marriage vows; but you have thrust Him aside and willfully stained your soul with scarlet sin. Through His Holy Spirit the Lord of life is asking you, troubled with affliction, tortured by evil, tormented by sufferings of soul and body, to take the unfailing comfort He offers you. Our heavenly Father grant that today will not be just another Sunday on which you hear of the Son of God's self-sacrifice for

Christ, Set Our Hearts on Fire! 213

you, but again stolidly refuse to receive and exalt Him as your Savior, your Sovereign!

Our Lord had appeared to console His two forlorn followers; and after they confess the cause of their sorrow, Christ's death, His supposed failure to redeem Israel, the false reports about His resurrection, Jesus begins to restore their faith with the most remarkable Easter sermon ever preached. The fathers often expressed the desire that they might have been hidden in the bushes along the roadside to have heard this testimony to the resurrection from the Lord Himself. The Holy Spirit has graciously preserved enough of Jesus' Emmaus-road conversation to teach us valuable lessons. Thus we see that the Master Instructor went back to the Bible for truth and comfort. He would not use men's frail, faulty word as the source of His assurance, and neither should we. If we are to find help for our age, we must discover it in Scripture. "Back to the Bible" must be the watchword of a repentant nation and of contrite churches.

Then, our Lord did not hesitate to preach the Law, when He said to the downhearted disciples, *"O fools, and slow of heart to believe all that the Prophets have spoken!"* That was strong language; but it was required for strong unbelief. Today, too, we must not overlook or excuse doubt and disbelief, but, following our Savior, regard those as fools, however highly trained they may be, who reject divine revelation. The other night, in Connecticut, during driving rain and darkness, an automobile somehow stalled on the main-line tracks of the New Haven Railroad just at the time when a Boston express train, only a few miles away, was speeding toward it. A young man who saw the danger tried to signal the driver, but his words and gestures were mistaken for a hitchhiker's appeal. Because every second counted, the alert young man rushed to the car, warned the occupants at the top of his voice, and pleaded with them to jump out. They did — only a few seconds before their auto was demolished by the streamliner. If we are to help save people from a calamity far worse than an automobile accident, the destruction of their souls, then we must warn them in loud, clear language, telling them unmistakably that without Christ they are lost. It did not bring our Lord joy to call His followers *"Fools, and slow of heart to believe,"* just as we experience no thrill in telling you that if you reject your living Redeemer, you are guilty of the worst folly, because you have spurned your only Hope of salvation, heaven, and life eternal, besides burdening yourselves with never-ending misery. Yet, if you are to receive God's Son as your Savior, you must recognize that without Him you are hopelessly lost. Dr. Einstein has published a new theory on gravitation, which is written in such complicated scientific language that the newspapers tell us, "No more than one person in a million can understand it"; but there is not one in a million normal persons who should misunderstand warnings like this: *"The soul that sinneth, it shall die."* Have I made it clear to you? If you refuse to believe the New Testament truth, you have allied yourself with the most abject fools; you are lost.

Then Jesus explained the glorious Gospel to the two doubting disciples. *"Ought not Christ to have suffered these things and to enter into His glory?"* He asked them; and to prove to them that He had to die on the cross and rise again, we are told that *"beginning at Moses and all the Prophets, He expounded unto them in all the Scrip-*

tures the things concerning Himself." The crucifixion was no accident, and the resurrection no mere wishful thinking; both were divine realities, guaranteed by God's Word. Jesus had to die and rise again, our Lord Himself explained, because Scripture had repeatedly predicted that He would; and not one word of its sacred truth could fail in its fulfillment. Christ had to lay down His life and then defeat the grave because only God could thus fully atone for all the sins of mankind. Only the Lord could break the bonds of death, and Jesus is — be sure of this! — the almighty and eternal God. The Savior had to give Himself as the Sin-Offering at Calvary and then triumph over the tomb, because in no other way than by His suffering, bleeding, and dying in payment of human transgression and then by breaking forth from His rock-hewn sepulcher could He remove the curse of guilt from your soul, fulfill Heaven's Law in your stead, and satisfy the demands of Heaven's righteousness.

It was no ten-minute sermonet that Jesus preached there on the Emmaus road, but a long, book-by-book study of the Old Testament, in which our Lord clearly showed how prophecy after prophecy was fulfilled at the cross and the open grave — the very message everybody always needs. This Scripture-searching and Scripture-teaching took so long that all too quickly for the disciples they had come to Emmaus. Then, we are told, Christ *"made as though He would have gone further."* Our Lord does not continually force Himself on us. There comes a time, after He has given us the assurance of our salvation, when we ourselves must decide whether we want to continue with Him or without Him. Eager to keep their new-found Teacher, although they still did not recognize Him, the two companions *"constrained*

Him, saying, Abide with us; for it is toward evening, and the day is far spent"; and, as it is recorded, the Christ who never spurns any invitation like this "*went in to tarry with them.*"

It was suppertime, and while Jesus sat at the table with them, "*their eyes were opened, and they knew Him.*" A few hours before they had been groping blindly in bereavement, mistakenly bemoaning a dead Lord; but now "*their eyes were opened*" to recognize that their Savior was really resurrected; and because they had been brought back to faith in His victory over death, Jesus left them. "*He vanished out of their sight,*" we are told; but the courage which their risen Redeemer had placed into their hearts was to abide with them. Astonished and filled with holy joy, "*they said one to another, Did not our heart burn within us while He talked with us by the way and while He opened to us the Scriptures?*" They had been inwardly chilled, frozen by doubt and disbelief; but now their hearts glowed with the fire of faith. They had left Jerusalem bemoaning their Leader's death; now they were ready to return and proclaim His resurrection. At noontime they said: "Christ has failed. He did not keep His word. He is defeated by death"; but by nightfall, having studied Scripture and met the living Savior face to face, their searing anguish had been turned to exultant joy.

II

CHRIST'S WORD WILL WARM OUR COLD HEARTS

What a marvelous promise this is for our cold, unbelieving age! Christ can likewise warm our chilled hearts when a score of sorrows seek to freeze our faith. Your letters give widespread evidence of heavy burdens. A New Hampshire listener says, "Five years ago I wrote you as a twenty-five-year bed patient; now it is thirty years that I have been in bed." A listener in Washington, who has had to stay in a wheel chair for fourteen years, finds her body slowly calcifying, her bones seemingly turning to stone. A California woman laments: "I am the mother of two boys who gave their lives for their country in the terrible war. I have no other children." A Florida widow writes: "The doctor states I have cancer of the stomach. I live alone next door to my aged parents and mentally unbalanced sister. All my savings are gone."

Besides this bodily anguish, miseries in the home weigh heavily on many of you. A Chicago woman's heart is torn by the horror of having a grandson deliberately lie on a railroad track and let the train cut his body to bits. In hundreds of cases that come to my desk, husbands desert wives, and mothers leave their families to run away with other men.

Especially does the load of sin's guilt crush happiness out of many lives. A Rhode Island listener confesses, "My mind is so upset with evil thoughts that I cannot find rest at all." A Texas friend sobs: "A filthy word has control of my heart and mind. Even in my prayers these dirty thoughts come into my mind. Oh, help me! I have prayed, pleaded, and begged God for help. Not a day goes by that I don't cry my eyes out appealing for peace, forgiveness, and a life for God. Can there be a chance for me, after being so sinful? Have I committed the unpardonable sin against the Holy Ghost? Am I doomed and lost forever?"

What can we say to help warm chilled hearts? Where is the true source of joy in an age when, despite the highest salaries ever paid, an official in the Department of Labor estimates that 20,000,000 people in the United States are unhappy in their work, and in many places throughout the country the number of divorces equals the number of new marriages? Where can you find the secret of soul happiness?

Not in any merely human theories! On his thirty-third birthday Lord Byron, acclaimed literary genius, wrote in his journal: "I go to bed with the heaviest of hearts at having lived so long and to so little purpose." When Tolstoy, the Russian novelist, was fifty years old, life was so dark that at his orders all ropes were hidden to keep him from hanging himself in his room. Genius, wealth, power, fame, cannot bring you the warmth of true joy.

For this you must meet the living Savior of the Emmaus road in spirit on your own life's road and have His Word set your heart on fire. You must believe and find in your risen Redeemer's love for you a mercy so mighty that only God could plan and grant it. You must be inwardly moved, assured, thrilled by Christ's compassion. You need not only a head knowledge of the Savior's devotion unto death, but a glowing heart exultation that the Son of God loved you, as the whole proud, sin-stricken, lust-filled, hate-charged, rebellious race of men, with such intense yearning that He gladly paid the full price demanded for complete, universal redemption, by suffering in His own soul and body the total death and damnation torment of humanity's teeming billions.

How matchless the Savior's mercy! An Illinois listener writes that for $5,000 he is ready to undertake any mission, however dangerous it may be. For $5,000 he will sacrifice any part of his body if thereby he can

Christ, Set Our Hearts on Fire! 219

help save a life. For $5,000 he will submit himself to medical associations or laboratories in their quest for cures of diseases, even infantile paralysis. He wants this sum and is willing to offer his life as collateral so that he can meet his financial obligations and return to his home in good standing. How infinitely greater is Christ's grace! He gave Himself into certain death without a penny's pay! A Washington man is asking the courts to award him damages of $1,300,000 for false arrest. Yet the sinless Son of God, in whom even His enemies' perjury and malice could find no trace of guilt, asks only that for the awful agony He endured in your stead on the cross you receive Him as your Redeemer.

May His Spirit open your eyes, as He enlightened the Emmaus disciples, and make you realize that your Savior, who is your God and present Help in every need, lives in eternal triumph to comfort you in moments of misery, to build your courage in hours of bereavement, to brighten your soul in the dark days of adversity, to warm your heart with the fire of faith in every affliction!

Once you truly know Jesus as your Deliverer from death, you will understand that because He gave His life to save your soul, defeated sin, death, and the devil in hell, to prove Himself your ever-living, ever-loving Rescuer from ruin, He assuredly will help you triumph over your troubles. He will refuse to permit the sorrows you must suffer to undo His saving work in your soul, nor the burdens you must bear to crush you into the dust of defeat. Learn to take refuge in His love, my afflicted friends who feel the ache of sudden sorrows, and you will then understand the surpassing promise of Scripture, *"All things work together for good to them that love God."* Trust the Savior's pledges, though with your human reason you cannot fully fathom the depth of devotion in these sacred statements: *"Whom the Lord loveth He chasteneth"; "We must through much tribulation enter into the Kingdom of God"; "As many as I love, I rebuke and chasten"; "If we suffer, we shall also reign with Him"; "Blessed are ye when men shall revile you and persecute you. . . . Rejoice and be exceeding glad; for great is your reward in heaven."* As surely as Christ is your Ruler and Redeemer, your suffering is the evidence of His love, the proof of His divine mercy, by which your faith is to be fortified, your reliance on His saving grace intensified, your self-confidence decreased, but your conviction of His almighty power increased; your pride lowered, but your assurance of answered prayer heightened; your attachment to the things of this world broken, but your search for *"those things which are above"* re-enforced. All of you who are God's children, weighted down by woe, should firmly believe that the Christ of the Emmaus road knows your grief even before your afflicted souls beseech His help, that often He appears before you ask Him, and that always He is ready to warm your cold hearts and to turn your anguish into joy.

He is eager to bless your home with His presence; but have you invited Him into your household with the prayer, *"Abide with us"*? Only God knows how much domestic misery, marital strife, and household unhappiness could be avoided, and in how many instances dying love could be revived, broken hearts mended, and unfaithfulness prevented, if the Lord of life were made a welcome Guest in sorrow-shadowed dwellings. The Savior wants to bless your family with His strengthening presence. Parents and children, while you hear this ap-

Christ, Set Our Hearts on Fire! 221

peal, resolve that from this moment on you will pray: "*'Abide with us!'* 'Come, Lord Jesus, be our ever-welcome Guest, so that we, fathers and mothers, sons and daughters, may be Thy guests in heaven's eternal bliss!'"

True, Christ does not now come to us visibly in His resurrected body. This joy He has reserved until we see Him face to face, when we stand before His eternal throne. Yet He has pledged, *"I will not leave you comfortless; I will come to you,"* and He does come to us, mercifully and marvelously in the words which He once spoke and which the Holy Spirit has written in our Bibles to assure us of the Savior's presence. Do you read God's Word regularly and study divine revelation, which by its own promise *"is able to build you up"?* We are astonished to learn that in Estonia, where Red atheism is already producing a harvest of ruin from its seeds of unbelief, a woman interpreter, hearing a religious leader from the United States say that the Almighty wrote the Scripture, laughingly asked: "That's funny. How could God write a book?" Even in our own country millions do not know the Bible nor find time to read it. More catastrophic, however, is the fact that most church members — and public opinion polls support this statement — do not daily delve into the sacred treasury of guidance and comfort. An Episcopalian leader in Washington correctly declares, "An entire generation or more has grown up, even within the churches, who have never heard the true Christian Gospel." Therein lies our country's greatest danger — the neglect of grace by those who know its glory. It is now revealed that during the war the Japanese had developed two supercraft of 72,000 tons each, 20,000 tons larger than the *Missouri*, our biggest battleship. These two dreadnoughts could have taken a heavy toll of our ships, yet they did no damage whatever. Why? Because the Japanese admiralty officials kept them hidden so long that finally, when they were sent out for combat, their officers did not know how to maneuver them successfully, and they were destroyed. What a striking picture of the tragedy in homes where God's Word is secluded on bookshelves or displayed only as an ornament in the living room! The cry which must re-echo throughout the land is not only, "America, Back to the Bible!" but also, "American Christian Families, Back to the Bible!" "American Believers, Back to the Bible!"

If some of you churchgoers, who have time for the many outside activities of your congregation but no time to meet the living Christ in His Gospel, feel lonely and soul-saddened, your cold hearts can be warmed by the radiance of a Scripture-searching faith! Probably none of you has ever heard of Pong Cho. He was a Christian leper in China, of whom the Bible Society reports: "He has not a whole finger left; his ears are twice their normal size, and his feet swollen so he can hardly walk. He can speak only in a hoarse whisper, and he is totally blind." This poor, disfigured, sightless, doomed man has memorized among other books the whole Gospel of Saint Matthew. When once in the presence of visitors he came to the end of the twenty-eighth chapter and someone asked him, "This painfully hard work of memorizing the whole Gospel — has it been worth while?" the blinded, diseased, mutilated leper answered: "It has given me a mind at peace with God. My faith has been strengthened. I have joy." "And death?" he was asked. Hear his reply: "The matter of death is not my business. That belongs to God. I see heaven in my mind." Get out your Bibles, read them reverently, search them to find Jesus, confess Him your Savior! Then, penetrating the gloom of grief, the darkness of death, you, too, will have peace and joy.

Because we in this broadcast believe Holy Writ to be the errorless and divinely inspired truth, in at Genesis and out at Revelation, from the record of the earthly Paradise to the vision of the heavenly, we must appeal to you skeptics and Christ-deniers who have been struck down by one blow of adversity after another [and the denial of our Lord never brings happiness and satisfaction, as infidels since the day of Judas know only too well], to be fair enough to read the Bible without prejudice and thus give the Holy Spirit opportunity to stir the flame of faith within your heart. How marvelously the Almighty has used Scripture in turning sinners from their evil ways to their merciful Redeemer! A salesman for a New York wholesale concern, who had systematically stolen money from his company and tried to stifle the voice of his conscience by further sin was shaving in a Chicago hotel. Searching for a piece of paper on which to wipe his old-fashioned razor, he tore from a Gideon Bible a page containing the sixth chapter of Romans, only to have his eyes fall on Saint Paul's words, *"The wages of sin is death."* Struck by this warning, he seemed compelled to read on in the same verse, *"but the gift of God is eternal life through Jesus Christ, our Lord."* This hope of deliverance led him to study this hotel Bible for two hours, until he knelt before God and declared himself a lost sinner, but the Crucified his Savior. Immediately the man returned to New York and confessed his theft. His employers did not prosecute him, nor did they discharge him. Instead they kept him in his position and permitted him to pay back his theft in monthly installments.

A current magazine prints the story of a lawbook salesman who was a complete failure. As Dale Carnegie quotes him, he relates: "I was broke. I didn't have the money to pay even my hotel bill. Neither did I have the money to buy a ticket back home; I was truly done for. . . . I had nothing but a glass of hot milk for dinner. Even that was more than I could afford. I understood that night why desperate men raise a hotel window and jump. I might have done it myself, if I had had the courage. Since there was no one else to turn to, I turned to God. I began to pray. After that prayer I opened my eyes and saw a Gideon Bible that lay in a dresser drawer in that lonely hotel room. I opened it and read those beautiful, immortal promises of Jesus — especially the passage ending, 'Seek ye first the kingdom of God.' As I read those words, a miracle happened; my anxieties, fears, and worries were transformed into heart-warming courage and hope and triumphant faith. I was happy, even though I did not have enough money to pay my hotel bill. I went to bed and slept soundly — free from care — as I had not done for many years. I was born anew that desperate night, twenty-one years ago, in a little hotel in Amarillo, Texas." You, too, can be born again through the Word, by the Holy Spirit; and as that lawbook salesman, under divine grace, became a successful attorney, so you can be turned from defeat to distinction and — what is vastly more important — directed from hell to heaven.

On the day after last Christmas, weather bureau experts predicted for New York City: "Occasional snow during the afternoon, followed by a partial clearing."

Christ, Set Our Hearts on Fire! 225

Instead, the city was hit by a blizzard which in twelve hours blanketed the streets with twenty-six inches of snow. Not only has the Bible never made a mistake in forecasting the future, but as Christ emphasized to His two disciples on Easter afternoon, Scripture has divinely foreseen and foretold many world events in exact detail and long centuries in advance. Here, then, is a book you can trust — a book you must heed if you would escape destruction.

You can be sure that the Bible is God's Word because, as Jesus emphasized on the Emmaus road, it does what no other volume can do: It gives definite proof of its divine nature in its prophetic statements. Men's predictions are mere guesswork and repeatedly fail. In the *Saturday Evening Post* of December 6, 1913, Senator Theodore E. Burton of Ohio made the assertion: "Wars for the aggrandizement of rulers have ceased." Eight months later the world was aflame in the first global struggle of aggrandizement; but when our Lord promises, *"Peace I give unto you,"* those who believe Him have the *"peace . . . which passeth all understanding"* in its divine and absolute certainty.

Because it is not the Bible that saves you but the Christ of the Bible, who shed His blood to cleanse you from your sins, search and study the Scriptures to find the atoning Son of God and have your hearts fired by faith! In Vienna, Austria, someone gave a New Testament to a brilliant young man named Gartenhaus, a teacher in a Jewish school. He had been warned to stay away from this book; nevertheless, in the privacy of his room, after he had locked the door, he sat down to scan its pages. Soon he compared Old Testament prophecies with New Testament fulfillment, just as

Christ on the Emmaus road began *"at Moses and all the Prophets."* Before the young teacher realized it, he had spent the entire night studying the Gospel record; but for days thereafter he kept on reading the faultless book, and without any instructor he found *"in all the Scriptures the things concerning"* the promised Messiah. He accepted Jesus as his own Redeemer; and because his soul had been set on fire by faith, he wanted other cold hearts to be warmed by the same wondrous Deliverer. So he traveled 5,000 miles to reach his own brother and convince him of the full and free salvation in the Virgin-born Messiah.

When officers of the Pocket Testament League gave President Coolidge a New Testament, he stated briefly and pointedly, "In this little book will be found the solution to all the problems of the world." President Coolidge was right. Let men everywhere accept the Gospel truth, and our international rivalries, class hatreds, and color discriminations will fade away in defeat. Today, as we offer you the whole Bible, I tell you: In this holy book, Old Testament and New, you will find the lightening of your burdens. It offers you, through faith in God's Son, forgiveness for your sins, guidance in darkness, peace of mind in a strife-torn world, unfailing comfort and courage in every affliction, the assurance of eternal life even here on earth! With that guarantee of grace we pray: O Christ, come to us, walk with us, talk to us, abide with us! By Thy sacred companionship, set our cold hearts on fire for Thee! *Amen!*

HEAVEN'S HAMMER AND SICKLE

"Is not My Word like . . . a hammer that breaketh the rock in pieces?" JEREMIAH 23:29

"And He that sat on the cloud thrust in His sickle on the earth; and the earth was reaped." REVELATION 14:16

GOD OF ALL GRACE IN CHRIST: Humbly we praise Thee for the countless blessings that are ours in this country as in no other land on earth, and contritely we beseech Thy pardon for our repeated ingratitude and our thankless neglect of Thy mercy. For the sake of Thy Son, our only Savior, who laid down His life in payment for our sins and then rose from the grave to seal our eternal salvation, forgive us these sins of selfishness, and fill us with a new fervor of faith! Make us a repentant people, wholly reliant on the redeeming Christ! Reject and restrain all who seek to overthrow Thy Church and destroy the blessings of our free government! To this end help us walk more closely with Thee, in greater love to our fellow men, and in deeper devotion to Christ's Golden Rule! In Thine everlasting compassion comfort all the sick and sorrowing, the destitute and dying, with the love which sent Jesus to the cross for them! Graciously provide for the homeless and hungry across the seas by leading us to share our bounties with them in their needs! Above all, loving Father, draw searching souls to Thee now, by this message, through Christ, the Friend of sinners, the Help of the helpless, the one but sure Guide to heaven's glory! *Amen!*

TODAY, April 18, 1948, has been called "the decisive date in modern history," and for weeks liberty-loving people throughout the world have anxiously awaited this Sunday. At first glance the fact which gives the day its importance, the election of a parliament for the new republic of Italy, may make you ask, "What has that to do with us in the United States?" Just this: Godless Communists are busily at work to bring Italy under their control. If they succeed, their task in taking all Europe will be much simplified, the danger of their infiltration into our own beloved country decidely enlarged, and the Red rebellion's sworn hostility to Christ and His followers disastrously increased.

We have reason to believe that in a free election the Italian people will reject atheistic Communism. However, as past years have shown, such setbacks only serve to spur the masterminds of Marxism to more determined efforts. April 18 will be followed by a score of similar days of decision in various parts of the world; for Communism, as its records and utterances show, definitely seeks to conquer the whole earth. On the cover of the *Communist Manifesto,* United States edition, we read this appeal and program: "Working men of all countries, unite! You have nothing to lose but your chains. You have a world to win."

Widely organized godlessness is drawing more closely to this goal. The Red flag waves not only over all Russia, but also dominates the lives of millions in a dozen other Communist-controlled countries. Within our boundaries, William Z. Foster, once listed as Communist candidate for the Presidency of the United States, is on record as declaring: "The workers of the country and the workers of every country have only one flag, and that is the Red flag; and the duty of the Communists is the abolition of the American form of government. I stated clearly that the Red flag of the revolutionary class is the only flag we recognize, and that we owe no allegiance to the American flag." Wherever the crimson flag's hammer and sickle are triumphantly unfurled, the Church of Jesus Christ has been oppressed. Within our own borders the Communist crusade parades under the slogan: "Down with the churches! Down with religion! Long live atheism!"

When we ask ourselves: "Will it be the hammer and sickle or the Stars and Stripes for the United States? Will it be the Red banner of Marxism or the red blood of Christ for American churches?" we ought to thank the Almighty that He has another hammer and sickle which can protect His Church against the brutal assaults of atheism! Therefore, to warn and strengthen you in faith, I show you

HEAVEN'S HAMMER AND SICKLE

described in the two passages chosen as our text (Jeremiah, chapter twenty-three, verse twenty-nine): *"Is not My Word like . . . a hammer that breaketh the rock in pieces,"* and (Revelation, chapter fourteen, verse sixteen): *"He that sat on the cloud thrust in His sickle on the earth; and the earth was reaped."*

I

THE DIVINE HAMMER AND SICKLE DESTROY GOD'S ENEMIES

In his twenty-third chapter, from which the first passage has been chosen, Jeremiah presents a powerful prediction of Christ, foretelling that *"He shall be called, The Lord our Righteousness."* Six long centuries before Jesus was born, this Old Testament Prophet knew that the coming Messiah would be both *"the Lord,"* the eternal God, and *"our Righteousness,"* the Savior who, through His suffering, death, and resurrection, removed all our sins and thus made us *"righteousness"* before God. Then this remarkable chapter hastens to put Jeremiah, and us, on guard against the treachery of false prophets, who change the divine record and substitute their destructive lies for Heaven's truth. As a warning to His people who were following these misleading teachers and as encouragement to His messenger, Jeremiah, the Almighty declared, *"Is not My Word like . . . a hammer that breaketh the rock in pieces?"*

A few years later the Lord proved how strong and devastating His threatened punishment could be. The judgments which He had uttered against his faithless followers were all executed to the letter. Nebuchadnezzar's battalions captured Jerusalem, made the streets run red with the blood of its slain defenders, led thousands of its gifted leaders, artisans, and craftsmen away as slaves to far-off Babylon. Only the poorest of the poor were left in the land. The Word of the Almighty, which they had despised, had indeed demolished their pride with hammerlike blows, razed the city walls, left the Temple in ruins, and the large buildings in debris.

Since that day, as before, Heaven's truth has wondrously shown itself a hammer in breaking to pieces the rocks of blasphemous unbelief; and God's triumph over His enemies will continue until the end of time. The second passage of our text, taken from the last book of the Bible, reveals *"the Son of Man, having on His head a golden crown, and in His hand a sharp sickle,"* and records, *"He that sat on the cloud thrust in His sickle on the earth; and the earth was reaped"* — a graphic picture of the Last Judgment, the final destruction which will overtake the foes of the faith, cutting down their rebellion against Christ, as a man swings the sickle to mow the grass.

Who are these enemies of the Almighty? In the widest of all uprisings against the Lord this earth has ever witnessed, believers in our generation face the "Down with God! Down with Jesus! Down with the Bible!" campaign conducted by Communism. Leaving entirely unmentioned any of its political practices, for the Church must not speak on purely partisan issues, we see that organized atheism has continually opposed Scriptural faith and has been guilty of gruesome crimes in persecuting believers. This attack on the Lord has closed most of the churches in the territories it controls, removed most of the clergy, prohibited most of the Christian education of its youth, cut off most of the church publications. It has demolished many places of worship, killed many of the clergy, and confiscated all church property. It has instituted an all-out antireligious campaign by turning one of its largest churches in Moscow into an antireligious museum, by starting nine antireligious universities in one month, by requiring trade unions to contribute to the down-with-the-churches fund, by urging its citizens to engage in atheistic propaganda. Communism has sought to change the calendar, abolishing the seven-day week, eliminating Sunday, leaving only five days in the year as holidays, each commemorating the Red Revolution. On Christmas Eve, to counteract the celebration of the Savior's birth, photographs of

Lenin as a baby are substituted for pictures of the Holy Infant, and Communist hymns for carols. Christmas trams in Moscow post warnings like this: "Religion is poison. Don't poison your children!" On Easter, the highest festival for orthodox Russia, officials schedule stage plays for the exact hour of worship and arrange concerts, motion pictures, and carnivals in the city squares, to keep the people from church. The constitution officially permits (and therefore encourages) each citizen of the U. S. S. R. to engage in anti-Christian propaganda. Public funds are used to spread atheism.

Special efforts are made to tear children from the faith. The Commissar of the Interior, Nikolas Jeshoff, issued a directive to local authorities, declaring that Christian names are forbidden for Russian babies, the only exceptions being those Biblical names which outstanding Communists have, such as Josef, Stalin's given name. Red mothers and daughters are told, "A good Soviet woman cannot be a follower of the doctrine of Stalin if she is not 100 per cent atheistic." The lower age limit for membership in the Communist youth movement has been reduced to eight years, and schoolteachers receive emphasized training in courses on atheism.

Do not think that this is the madness merely of individual extremists! These are truly the principles of all Communist leaders and their government practices. Listen to the screaming hatred from official Red sources: The newspaper *Pravda*, government mouthpiece: "The local authorities must, without loss of time, throw all necessary forces onto the anti-God front . . . we must declare a war to the death on all forms of religion." Lenin: "Every sort of religious idea . . . is inexpressible baseness . . . the most hideous source of infection." Dimitrov: "Every religion, especially the Christian religion, is the worst enemy of Communism and must be completely destroyed. It is not enough in the fight against religion to give illuminating talks or write books, weapons must be used against religion also." Stalin: "There shall not remain in the territory of the U. S. S. R. a single house of prayer to God, and the very conception 'God' will be banished from the boundaries of the whole Soviet Union."

Avoid the further mistake of assuming that this hatred of Christ and of His Church marked only the beginning of the Communist control, that its leaders have now changed their minds. This year official pronouncements by the Kremlin plainly tell the members of the Young Communists' League that they cannot be good Reds if they are religious. They cannot serve both God and Stalin. This very month *The New York Times* prints a report from its European correspondent who announces: "A new campaign to stamp out religious movements in the Soviet Union is reported under way." This new anti-God offensive would combat the clergy in small towns and villages, who are "struggling against the Kremlin's atheistic tendencies." The Central Committee of the Young Communists' League only a few weeks ago called for "an intensified struggle" against all religion. On the basis of Scripture we maintain that Communist leaders will constantly increase their opposition to the Savior.

Once more we beg you not to shrug your shoulders nor object: "What's he talking about, anyway? Communism is in Russia, and Moscow is 5,244 air miles from Washington. We have almost a quarter million churches in the United States, and no one can take these away from us." Are you sure? Do you know that the world's oldest atheistic publication is printed in our country? Do you know that infidels and enemies of Christ, supported by large legacies and financed by wealthy supporters, have issued blasphemies which stand side by side with the Red ridicule of the Almighty? American Communists, too, threaten to take over the churches; they, too, publish vile assaults on our holy Lord. Infidel folders on "Atheistic Poetry" contain vicious blasphemies under such titles as "Onward, Atheistic Soldiers!" "There Is No God," "Don't Talk to Me of Heaven!" Happiness Here, Not Hereafter," "Forget About God!" They feature such shocking lines as these:

"Glory to man in the highest, for man is the master of things."

"Plant Freethought on the ruined creeds,
  Till, in the world all o'er,
To science, as the only Lord,
  Be glory evermore."

"Away with parsons and with priests!
  But why?
Because they falsely claim to know
That God exists, and strive to show
That they're his agents here below!
  That's why!

"Away with parsons and with priests!
  But why?
Because they've filled the earth with fears,
Dissensions, hopeless hopes and tears,
Throughout a thousand wasted years.
  That's why!"

The editor of a leading atheist paper protests against kneeling in prayer, claiming that only those resembling savages "who first imagined God . . . will fall on their knees." However, visitors to our first Continental Congress in Philadelphia could always tell George Washington because he was one member who regularly knelt when that body united to entreat the Lord.

Thank God, as our text emphasizes, the Almighty has a hammer with which to smash all opposition to pieces; and His divine hammer never fails to crush. The last great attack on the Gospel before the Communist upheaval was the French Revolution, 150 years ago. It used almost the same language, the same blasphemies, the same ridicule of our faith, the same brutal procedures which today mark the Red assault on religion. Some of those atheist chiefs in France boasted that they would not halt "until they had dethroned the King of Heaven as well as the kings of earth." The churches in Paris and other large cities were closed; their treasuries confiscated; their altars pulled down; their bells melted into cannon. Statues of Christ were replaced with images of the revolutionists. A popular actress was enthroned on the altar of Notre Dame Cathedral and worshiped as the goddess of reason. "The Holy Guillotine," as they called it, took the place of the cross in working for the freedom of the world. Sunday was abolished, and in its place every tenth day meetings were held at which atheist orators propagandized the people. Those who opposed this godlessness had their heads cut off. In a seven-week period 1,326 people were guillotined in Paris alone, twenty-seven every day. One of the French revolutionists stood up in a Parisian church and cried to the mob, "Here am I in this pulpit from which lies have so long been told to the sovereign people, making them believe that there is a God who sees all their actions. If this God exists, let Him thunder, and may one of His thunderbolts crush me!" Then, after pausing dramatically, he continued, "He does not thunder, so His existence is a chimera." Another French revolutionist who gave himself the title "Personal Enemy of Jesus Christ," wrote in language which present-day atheists have copied: "Religion is a social disease.... A religious man is a depraved animal; he resembles those beasts that are kept only to be shorn and roasted for the benefit of merchants and butchers. The people is the Sovereign and God of the world; ... only fools can believe in any other God, in a Supreme Being."

Suddenly, however, the Almighty took out His hammer, struck this rebellion in France one blow, and as it collapsed in its ruins, its founders fell with it. Shocking despair marked the last hours of those who mocked the Lord of Lords and sent guiltless souls to the guillotine. The people whom Clootz had elevated to be God now quickly became a devil for him and had him executed. The beautiful goddess of reason ended as a repulsive hag; closed churches were reopened; Sunday, not the tenth day, was again honored; cannons were recast into church bells; and those who called themselves the enemies of Christ ended in hell.

Today's Red rebellion against the Almighty is doomed to the same defeat. No matter how much power His enemies amass, how much territory they seize, how many opponents they kill, God still has His hammer, and one blow can demolish the most formidable human foes. His divine truth, which heathen hordes, atheist armies, and Communist campaigns can never suppress nor silence, tells us twice, *"The fool hath said in his heart, There is no God. They are corrupt, they have done abominable works, there is none that doeth good."* The unbreakable Scripture also says: *"He that sitteth in the heavens shall laugh; the Lord shall have them in derision. Then shall He speak unto them in His wrath and vex them in His sore displeasure."* Yes, the Psalmist adds, *"Thou shalt break them with a rod of iron,"* really a club of iron, a hammer, *"Thou shalt dash them in pieces like a potter's vessel."*

The Most High uses this hammer in various ways and at various times. Even now Russia feels the blows of His wrath. Millions of its peasants have been liquidated, and masses are groaning in concentration camps. *"Be not deceived; God is not mocked!"* If we could know what was happening behind the Iron Curtain, we could realize that Heaven's hammer is striking. Sometimes reports leak through to confirm this. An eyewitness, whose account is printed in the National Lutheran Council *News Bulletin,* describes a Communist antireligious festival at Kursk. The procession was led by standard bearers carrying posters with blasphemous inscriptions like these: "Away with God!" "We need no God." "God did not create man; men created God." "Christ is a fabulous creation and has never existed." The feature of the parade was a float with a young woman defaming the Virgin Mary. In her arms was a doll, a Red soldier fully armed, labeled "The Modern Christ Child." Around the barrel in which this woman stood were caricatures of robed Russian clergymen; and behind the wagon, a carnival of dancing devils and jumping saints. For a few blocks the procession marched on; then suddenly the horses shied and ran wild. The wagon carrying this blasphemy struck a pillar and overturned, throwing the mock virgin to the pavement. She was rushed to the hospital, where it was necessary to amputate both her legs. Two days later she died of blood poisoning.

If God's hammer blows are sometimes delayed, He will finally *"thrust in His sickle on the earth; and the earth"* will be *"reaped."* An inescapable judgment must overtake all who rise up against their Ruler and Redeemer. In His own good time the Almighty brings every unforgiven sinner to account; and, as ten thousand pages of history show, His hammer and His sickle combine to destroy all persistent rebels against His grace. Atheist Communism is doomed.

In almost the same breath, let me tell you that the heavenly hammer and the celestial sickle will also strike those responsible for the conditions which help provoke Communism. Why did this evil get its first foothold in Russia? Because there, under the Czarist regime, millions of poor peasants were exploited by wealthy landowners, by military leaders, and — may God forgive them! — by churches themselves. Too frequently the clergy over there worked hand in hand with the men of money and did nothing to help the underpaid laborers and the overtaxed farmers. In far too many instances the priests neglected the saving Gospel with its sustaining love, substituting superstitions for Christ's comfort. The Russian churches could have saved their country from Communism, had they consistently preached and practiced Heaven's Word of warning and welcome; instead, they lost themselves in ease, error, and selfish ambition. Then God's hammer, using Communism, just as in the Old Testament the Almighty employed a dozen different foreign foes to punish unfaithful Israel, sentenced this selfishness and pride and coldness to the most grievous calamities the records of religion show.

In the same way, God's hammer will strike all those in the United States who help create the conditions under which Red ruin thrives. The worst enemies of our country are the heavily rich who have no interest, love, or concern for the downtrodden poor; the greedy employers who forget that *"the laborer is worthy of his hire";* the cruel exploiters who cheat, defraud, and exploit the Negro, treat him as though he were a dog, and drive him into the open arms of atheist agitators; the 200-per-cent Americans who despise the honest, thrifty foreign-born worker; the tax-supported teachers who deliberately exalt the U. S. S. R. system and sneer at the heroes who made our country; the corrupt politicians whose bribery and graft are used by the radicals as Exhibit A in the case against democracy; the rabble rousers who pit race against race, color against color, class against class; especially the infidels and scoffers outside the Communist circles whose ridicule of the Christian religion has helped bar many from that personal trust in the Savior, which alone can make men really love their fellow men, give them peace of mind, the guarantee of God's grace, and the assurance of redemption.

Particularly in these critical days you should recognize clearly that Heaven's hammer which shatters the rocks of resistance is not the force of arms. The opinion is gaining ground that, to retard the Communist conquest, we should start World War III and wipe out the Red advance. Indeed, voices already have been raised calling for a holy crusade, a sacred struggle to defend

Christianity. Yet our Lord, who commanded, *"Put up again thy sword into his place,"* and who declared, *"They that take the sword shall perish with the sword,"* does not want, nor does He need, bloodshed to defend His kingdom. Besides, have we forgotten after less than three years, the one third of a million American lives sacrificed in the last global struggle? Have we studied the price paid by the army of the permanently injured, the hopelessly crippled, the mentally deranged in veterans' hospitals across our country?

The first world conflict produced 21,000 millionaires in this land, one millionaire for every six boys slaughtered; and only God knows the total of private gains heaped up in this last war. Still we can see some of our losses: the heaviest debt in our national existence; the gravest international problems we have ever had to face; the highest crime wave; the deepest divorce depravity; the widest spread of irreligion; the greatest increase of profanity; the heaviest upswing of marital unfaithfulness; the most alarming growth of juvenile delinquency. A European general was right when he said that a victorious war is a misfortune, not only for the conquered, but for the conquerers as well. One conflict usually creates another. If only half the effort directed toward waging war were channeled into waging peace, the catastrophe of world struggles, under God, might be averted. When interviewed in 1936, Winston Churchill said: "America should have minded her own business and stayed out of the World War. If she had done so, the Allies would have made peace with Germany in the spring of 1917, thus saving more than a million British, French, American, and other lives, and prevented the subsequent rise of . . . Nazism." We read the startling claims by Professor Beard, one of our foremost historians, as published by Yale University, declaring that we provoked World War II; and we realize with what urgency we need to pray, *"Scatter Thou the people that delight in war!"* asking the Almighty to use His hammer in crushing all who seek personal profit, personal glory, personal power by involving our nation in the atomic horrors of a new war. My countrymen, pray for peace as never before! Pray contritely; pray earnestly; pray in Christ's saving name!

God's hammer, as our text clearly points out, is His Word, His Bible, His Gospel of grace in the Savior. See how marvelously this has proved its rock-splitting strength! The Son of the Highest is nailed to a cross to suffer the penalty of all human sins and to die for all sinners. Cold, silent in death, and apparently a failure, He is laid into a stone sepulcher. Yet the hammer of divine Omnipotence strikes that granite grave, the imperial Roman seal is broken, the boulder closing the entrance to the tomb is miraculously pushed away, and Jesus comes forth, as He promised, resurrected in glory. A few unlearned Galilean fishermen and their followers take up the cause of His kingdom and defeat mighty empires sworn to destroy them. As the disciples preach in the Savior's power, the rocks of resistance crumble into pieces, heathen hatred and pagan pride are defeated. How? By the hammer of God's Word. Polygamy is checked, the degradation of womanhood stopped; the exposure and murder of children outlawed, and these evils are supplanted by self-sacrificing compassion. Why? Because Heaven's hammer broke through the barricades of sin, while the Gospel of grace in Jesus brought multitudes to faith and therefore to service, not selfishness, mercy, not might. Millions of the enslaved, their backs bleeding from the lash, their minds paralyzed by fear, their hearts hungry for liberty, are set free, emancipated from misery. Why? Because the hammer of the victorious Word broke down the brutality of the human heart, and the Holy Spirit supplanted cruelty with Christ's Golden Rule. Even the horror of war can be reduced by this hammer. Go over to New Guinea, and you will learn that a pioneer Lutheran missionary worked there for thirteen years before winning a single soul, but today, through the Spirit's blessing on this one missionary's effort, 40,000 Papuans have been baptized, having forsaken war to *"seek peace and pursue it"!* Why? Because the hammer of the Almighty's Word has demolished their old hatreds, and the new peace they received through faith in the sin-atoning Savior has made them hate bloodshed and love their fellow men.

This heavenly hammer can break the granitelike opposition in hearts of utter unbelief. Giovanni Papini was called "an anarchist, an atheist, a Nihilist"; but as he studied the Bible, his vile blasphemies were shattered by the sacred pledges of Scripture. He could then exult with Peter, *"We believe and are sure that Thou art that Christ, the Son of the living God."* In this new-found faith he called Jesus "The Prince of Peace, the Son of Man sent by God, the Savior, the Anointed . . . for whom the poor, the wounded, the hungry, the afflicted, had been waiting from century to century as dry grass waits for rain, as the flower waits for the sun, as the mouth awaits the kiss, and the heart, consolation; the Son of God and of Man, the Man who hid God in human flesh, the God who cloaked His divinity in Adam's clay . . . the dear Brother of every day." Pray today that masses of anarchists and atheists in Italy may experience the same powerful change which brought Papini, their countryman, to Jesus!

A woman doctor, assigned to help wounded Red soldiers, writes, "I had to hide my little Gospel in order that they would not take it away from me, for it was a sign of a counter-revolutionary to have a Gospel in the army." Then she adds: "Especially during the nights when there were no attacks, I spoke to my wounded and sick of God, of their families, read them what I could of the Gospel. You cannot imagine what I felt when men, sometimes great sinners — murderers of women and men, even of children sometimes — confessed . . . to me, asking me to read to them about the robber on the cross and what God said to him." Here, too, God's hammer cracked the resistance of atheism, for the doctor continues: "Not one Red soldier of mine died without confessing his sins. They all died Christians."

"Will you not agree that when the Lord says, *"Is not My Word like . . . a hammer that breaketh the rock in pieces?"* we must try to bring this truth to His enemies? Followers of the Savior throughout the world on their knees, beseeching the Almighty to hammer down the strongholds of atheism, pleading in behalf of Red rebels against the Almighty, as the Christ of all compassion directed, *"Love your enemies";* Bibles and Gospel tracts printed in the language of Communist-controlled countries and distributed among the masses; high-powered broadcasting stations beaming the promises by the Lord of life into many hearts and homes in these Red realms — such a mighty spiritual offensive for the Redeemer will do more to stop atheist attacks on the Church and to help the unhappy victims of this aggression than any war can ever accomplish. While we still have time, let us work and pray to bring the divinely dynamic Word to the suffering masses of our fellow men, for whom the Son of God shed His holy blood! Then the heavenly hammer will truly break the boulders of blasphemy in pieces.

II

THE DIVINE HAMMER AND SICKLE WILL DESTROY YOUR ENEMIES

For your own lives, believe that the heavenly hammer can break down the stony barricade of unbelief which keeps you from your Savior or reduces your reliance on His mercy! Be fair enough and wise enough to read God's Word with its glorious Gospel grace in Christ, even though throughout your entire life, until today, you have spurned Scripture and rejected Jesus! Infidel Voltaire, of whom his doctor wrote, "He expired under the torment of the furies," had a disciple named LaHarpe, whom he regarded as his successor in spreading unbelief. Suddenly, however, LaHarpe with others was thrown into prison, to await the death sentence. The monotony of being locked up day after day without any book whatever almost drove him mad. By contrast he noticed an old man among his fellow prisoners with a book which he read constantly and which somehow produced ever-increasing assurance. In his solitude LaHarpe begged permission to borrow the book for a few moments; and the man who had dedicated his energies to ridicule the Gospel found that the volume he requested was the Bible. With nothing else to do, he read it for the first time in his life; and then the divine hammer began to strike at the citadel of his cynical atheism. Soon he exclaimed, "Here is everything to excite curiosity; and here is also everything to satisfy it." His life was saved, and he left prison; but far more important, his soul was saved by the Bible's hammerlike power. Now he preached the faith which before his imprisonment he had sought to destroy.

In His merciful wisdom God has perhaps directed the sledge hammer of adversity to lay some of you low on sickbeds, or otherwise to give you time and reason to learn Christ's love. If you value your soul, don't neglect this opportunity! Study the Bible! Start with the Gospel of Saint John! Prayerfully read the record of your redemption! We can warn you in advance that hammerlike blows will knock down much of your pride and pretense to show you that, however good you think you may be, in Heaven's sight you are false and full of sin, guilty of grievous crimes against the Lord, your fellow men, and yourself, doomed to death, sentenced to hell, utterly hopeless and helpless in rescuing yourself from this eternal ruin. You may have thought that you yourself could earn your Father's favor and forgiveness; but the hammer of His Word cracks that delusion when sweepingly it asserts, *"All our righteousnesses are as filthy rags."* You may have felt that others, godly men or sinless angels, pious parents, a churchgoing husband or wife, could somehow bring you into Paradise; but Scripture pulverizes that opinion, declaring, *"None of them can by any means redeem his brother."* You may have sought false peace by denying that there is a God, a hereafter, a judgment to come. Still your own reason rebels against this absurdity, and as you page through Scripture, your conscience supports this statement of divine truth: *"As I live, saith the Lord, every knee shall bow to Me, and . . . every one of us shall give account of himself to God.*" You may boast that you live without a heavenly Master and then die as a beast, disappearing forever; but Scripture can force that folly from your mind and tell you that you are headed for hell.

Thank the Lord with me, however, that the heavenly hammer of His Word can destroy the doubt, delusion, despair, which seize men's hearts when, terrified by the torturing thought of damnation, they cry, "What must I do to be saved?" Then the Gospel directs you to Jesus, God's Son and Mary's, your Savior and the whole world's, who, led by His limitless love, perfected the only plan of pardon which can save sinners. Rejecting the claims of your own righteousness, the Gospel takes you first to gloomy Golgotha, points to Christ, the Lamb of God, nailed to the sin-cursed cross, and tells you in a message of the most marvelous mercy your all-powerful Father could offer and His stainless angels proclaim, *"The blood of Jesus Christ, His Son, cleanseth us from all sin." "He was wounded for our transgressions, He was bruised for our iniquities . . . and the Lord hath laid on Him the iniquity of us all."*

My beloved, I ask you: Has the Word struck down the idol of self-worship in your heart? Has it broken down the barrier of unbelief so that you can truly call Christ "My God and my Savior"? Are you really persuaded that Christ died to deliver you from eternal death, that by your faith in what He did for you, not by the puny, little things you may try to do for Him, your sins are removed forever, and that as God beholds you, you have no more guilt, since your transgressions were transferred to His Son? Do you surely know, not in a church faith, a family faith, a mouth faith, but in inner heart-and-soul conviction, that through Jesus' blood and righteousness you, who were a child of wrath, have become a child of grace and an *"heir . . . of salvation"?*

If you have this assurance (and many are praying that you who up to this Sunday have steadily and stolidly turned from your Redeemer may today confess Him your Savior), then the divine hammer is for you, not against you. In this twentieth century it will strike down the enemies of your soul just as it overcame evil in the first century, after a dozen disciples began to conquer the world. If you can truly say, *"If God be for us"* (and you are convinced He is because Christ went to the cross to reveal the heights and depths of divine love) *"who can be against us?"* you know that the Holy Spirit will hammer down the assaults of unbelief and help build your trust more firmly. This confidence in Jesus will mightily repulse the satanic attacks which would make you feel that you have sinned too frequently and frightfully to be forgiven. If your own resistance is too weak to overcome temptation, you can wield the hammer of God's Word and send the foes of your faith into flight with your Lord's command, *"Get thee behind Me, Satan!"* When sorrows overwhelm you and one after another of your hopes collapses; when sickness, losses, family quarrels, unfaithfulness, loneliness, and the scores of other sufferings laid on men's souls in these disquieting days combine to make you doubt or deny your Savior's compassion, then His Word, the mallet of mercy, will break its way through disaster or despair and, as you cling to God's Son, make you exult: *"Nay, in all these things we are more than conquerers through Him that loved us. For I am persuaded that neither death nor life nor angels nor principalities nor powers nor things present nor things to come nor height nor depth nor any other creature shall be able to separate us from the love of God, which is in Christ Jesus, our Lord."* Even if the thoughts of your last hours and the fear of your farewell to this earth rise to dispel your peace of mind, resting on the Easter reassurance, you can cry out: *"O death, where is thy sting? O grave, where is thy victory? . . . Thanks be to God, which giveth us the victory through our Lord Jesus Christ!"* For then you can be sure that one day the hammer of heaven will pound at the door of your grave, and after the Lord of life commands, "Arise," you come forth with a glorious resurrection body, in the likeness of the risen Redeemer.

If, however, you do not have this faith; if stubbornly you resist your Savior, not only will God's hammer smash your pride and unbelief, but God's sickle will also cut you down. You can go on cheating, lying, stealing; you can run around with other women, or, forsaking your husband, you can follow other men and bring heart sorrows to your own family; you can live in drunkenness and lust, in cold hatred and crime; you can curse and blaspheme the Almighty, sneer at the Savior, and shake your fists in challenge against Heaven; you can do all this for a little while, and in your blind conceit boast that sin pays, that you receive rich dividends from your denial of God; yet during this time the celestial sickle is being sharpened! *"Like the grass which groweth up, in the morning it flourisheth . . . in the evening it is cut down, and withereth,"* so your short day of scoffing will suddenly end. For you in hardened unbelief, the Redeemer will become the Reaper; the saving Gospel which you opposed will give way to the sickle; and you will be cut down forever. For some of you this sickle, now raised high, will swing down before you know it.

As we read these words of doom on unbelief, *"He that sat on the cloud,"* our risen and ascended Deliverer, *"thrust in His sickle on the earth; and the earth was reaped,"* may we repent of our transgressions, *"return unto the Lord"* of life, and pray:

O true and Triune God, wield Thy hammer in breaking the crags of crass resistance to Thy saving truth! Yet withhold the sickle of Thy judgment until men accept Christ, our Deliverer. Restrain the reaping of the nations until, by the guidance of the Holy Spirit, we can bring all people the promises of Thy saving Word! We ask it in the blessed name of Jesus, our only but sure Redeemer. *Amen!*

SEEK THE SAVIOR NOW!

"Seek ye the Lord while He may be found, call ye upon Him while He is near. Let the wicked forsake his way, and the unrighteous man his thoughts; and let him return unto the Lord, and He will have mercy upon him; and to our God, for He will abundantly pardon." ISAIAH 55:6-7

O GOD, MERCIFUL AND MIGHTY: We glorify Thee for Thy patient love which repeatedly has reassured us that though we have sinned much, nevertheless Thy greater grace in Jesus, Thy Son our Savior, has remitted and removed our guilt. Preserve us from doubt and despair by leading us ever anew to behold our crucified, risen Redeemer and to trust the promise of Thy Word: "He will abundantly pardon!" We thank Thee also, Father, that Thou hast kept close to us in this country and that Thou hast promised to be found by all who seek Thee. May Thy Spirit lead those sorrowing because of sin and burdened by its weight to acclaim the Christ of all compassion as their Ransom from eternal ruin and their Reconciliation with Thee, our heavenly Father! We praise Thee, that Thou wilt welcome even the worst if only they approach Thee penitently and in humble faith! Use every message which this Lord's Day proclaims Thy divine Word to convict, convince, and convert many! As we plead with Thee to make America contrite and keep it out of war, we beseech Thee to bring the comfort of the Cross into sore, sorrowing hearts, into broken, bereaved homes. Thy saving Son is our last and only Hope for pardon, peace, and Paradise. O give us all full joy in Jesus! *Amen!*

Seek the Savior Now!

As this broadcast, Bringing Christ to the Nations, increases, the opposition to its emphasis on Jesus also grows. In the letters we receive every week from more than one hundred countries and territories outside the United States we find repeated, often blasphemous resistance to the Savior's truth. In Tangier, North Africa, for example, the superpower station Radio International until recently featured our messages in English, French, Spanish, and Arabic. However, the use of this last language started trouble. A local Moslem newspaper protested loudly against airing the Gospel in Arabic and even threatened violence if the station continued to transmit our program in that tongue. Soon the issue became highly political, and excited people took the matter to the Sultan. The owners, unwilling to have Radio International boycotted or to suffer personal injury, gave in to the Moslem demand and dropped our Arabic broadcasts. Temporarily the mosques of Mohammed have defeated Christ's cause; finally, of course, our Lord must win.

This animosity toward the Gospel is particularly impressive since it comes from a part of the world which once was strongly Christian. In the first six centuries after Jesus, His Church spread over North Africa with remarkable rapidity. Forty thousand congregations once flourished there; millions were brought to the saving knowledge of their Redeemer; many Christian schools and charitable institutions were established; mighty religious leaders arose to proclaim the power and permanence of the faith. No fewer than 270 bishops once met in Carthage. In North Africa, it seemed, the Kingdom had a secure stronghold. Yet, as often, prosperity made the churches lazy, worldly, disobedient to the divine Word. Then suddenly came the Mohammedan conquest with its uninterrupted victories. The Crescent supplanted the Cross; the Koran took the place of the Bible; the mosque minarets rose triumphantly over the Christian churches. In our generation, throughout certain North African areas, where faith once flourished, no followers of the Savior survive, no divine Deliverer is worshiped, no hymns are sung to our Lord, no prayers raised in His name.

The Holy Spirit help over-blessed America learn the all-vital lesson that Heaven's grace will not perpetually remain with people who despise it! Russia once had the Son of God, but today, after His name has been blasphemed, His mercy mocked, His redemption ridiculed, Jesus is far from millions. The Almighty highly favored Germany; but it gave the world Bible critics who contradicted divine revelation, atheists who delighted in scurrilous scoffing, Nazi leaders who systematically opposed Scripture; and today thousands of its churches lie in war's rubble. Great Britain, whose colonists once brought the New Testament message to many new settlements throughout the world, is today losing its empire lands and its devotion to the Lord. Hardly 10 per cent of the people in England attend church on Sunday.

We in the United States should remember with pointed warning that our heavenly Father will not indefinitely remain with us if we do not want Him. Should increasing numbers of our citizens constantly reject Him, He will not always shower His blessings on an ungrateful, unbelieving America. The Gospel can continue its westward course to make China, with its 461,000,000 people, and India with its 389,000,000 the world's largest Christian nations.

Seek the Savior Now!

Realize similarly that for your own soul's salvation you cannot go on postponing your decision for God's Son without running the fatal risk of losing Him when you need Him most! Because the Holy Spirit will not everlastingly plead with those who again and again and again push Him aside; because in life's uncertainty delay in acclaiming Christ the Redeemer is more dangerous than ever before, Scripture calls out to you,

SEEK THE SAVIOR NOW!

Heed the words of warning and appeal in our text (Isaiah, chapter fifty-five, verses six and seven): *"Seek ye the Lord while He may be found, call ye upon Him while He is near. Let the wicked forsake his way, and the unrighteous man his thoughts; and let him return unto the Lord, and He will have mercy upon him; and to our God, for He will abundantly pardon!"*

I

WHY? BECAUSE HE IS NOW NEAR
AND CAN BE FOUND

In Jerusalem a manuscript of the Prophet Isaiah's book was recently found which dates from the first century before Christ, at least nine hundred years before the earliest copy heretofore known. For a long time Bible critics confidently asserted that Isaiah did not write the last half of the book bearing his name, and that the fifty-fifth chapter, from which our text is taken, is not his work, but the product of an unidentified author who lived hundreds of years later. The newly discovered manuscript of his prophecies will help disprove these claims and will give added testimony to the truth, endorsed by our Bibles, that Isaiah wrote the entire sixty-six chapters which Scripture ascribes to him. In God's mercy another false theory which men have invented to desecrate the Bible will be overthrown completely, as human investigations confirm our Savior's verdict, *"Thy Word is truth."*

Isaiah himself, no unknown and unnamed person, therefore, penned this magnificent fifty-fifth chapter, the thirteen verses of which, I suggest, you memorize. The opening of this golden section, *"Ho, everyone that thirsteth, come ye to the waters; and he that hath no money, come ye, buy, and eat,"* the marvelous pledge, *"I will make an everlasting covenant with you,"* the strengthening assurance of our text and all the promises of its grace, are rooted in Christ; for only two dozen verses before, in chapter fifty-three, we have eleven plain statements of our Lord's atoning self-sacrifice for our redemption — such radiant guarantees of grace as: *"He was wounded for our transgressions, He was bruised for our iniquities. . . . The Lord hath laid on Him the iniquity of us all." "For the transgression of My people was He stricken." "He bare the sin of many."* Then, beholding this sin-bearing, sin-atoning Son of God, Isaiah, in four short, simple words, gives the most necessary directive and the most blessed instruction men can ever receive, *"Seek ye the Lord!"*

I pray that today the Holy Spirit will indelibly imprint this *"Seek ye the Lord!"* on your soul and make you recognize this finding the Almighty as your highest duty. May the Lord so bless our message today that when it is finished, you who have lived against your heavenly Father will resolve, "The Holy Spirit helping me, henceforth I will seek my God, find Him, and keep Him!"

Seek the Savior Now! 255

It is no secret that our proud world does not heed Isaiah's appeal, *"Seek ye the Lord!"* Despite what we call the advance of civilization, with its increase in schools and culture; despite the heaped-up woes of our generation, the ten millions of military and civilian dead, sacrificed in two gory, global wars, the world is not seeking God. Indeed, this year witnesses history's all-time high in the rise of atheism. Never before, even under the horror-reigns of the worst heathen hellhounds, have so many leaders and so many people in so many lands blasphemously boasted: "There is no God. There is no Christ. There is no heaven, no hell."

Even in countries opposed to organized political godlessness the search for the Almighty is often weak and suppressed. The Pan-American nations recently met in Bogota, Colombia, to emphasize Western Hemisphere solidarity. The question was raised in these conferences whether the convention of all American countries should not invoke divine aid. Both Bolivia and Peru led a movement to recognize the Sovereign of the world; but a Nicaraguan representative objected that this might touch off an undesirable debate. So no prayers for Heaven's guidance were heard at these meetings; and there should be none, since some of the delegates are rabid blasphemers, sworn enemies of the Lord. What happens, then, when men who want to build our Western World cannot meet in prayer, as the First Continental Congress in Philadelphia regularly did? You find the answer in the civil war which shook Colombia, leaving more than a thousand dead on the streets. In Bogota, the very city where the Pan-American conference met, government buildings were set on fire, and property worth millions of dollars destroyed. May we be warned in time! Forsaking God we can expect nothing but resistance, revolution, and ruin. If we need the Almighty properly to preserve a single community, since Scripture declares, *"Except the Lord keep the city, the watchman waketh but in vain,"* how can we hope to keep a continent without Him?

Here in the United States, which of all nations has the most reason to find God, large numbers refuse to seek Him. The quest for His Word is by no means so earnest and persistent in these days of atomic superdestruction as it was in America's yesteryear of peace and prosperity. Recently I came across a collection of official proclamations by governors of various States and was thrilled to read in them the repeated acknowledgment of Christ. Governor Buckingham of Connecticut thanked the Almighty in this statement: "The door of mercy is yet open, through which the guilty may enter and obtain eternal life, by faith in the atonement of Jesus Christ, His Son." Governor Lowe of Iowa declared: "Praise Him [the God of our fathers] for the Christian faith and the spread of our holy religion!" Governor Andrew of Massachusetts asked his people to praise God "for the redemption of the world by Jesus Christ, for the means of grace, and the hope of glory." One of his successors, Governor Rice, directed his fellow citizens to praise God "for the redemption of the world by our Lord and Savior, Jesus Christ, for His holy Word." Governor Olden of New Jersey told the citizens of his State that their greatest reason for thanksgiving was Almighty God's "inestimable gift of His dear Son, Jesus Christ," and "all the blessings of free salvation through Him." See how New York State leaders officially recognized divine grace! Governor Jay magnified the Almighty for the "light and influence of His holy Gospel." Governor Seward praised the Lord for the "blessed hopes of the Gospel of His Son, our Savior," and requested his people to join him in prayer for "that heavenly grace which, with faith in the Lord Jesus Christ, leads . . . to the blessed society of the redeemed in His everlasting kingdom." Governor Bouck raised his voice to exalt God for "the blessed Gospel" and for missionaries who have "gone forward to proclaim *'Christ, and Him crucified.'*" Governor Wright stated, "The gift of a Savior and the full light of divine revelation are spiritual blessings which should awaken to expressions of devout thankfulness the hearts and the voices of a Christian people." A score of other proclamations bring similar convincing proof that in the past our people earnestly sought the Lord.

In our time, however, the picture is changed. Seldom, if ever, do we hear the sacred name of Jesus mentioned in such pronouncements. Even the name of God appears less frequently in our national documents. As the Savior recedes, lawlessness increases. We are the most crime-ridden nation on earth. In a ten-year period more Americans were murdered than were killed in wars during the first century and a half of our existence. The army of our criminals, almost 8,000,000, is larger than our total military forces used against Germany and Japan in the last war. J. Edgar Hoover, head of the Federal Bureau of Investigation, warns, "A creeping rot of moral disintegration is today entering our nation."

Neither do we seek the Lord in education. Now that the Supreme Court has declared illegal the use of school buildings for voluntary released-time religious instruction, some of our school boards have hastened to ban released-time study even in churches. God help the

United States if our children, kept ignorant of the Bible, are instructed daily in courses which do not mention our heavenly Father, and by some teachers, as your letters reveal, who do not hesitate to raise claims contradicting Scripture! The Christian day schools of my Church, open to your boys and girls, will give them instruction in secular knowledge and the necessary guidance in heavenly wisdom. What greater blessing can you offer your child than enrollment in a school where *"the fear of the Lord is the beginning of wisdom"* and the love of the Lord Jesus its glorious end? An educational authority warns us, "What you now put into your schools, in from twenty to thirty years will be the controlling force in the lives of the people." Must we not shudder, then, to think of 1970 or 1980, if the world stands that long, when 17,000,000 of our present school children, without Sunday school training, will be in charge of this country's affairs?

Multitudes in American households are not seeking God. Parents who in selfish, sensual sin have no love for each other, no love for the Savior and, therefore, no love for His Word, refuse to dedicate their dwellings to Christ and to bring up their sons and daughters *"in the nurture and admonition of the Lord."* We bemoan our juvenile delinquency; yet we should be honest enough to admit that masses of our youth have never been equipped to resist evil and find guidance in God. How can we expect our heavenly Father to look graciously upon this nation, when in too many homes the doors are closed to Jesus; when children, who should be esteemed as *"an heritage of the Lord,"* are considered burdens, hindrances, nuisances, and too often destroyed? On this Sunday hundreds of thousands of husbands and wives are scheming and conniving to break their marriage vows. Millions, according to University of Indiana investigations, are serving lust and have deliberately broken their wedding vows. If you are plotting to flout God's holy Law and your own marriage promises, I warn you that these sins of the flesh, far from being smart and fashionable, as their frequent mention in the newspapers may indicate, can destroy your soul in hell! Scripture pleads with you, *"Seek . . . the Lord!"*

Instead of seeking God, great numbers are madly seeking gold. One hundred years ago in Coloma, California, James Marshall happened to spy glittering pieces of the precious metal in a millstream. When soon his discovery was made known, the gold rush was on. Within a year 80,000 men had hurried to California, and within twenty years $600,000,000 worth of gold had been found. Books of great length would be required to describe the ruin, curse of crime, madness of murder with which these riches were secured.

Far outside the gold fields, Scripture's warning, *"The love of money is the root of all evil,"* has proved its truth, as greed leads men to bestiality, war, and massacre. Let people serve the Maker rather than Mammon; take the profit out of bloodshed; draft money as well as men; do this over the entire globe, and you will have the best possible human guarantee of peace.

Are you seeking gold instead of God? Are you so engrossed with business and profit making that you have no interest or energy left for your Lord, your home, your own soul? Have you, Judas-like, betrayed your Savior and sold yourself for silver? Are you so money-mad that you strive for gain at others' loss, gain for yourself by helping destroy the purity and decency of your fellow men? Is money your master? Then the Holy Spirit has led you before your radio to tell you: "*Seek . . . the Lord!*" Your riches, though you have millions, can disappear overnight. Even if you heap up billions and keep them — far from buying your way into heaven, they can help send you to hell.

In place of seeking God, multitudes throughout the world are pursuing sordid sin, *"the lust of the flesh and the lust of the eyes and the pride of life."* For every dollar given the Church for spreading the Gospel, a thousand dollars are paid for evil which can destroy the soul forever. Many think more of liquor than of the Lord. We have 437,000 taverns within our borders, two for every church, and the arrests for drunkenness constantly increase.

This "*Seek . . . the Lord*" is the repeated appeal of divine truth in more than seventy Old Testament passages. Listen to these heroes of faith: David: *"Set your heart and your soul to seek the Lord!"* Zephaniah: *"Seek ye the Lord!"* Hosea: *"It is time to seek the Lord!"* They speak to your soul. You need God if you would have joy here and eternal happiness hereafter; if you are to overcome the power and punishment of your guilt, defeat the grief and gruesomeness of the grave, escape the agonies of hell and the anguish of eternal damnation. Do you want a sure Rock of Refuge to which you can cling amid the storm of life's sorrows? Then *"seek . . . the Lord"!* Ignore Him, reject Him, as some of you now do, and you will be crushed more completely than a caterpillar beneath a steam roller. The Almighty will wipe out your resistance to His will more quickly than a bulldozer crushes an anthill. You can live your short life in defiance of your heavenly Father, but you cannot escape His final judgment.

Infidels, of course, scoff at the mention of judgment and hell. Atheists in our country sarcastically advertise an imaginary liquid, "Asbestosin," which, they sneer, "fireproofs the soul." They report in ridicule, "Rubbed briskly on the chest, Asbestosin penetrates the entire body and renders the soul of even the most hardened sinner immune to hell's hottest flames." Hell is no joke. The rich man who there pleaded for a single drop of water learned this, just as every modern blasphemer must. Why is it that such mockery often turns to stark, raving madness in life's last hours? Is it not because scoffers can no longer smile away the dread of eternity and the doom of damnation?

Marvelously merciful beyond everything we deserve in our rebellion against God is Scripture's pledge, *"If ye seek Him, He will be found of you,"* stated almost in the same language for your personal reassurance, *"If thou seek Him, He will be found of thee!"* In hundreds of thousands of instances fathers have disowned their ungrateful, disrespectful children, banished their own flesh and blood from their homes forever. Men's laws, some of the earliest we know, permitted parents thus to cut off their sons and daughters from family and inheritance rights. How much more would the Most High be justified in disowning every one of us because of our thankless unbelief, our continued disobedience to His Law, our utter disregard of His love? How completely even our human sense of right and justice would be compelled to agree if the Holy One had decreed for us: "You chose sin instead of Me; you preferred lust to your Lord; you decided for gold rather than God; you deliberately selected hell instead of heaven. I am through with you. Don't seek Me, because you will never find Me!"

What measureless mercy our Father's love for us eternally, hopelessly, helplessly lost sinners, that His Word issues the urgent directive, *"Seek . . . the Lord,"* and that on the basis of Christ's Gospel grace we can tell you: If you really want to find God, you can. Whatever your sins have been — and our large listeners' mail brings confessions of shocking crime, including murder; wherever you are — and we hear from prisoners in State and Federal penitentiaries; from distressed souls, fugitives from their own home, who are ashamed to continue staying with their loved ones; however your life is burdened and blighted — and never before have so many been disquieted by nervous disorders, shaken by the fear of having committed the unforgivable sin; whoever you are, high or low, rich or poor, white or black, cultured or unschooled, and whyever you are what you are, listen as in divine truth we assure you: if you want the loving Guide to glory, seek Him now, and by His own promise you will find Him!

Do I hear you ask, repeating unconsciously this ancient question recorded in Scripture, *"Oh, that I knew where I might find Him!"?* Do you really want to know the way to the Lord from your sins, sufferings, and sorrows, the path to pardon, peace, the guarantee that God is with you and because He loves you, He will never forsake you? Then let me give you, not a human guess or wish or theory about the Almighty, but in Heaven's highest truth let me show you your God in Christ, whom these messages, on the basis of Old Testament and New, Prophets and Apostles, Psalms and Epistles, declare to be the one God, the eternal God, together with the Father and the Spirit the true, the only God!

Because Jesus said, *"He that hath seen Me hath seen the Father,"* and again, *"I and My Father are one";* because He was acclaimed by Heaven and the holy angels as God; because His divine power and knowledge and love proved Him God, we will not be satisfied with any acknowledgment of the Master, however high-sounding it may be, which does not go all the way and, bowing humbly in His presence, acclaim Him, *"My Lord and my God!"*

If, then, you have been seeking God, your search is over. Here, in the Christ who trod the pathways of Palestine, is your God, my God, everyone's God, with all the love and power required to bring you into heaven. Jesus is also your divine Redeemer from ruin, your Savior from sin, your Deliverer from death. If until this moment you have thought of Christ only vaguely as a figure in ancient history who brought men a message of hope and who was mistakingly nailed to a cross, then give me your close attention! He is as much greater than all this as the wide Atlantic is larger than a single drop of water. He did what only God-made-Man could do: He took your place in suffering the penalties of your rebellion against the Lord; He removed your iniquities, transferring them to Himself, so that you could escape their penalty. He pleaded an unconditional "Guilty" to the charges raised against you, so that your punishment is paid and the true indictment against you canceled. This He did in the mightiest masterpiece of mercy when, tortured in soul and body in your stead and your behalf, He died your death on Calvary's cursed tree in full, final atonement of your sins.

Therefore find *"the unsearchable riches of Christ,"* which are yours when you acclaim Him the Savior of your soul! He offers forgiveness of all your guilt, the complete, eternal removal of every transgression, so that once you believe your iniquities are washed away by His blood, no power in earth or hell can ever bring them back. Christ offers you, whom He purchased with His death agony, the divine comfort which many of you need, that trials and tribulations come to God's children from His love, to chasten, purify, refine them, to weaken their reliance on men and fortify their trust in the Almighty. Jesus grants those who are His strength to resist temptation and reject evil. He makes every believer, reborn by His Spirit, a new creature dedicated to godliness, honesty, cleanness, courage. In His all-powerful, all-knowing love, by day and by night, He guards the bodies and souls of His faithful and gives His angels charge over them. Reliance on His mercy fills fear-beset hearts with contentment that "whatever God ordains is good." When you can say, "I am trusting Thee, Lord Jesus, trusting only Thee," you are guided by His constant comradeship, as, unseen yet certainly, He walks at your side and fulfills His promise, *"Lo, I am with you alway."* By faith in Christ you are filled with inner joy, however heavy life's outward sorrows may be. You have peace in a world of strife, because you know that your heavenly Father loves you, that your conscience has been quieted. Following the Savior's example, your soul is stirred by sympathy for your suffering fellow man, and instead of giving way to dark thoughts of revenge and retaliation, you ask that your enemies be forgiven, and you strive to lead them to the Lord. When the Son of God is truly enthroned in your heart, you have His own promise of answered prayer. When you can sing in truth, "My hope is built on nothing less than Jesus' blood and righteousness," you enjoy, even here on earth, the beginning of an eternal life with unspeakable bliss; you have the guarantee of a personally prepared place in heaven, the pledge of marvelously resurrected bodies, and the promise that you *"shall be like Him,"* ever privileged to behold the living Son of God, together with the Father and the Spirit, in the radiance of the heavenly realms.

Do you wonder, then, that all these blessings combine to cry out: Seek the Savior *now?* You must start your search for Him during this life, since it will be too late in the next. You will have no second chance to accept Christ after your body is laid into the grave. When Scripture says clearly, *"It is appointed unto men once to die, but after this the judgment,"* dare you contradict this and claim that besides heaven and earth there is a third place of purging, where after death you can undo your unbelief? You must *"seek . . . the Lord"* now.

Again, don't make the mistake of thinking that you will come to Jesus at some indefinite, later time. The Almighty is not like a machine which can be set into motion by pushing a button. You should not keep on rejecting Him in incessant unbelief and then, when sudden sorrow comes, quickly summon Him. Divine patience is long-suffering, but it is not endless. See how God dealt with His people in the Old Testament! Repeatedly they provoked Him to anger by their idolatry but just as repeatedly He forgave and restored them. He led them out of Egypt, but they rose in rebellion to worship a golden calf. He guided them through the desert, but they murmured against Him. He divided the Jordan before them and brought them into Canaan, but they departed from Him. He awakened judges and leaders for them, but they forsook Him. He sent them Prophets and priests, but the masses rejected them. He gave them kings and princes, but these turned from Him. He dispatched messengers who appealed for repentance and return, but they killed them. Century after century He stretched His arms toward His people, but they turned their backs on Him. Then, after almost endless appeal and affliction had proved useless, His patience was exhausted, and Israel sentenced itself to suffer the punishment of divine wrath. Its cities were destroyed, its territory taken, its people exiled and dispersed.

No wonder our text cries out, *"Seek ye the Lord while He may be found!"* The time may come when you cannot find God. How often fatal accidents leave no time to *"seek . . . the Lord"*! How frequently, in lingering sicknesses, do long periods of coma, unconsciousness, delirium, loss of mind, make it impossible to *"seek . . . the Lord"*! How completely can atomic destruction — and experts see other nations making these bombs within a few years — cut off church services — even in this country! When our text directs, *"Seek ye the Lord while He may be found,"* believe that the Holy Spirit Himself pleads that you stop resisting your Redeemer and from this moment on begin to *"seek . . . the Lord"*!

Emphasizing this sacred appeal, the text continues, *"Call . . . upon Him while He is near!"* Often when God has remained close to a people only to have them shun His mercy, He turns away. Today in Europe He is far from the army of atheist Communists who blaspheme His name, much farther than ever from masses in nations where churches have been destroyed, Bibles burned in bombings, clergymen killed or captured in war. Yet He is coming closer to others who have never really known Him, in countries like Japan, where the door has been opened for Christian teachers, where state Shintoism is being discarded as a failure, where the demand for Testaments constantly increases and the opportunities for mission work register new heights.

Similarly the radio has brought the Gospel close to you, right into your homes. God's Word, distributed in millions of copies throughout these United States, puts the saving truth into your hands. If for twenty, thirty, forty, fifty, sixty years you persistently spurn the Lord, can you blame Him if, as you harden your heart, He will not always remain as close to you as He is in this moment, when He asks you to seek your Savior now?

In His compassion God *"is near"* in your trials and troubles. A Texas listener writes: "It was through you that I came to know the Bible, and through the Bible I came to know Jesus as my Savior from sin. My husband, who formerly was a drunkard and mistreated my eight children and me, is now changing into a better person through reading the Bible."

God *"is near"* in your moments of deep despair. A friend in Cuba says: "Last Sunday I was on the verge of taking my own life when I happened to tune in your message and hear that there is peace for me in Christ. That sermon changed my attitude toward life, and I have surrendered my soul to God."

Praise divine goodness, God *"is near"* in your sickness and pain! A deeply afflicted person in British Guiana testifies: "It has taken me two years and nine months in the best sanitarium to come to the knowledge of God.

Through your goodness, by your spreading the Gospel to all nations of the world, through your efforts before I left the sanitarium, I came to the knowledge of God. Your words have brought hope, courage, faith, and strength to me."

An Alabama young man sends us these lines: "I had an uncle who in his younger life and also in his middle age was a very wicked man. Then suddenly he became blind, and at first he was as mean as Satan wanted him to be; but my grandmother bought a radio for him, and your broadcast helped win his soul for Christ. He would sit by his radio and weep and pray over his sins. He died in the faith." After you hear these letters, ask yourself if your sufferings have not been sent you so that, finding God close, you will *"call . . . upon Him while He is near"!*

The Lord may be nearer to you today than ever again. Seek Him and find Him! *"Seek the Lord, and ye shall live,"* He promises. Why run the risk of living another week without Jesus? Why delay another day, another hour, another minute, before coming to Him? Find Him, on this Sunday, through this broadcast! Seek your Savior now!

II

HOW? BY REPENTANCE AND FAITH!

"How," some of you are asking, "can I, sin-stained and sin-cursed, ever approach the holy God? How can I, with all my guilt, draw near to the Almighty, sinless, stainless as He is?" Because this Gospel message may be the last some of you will hear, I give you a clear answer on the basis of Scripture itself, our text's golden guarantee of grace. How can you come before the Most

High? Isaiah replies, and we join him, *"Let the wicked forsake his way, and the unrighteous man his thoughts!"*

You see, then, first of all, that because God does not exclude *"the wicked"* and *"the unrighteous,"* He is ready to receive you. No sin is too great, no crime too shocking to bar you from His presence, if only you come before Him in the one way, the sure way, the only way His mercy and wisdom have decreed.

Our text outlines the start in this approach to God when it says, *"Let the wicked* FORSAKE HIS WAY, *and the unrighteous man* HIS THOUGHTS!*"* To begin with, your heavenly Father requires repentance. He wants you to confess your sins, show heartfelt sorrow for the evil which has stained your mind, mouth, and hands.

If up to this time you have thought lightly of your transgression, compared yourself favorably with hardened criminals, repeated the prayer of the proud Pharisee, *"God, I thank Thee that I am not as other men are, extortioners, unjust, adulterers,"* remember, as our Scripture warns, that selfish, impure, hate-filled *"thoughts"* condemn you! The lustful longings of your heart, the greedy, grasping impulses of your soul, the envy and malice in your spirit — the All-knowing sees these, for it is written, *"The Lord knoweth the thoughts of man."* He wants you to repent of them, renounce and reject them.

In all the world and in all its ages there is one path to the pure life God demands — faith in Jesus Christ. Nothing but His atoning love can make and keep the pledge, *"Though your sins be as scarlet, they shall be as white as snow; though they be red like crimson, they shall be as wool."* Our Savior suffered for all sins, the transgressions in thought, word, act; and when, firmly relying on His redeeming love, we, *"the wicked"* and *"the unrighteous,"* *"return unto the Lord,"* then, as Isaiah's faith-building fifty-fifth chapter says at the beginning, *"Without money and without price,"* without good intentions or good works, without penance or payment, we have this double, divine pledge: *"He will have mercy,"* and *"He will abundantly pardon."* All that any arch scoffer needs to find a gracious God is contrite trust in his Lord and Redeemer. Then, without any condition or credential, without any question or qualification, without any exception or exaggeration, the vilest criminal is pardoned and purified by faith because Jesus *"bare our sins in His own body on the tree"* and by His atoning self-sacrifice made us sin-free in Heaven's sight.

"He will abundantly pardon." Believe that all-embracing guarantee of grace! The love of the Almighty is not limited, nor does He forgive grudgingly. His mercy is offered everyone, regardless of country, class, color, condition, for His promise proclaims, *"God so loved the world that He gave His only-begotten Son, that whosoever believeth in Him should not perish, but have everlasting life."* His abundant mercy atones for every sin, even those transgressions the memories of which leave you sleepless, remorseful, and wretched; for the truth which can never be mistaken testifies, *"The blood of Jesus Christ, His Son, cleanseth us from all sin."* You may be a great sinner, but thank God, Christ is a greater Savior. He does not draw fine, narrow lines when He forgives; He does not measure His mercy under a microscope nor restrict it to the lowest hairbreadth mark. By His abundant atonement we know that *"where sin abounded, grace did much more abound."* One drop of

our dying Redeemer's blood can cleanse a world of wicked men. One prayer from a dying thief was answered by the promise of Paradise.

One plea for His mercy will make Him your Deliverer this day. In this moment, when the Holy Spirit urges you to seek Jesus *"while He may be found"* and *"while He is near,"* resolve, with divine help, to forsake sin's way, to *"return unto the Lord,"* whom many of you once knew but traitorously denied, to call upon Christ in this very hour! Then, trusting His victory over death and hell, you can bow down before your Lord in the joy and exultation which rejoices, "*'He will have mercy'* on me and *'He will abundantly pardon'* my sins." Above every other blessing, God give you that faith now, for Jesus' sake! *Amen!*

JESUS NEVER LEAVES US

"He led them out as far as to Bethany, and He lifted up His hands and blessed them. And it came to pass, while He blessed them He was parted from them and carried up into heaven. And they worshiped Him and returned to Jerusalem with great joy; and were continually in the Temple, praising and blessing God. Amen." SAINT LUKE 24:50-53

JESUS, OUR RULER AND REDEEMER: Thou art eternally enthroned in heaven, at the right hand of Thy Father; yet, praise Thine eternal love, Thou art also ever with us both in our joy and in our sorrow. Thou didst give Thyself, Thine own holy body and sinless soul, into death on the cross of pain and shame, so that merely by believing this grace in repentant, trusting hearts we are saved freely and forever; yet in measureless mercy, ascended in glory, Thou dost still intercede for us when we forget Thee and thanklessly rebel against Thee. Thou hast returned to Thy celestial realm, yet Thou wilt also come again in power and glory to judge the quick and the dead and to take Thy faithful home to heaven with Thee! Oh, what a wonderful Savior Thou art, with pardon for every transgression, comfort for each heartache, power in all weaknesses, peace in a world of war, and after life's end the pledge of Paradise with Thee! Bring many this day to faith in Thy forgiving love! Bless the United States with repentance and reliance on Thee! Sustain the sorrowing, supply the starving, support the sick and dying! We have no help or hope but in Thee; therefore bless us now with firm trust in Thy saving truth, and in Thy good time bring us all to Thee in Thy Father's many mansions! *Amen!*

Jesus Never Leaves Us

WHEN Gandhi, liberty-loving Indian patriot, died, his funeral drew larger throngs than any other burial in our age. A million Hindus and Moslems gathered mournfully at the burning ghat on the banks of the sacred Jumna River, where a pyre with 1,200 pounds of sandalwood, 320 pounds of melted butter, 160 pounds of incense, and 30 pounds of camphor cremated his body. Multitudes — far greater than those which visited the funeral train of Abraham Lincoln — lined the 500-mile railroad right-of-way to see the draped coaches slowly carry his remains to the Ganges River. More than two million Indians, priests and politicians, fakirs and farmers, dancing girls and destitutes crowded the river edge, thousands up to their necks in water, while Gandhi's third son mixed milk from a "sacred" cow with his father's ashes and poured them into the Ganges River. Similar exercises were held on the shores of six other "sacred" streams, while cannon roared seventy-nine salutes, one for each of Gandhi's years. Thus, on the day after India's apostle of freedom said he might live to be 125 years old, his mortal frame disappeared from view.

How different, in contrast, was Christ's departure from this earth in the Ascension which His churches commemorate on Thusday of this week! Not eleven million mourners, only eleven hopeful disciples were with Him when He left this world. No military might was displayed in His final hours, for Jesus was the Prince of Peace. No long funeral cortege, no rose-strewn procession marked His last journey, which was only a few short miles filled with quiet teaching. No fire consumed His body, and no river received His ashes; for our Lord, who bade His followers farewell, was not dead, but resurrected from the grave, alive in radiant love. No wailing or lamenting was heard when He left His friends; rather were they filled *"with great joy,"* for they knew in exultant assurance that, though their Master had disappeared from their sight, He still would be with them always, ready to sustain and strengthen them in their weaknesses and fears.

What a wonderful Savior and Sovereign Jesus is! Visibly He ascends into heaven and leaves His messengers; but spiritually and unseen He is ever with them! As we study the story of His majestic return to His heavenly realm, I tell you, especially the deserted, the downhearted, the distressed, the despairing, that once we are Christ's in trusting, triumphant faith, we have this guarantee of glorious grace:

JESUS NEVER LEAVES US

We find this personal assurance in the Ascension record, chosen as the text for this Sunday, the closing words of Saint Luke's Gospel (chapter twenty-four, verses fifty to fifty-three): *"He led them out as far as to Bethany, and He lifted up His hands and blessed them. And it came to pass, while He blessed them, He was parted from them and carried up into heaven. And they worshiped Him and returned to Jerusalem with great joy; and were continually in the Temple, praising and blessing God. Amen."*

I

HE MAY SEEM TO DISAPPEAR AS HE DID
AT HIS ASCENSION

A month and a third after His glorious resurrection, according to the Savior's schedule of salvation, the time had come when He was to return to His Father. It would have been abundant grace if our Lord, having emerged from His grave, triumphant over death, had appeared only once to His disciples and then left this world forever. Yet in His radiantly resurrected body He repeatedly came to His followers during almost six sacred weeks. Today it takes influence and favor to secure a ten-minute appointment with big-name political leaders; but in our blessed Redeemer's abundant compassion, Jesus never did anything in a small, narrow, restricted way. He reserved forty full days for the men who were to be the messengers of His mercy.

He has given some of you more than forty years; during this time, however, you have spurned His love. Or, if you have pledged yourself to Him, you still show fear, smallness of faith, lack of true trust in His divine power to *"save . . . to the uttermost."* Some of you are believers in name only, with head creed and lip worship which permit you to live for the world, without the fire of true zeal, the joy of salvation, and the assurance of your redemption. Ask your heavenly Father to forgive you for Jesus' sake; and when Christ, through His Spirit, seeks entrance to your soul, open your heart to Him and make every day a treasured time for coming closer to your divine Deliverer!

If you unbelievers would spend some of your leisure with God's Son, meet Him regularly in His Word — the Savior had His lifetime for you — then you could be brought to full faith. In the land for which Gandhi lived and died, a lad grew up in a Brahman family utterly opposed to the Christian truth. A preacher of the Gospel frequently visited their village; but each time this man of God appeared, this boy gathered his gang, hid them in the thicket beside the road, and had them stone the teacher when he passed. One night, after the routine rock-hurling, one of the believers caught the lad and brought him to the missionary. Instead of punishing the lad, the preacher of New Testament peace treated him kindly and spoke to him in words of love. When they parted, the boy promised his new-found friend to read the copy of the Gospel he there received. Spending this time with his Redeemer, the lad was converted by the Spirit, and some years later the former ruffian became the principal of a Christian training institute in Madras. He writes, "Life has not been easy . . . but in return I found Christ as Lord." If you would dedicate only one hour during each of the next forty days to Him who gave His entire life for you, you could learn the marvelous treasures of truth in His Word.

The disciples needed these forty days with Jesus, for their all-too-human hearts were still entranced by dreams of power and prominence. They were to take the Lord's place, serving as His representatives in spreading the Gospel, and they needed encouragement for the hardships ahead. Christ's farewell instruction was short and unmistakable: *"Go ye into all the world, and preach the Gospel to every creature!"* These six words, *"Preach the Gospel to every creature!"* are the Church's charter. If only, with the wealth and opportunities at our disposal, we had the fire required to fulfill this command as fully as did those persecuted disciples! Bring this message of Christ's full, free, and final salvation to the far corners of the six continents — and who has been as eminently able to fulfill this commission as our generation, with its money and manpower, its radios and printing presses, its streamliners and airplanes? — make the Gospel of Christ's blood-bought salvation truly global by teaching uncounted myriads of souls in all heathen strongholds the message of God's Son, who died for them; and merely as a by-product of world evangelization, we will check international slaughter, restrain the conflict between class, creed, color in our country, and enjoy the highest happiness men and nations can ever know.

Because, as our Lord Himself declares, the *"prince of this world"* is the devil, men resist the saving Gospel. Even the churches, on the conscience of whose members our Lord has laid the world-wide preaching of His cleansing blood and atoning death, are often cold, slow, timid in fulfilling His final directive. Our hope lies not in the United Nations (a committee of experts appointed by the President reports that no international covenants, treaties, or organizations are yet a sure pledge of peace); nor in military might (for the pages of the past have shown that those who thought they possessed the strongest armies and navies were the first to use them). The promise for a war-weary age lies in fulfilling the divine commission to spread the Good News of a Savior slain for the sins of an evil world. Therefore, while political leaders, many of them violent atheists pledged to destroy the churches, make proposals and veto them; while secret laboratories behind well-guarded walls in this country and iron curtains in Europe feverishly work to produce more frightful means of mass destruction, may you know Jesus, hear Him say before His ascension, *"Ye shall be witnesses unto Me,"* and resolve that by your prayers, gifts, and personal testimony you will spread His saving grace! Plead for Bringing Christ to the Nations, as never before, so that in heroic advance we may soon bring the Gospel not only, as at present, to one hundred countries and territories, but to two hundred, and finally to all lands!

For the tremendous hardships of their task the disciples needed divine comfort and strength; and their loving Savior would not leave this earth without offering them the rich resources of His unfailing counsel. The other day a man died suddenly in New York, without telling anyone, even his wife, where he had hidden one million dollars in bills. Far worse, some of you are on your way to the grave without ever having opened your mouths earnestly to reveal *"the unsearchable riches of Christ"* to a single poor, struggling soul. Our Lord does not keep His counsel silenced. As Saint Mark fully records, He assured His questioning disciples, overcome by the heavy responsibilities of their world mission, that He would bless their efforts, protect them in danger, and support them by His miraculous power.

He is the God of consolation for you, too. His guarantee of grace, *"Come unto Me, all ye that labor and are heavy laden, and I will give you rest,"* is offered you. If only you truly trust Him and believe that when He says, *"Let not your heart be troubled," "My peace I give unto you," "I will not leave you comfortless,"* He voiced Heaven's own truth, which can raise your soul from the depths of gloom, you, too, will experience that when the time comes for a loved one or even you yourself to leave this earth, Christ's victory over death will help you triumph over fear.

Finally, then, the hour struck for Jesus' return to His heavenly Father. His work was done; mankind had been redeemed; the blood which flowed from the wounds of His martyred body, nailed to Calvary's gory timbers, had cleansed the world of all sin. Nothing necessary for your salvation remained undone. Had He not cried on the cross, *"It is finished"?* Does not His Word assure us, *"Ye are complete in Him"?* Do not let men of unbelief or the devils of doubt tear this truth from your heart: the Son of God gave His soul and body as the full and final atonement for humanity throughout the centuries! By His taking the sinners' place, suffering the penalty of their transgressions, enduring the curse of their crimes, dying the death we had deserved as the penalty of our rebellion against the Almighty, Christ paid the whole price of our redemption, left nothing unsaid, unfulfilled, unearned, unfinished, uncertain concerning our eternal deliverance. We do not preach a possible pardon in the crucified and triumphantly resurrected Redeemer; but we do proclaim a finished forgiveness, a perfected pardon, an accomplished atonement.

In 1937 the court of Ebensberg, Pennsylvania, ordered a man in that city to pay a doctor's bill of $128 at the rate of $1 every week. In a little more than two years, the obligation was fully met; but for nine years thereafter, until the present, the Pennsylvania man who moves from place to place about the country, continues to send in the dollar every week, and court officials feel that, having misunderstood the order, he will continue to pay and pay until he dies. You may be guilty of a far more serious error. Twice the Bible tells us, *"Whosoever shall call on the name of the Lord shall be saved";* but you set yourself above this doubly divine statement and think that you must earn what Christ Himself earned forever and for everyone with His crucifixion. Entire chapters of Scripture, like the fourth and fifth of Romans, assure you that *"we were reconciled to God by the death of His Son,*" and declare, *"Therefore we conclude that a man is justified by faith without the deeds of the Law"*; yet you hold that you know more than God, that Calvary's grace is not sufficient for you. You set yourselves to the treadmill task of substituting your merit for the Savior's mercy. Be assured, then, that Jesus would not have gone back to heaven had the smallest part of His redemptive work remained uncompleted! If after they have bombed cities to ruin, wartime fliers strive to return to their base and report, "Mission accomplished," do you believe that the perfect, all-powerful Son of God would go home to heaven without being able to say, "Father, Thy mission of rescuing the human race from ruin is accomplished for all times?"

Our Lord ascended also because Scripture, as He Himself, had repeatedly foretold this triumph. Old Testament Prophets predicted, *"God is gone up with a shout,"* and again, *"Thou hast ascended on high."* The Savior plainly promised, *"I go My way to Him that sent Me"*; and again, *"I leave the world and go to the Father"*; still again, *"I ascend unto My Father and your Father, and to My God and your God,"* and in His merciful abundance once more, *"Ye shall see the Son of Man ascend up where He was before."* These are sacred pledges which had to be fulfilled. Christ always keeps His Word. In the turmoil and treachery of our war-cursed age, world figures have often broken their treaties. Those battling in Palestine know that national leaders can contradict themselves and nullify their previous guarantees; but you can always trust the Lord. *"Try Me,"* He says; and if in all sincerity you do try Him; if you scan the pages of history to see whether He has fulfilled His threats and kept His covenants, you will

Jesus Never Leaves Us 281

be confronted by a convincing demonstration of divine power. Though you may not realize it, the prophetic warnings of His consuming anger are being executed on atheist lands, as on the lives of unbelievers who have risen up against the Almighty but are being crushed by the agonies of His judgment. Why do you not stop resisting the Lord and learn with Paul that *"it is hard for thee to kick against the pricks"?* Why not trust Christ and experience the gentle healing mercies of His grace?

As the exact hour of departure drew near, our text tells us, *"He led them"* [His disciples] *"out as far as to Bethany."* Today, when world figures leave, they lead no more; but because Jesus is our God, and *"death hath no more dominion over Him,"* even after Golgotha, He still leads, and blessed are those who follow Him. Do you walk in His footsteps, as His will and way are outlined in the Bible? If you can truly sing, "Savior, I follow on, guided by Thee," then in the cruelest hours you will be assured that His direction is always right, planned to bring you from sorrow to joy, from question to conviction, from cross to crown.

Note also that our blessed Redeemer *"led them out as far as to Bethany,"* the village just outside Jerusalem in which He had often found warm welcome. Our Lord comes back in His last moments on earth to the place which had eagerly greeted Him. Repeatedly will He return to your home if you receive and revere Him. He plainly shows His preference for those places where His love reigns supreme. Communities most loyal to the Gospel are usually the happiest, the most crime-free and the most richly blessed. Help make your town a

"Bethany," by bringing Christ into the hearts of its people!

It took only a few moments for the Master and His eleven followers to climb to the spot on the Mount of Olives where His feet would touch the ground for the last time. Before Jesus returned to His Father, He imparted one farewell token of His devotion. Our text tells us, *"He lifted up His hands and blessed them."* If only we knew the words of that final utterance on earth, which stands out in sharp contrast to the curses with which unbelievers often breathe their last! Whatever that parting prayer and promise was, thank God that His Son wants to give you His benediction! Have you read these glorious six words of marvelous mercy, *"God . . . sent Him to bless you"*? The Savior has blessings for soul and body, blessings for home and country, blessings for parents and children, blessings for white and black, blessings for rich and ragged, blessings for healthy and sick, blessings for life and death. Why stubbornly deprive yourself of His heavenly help, when He is ready to bless you this day, if only you come before Him penitently and prayerfully to proclaim Him your Redeemer?

Then our text records, *"It came to pass, while He blessed them, He was parted from them and carried up into heaven."* Skeptics have denied that this happened; but pre-announced in prophecy, twice recorded in the Gospels, and repeatedly mentioned in the Epistles, this Ascension is the absolute, eternal, unchangeable truth. God stop you from tampering with His Word! If you must, rather play with forked lightning or atomic bombs; but keep your blasphemous hands from slashing Scripture! We cannot understand how Jesus could defy the laws of gravity; but this is because of our own limited reason. Men require airplanes or balloons today when they seek to explore the skies above; and if mere mortals by their own invention can soar high into the stratosphere, why should we doubt that the Almighty who made man, the materials of his aircraft, and the ether itself, cannot ascend as the Bible says He did? Saint Luke closes our text and his book with the word, *"Amen."* This gives double assurance to the fact which all believers confess in the Apostolic Creed, "He ascended into heaven."

Learn to regard the Savior's return to the realms of glory as the mighty climax in His career of compassion, the victory of victories! The ascended Christ is no longer the humiliated, crucified *"Man of Sorrows,"* but the Lord of Lords, the King of Kings, the Sovereign of Sovereigns; and now, His battle won, He proceeds in triumph to the celestial splendor. Do you remember the parades held a few years ago when our victorious troops came back from overseas? The cheering and shouting then was a hoarse whisper in comparison with the acclaim at Christ's majestic entry into the eternal Paradise. He is greeted by the hosts of angels; and remember, according to Scripture, these emissaries of divine might could devastate cities or wipe out armies. He is received with glory by archangels, the mightiest of these mighty messengers who sang God's praises when the earth was created. In a moment of supreme magnificence, He is welcomed by His Father in a scene of celestial splendor far beyond our poor powers of perception. The Conqueror of sin, death, and hell is ascended, amid the acclaim of angelic hallelujahs, to occupy His throne at the right hand of the Almighty.

II

YET HE WILL ALWAYS SURELY BE WITH HIS OWN

If such jubilation re-echoed through the new Jerusalem, how sad, you may feel, the eleven men must have been when their Lord left them near the Judean Jerusalem! Yet our text contradicts the thought that the disciples were distressed by Christ's departure. At first we may be surprised to read, *"They worshiped Him and returned to Jerusalem with great joy";* but when we find the deeper meaning of the Ascension, we can understand their reason for rejoicing. Saint Matthew tells us that in one of His last utterances Jesus assured them, *"Lo, I am with you alway, even unto the end of the world";* and because these eleven faithful followers believed every word of this promise, they knew that though their Teacher might physically disappear from their sight, yet by His pledge of everlasting comradeship He would ever be close to them.

This is the strengthening comfort the Ascension gives today after nineteen crime-marked centuries: Christ is ever with those who worship Him. Believers, risen triumphantly over sin and sorrow, can confidently exult: Jesus never leaves us.

Though the Savior has ascended into heaven, He still is with us in His omnipotent might. *"All power is given unto Me in heaven and in earth,"* He told His messengers in those farewell moments. During the First World War many thrones collapsed in Europe, and crowns were removed as the Romanovs, the Hapsburgs, the Hohenzollerns, all royal families, fled or were assassinated. After the Second World War, more monarchs lost their scepters. One Italian king abdicated, another, banned from office, went into exile. A Communist replaced a king in Yugoslavia, Bulgaria, Albania, and recently in Romania. Throughout Europe only six thrones of importance remain, and some of these are tottering. Thank God with me that our divine Ruler will never desert us! Atheists may boast, "We have destroyed the kings of the earth; now let us destroy the King of the skies"; but will they? In their most vicious attacks they cannot even touch the Almighty. Once the hour of divine vengeance comes, these infidel blasphemers, however powerful they may seem at this moment, will be pulverized in defeat.

Find assurance, therefore, for your own soul in the fact that Christ, Ruler of heaven and earth, is with you, His disciple, in every need! He has fully defeated the foes of your faith. If the devil of doubt makes you wonder whether your sins are not too great to be forgiven; if you seem to be losing in life's battle; if you feel overwhelmed by the opposition before you; if you greet each day with fear and trembling, remember Jesus still reigns! With Him at your side you can batter down every boasting enemy of your soul, confidently believing, *"This is the victory that overcometh the world, even our faith."* Our Lord has never been conquered. Receive Him as your divine Redeemer, trust Him without question, and you can join the Apostle in this challenge: *"Who shall separate us from the love of Christ? Shall tribulation, or distress, or persecution, or famine, or nakedness, or peril, or sword? . . . Nay, in all these things we are more than conquerors through Him that loved us."*

Because Jesus promises every believer, *"I will never leave thee nor forsake thee,"* your heart, as was the disciples', can be filled with *"great joy."* His followers never have reason to hang their heads in defeat. Through the

Savior they have become sons and daughters of the almighty God. *"I can do all things through Christ, which strengtheneth me,"* the Apostle declares, and with a firmly rooted faith, built on our Lord's promises, you enjoy the same guarantee of grace. When the unbreakable Word declares, *"Fear thou not, for I am with thee; be not dismayed, for I am thy God; I will strengthen thee; yea, I will help thee; yea, I will uphold thee with the right hand of My righteousness,"* trust it, and you will truly triumph over the grim terrors now defeating many of you: the fear of death, the fear of loss, the fear of sickness, the fear of exposure, the fear of having placed yourself outside the pale of the Savior's mercy!

Therefore, don't torture yourself any longer by halting uncertainly between the two opinions: Christ can help me, and Christ cannot help me! Think of Him, enthroned, higher than the cherubim and the seraphim, in eternal omnipotence! Recall His pledge, *"If ye have faith . . . nothing shall be impossible unto you"!* Believe this, and, Jesus with you in His limitless might, you will overcome the world!

The disciples were filled with joy, although such partings are otherwise marked with sorrow, since they knew that the Son of God, who had ascended into the realm of glory, would still be with them. He would be at the right hand of His Father, not only as the Ruler of heaven and earth, but also as their Representative before the celestial throne. The other night I explained to a businessman the intercession which Jesus constantly raises in behalf of His believers. He exclaimed, "That makes Him almost a lawyer, pleading for us, doesn't it?" I answered that the New Testament deliberately calls Christ our defense Attorney when it says, *"If any man sin"* [and that includes you, no matter how frequently and fiercely you have broken God's Law], *"we have an Advocate with the Father,"* a Barrister before the bar of divine justice, who in all the centuries has not lost one case. There our Redeemer appeals for those who call Him their Lord. Though we are born again by faith in Him, in the weakness of our flesh we daily and heedlessly transgress divine Law; how reassuring, then, no matter how frequently and seriously we fall, to have the blessed Savior as our Attorney, who, basing His defense on His own removal of our guilt on cross-crowned Calvary, declares: "Father, I suffered for them. I endured the complete punishment of their transgressions. I laid down My life to save their souls. They have been washed and cleansed by My blood. *'There is therefore no condemnation to them.'"* Because His justice has been fully satisfied; because those who place their trust in Jesus, according to Scripture's repeated reassurance, are without sin, the Almighty will declare us innocent and guiltless, saved forever.

What a wonderful Attorney Jesus is! A well-known lawyer told me that he would not knowingly accept the defense of a guilty criminal and try to have him set free; but Christ has not refused a single client, according to His own promise, *"Him that cometh to Me I will in no wise cast out."* Attorneys in our courts often drop a case after they have started to act as counsel, but the ascended Savior — praise His divine love! — will not discontinue His appeal for a repentant sinner. Jesus never leaves us. He always remains with those who love Him until the final victory is theirs.

We repeat: Jesus never leaves us so long as we do not

leave Him. We can always come into His abiding presence through prevailing prayer. At God's right hand we see not only the evidence of our Lord's divine power, but also the proof of His divine intercession, His mercy and might in answering pleas directed heavenward in His name. People in our country consume 10,000,000 pounds of aspirin every year, so great are the headaches which this outwardly prosperous but spiritually impoverished age has brought; yet no statistics can reveal the heartaches and soul-aches you needlessly suffer. If you would follow Scripture's merciful direction and, casting *"all your care upon Him; for He careth for you,"* learn the priceless privilege of prayer in Jesus' name, you could be freed from the fears and phobias which attack you. This is the time — and Chief of Staff Omar Bradley declared that we are nearer war than we were three short months ago, with no guarantee that bloodshed cannot break out at once — for the people of the United States to pray as never before. In *Mein Kampf* Adolf Hitler claims that "prayer alone can never save a people in war." We register our emphatic protest against this and any similar delusion in our own land. While military might, money, men, munitions can give an outward victory, conquest by force, it takes God to grant us true triumph and peace which do not involve worse and wider warfare. Let the people of our country get down on their knees and daily, humbly, earnestly plead with the Almighty in our Savior's name, to preserve us, unworthy as we are, from the massacre and a-million-lives-an-hour destruction schedule which experts foresee for the next world holocaust! Keep Christ with our country, and because masses petition Him on His heavenly throne, we will have the nation's surest and strongest defense.

Jesus Never Leaves Us

You who love the Lord know that Jesus never leaves you in your prayer. In your shortsighted, impatient, imperfect faith you may feel that the Savior does not hear your petitions. A Rhode Island young woman writes us: "I am completely bewildered and confused and tempted far beyond what I can endure. Won't you please pray for me? My prayers don't seem to help." We will consider it a privilege to put your name on our intercession list, but we also tell you that you yourself must pray and keep on praying, especially when it seems that your pleadings are in vain. Scripture gives us the guarantee, *"This is the confidence that we have in Him, that if we ask anything according to His will, He heareth us."* Christ Himself has promised, *"Whatsoever ye shall ask in My name, that will I do."* Before one jot or tittle of the eternal truth changes, everything in the universe will pass away. So we tell the Rhode Island young woman and every one of you: "Keep on praying! God loves you so much that He *'will not suffer you to be tempted above that ye are able.'* " He will help youth fight the sins of the flesh and give them the power of purity.

He may not reply at once, when, where, or how we demand; but the truth that He does answer is as sure as the fact that the ascended Jesus will never leave us if we stay at His side in prayer. A group of young folks were studying the story of the Savior's ascension. Pointedly the eldest son asked, "How do we know that Mother is upstairs?" Someone answered, "I saw her go." "You mean that you saw her start upstairs," another said. "Perhaps she never got there or did not stay there." Then the youngest in the family interrupted, "I know that Mother is upstairs, for a moment ago I went to the stairway, called to her, and she answered me." When you raise your voice to plead with God's Son, you, too, will learn that though He is in heaven, He is still near you, because He hears you and replies to your requests.

Jesus never leaves us who believe, we say, for though He is not with us physically and visibly, He will return to the earth. The holy angels standing on the mount of the Ascension assured the wondering disciples, *"This same Jesus, which is taken up from you into heaven, shall so come in like manner as ye have seen Him go into heaven."* The time of His second coming is drawing close. Even men who have never supported divine truth speak out in warning. Henry L. Mencken, who likes to write satires on modern society, recently stepped out of role to warn preachers that "in these dangerous days they are too silent on Bible prophecy." He declared, "All I desire to point out is that the New Testament offers precise and elaborate specifications of the events preceding the inevitable end of the world, and that a fair reading of them must lead any rational man to conclude that these events are now upon us." The *"wars and rumors of wars"* in our age, the nation rising against nation, the *"famines,"* *"earthquakes,"* self-love, covetousness, boasting, pride, blasphemy, disobedience to parents, ingratitude to God, sex perversions, promise breaking among individuals and nations, the false accusation of slander and gossip, the intemperance of passions and appetites, the despising *"of those that are good,"* the two-faced deceit of traitors, the headstrong stubbornness, the love of pleasure more than the love of God — all these and other clearly specified signs of the Savior's return, fulfilled before our eyes as in no previous generation, call out to us: "Christ is coming! *'The Lord is at hand!'* "

Jesus Never Leaves Us

While the Second Advent means the end of the world, and for those who reject their Redeemer the start of sin's awful penalty, to the believer it is the beginning of bliss eternal, joy everlasting, and peace never-ending; for then our Ascension assurance, "Jesus never leaves us," comes into its full and blessed reality. Our Lord Himself emphasized, *"I go to prepare a place for you."* There, in the heavenly mansions, those who entrusted their souls to the divine Deliverer will always be with Him. What radiance beyond compare! What magnificence beyond understanding! We speak of "the pearly gates," "the crystal fountain," "the golden streets," "the jasper walls," but all this and whatever else we can see within the range of human vision, think within the limits of human thoughts, or express within the restriction of human words, cannot begin to picture the celestial beauty in *"the glory which shall be revealed in us."* Both the Old Testament and the New Testament, using the same terms, exult, *"Eye hath not seen, nor ear heard, neither have entered into the heart of man, the things which God hath prepared for them that love Him."*

Beloved, begin now, this hour, through humble faith in Christ, to secure your title to the prepared place in the heavenly mansions! He alone can defeat and dispel death's terror and give you the positive assurance of the resurrection and the glory eternal. The best that Robert Ingersoll, self-confessed skeptic and agnostic, could say when he stood at the casket of his dead brother, was limited to a one-minute oration, in which he declared: "Life is a narrow vale between the cold and barren peaks of two eternities. We strive in vain to look beyond the heights, we cry aloud, and the only answer is the echo of our wailing cry. From the voiceless lips of the unreplying dead there comes no word; but in the night of death, hope sees a star, and listening love can hear the rustle of a wing." How cold and empty and hopeless! Yet, as you behold the ascending Savior, returning to the heavens, now ready to receive the souls of all who trust in Him, receive Him as your Redeemer now. Then, when your last moment comes and He holds His cross before your closing eyes, you too can exult: "Jesus never leaves us, even in death!" Faithful unto the end, you will awaken in heaven, in far loftier than earthly strains to sing the celestial song of praise. There Jesus never leaves us! The Holy Spirit grant us this heavenly reunion, for Jesus' sake! *Amen!*

CHRIST FOR UNHAPPY HOMES!

"The name of the man was Nabal and the name of his wife Abigail; and she was a woman of good understanding and of a beautiful countenance, but the man was churlish and evil in his doings. . . . And David said to Abigail, Blessed be the Lord God of Israel, which sent thee this day to meet me; and blessed be thy advice, and blessed be thou, which hast kept me this day from coming to shed blood."
1 SAMUEL 25:3, 32-33

GOD OF OUR FATHERS: With all our hearts we thank Thee this day for our homes and for the love which has preserved them from the ravages of war's destruction. As we contrast our dwellings with the widespread wreckage across the sea, fill us with a new, deeper sense of our indebtedness to Thy grace and with a more self-sacrificing love for our hungry, destitute fellow men! Forgive us our family faults! Remove them all for Jesus' sake, who assumed their guilt and paid their full penalty when He died our death on Calvary's cross! Through Thy Holy Spirit show us clearly today that Christ offers us a divine cure for unhappiness in the home, heavenly light for the darkness of suffering in our family circles! Use the mighty Gospel in leading many henceforth to dedicate their households to the Son of God, in guiding mothers to teach their children the Savior's mercy, in prompting fathers to unite their loved ones for prayer and Scripture study, in showing children how to honor, obey, and support their parents! Stop the spread of divorce, the increase of unfaithfulness, the rejection of parenthood, and the other heavy sins against happy home life! Amid wars and rumors of wars, make the dwellings of Thy children all over the earth foregleams of the place Thine atoning Son prepared for them in Paradise above! We ask it in His saving name! *Amen!*

THERE are two kinds of weddings, one like the happy festival in Cana, where a young man and his bride invited the Lord Jesus to be present and started their new home life with Him; and the other like a recent widely publicized ceremony which united a motion-picture actress and a wealthy businessman, each previously three times married and three times divorced.

There are two kinds of wives, the true, clean, honest, and the untrue, unclean, dishonest; those who stay with their husbands through thick and thin, and those who follow an unmarried San Francisco psychologist's claim that the "love, honor, and cherish" promise in the nuptial vows ought to be "torn to shreds."

Again — and this comparison comes close to us on Mother's Day — there are two kinds of mothers, those who love children as *"an heritage of the Lord,"* like one Michigan woman, who last week presented her husband with triplets to enlarge the family to nineteen members, yet who is unusually contented in her crowded four-room house; and those like another Michigan mother, who, hailed into court for neglecting her three boys, aged five, four, and one, screamed, "I hate the children and want them in an orphanage!" Two classes of mothers, one pictured on greeting cards, featured by song, poetry, art, and represented in actual life by the Carlsbad, New Mexico, heroine who fought off an eagle, its talons imbedded in her four-year-old child, after removing those claws with a pair of pliers; and the other found too often in tragic truth, like a Minneapolis young wife, who placed her newborn baby into a garbage can!

Consequently there are two kinds of homes, the happy and the unhappy — some in which love and loyalty bring the closest approach to heaven earth knows,

Christ for Unhappy Homes! 295

and others in which cruelty and hatred point to the horrors of hell itself. More than any previous age, our generation has steadfastly sought solutions for these domestic difficulties; and likewise more frequently than ever before men have produced human panaceas which have often failed in practice. A New York psychiatrist, counselor in matters of the home, and his wife were reprimanded by a judge for leaving their eight-month-old daughter, half-naked and crying, on the back seat of their unlocked car late at night in the crowded Manhattan theater district, while they attended a lecture on "The Cultural Importance of the Theater in Our Present Civilization." Across the country the leader of a San Francisco marriage clinic asked the court to postpone his divorce hearing because of his engagement to speak on the subject "How to Be Happy, Though Married." Between the Atlantic and the Pacific, a Pennsylvania child psychologist, department head at a large university, took a lad from an orphanage and reared him according to the principles of "progressive education," which, banning discipline, permit youngsters to have their own way. Some years after the adoption, two Pennsylvania policemen, stopping a stolen car, were shot to death by the driver — this orphan adopted by the child psychologist. In the police hospital the wounded boy screamed at his father: "Get away from here! I want to die alone!"

In this immodest and immoral age, when a British clergyman declares that unmarried women schoolteachers should be permitted to have children if they so desire; in this selfish day, when wives without babies (more than a third of our families are childless, many deliberately so) for $1.98 can buy their poodles a box of cosmetics called "dogmetics," while this $1.98 could help give an undernourished European child a chance to live, we need God's guidance to secure domestic blessings; more pointedly, we should realize that only Jesus can bring joy to the members of a household marked by misery. Therefore, if your home is grief-filled and sorrow-swept; if painfully you contrast the eager engagement-day hopes and the roseate wedding-day dreams, with the present reality of remorse and disillusionment, then listen carefully when, to warn the faithless and to cheer the faithful, to instruct the young now entering marriage, and to encourage those who want to celebrate a joyous silver or golden anniversary, we exult:

CHRIST FOR UNHAPPY HOMES!

and ask the Holy Spirit's help in teaching you the modern lessons from this ancient text (the First Book of Samuel, chapter twenty-five, verses three, thirty-two, and thirty-three): *"The name of the man was Nabal and the name of his wife Abigail; and she was a woman of good understanding and of a beautiful countenance, but the man was churlish and evil in his doings. . . . And David said to Abigail, Blessed be the Lord God of Israel, which sent thee this day to meet me; and blessed be thy advice, and blessed be thou, which hast kept me this day from coming to shed blood."*

I

MANY LIKE ABIGAIL ARE UNHAPPY IN THEIR HOMES

These words take our thoughts back three thousand years to the days before David was crowned King of Israel; but we see the same problem — the unhappy

Christ for Unhappy Homes! 297

home — at all times, whether we go back to the early records of the race, as perpetuated on cuneiform tablets, or forward to the years ahead when, social experts assure us, the number of families divided by divorce will reach a figure far higher than the present danger mark.

The scene of our text is the vicinity of Mount Carmel in far-off Palestine, but it could well be Carmel, California; Carmel, Indiana; Carmel, New Jersey; Carmel, New York, or any other community in the United States. As the letters which come to us from a hundred different countries emphasize, domestic difficulties, like the sins which provoke them, have no geographical limits.

In our Scripture we meet a man with the significant name Nabal, and his wife, Abigail, apparently childless. This couple should have been unusually happy, for we are told that Nabal was a *"very great"* man, a leader with authority and power throughout the whole vicinity. Despite this prominence, however, his home was anything but exemplary. Position and public applause in themselves are no guarantee of household joy. You can see this clearly when you read the life stories of *Fuehrers, Il Duces,* dictators, headmen in European democracies, public figures in the United States, who, in their swollen pride, thought themselves above God's marriage standards and became a law unto themselves.

Nabal's household should have been blessed with peace and gladness, because, far from being pinched by poverty, as are millions in war-ruined Europe, he owned great stretches of land; in only one of his enterprises he had, according to recorded inventory, *"three thousand sheep and a thousand goats."* Money alone can never purchase permanent happiness. In New York, wreckers are battering down one of the last show-place mansions in that city, a Riverside Drive residence with seventy-five rooms, which, with its furnishings, cost more than $8,000,000. Even this magnificence, however, could not bring real, lasting joy; for its owner, a former steel king, died in sorrow and bankruptcy. You young folks, eager for a successful marriage, do not make high financial rating the first requirement in your wedding plans! You need money, of course, more in the present inflation than ordinarily; but let money be a means to a higher purpose, not the end itself! Whose multimarital extravagances make the newspaper headlines, the rich or the ragged? Who heap up the highest number of divorces, the plutocrats or the paupers? You know the answer: the men and women of wealth, who have enough to buy whatever they want. *"Better,"* the Bible declares, *"is little with the fear of the Lord than great treasure and trouble therewith. Better is a dinner of herbs where love is, than a stalled ox and hatred therewith."* Or, in more modern language, better a hamburger in a small flat with one whom you truly love and who just as truly loves you, than a ten-course dinner in a gold-coast penthouse with one who is your husband or wife only in name!

Why, then, we pause to ask, was Nabal's household cursed by unhappiness? The answer becomes clear when we learn that the master of the house lived up to his name, Nabal, which means "fool." We wonder why his parents called him that, just as today we are dismayed by some of the nonsensical or blasphemous names selected for children. Bible names are still among the best; and while they have been prohibited in some countries by atheist decrees, those of you in this land who will soon be privileged to become parents should gratefully accept the freedom afforded you and select for your boys and girls names of Biblical or Christian leaders.

Strange as this selection by Nabal's parents may seem, he was not only called Nabal, he was Nabal, a fool; and he showed his folly in many ways. The text tells us that he was *"churlish."* This old English word has much present-day meaning. It describes a surly, sullen, sordid, stingy person. When the Bible otherwise speaks of the churlish man, it describes him in these words (Isaiah 32:7): *"He deviseth wicked devices to destroy the poor with lying words, even when the needy speaketh right."* Nabal showed these base qualities; for when David and his men, fighting God's cause in Israel, came into the vicinity of rich, productive Carmel, Nabal studiously insulted them and withheld the food they requested. Here was David, long in exile from his home, battling for the Lord, and ultimately this meant for Nabal himself; yet instead of helping his cause, Nabal contemptuously classified the future king of Israel as a run-away slave, a disdainful upstart, with whom he refused to share the smallest part of his abundance.

We have too many churls today, even in public and international affairs, uncouth, swaggering braggarts, who delight in hurling challenge and shouting abusive profanity. Nabal's coarse, headstrong action almost started a small war; and if some of the name-callers on both sides of the ocean are permitted to continue unrebuked, they, too, may serve the devilish design of helping provoke bloodshed. Besides, many modern Nabals show the selfishness which marks their counterpart in Carmel. He was ready to let David risk his life, suffer hunger and danger in his campaign for the Lord; but help God's cause by contributing food to his army, encourage David with words and action? Never! The same blank refusal is re-echoed by twentieth-century churls, eager to make money, especially through war, though unwilling in their niggardliness to provide for veterans, completely opposed to sharing any of their abundance with sick, starving masses, and stone deaf to every appeal for contributions to the advancement of God's kingdom. Stinginess is a calamitous crime; it stunts the soul, shrivels the affections, and ruins homes where money problems are among the first causes of discontent. How many wives are forced to maintain the household on pittances grudgingly bestowed by a husband who spends lavishly for his own enjoyment! How many women, in senseless extravagance, have ruined their families! Far more seriously, how often has not *"the love of money"* proved itself *"the root of all evil"* in tearing souls from the Savior! For while *"God loveth a cheerful giver"* who has compassion on his suffering fellow men, it is equally true that those who madly worship gold have *"erred from the faith and pierced themselves through with many sorrows."*

Again, Nabal was a real fool, because, as our text charges, he was *"evil in his doings."* He resembled the wicked-minded men in this generation who think evil, plan evil, practice evil, glorify evil, in short, live for evil and die for evil. You have seen people like that. They never have a word of encouragement for anything good, but are constantly on the lookout for opportunities to cheat and defraud their brothers; they revel in ob-

Christ for Unhappy Homes! 301

scene jokes; they cannot speak without abusing God's holy name. They are living proofs of the shocking fact that human beings can sink lower than the brute. The Lord keep us from the unbelief which produces such utter depravity!

Nabal lived the meaning of his name also in his gluttony and drunkenness. After he had insulted David and sent away his messengers empty-handed, *"he held a feast in his house, like the feast of a king; and Nabal's heart was merry within him, for he was very drunken."* We can almost hear him boasting: "I told that upstart David to keep out of my way. Who does that shepherd boy think he is? I wouldn't give him a crust of bread if he was starving! I'll fix him if he dares set foot on my land! Boy, bring me another flagon of wine!" Everybody who like Nabal becomes a slave to liquor is a fool. The drunkard injures his body, weakens his mind, shatters his morals, sacrifices his self-respect, endangers his loved ones, and unless he repents and turns to God in Christ, sends his soul to hell. Do not be a fool like Nabal and pride yourself on the number of cocktails you can take! His alcoholic orgy ended in disaster, and so can yours. If you are addicted to drink, let Jesus free you! You cannot overcome this demon of drunkenness only through your own strength and by your own resolution. Let the Lord give you the victory! Any believer can defeat this degrading habit, which is responsible for more broken bodies, broken hearts, broken homes, broken happiness, and more broken hopes of salvation than we can ever compute. Here is Scripture's unfailing promise: *"If any man be in Christ, he is a new creature; old things are passed away; behold, all things are become new."*

In his unbelief Nabal refused divine help. This disregard of the almighty God, more than anything else, made him the veritable fool of fools, just as in our time no man is a worse imbecile than he who sets himself above the Lord. Because the Bible is right when it declares, *"The fool hath said in his heart, There is no God,"* and again, *"Fools make a mock at sin,"* and once more, *"He that trusteth in his own heart is a fool,"* our age, with the widest spread of education, higher and lower, the world has known, is producing a shocking aggregate of spiritual fools and moral morons who oppose their own reason and belittle Scripture truth, blatantly denying that there is a God. They contradict their own conscience as they laugh at sin and ridicule Heaven's retributive justice. They deliberately reject their Savior and in the greatest mistake a man can make substitute their own miscalled merits for Christ's sure mercies. Does your lack of faith show that you are in the same class with notorious Nabal, because you endorse his unbelief by setting yourself above the Almighty? Then may the Most High be more merciful to you than He was to that ancient scoffer and teach you, starting today, if necessary by reverse and rebuke, this truth laid down in His Word: *"The fear of the Lord is the beginning of wisdom!"*

Now for the brighter side in Nabal's family. We find this in his wife Abigail, whom Scripture describes as *"a woman of good understanding."* Her actions, as recorded in this twenty-fifth chapter of First Samuel, show her keen recognition that a wife's interest should center in her husband and her home. When a Hollywood singer, torn between her public career and her coming baby, recently gave up a $1,500-a-week engagement, she was pictured in the newspapers as depressed and temperamental; yet the woman who puts maternal interests first is truly intelligent. In Minneapolis a five-year-old boy, standing forlorn on a street corner, at ten o'clock at night, when asked "Why don't you go home?" replied: "There's no one home. My mother's at a card party." In cruel truth, many parents do not know exactly where their children were last night, with whom they associated, what they did. Tonight hundreds of thousands of our teen-agers will be anywhere except in church, with anyone except clean-minded companions, doing almost anything except fortifying their own resistance to evil. The Holy Spirit give us parents *"of good understanding,"* who realize that God holds them responsible for bringing their children to the faith and keeping them clean through Christ!

As our text further explains, Abigail was *"of a beautiful countenance."* Too frequently physical attraction outweighs inner comeliness, when women misuse the gift of personal charm for selfish, sinful purposes. Abigail who thus combined beauty of body with beauty of spirit, has this message for American mothers and daughters: If the Lord has given you good looks, thank Him and show your gratitude by a pure, faith-filled life! Never under any circumstances permit the advantage of your attractiveness to become a hindrance to your holiness! The Almighty has endowed you more richly than your plain, unattractive sisters. *"Unto whomsoever much is given, of him shall be much required"!* Our country needs more of that loyalty to the Lord shown by a Memphis girl, nationally acclaimed for her beauty. Although selected as Miss America, she still teaches Sunday school. Like Abigail, she adds to beauty of countenance beauty of consecration.

This obedience to the Almighty gave Nabal's wife her most notable quality. She feared and loved God; she implored and exalted God; she testified and showed unswerving reverence to God. Her coarse, cruel husband might try to oppose the Most High, but even more resolutely she was determined to treasure His Word.

It is a mystery to us, of course, how a woman of such physical charm and spiritual grace could ever marry a churlish, boastful brute like Nabal. Perhaps for the same reason which today leads many heedless young women into unfortunate alliances — the fear of never finding another husband, the mere desire for marriage, the hope of compensation for an earlier disappointment in love, the heartless insistence of money-loving parents, or some similar misplaced motive — Abigail gave herself to Nabal. Apparently she made two tremendous mistakes: she married without genuine love and without requiring unity in faith. You young folks, for whom marital happiness must be a matter of prime importance, warned by the heavy afflictions Abigail suffered, should refuse to pledge yourselves to anyone whom you do not truly love. Do not marry merely for convenience, position, protection, support, shelter! Marry for love! Be sure, too, that the person to whom you entrust your happiness has the same trust in Christ which you confess! The religiously mixed marriages, in which the husband goes to one church while the wife attends another of diametrically opposed creed, or in which the mother is a believer, the father a scoffer, the children halfway between and finally lost to the Lord, are menaces to marital understanding and family joy. *"Be ye not unequally yoked together with unbelievers,"* Scripture tells all who love the Lord, and this includes a pointed warning against marrying

Christ for Unhappy Homes! 305

anyone with whom you cannot worship, pray, attend Communion, and come before God in the same, sacred trust. You may think that your love is strong enough to overcome the handicap of living in a house religiously divided against itself; but you are wrong. A study of broken homes and wrecked marriages reveals among the foremost reasons for marital misery and household hatreds this absence of spiritual unity. The family which does not pray together will not stay together. The couple whom the blessed tie of faith does not bind may be cut apart by cursed unbelief. Indeed, as some of your letters tragically show, the godless husband often leads a godly wife into the misery of unbelief and atheism. Before you give your heart and hand, be sure that your beloved worships your Savior with you in the same true church! Do not be satisfied with vague promises that somehow, somewhere, sometime later the person of your choice will join the Church; be sure your loved one joins now, before marriage! Rather refuse to enter a mixed union than burden your home with the handicap of conflicting creeds! The Almighty will honor you for such loyalty.

Abigail kept her faith, despite her churlish husband's tyranny and unbelief. She remained loyal to Nabal, boorish and brutal as he was. She had taken him "for better or for worse," and though the "worse" predominated, she still saw in Nabal the husband to whom she was pledged until death would part them. She could have played the role of the misunderstood, mistreated wife and sought sympathy from other men, as many unhappy women do today; but give her credit for her unswerving loyalty: she remained true to Nabal, *"son of Belial,"* and was even ready to have his guilt fall on her. Thousands of women with her drab, dreary outlook today seek solace in divorce. A women's national magazine prints a social service expert's complaint that only one of the forty-eight States grants divorce for incompatibility, that is, for disagreement in thought, words, action, and pleads that every person joined in an incompatible marriage be given the freedom of divorce. The Lord prevent that! The United States needs not laxer divorce laws, but more rigid regulations for marriage maintenance. The Bible recognizes only two kinds of divorce: first, that granted on account of unfaithfulness, and second, that granted on account of desertion. The score of other "reasons" advanced in this greedy age, when certain States try to make money by easy separation laws, are all condemned by God. If you are consulting a divorce attorney, check the advice he gives you with Holy Writ and refuse to do anything contrary to Scripture! Follow Abigail's allegiance to her husband, unreasonable and incompatible as he was!

Her loyalty saved Nabal's life; for when David determined to destroy the man who had opposed his cause, Abigail urgently entreated him to spare her husband. He did, and Abigail thus became one of many wives who rescued their own husbands from death. History records, for example, that when the city of Weinsberg in the Old World surrendered, and the women in the besieged city were permitted to escape and take with them whatever they could lift, they carried their husbands to safety. In a less dramatic but equally definite way, many a present-day wife has rescued her husband by nursing him in his sickness, protecting him in danger, and by such daily tasks as watching his food and diet. Many a mother has saved her child even after the doctor shook his head and said, "There is no chance!" Christian mothers have helped rescue their loved ones from eternal ruin, and on Mother's Day we do well to declare:

> "Who went to the door of death for me?
> Who held me long upon her knee?
> Who sat for hours beside my bed?
> Who soothed my pain and stroked my head?
>   'Twas Mother.
>
> "Who worked from early morn till night?
> Who always taught me wrong from right?
> Who pointed me to Christ the Lord?
> Who led me to His holy Word?
>   'Twas Mother."

However, gratitude should be expressed not only in poetry, with flowers, and on a single day, but with love, thankful prayer, and the determination to share with our mothers the best we have. Such devotion has the promise of divine blessing.

In dissuading David from attacking her husband, Abigail thus prevented the start of another war. Today, too, Christian women likewise have the mighty privilege of helping to restrict bloodshed and to save our generation from the horrors of atomic annihilation. If God-fearing wives help make their homes dwelling places of the Lord; if they bring up their *"children . . . in the nurture and admonition of the Lord"*; if by their prayers and church work they help extend the Savior's kingdom and thus increase the righteousness which *"exalteth a nation,"* they will do more to insure divine favor and preserve peace than a hundred political conferences in which atheists help direct world affairs. Our text relates, *"David said to Abigail, Blessed be the Lord God of Israel, which sent thee this day to meet me; and blessed be thy advice, and blessed be thou, which hast kept me this day from coming to shed blood";* and we, too, should greet every true wife and mother with this grateful recognition, "*'Blessed be thou'* for helping to avoid more bloodshed and far worse slaughter!"

II

EVERYONE, LIKE ABIGAIL, CAN FIND HAPPINESS IN THE LORD

At first it seemed that Abigail was anything but blessed; for on the morning after his excessive drinking, Nabal, learning how close he had been to death at David's hand, was gripped by paralyzing fear, and, we are told, *"It came to pass about ten days after that the Lord smote Nabal that he died."* The shameful, painful end of a drunkard!

His sudden death unquestionably gave his wife relief, just as sometimes in our day the removal of a brutal, profane husband may be a blessing in disguise. This bereavement, however, also brought Abigail new hardships. She was left a widow; in those distant days, a solitary woman bereft of her husband suffered heavy handicaps. Widows then had few rights and were constantly exploited. For this reason God's Word repeatedly pleads for kindness to them, as Christ's Gospel seeks to create compassion for their loneliness and sorrow. However, the Almighty showed solitary Abigail His love. He led David to ask her hand in marriage, moved her to accept, and thus gave the young woman who had trusted divine guidance an abundant measure of happiness. Abigail who had been humiliated by a brutal husband was exalted by becoming the wife of a leader whom the Lord had chosen to rule His people.

We are separated from the time and scene of this

Christ for Unhappy Homes!

record by almost 3,000 years and 7,000 miles. In some respects we have advanced beyond that age, when a wife cringed in fear of her husband, or when kings, like David, took more than one woman in marriage. Thank Heaven especially that we have a far mightier means of fortifying family happiness than Abigail knew; we have God's Son, the world's Savior, the Hope and Help for every believing home! If our Old Testament text says, *"Blessed art thou!"* to a woman who could see the Messiah only dimly and from the distance of prolonged prophecy, how much more bountifully enriched are all who trust the New Testament record of the Redeemer's love! As David could tell Abigail, *"Blessed be the Lord God of Israel, which sent thee this day to meet me,"* so every Christian bridegroom can tell his believing bride at the altar, *" 'Blessed be the Lord* Jesus, *'which sent thee this day to meet me!' "* If David could say, *"Blessed be thy advice, . . . which . . . kept me this day from coming to shed blood!"* then surely every husband can similarly declare his Christian wife blessed for her counsel and guidance in leading him from sin and its sorrows. If Abigail was greeted with the benediction, *"Blessed be thou,"* then assuredly, not only on the second Sunday in May, but every day, the children of a God-fearing, Christ-revering mother should *"arise up and call her blessed"* in the Lord Jesus. The wife, the mother, the daughter, who love the Savior and live in Him are God's mighty instruments for bringing immeasurable joy into their households. The home united in true Christian faith, which exalts the Son of God as the Head of the house, the ever-present Guest, the Counselor in family problems, the Comforter in its sorrows, the Light of Life in the darkness of its bereavements, will have Heaven's own power in banishing misery, counteracting calamity, and insuring inner joy.

For Christ, unlike our so-called experts who claim to have the solution to domestic problems yet often touch only the surface and therefore fail, probes deep below the outward circumstances to reach the heart of every family difficulty, sin, the violation of God's Law, which, as in Abigail's case, is at the root of all household sorrow. To give us joy both here and hereafter, Jesus removed our transgressions, all of them, completely and forever, when He, pure and perfect, deliberately assumed our sins, transferred their punishment to His own soul and body, took upon Himself their guilt, their curse, their sorrow, and thus having fully satisfied the demands of divine justice, made us sinless, freed from death's dominion and hell's horror. All this He, the self-sacrificing Son of God, did for us when on Calvary's cross of crime and cruelty He died the death we deserved and when at the open grave He rose again to prove Himself our Lord, whose self-sacrifice for the redemption of the world had been accepted.

This *"promise"* is *"unto you and to your children,"* to everyone who hears the appeal of grace. However shockingly you may have sinned; however surely you may feel that you have made too great a mess of your home life to expect pardon or to rebuild the ruins of its wreckage; however insistently the agents of hell may try to convince you that you are doomed and that it is useless to begin a new chapter of family happiness with Christ, I give you His own assurance, *"Him that cometh to Me I will in no wise cast out,"* and the Gospel guarantees that Jesus is always ready to receive you just as you are, sin-burdened and sin-broken, if only you come to Him, contrite because of your guilt, yet confident of His grace. You honor your mother, but you dishonor her faith by rejecting the Redeemer. Bring your believing parents the greatest joy you can, the soul-satisfaction for which they have prayed the Almighty a thousand times, by giving yourself wholly to God, by returning to the compassionate Savior, whom you once worshiped and welcomed but whom you have belittled, betrayed, or even blasphemed.

Ask yourself in a precious, personal moment what the money, the sin, the pleasure, the profit you have chosen in preference to Jesus have brought you, if not a disquieted conscience, loss of inner peace, fears for the future, dread thoughts concerning death and the judgment to come! Then, by contrast, consider what God's Son unfailingly guarantees you: forgiven guilt; peace with your heavenly Father and your own conscience; the comfort of the Redeemer's constant companionship to protect you and provide you with all you need for soul and body; the full victory over sorrow, weakness, doubt, temptation; the joy in the Lord which comes with the inner assurance that *"we are more than conquerors through Him that loved us"!* As you make this comparison between the life without Christ and with Christ, how can you end another day before acclaiming the sustaining Son of God your Deliverer? Come to Him now! Someone has counted the number of instances Scripture uses this word *"come"* and has found it 400 times in the New Testament alone. Every occurrence is a personal invitation to you, just as each of the more than 400 broadcasts during the past fifteen seasons has urged sinners, *"Come; for all things are now ready."* God wants you with Jesus. That is why He has issued these hundreds of appeals urging you to *"come"* to the cross. The Holy Spirit grant that you will not refuse!

When the Christ of all compassion is welcomed into any dwelling — and the records of His Gospels show that He entered both the mansions of the rich and the hovels of the poor — He will surely bring the peace, contentment, trust, humility, reverence, hope, comfort, which can banish gloom and grief. He may not strike down an unbelieving, unrepentant husband, as He did in Abigail's house, for He has other, happier ways of bringing help. In His mercy He often strengthens a consecrated wife to lead her careless, churchless, godless husband to the faith, as many of your grateful letters reveal. Therefore, Christian mothers, stand up and speak up for the Savior wherever you can, but *"learn first to show piety at home!"* With the Spirit's blessing your *"chaste conversation,"* the Biblical term for "godly conduct," may win your loved ones for the Redeemer.

Jesus can remove the petty quarrels and the heavy hatreds which too often wreck marriages; for through His indwelling selfishness is checked and the miracle of grace fulfilled, *"If any man be in Christ, he is a new creature."* Christ can revive dying love, reawaken and restore dead affection. Even if the specter of divorce draws close and, against clear Scripture, arrangements for separation have been made, our Lord, with whom nothing is impossible, can keep you from the disaster of a broken home. While we thank the Almighty for the many letters you have sent to prove this, we also tell you husbands and wives who in wounded pride or sinful lust want the courts to sever your marriage bonds: For real, lasting happiness, follow the Savior, not your

Christ for Unhappy Homes! 313

selfish or sensual desires! Confess your guilt to Him now, before it is too late and you have burdened yourselves and your children with a heavy handicap! Ask Him to help you, and the Lord who could revive a corpse when this was necessary to make a home happy, can still prove His miraculous power by granting you mutual devotion instead of selfish divorce. Especially when you recall the Son of God's willingness to forgive, forget, and forego, as He laid down His life in your behalf, you should be ready to receive and restore your erring helpmate and to forgive even the sordid sin of unfaithfulness.

Christ's love can bring peace into dwellings hit by heavy hardship. As you behold Him who *"loved us and gave Himself for us,"* the Holy Spirit will grant you the triumphant trust which through tears of sorrow hears Jesus say, *"What I do thou knowest not now, but thou shalt know hereafter,"* and gains assurance in the conviction, *"He hath done all things well."* The faith firmly founded on Christ gives you God's own guarantee that your afflictions are evidences of Heaven's mercy, since it is written, *"Whom the Lord loveth He chasteneth,"* and that *"the sufferings of this present time,"* severe though they be, *"are not worthy to be compared with the glory which shall be revealed in us."*

Do you not see, then, that your family needs the Lord? Even if today your household is marked by peace and prosperity, tomorrow some of you may suddenly meet disaster and death. For unfailing guidance and unchanging help turn to *"Jesus Christ, the same yesterday and today and for ever"*! Find regular and reverent time daily to have your household worship the heavenly Father in family prayers, Bible reading and hymn singing! Plead earnestly with God's Son for the salvation of each member of your home! Have parents and children attend the same true church every Sunday, but do not keep your Christianity restricted to the Lord's Day! See to it that the children learn their prayers and acquire a treasury of spiritual strength which neither age nor weakness can remove. John Randolph, early American statesman, emphasized that he would have become an atheist had it not been for the memory of the moments he spent in His mother's arms when she taught him his childhood petitions to the Lord. Enroll your boys and girls in a Christian day school! As they grow up, give them the best education you can, teach them to select good companions, read helpful books, engage in worth-while activities!

In the colonial days, when our forefathers pushed the frontiers westward, they had to fight, mile after mile, against the Indians whose territory they invaded. In these battles the red men, who frequently pillaged and burned outlying settlements, kidnapped hundreds of children. When finally the Seneca, Shawnee, and Delaware redskins were defeated, the peace terms demanded that they return the captured white boys and girls. At an appointed place and time the long-lost children were restored to their families in scenes of truly indescribable joy. It often happened, however, that the little ones had been kidnapped so early, or remained with the Indians so long, that they could not be identified. Then someone suggested that the mothers move through the ranks of the unrecognized youngsters to repeat the songs and hymns which they had sung as lullabies. You can imagine the surge of joy which must have swept through the hearts of parents and children when one of the captives after another, recognizing these

Christ for Unhappy Homes! 315

early melodies, ran out to embrace a searching woman and cry, "Mother!"

How much happier and more radiant will be the heavenly reunion of those who love the Lord and die in the faith! What raptures when the greetings of celestial rejoicing ring out: "Father! Mother! Son! Daughter! Brother! Sister!" In the eternal homeland no songs will be required for recognition, since Scripture promises, *"Then shall I know even as also I am known."* There our hymns will hallow the precious name of our eternal Deliverer, whom we shall behold face to face. Make sure that you will be there by acclaiming Christ your Savior now! This is your first duty. The second is, do everything you can to bring your whole family there, with the risen Redeemer! The Holy Spirit guide you and yours to reach that home in Paradise! God be with you " 'till we meet at Jesus' feet"! *Amen!*

PENTECOST POWER FOR YOU!

"Peter said unto them, Repent and be baptized, every one of you, in the name of Jesus Christ for the remission of sins, and ye shall receive the gift of the Holy Ghost. For the promise is unto you and to your children, and to all that are afar off." ACTS 2:38-39.

SPIRIT OF POWER AND PURITY: On this day of Pentecost nineteen centuries ago, Thou didst come to the disciples, the first messengers of the saving Gospel, in the sound of a rushing, mighty wind. Teach us that we should not keep the glorious Gospel of a Savior, slain to atone for the sins of an evil world, quiet and unnoticed! Thou didst descend on these heralds of Heaven's mercy in "cloven tongues like as of fire." Oh, stir our hearts into flame so that our faith is fortified with new fervor! Filled with Thy strength, the Apostles, untrained as they were, received the wisdom to proclaim the Son of God's grace and the ability to make His mercy known in many different languages. When Thou didst dwell within the Pentecost disciples' hearts, their fears vanished, and they were strengthened by new courage. Oh, endow the present-day preachers of the risen Redeemer's grace with unflinching loyalty to the Cross. Give us the same holy zeal, the same power to bring the Gospel to every man in his own language, the same rich returns in souls led to their Lord! As these words speed through the air, accompany them with Thy power and penetration so that many all over the globe may be drawn to the compassionate Christ, whom to know is life eternal! Come, then, divine Comforter, into many sick and sin-torn hearts to bring light and love! We ask it all in Jesus' name and by His promise. *Amen!*

Do you want to start life over, commence a new career with a clean slate? Are you eager to break with the sins of the past, to face the future, confident and courageous? Would you like to become a new person, with love supplanting lust in your heart, mercy replacing meanness, rejoicing crowding out remorse, the guarantee of heavenly glory expelling the grim fear of hell? Then the Holy Spirit has placed you before your radio this Lord's Day to have you hear the divinely sure and eternally certain Scripture truth that you can begin a radiantly new life and be born again in the beauty of an incomparably higher existence.

Almost in the same breath, however, I must tell you that science will not achieve this change. Plastic surgery may perform marvels, but it cannot touch the soul. Doctors develop new facial features for a Chicago youth whose appearance was so repulsive that it drove him to crime; Uniontown, Pennsylvania, physicians can give a misshapen baby girl mouth and lips; New York specialists supply a deformed child with ears; but by no operation can medical experts reshape a repulsive heart or make mouths speak the pure, God-pleasing truth. Delicate surgery which actually cuts away brain tissue is now said to heal certain mental illnesses hitherto classified as incurable; yet no lobotomy, the technical term for this treatment, will cut away the sins and sorrows of the human soul.

Similarly, the political pledges of presidential election campaigns alone cannot insure a happier day. The platforms offered by opposing parties are based on the multiplying of new laws; but legislation itself cannot improve and ennoble men. For example, the United States today has the most numerous, most varied, most complicated divorce regulations ever known; still marriage massacres flourish in these United States more flagrantly than in sensual Sodom and ghoulish Gomorrah. A few days ago the lawyers in the American Bar Association denounced our divorce statutes as "rotten," productive of "deceit, trickery, mockery."

Communists commit themselves to change this world by destroying Christianity along with democracy; but the concentration camps behind the Iron Curtain; the millions of Ukrainian peasants who were liquidated because of their refusal to accept collective farming; the wail and woe of persecuted people in a dozen tyrannized countries, show that atheism can indeed alter conditions, but only for the worst.

A widely popular theory today holds that we must change men and their environment by force of arms, slaughter of war, annihilation by atomic bombs; but the past has proved that global struggles inflict more miseries as they promote the grief of utter godlessness. Pray as never before that the Almighty will thwart the threat of a third world struggle!

Contrary to popular opinion, people cannot be inwardly improved by money. The costliest beauty treatments do not leave the human heart more attractive. Perfumes at forty-five dollars an ounce will not make our lives a *"sweet-smelling sacrifice"* to the Lord. Wardrobes of ultrafashionable and ultraexpensive clothing cannot cover the disgrace of damnable guilt. In a Chicago court recently a woman sought to secure $900 a month from her estranged husband, only for clothing; but if this amount were granted and she could have accumulated entire rooms filled with garments, as did the best-dressed woman in Europe, who left a thousand fashionable frocks, the plain apparel of a Christian nurse, a deaconess, a self-sacrificing missionary teacher, would mean far more in God's sight than all such lavish attire.

Thank the Lord with me, then, that while men cannot purify the human heart nor cleanse the soul, the Almighty has provided a superhuman power which can reform our sinful lives according to His perfect pattern. That majestic power is mightier than the Rockies, stronger than the deep Pacific, more radiant than the azaleas, camelias, and rhododendra that this spring bloom in exquisite beauty. For this divine might, which can truly make and keep us new creatures in Christ, is the converting, regenerating, sanctifying, sustaining power of the Holy Ghost.

We devote this Sunday to the Holy Spirit, the Third Person of the glorious Deity, together with the Father and the Son, the true, triune, triumphant God, because today — how many of you realized it when you awoke this morning? — is one of the foremost festivals of our faith, Pentecost, the fiftieth day after our Lord's resurrection, when the Spirit visibly descended on the disciples, victoriously changed their lives, and led them to teach and preach the glorious Gospel of their risen Redeemer.

Because this Sunday can be a powerful Pentecost for each of you as the divine Enlightener enters your souls, I call out in both plea and promise:

PENTECOST POWER FOR YOU!

This is the assurance you should gain from our festival text (Acts, chapter two, verses thirty-eight and thirty-nine), which tells us: *"Peter said unto them, Repent and be baptized, every one of you, in the name of Jesus Christ for the remission of sins, and ye shall receive the gift of the Holy Ghost. For the promise is unto you and to your children, and to all that are afar off."*

I

HOW BOUNTIFUL THE BLESSINGS OF THIS POWER!

This pointed promise, *"Ye shall receive the gift of the Holy Ghost,"* is taken from the conclusion of the mightiest sermon any man ever preached, Peter's Pentecost appeal. The Holy Spirit had just descended on the disciples to change their hearts and lives, and now they were offering the proof of His indwelling to the multitudes assembled before them. They were speaking not in untried theory, but on the basis of real, personal experience.

What exactly happened on Pentecost? We are told that the disciples *"were all with one accord in one place."* If only it could similarly be said of the quarter million churches and the 70,000,000 nominal Christians in the United States that doctrinally they are *"all with one accord in one place"!* How marvelous if the differences, prominent and petty, which separate believers into several hundred groups would disappear! Atheists in political parties are more solidly united than many believers in competitive, contradictory groups which oppose and denounce, yet do little to win the oneness for which the Savior Himself repeatedly prayed and which God's Word frequently exalts!

However, nowhere in the Bible are we told that the Lord will force unity of faith on churches which do not want it and are unwilling to pray, work, sacrifice in seeking it. A fatal failure of Christian churches throughout the world today is their reluctance to study and discuss the differences which separate them, and to continue, if necessary, for many years, to learn what sacred Scripture teaches in these disputed doctrines. Believers should work and pray until by the grace of the Almighty, *"with whom nothing shall be impossible"* and of whom it is written, *"If we ask anything according to His will, He heareth us,"* the churches reach, not an agreement to disagree nor a compromise with error, but a complete, honest, open unity in every article of our faith. God speed that day! You who want the churches to present a united front, not for political power and earthly esteem, but for spiritual growth and triumph over our Lord's enemies, pray fervently that all who bow before the Bible as the errorless Word and who look to the Savior as the only Redeemer may be Spirit-led to find and follow faith's oneness, as they place the Son of God before personal, private, denominational teachings or traditions which oppose His will.

It may be that this *"one place"* in which the twelve disciples were gathered was a part of the Temple grounds. The Pentecost blessing thus came upon them while they were at church, worshiping and studying Scripture. Suppose one of the Twelve had stayed home to look after private interests! He would have been cut off from receiving the strengthening Spirit. This happens to many of you who sleep too long on Sunday mornings or who find a dozen other unworthy excuses for keeping your distance from divine worship. Get this straight: The Church will march along without you, but you cannot experience Heaven's blessing if you despise the Church of the Lord! This broadcast, as any other religious radio program, can never be a permanent substitute for your church attendance. Rather do we pray God that this mission of the air will be His means of leading many of you into a Gospel Church and to the fellowship with the faithful.

While the disciples were studying the Old Testament, a stupendous miracle occurred. Repeatedly Jesus had assured His followers, *"Ye shall receive power after that the Holy Ghost is come upon you";* and the Son of God is the only One in all the ages who has never failed to carry out His promise. The Holy Spirit did come, just as every one of our Redeemer's predictions will be literally fulfilled. Trust the Lord with childlike faith, and you will never be disappointed! The blessings crowded into your life will help you repeat this reassurance: *"There hath not failed one word of all His good promise."* Believe Scripture's sacred guarantee, *"All the promises of God in Him* [Christ] *are yea and in Him Amen"!*

Learn also the lessons taught by the manner in which the Holy Spirit descended on the disciples! We are told, *"Suddenly there came a sound from heaven as of a rushing mighty wind."* There was nothing silent, soft, and secret about the Pentecost miracle; it was public, powerful, impressive. Let the Church today send its Gospel throughout the world, truly *"a sound from heaven,"* as a *"rushing mighty wind"* by following our Lord's command, *"Preach ye from the housetops!"* by proclaiming from the antenna tops of superpower radio stations! Give us servants of the Most High in our pulpits who speak not only in smooth, dulcet tones, but, like Saint Paul before Agrippa, raise their voices in unmistakable warning, with all the energy the Spirit gives them, to urge sinners to receive their Redeemer! Give us congregations which, instead of halfheartedly singing or whispering the Savior's love, "shout the glad tidings, exultingly sing!" Residents of a fashionable district in Richmond, Virginia, were circulating a petition to have a church closed because the congregation sang too loudly. Seeking signatures in support of their request, they came to the home of a Jewish gentleman. He refused to sign, stating, "If I believed, as these people do, that the Messiah had come, I would shout this out at the top of my voice." Fellow Christians in the United States and Canada, testify to Christ in clarion, clear tones, with the full urgency, appeal, persuasion the Spirit grants! This is the day for the longest alarm, the most penetrating invitation to accept Jesus this world has ever heard. Let everyone know that you are the Lord's! Never disguise your discipleship!

The Spirit's coming was also shown *"by cloven tongues like as of fire,"* descending on each of the twelve. How sorely we need the flame of burning faith today! Many churches are spiritually barren and dead. The Bishop of Salisbury gave a British conference this shocking report: "Out of every 100 babies born in England, 67 are baptized. Out of the 67, only 36 are found in our Sunday schools. Out of those 36 no more than 26 go on for confirmation. And of these 26 only 9 remain as communicants." The growth of indifference and disloyalty within religious groups in our own country, as witnessed by shrinking memberships, decrease of converts, and absence of fervent zeal, makes us pray: Send the Spirit's fire to stir our hearts into flame for the Savior!

Not to praise this radio program — for nothing could be cheaper and more unworthy of Heaven's grace — but to praise God from whom all broadcast blessings flow, I share with you this portion of a letter from a Detroit pastor: "I want you to know that as a result of your broadcast we confirmed (this means, received into membership after careful instruction, often after Baptism) 107 adults in 1946, and 127 in 1947. Almost all these people were brought to Christ through the . . . messages of your broadcast." Think of it, 234 men and women led to the Lord in only one congregation, through divine benediction on this mission of the air and the tireless service of a fervent, faithful pastor! What miracles of divine mercy could be accomplished if every one of you were similarly afire for the Savior!

We cannot sidetrack the Spirit without sacrificing power and blessing. By far the greatest need in the United States today, more important than any political panacea or military proposal, is a real, fire-filled revival in the Christian churches, which will re-emphasize and restore the preaching of Jesus as the Savior of mankind and lead the laity to work with flaming zeal.

When the disciples *"were all filled with the Holy Ghost,"* they *"began to speak with other tongues."* The fact that these companions of Christ, mostly unschooled fishermen, used at least sixteen different languages in preaching the Gospel is a challenge, asking our age with its many schools and its advanced culture to publish Heaven's grace in every known language and bring the glad tidings literally to the ends of the earth. When men of different races, colors, nations learn to look to the same divine Deliverer and believe the same truths of faith, the perils of global wars will have been drastically reduced. The churches must redouble their efforts in the race with godless Communism to win the world; and they can triumph only, as that handful of believers at the first Pentecost, by preaching the comfort of the Cross with increased power and persistency in all the languages of our Babel-like world. Keep on praying with us that our heavenly Father, rich both in resources and redeeming grace, will soon open a way for us to build superpower broadcasting stations in Europe, Asia, and Africa! This mission of the air uses only eight languages, while the Spirit strengthened those Pentecost preachers to speak in twice as many tongues. Beseech God with us that we may soon tell the story of salvation in scores of languages and over many more than the thousand-plus stations now affiliated with us in Bringing Christ to the Nations!

The Spirit produced marvelous inner changes in the disciples' hearts and minds. Before the Holy Comforter took possession of their souls, these eleven frightened men had huddled terror-stricken behind locked doors; but now fear fell away. A few days ago they had not given a single word of testimony for the Savior; but filled with the Spirit, they clearly told their hearers that Jesus had died on the cross and had been resurrected at the open grave for their eternal redemption. A few weeks earlier they had been a selfish group, each looking for his position in a worldly kingdom, which they mistakenly thought our Lord would establish; but after the cloven tongues of fire had purified their understanding and desires, they were ready to lay down their lives — as all but one did — in spreading the saving Gospel. They were completely changed men. No longer would they doubt, deny, or desert their Redeemer; no longer would they seek earthly, privileged position through following Jesus. No longer would they try to punish and destroy those who opposed them. From the moment the Holy Spirit refined their faith and purified their mind, they became new creatures in Christ, their entire existence dedicated, not to self, but to the Savior.

Do not picture this Pentecost outpouring merely as ancient history, a beautiful occurrence in a far-off land, with little modern meaning or personal help! Peter was thinking of you when he spoke these words of our text: *"The promise is unto you and to your children, and to all that are afar off."* What marvelous mercy! Only a few minutes before Peter had pointedly indicted his hearers on the murder charge: *"Jesus of Nazareth . . . ye have taken and by wicked hands have crucified and slain";* now, however, he tells the same killers of Christ, *"The promise is unto you."* When Justice Minister Ladas was assassinated in Greece a few days ago, the Athens government ordered that 1,000 captives of the party which opposed him be shot to death in retaliation. Yet after the vilest crime in history, the Crucifixion, the Savior's slayers are offered peace and pardon by faith in His atoning love. You see, then, that our Lord has mercy for you, no matter how terrifying your transgressions.

Distracted young women write us after they have fallen, anxiously inquiring whether they have forfeited the hope of their salvation. Wives who have cheated their husbands and are now overwhelmed by this cheap deceit want to know, as their conscience accuses them, whether Christ has completely cast them off. Deeply distressed listeners who have had evil thoughts against God or spoken blasphemous words, plead for proof positive that they have not placed themselves beyond the pale of divine pardon. Here is the Lord's own guarantee of grace for them in Peter's Spirit-filled pledge of mercy to the murderers of the Messiah, and therefore to every evildoer. Take the Almighty at His Word and believe this: The promise of forgiveness, the promise of crimson-stained sins washed away forever, the promise of the Holy Spirit, the promise of redemption, resurrection, and restoration to the heavenly Father, *"is unto you"!*

Praise God, the Holy Spirit also directed Peter to add, *"The promise is . . . to your children."* In the first sermon preached by an Apostle, youth is thus emphasized. What an example for our pulpits! The boys and girls in Jerusalem at that time needed special consideration because they were to inherit the destiny of death and disaster when their capital would be destroyed, their country devastated, their people enslaved in a national calamity, still notorious in these days of atomic disaster. How can we, realizing the crushing burdens we have placed on our children's shoulders, refuse to multiply tenfold or a hundredfold the efforts directed to bring the rising generation to their Savior? They have inherited from us the heaviest Federal debts, the most complicated international problems, the most alarming increase of crime and immorality, the most dangerous attacks on the Church any generation has received from its predecessor. My countrymen, work and pray to strengthen the faith of our young people, because the pledge of Heaven's mercy is to them! Intensify your efforts, sacrificing what you must, in bringing Christ to them and them to Christ!

The Pentecost promise, Peter adds, is also *"to all that are afar off,"* to those separated from the time and scene of the Spirit's outpouring by many thousands of miles or hundreds of years. *"God . . . will have all men to be saved"* and to be reborn into a new existence. Only your obstinate unbelief and your stubborn refusal to receive your Redeemer can keep you away, however *"afar off"* you may be in distance or in obedience to the Savior. Your heavenly Father loved you and gave His Son to save you. It will not be His fault, but your own, if you go to hell instead of heaven.

See the remarkable present-day proof of the Holy Spirit's power to change lives, as He reveals this in our broadcast! A friend in Mexico reports: "A great blessing has come to us through your messages, for my husband did not know the Savior when I first met him. One night God in His mercy permitted us to tune in your station, and since that day we have been listening faithfully to your sermons, giving thanks to God in the name of the Lord Jesus that He finally led my husband to feel the call of the Holy Spirit in his heart." A mother in Chile confesses: "Each Sunday that I hear your sermons over the radio I feel very happy over the hope of salvation they give me. Sometimes I weep for shame at having sinned; at other times I weep for joy at knowing that we have such a kind heavenly Father." From the far-off Fiji Islands a listener sends us this marvelous news: "You were the means of bringing me to Christ. Words cannot express how happy I feel in accepting Him as my personal Savior. What can separate me from His love? Nothing!" A man in North Wales, Great Britain, informs us: "I must write you personally to express my gratitude for showing so plainly over the radio the way of salvation. I was tuning in various American stations, when suddenly I heard your program. It had such an immediate grip on me that I stayed tuned to the station. It seemed that you were telling me what to do to live a better Christian life. I cannot describe the feeling I had inside me; it was uncanny. I felt something taking place within me, and I was really happier spiritually after that sermon. You were speaking about the American soldier who rescued a Bible from a bombed church on a South Pacific island. The Japanese captured him, and he was able to conduct services in the prison camp with the help of the Bible he saved. All the time you were repeating the words, 'Take me!' In the end I said, 'Take me, Lord, too!' Since that time I have listened regularly to your broadcasts and derived great blessings from them." A pastor in British Guiana reports: "In the congregation at New Amsterdam is a family that your hour over the air has been largely responsible for converting. The family has three children, two boys and a girl. The man is a very keen listener and a hard worker for the Lutheran Hour. He gathers all the friends he can in his house to listen every Monday night. Last Monday he had another idea, to borrow the records from the radio station and on other afternoons to invite his friends to hear the records on his pickup." A Smith's Parish, Bermuda, listener relates: "Last Sunday I had become a member of the Lutheran Hour audience, and I am telling everyone here to tune in the program. I shall also write my family in Trinidad, asking them to listen. I gave my heart to God after hearing one of your broadcasts, and I went to church. The Lord bless you and keep blessing the Lutheran Hour!"

More important for you personally is the fact that the Holy Spirit wants to change *your* life and give *you* the Pentecost power. He is the almighty God Himself, with Heaven's resources, wisdom, and love. Therefore He can re-create you as an entirely new being, enlighten your mind by dispelling doubt, drive away the fears and phobias which haunt you, help you gain the victory over vices which beset you, empower you to defeat drunkenness and break the chains of any evil habit.

Besides, He who is called *"the Comforter"* can *"turn your sorrow . . . into joy"* and make your afflictions your advantages. A resident of Champaign, Illinois, planted asparagus in his yard three years ago, but it did not grow. Then he built a driveway over the barren patch, using four inches of gravel and two inches of solid asphalt. Now the asparagus is beginning to sprout and split the driveway. The Holy Spirit is far stronger than such forces of nature. If you will not continually resist Him, He can break through the hardest of your sorrows and your multiplied miseries. Through His divine indwelling you can be born again; and if you want to *"see the Kingdom of God,"* remember that Jesus Himself has said, "You *'must be born again!'* "

II

HOW CLEAR THE WAY TO SECURE THIS POWER!

In His marvelous mercy your heavenly Father not only offers you the Pentecost power through rebirth by the Holy Spirit; His Word, in plain, direct, unmistakable language, also tells how you can be assured of this blessing. When Saint Peter, filled with the Holy Ghost, preached the Law and the Gospel to that festival throng in Jerusalem, *"they were pricked in their heart"* and asked, *"What shall we do?"* As we now repeat the climax of Peter's appeal and tell you that you *"have sinned and come short of the glory of God"*; that no matter how virtuous you claim to be and how respectable men think you are, you have repeatedly broken the divine Law and invoked its penalty; that your sin also helped nail Christ to the cross; that if these transgressions remain charged against you, and your guilt unremoved, you are headed for hell; when those of you who have lived without the Savior and against Him find yourselves peace-robbed and fear-filled, we pray that you will likewise ask, *"What shall we do?"* and follow Peter's Spirit-given directive, *"Repent and be baptized, every one of you, in the name of Jesus Christ for the remission of sins."*

You see, then, the first sermon preached by our Lord's followers featured repentance. Indeed, every great Biblical preacher urged his hearers, *"Repent!"* The Prophets of the Old Testament cried out, *"Repent!"* John the Baptist, forerunner of our Savior, appealed, *"Repent!"* Jesus Himself started His public ministry with a repeated and re-emphasized *"Repent!"* Martin Luther began his ninety-five statements of Reformation truth with *"Repent!"* Today in our sinful, self-willed generation the only message which can have Heaven's approval and the Spirit's blessing is the fearless indictment of evil, personal and national, which begins, *"Repent!"*

In the eyes of the all-holy God, sin is not a slight matter, only bad judgment or a crime against society; it is an insult to God, an outrage so destructive that, if unforgiven, it damns souls to hell; so guilt-cursed that to free us from its appalling penalty the Father sent His own Son, Jesus Christ, to suffer the full punishment of our trangressions, to give His own life in place of ours, to serve on the cross the sentence of death divine Judgment has decreed for every sinner. Therefore this broadcast, cries out: *"Repent,"* you unbelievers and blasphemers who brazenly mock the Almighty and ridicule your Redeemer! *"Repent,"* you who profane the holy name of God and drag the Savior down into the dirt! *"Repent,"* you sophisticates and skeptics in universities, who proudly think yourselves above the necessity of hearing God's Word! *"Repent,"* you cruel killers of morality and decency, who lead our youth astray through printed filth, sensual entertainment, commercialized vice, drunkenness, and debauch! *"Repent,"* you adulterous husbands and unfaithful wives, who laugh at the Almighty's command, *"Keep thyself pure,"* who deliberately refuse to obey His mandate, *"Be fruitful and multiply!"* *"Repent,"* you ungrateful sons and daughters, who disobey and dishonor your parents! *"Repent,"* you godless fathers and mothers, who refuse to teach your own children the truths of the Lord! *"Repent,"* you dishonest, who lie and steal as you seek your own enrichment at others' loss! *"Repent,"* you liars, scandalmongers, perjurers, promise-breakers! *"Repent,"* you greedy and covetous! *"Repent,"* all of you who in a hundred different ways and unnumbered instances have flagrantly broken Heaven's Law!

Repentance means more than simply admitting your guilt. The French skeptic Rousseau wrote a book called *Confessions,* in which he describes, often with much detail, his bad habits and vices; but sometimes he gloats over his crimes. Repentance does not mean stopping your sins because you cannot continue them. Recently Great Britain's oldest burglar retired from his evil profession at ninety years, almost half of which were spent in prison. He stopped stealing, not because he regarded it as wrong, but because, as he stated: "I can't run as I used to. And besides, I'm getting clumsy; I knock things over on the job." Again, repentance is not mere sorrow over your wrongdoing. Judas was seized by remorse for betraying Jesus; but he did not repent. Almost every girl who gets into trouble regrets her downfall, but not all, by far, repent.

Pentecost Power for You! 333

When Scripture records, God *"commandeth all men everywhere to repent,"* it tells us, wherever we may be, that we must confess our transgressions in thoughts, words, actions, realize that they are vicious violations of the divine will, which can doom us to eternal damnation, and feel heart-deep sorrow over our evil ways. To show our sincerity we must resolve, with the Lord's help, to restore whatever we have taken, compensate for any loss we have caused, and then, with the Spirit's guidance, to amend our sinful lives and walk more closely with Christ. God grant that now, with the vision of your Savior suffering for your guilt impressed on your heart, you will thus honestly and unreservedly repent of the wrong in your life! You who know the Lord Jesus must be ready for daily repentance and constant re-examination of your conduct. Do you recall the tragic Atlanta hotel fire which took many lives? City inspectors had reported the building fireproof, and only a few days before the fatal flames gutted the structure, authorities had inspected the structure and declared that it met all safety requirements. In our lives we need, with even greater urgency, daily, repeated self-inspection and the repentance which must follow.

Then, showing us how we are to receive the *"gift of the Holy Ghost,"* Peter continues in his Pentecost appeal, *"Be baptized!"* With the urgent plea for Baptism thus emphasized in the first Apostolic sermon; with the Savior Himself instituting this sacred rite for His followers and promising, *"He that believeth and is baptized shall be saved";* with the Apostles baptizing their converts wherever they preached, in proud Jerusalem and in outcast Samaria, down in Gaza or up in Ephesus, across the Mediterranean, in Philippi or in Corinth, how can people today speak lightly of this *"washing of regeneration"* and set aside Christ's directive, insisting that it does not matter whether or not you are baptized? When our text commands, *"Be baptized, every one of you,"* and this certainly included the children in that Pentecost audience; when Peter particularly emphasizes, *"The promise is unto you and to your children,"* why do some teachers claim that the benefits of Baptism are not meant for our boys and girls?

Whatever men may say in contradiction, the unbreakable Bible declares, *"Baptism doth also now save us,"* that is, the faith which accepts Jesus' promise in Baptism saves us. Believe this! Then obey this other appeal of Scripture: *"Why tarriest thou? Arise and be baptized and wash away thy sins!"* We have never broadcast an invitation to Baptism without receiving definite assurance that some in this mission of the air have followed it. Listen to letters like these, just a few of many: *Wisconsin:* "Seven members of my family have been baptized and have accepted Christ as their Savior, through listening to your broadcasts." *Louisiana:* "All in our family have been baptized since hearing the Word proclaimed on the Lutheran Hour." *Nebraska:* "Every member of our family was baptized as a direct result of your Scripture-founded messages." *Missouri:* "Two in my home were baptized after hearing your constant plea for a rebirth in His name." Because we want you to experience this blessing, we beg you, *"Be baptized!"* We will gladly help and direct you if you will write us that you and your entire household want to join the Church in this way.

"In the name of Jesus Christ," so the Apostle states, we must repent, believe, and be baptized. We cannot

come before God in our own names, nor in the names of saints and martyrs, for everything human is stained with sin; but — praise the Lord with me this Pentecost Day — we can draw near to the mercy seat *"in the name of Jesus Christ."* Trusting in His full, free forgiveness of our faults and failings; believing assuredly that *"the blood of Jesus Christ, His Son, cleanseth us from all sin,"* we can come all the way to our heavenly Father. Then we have *"the gift of the Holy Ghost."* We are born again. Our lives are changed.

Be sure that the Holy Spirit has changed your life! Bishop John Taylor Smith, former Chaplain General of the British army, once preached before a large cathedral audience on the words *"Ye must be born again."* To emphasize the necessity of this rebirth, he pointed to the archdeacon who sat near the pulpit, and said: "You might even be an archdeacon, like my friend here, and not be born again; and *'except a man be born again, he cannot see the Kingdom of God.'*" Can you imagine Bishop Smith's surprise when, a few days later, he received a letter from the archdeacon with these words: "My dear Bishop, you have found me out. I have been a clergyman for more than thirty years. . . . Mine has been hard, legal service. I did not know what was the matter with me, but when you pointed directly to me and said, 'You might even be an archdeacon . . . and not be born again,' I realized in a moment what the trouble was. I had never known anything of the new birth." The next day the Bishop was on his knees with the archdeacon, who humbled himself before his God "as a poor, lost sinner . . . telling the Lord Jesus he would trust Him as his Savior." Do not rely on church membership, emotions, congregational offices, religious ancestors, but repent, trust your Redeemer, and by "the water and the Spirit" you will truly be born again.

For the blessing of Pentecostal power, for the cleansing by Baptism, come to your Redeemer now, you who have never known Him! Draw near to the Almighty, not in the name of any creed or congregation, but in the *"name which is above every name,"* Jesus Christ, God's Son and your Savior! Then this Pentecost marking the birth of the Christian Church will be a blessed day marking your rebirth into a new, victorious life. Spirit of God, give us all this Pentecost power, for Jesus' sake! *Amen!*

GOD, TRUE AND TRIUNE

"Jesus, when He was baptized, went up straightway out of the water; and, lo, the heavens were opened unto Him, and He saw the Spirit of God descending like a dove and lighting upon Him; and, lo, a voice from heaven, saying, This is My beloved Son, in whom I am well pleased."
SAINT MATTHEW 3:16—17

FATHER, SON, AND HOLY SPIRIT: Angels perpetually glorify Thee, our triune, ever-triumphant God. How, then, can we, weak and sinful as we are, worthily proclaim Thy might and mercy? Yet, we beseech Thee, accept our praise and receive our thanks for Thy limitless love toward us! O blessed Father, who didst create us and hast sustained us until this day with numberless blessings; O precious Savior, who didst give Thyself as our Ransom from ruin, when at Calvary, giving Thy soul and body the Sin Offering for all mankind, as Thou didst suffer the penalty of our sins; O sanctifying Spirit, without whom we cannot call Jesus Lord, through whom we are brought to faith, be with us during these trouble-weighted days, when war's shadows hang lower and heavier over the earth! Revive Thy work in our country, and help masses in the United States build their hope for both time and eternity on Thine unchanging Word! Awaken within the churches anew the voices of loyalty and allegiance, which will constantly denounce error and valiantly testify to the truth! O triune Lord of life, love, and light, bless our homes and our hearts with firmer trust and more resolute reliance on our risen, ruling Redeemer! O ever-glorious Trinity, hear us, uphold us in our sorrows, deliver us from our doubts, help us triumph over our temptations; above all, keep us ever with Thee and for Thee! We plead with assurance because we pray in Jesus' saving name. *Amen!*

According to public opinion polls about 5,000,000 people in the United States say they are not certain that God exists, and 5,000,000 more, self-confessed atheists, declare that no almighty Creator rules the world. In a problem-weighted day, when this country urgently needs divine guidance and Heaven's blessing, more of our people than ever before, 6 per cent of the population, either doubt or openly deny that there is a God. Heaven have mercy on America if this rebellion against reason and true religion increases!

Of course, many of these skeptics and scoffers, atheists only in name, forsake their folly when danger or destruction draws near. The war showed us that there are no atheists in foxholes, in fire-filled planes, on lost life-rafts, or in sunken submarines; and no less forcefully do the perils of peace constantly emphasize that in life-or-death emergencies, blasphemers quickly discard their unbelief and frantically seek the Almighty's protection. Down in High Shoals, North Carolina, William Hague Wood, a sworn infidel, so hated God that during a revival there he conducted opposition meetings in front of the church. In swaggering, boastful falsehoods, he claimed that the idea of God was fiction, invented by preachers for their own profit. When Sunday came, in the midst of a hate-filled harangue, he suddenly stopped. He could speak no more, since his tongue was paralyzed. For the crowd gathered to hear him, this was divine judgment, and they hurried into the church. That night Wood himself attended the service, where he, the infidel who had ridiculed the Almighty, handed to the preacher this note: "I now believe that there is a hell, and I am doomed for it. Pray for me!"

Much more widespread, however, than the denial of

the divine, omnipotent Lord is the appalling ignorance as to who He is. In Tsinan, China, a large temple is dedicated to five different religions: Christianity, Mohammedanism, Buddhism, Taoism, and Confucianism. The underlying thought in this pentagon-worship is the delusion that if one of these creeds fails, the people can fall back on another. Similarly, masses of the cultured in our country have only a hazy, self-contradictory idea of God. To them, too, religion is a try-it-and-see-what-happens experiment.

This Tsinan temple also claims to have an actual photograph of God displayed over the altar. This picture, it is asserted, was taken exactly at noon, on the ninth day of the ninth month, in 1929. Visitors to the temple are not allowed to come closer than within ten feet of this so-called photograph. Actually, however, it contains only a shadowy smudge, in which, attendants explain, a faithful believer can finally find the likeness of the Almighty. By the same error, again, too many in our country create a non-existent god of their own imagination. Ask the man in the street who the Lord is, and because half the population of the United States is outside the churches, generally ignorant of the fundamentals of faith, and because half of the half inside the churches is uninformed in the realities of religion, most people will stammer and stutter as they grope unsuccessfully for the correct answer.

Since dangerous days have dawned for our country, when millions in America point-blank declare, "There is no God," and when more millions do not know who the Almighty is; since many of you are ruining your lives by insisting, "No God made man, but man made God," or by speaking of the "Supreme Being" as "The Great

Unknown and Unknowable," we point you, in answer to the two questions, "Is there a God, and if there is, where can I find Him?" to

GOD, TRUE AND TRIUNE

and say, "Yes, there is a God, and He is the Father, Son, and Holy Spirit, revealed in the Bible." This Trinity Sunday lesson is clearly outlined in the words of our text (the Gospel of Saint Matthew, chapter three, verses sixteen and seventeen): *"Jesus, when He was baptized, went up straightway out of the water; and lo, the heavens were opened unto Him, and He saw the Spirit of God descending like a dove and lighting upon Him; and lo a voice from heaven, saying, This is My beloved Son, in whom I am well pleased."*

I

THERE IS A GOD

The scene of our text is the bank of the River Jordan, close to that section of Palestine now in the new, independent nation, Israel. The Lord Jesus had come down from Galilee to Judea to be baptized by John, the mighty preacher of repentance and return to the Almighty. If Christ, the sinless Son of God, Himself received this sacred rite at the beginning of His ministry, and if later, at its end, when He was about to ascend the heavenly throne, He commanded that all His followers be baptized, certainly you should accept the blessing of this holy ordinance. Our Lord Himself declared, *"He that believeth and is baptized shall be saved; but he that believeth not shall be damned."* This clear statement settles the issue. No matter how men may belittle Baptism, your Savior wants you and your family to be strengthened by this Sacrament. Therefore I repeat Peter's Pentecost appeal, *"Be baptized, every one of you, in the name of Jesus Christ for the remission of sins!"* Once more I offer you help and guidance in bringing you, wherever you may be, the new life and the blessed assurance of salvation which come through faith and Baptism. Write us, and we will thank the Lord for the privilege of assisting you!

Here on the banks of the Jordan, and here in Matthew's Gospel, the question "Is there a God?" finds its definite answer. For the *"voice from heaven"* declaring, *"This is My beloved Son, in whom I am well pleased,"* was not a rumble of thunder, which, unbelievers claim, the people mistook for words, but the utterance of God Himself. Hundreds of Scripture passages, in the Old Testament and the New, likewise proclaim that a divine Creator made, rules, and sustains the universe. The Bible never spends time in arguing or debating the fundamental fact of God's existence. It contains surprisingly few passages on atheism. From Genesis to Revelation, Holy Writ teaches in practically every chapter and every book that there is an almighty and all-knowing God, who gave you life and whom you must face after death, an all-powerful Ruler of this universe, who designed our world and who will destroy it, who is *"upholding all things by the word of His power,"* and before whom you, as indeed the strongest and best of men, are weak, fragile, puny, helpless mites of humanity.

Today, however, in the widest advance atheism has known, proud, willful unbelievers brazenly cast Scripture aside and deny that any kind of God ever existed. According to the claims officially endorsed, supported, and spread by Red leaders and their government, the very idea of God — and these are the words of Karl Marx, who a hundred years ago published his *Communist Manifesto* — "is the keystone of a perverted civilization." The present dictator of the U. S. S. R. is on definite record declaring that no good Communist, old or young, can believe in God. The sacrilegious slogan invented by Lenin: "Down with religion! Long live atheism!" summarizes the godlessness of Communism.

To tear the Almighty from the minds of the masses, Communism has practiced a ruthless program. First, its teachers have published infidel literature and attacks on the Almighty in quantities never previously equaled. Second, they have established many atheist "universities." Third, they have systematically had the denial of God taught to children. Fourth, they have supported and financed the formation of antireligious youth organizations. Fifth, they have placed into state constitutions provisions which encouraged their people to engage in blasphemous propaganda. Sixth, they have officially glorified godlessness by placing atheist slogans on public buildings and and on busses. Seventh, they have used the stage, motion pictures, and other public entertainment to promote the attack on Heaven. Eighth, they have printed and displayed some of the vilest pictures depraved minds could produce, all in ridicule of God. Ninth, they have brought the battle against the Lord into the homes. Tenth, besides all this, they have fought God with force, closed churches by the ten thousands, deposed equally large numbers of clergymen who proclaimed that there is a God, and in general instituted the widest persecution of believers history has recorded.

Some people claim all this is passé, that the Reds

have seen the error of their way and are now actually favoring religion. At a Round Table discussion with members of the faculty and students of the Oregon State College in Corvallis, a young woman objected that Communism has so changed, especially in the last ten years, that today it is no longer anti-God and anti-Christian, that people ruled by Marxism enjoy complete, unrestrained religious liberty. This type of propaganda is fed especially to American campus youth to discredit Christianity and democracy. Here are the facts: No Red leader has ever disavowed or denied atheism. I challenge you to produce evidence proving that Marxist Communism has officially altered one iota of its godless teachings. Second, in February of this year, *The New York Times* announced a new Communist campaign against the village churches and the village priests in Red-controlled territory. Organized atheism, far from losing its principles or power, is stronger than ever.

We in the United States are face to face with widespread denial of God in our own midst. This country, which should acclaim the Almighty more gratefully than all other nations, since our blessings, material and spiritual, are far above theirs, has atheists among its rich and poor, its whites and blacks, its educated and illiterate, its authors and readers, its politicians and common people — so many, in fact, that if the Gallup Poll figures are correct, the total number of the godless within our borders represents a force equal to that of fifteen States with the population of Idaho. These radicals support the slogan: "Down with religion! Long live atheism!" Enthusiastically they insist: "No God created this earth; it came into existence by mere chance. No God designed the systems of this world; they happened haphazardly to come into their present order. No God created man; he was accidentally evolved from lower animal orders. No God preserves and sustains the human race; it simply goes on by itself. No God awaits man in the next world; when we die, we disappear forever."

Scripture has one short ugly term for those who thus refuse to recognize a divine Creator, Ruler, and Sustainer. Twice the Psalter pronounces this verdict: *"The fool hath said in his heart, There is no God."* We stand with the Bible and declare that no matter how many degrees a university atheist may have, however much money a godless capitalist may have acquired, regardless of the huge power any infidel leader may wield — all who blaspheme God are guilty of the worst possible folly. They contradict their own reason. What normal human being, for example, can travel through our country and claim that these myriads of natural wonders came into existence by sheer accident? The British poet Shelley, outspoken infidel, once went to Switzerland and, beholding the sublime scenery of the Alps, found himself confronted by evidence of the Creator's omnipotence. Asked to enter his name in the guest register of a Swiss mountain inn, Shelley did, adding, "an atheist." The next visitor at the same inn, ready to sign the register, wrote in protest beneath Shelley's blasphemy, "If an atheist, a fool; or if not, then a liar!" He was right; no man in his normal senses can see the majesty of mountains, the almost limitless sweep of oceans, the vastness of continents, the entire grandeur of the globe — and then maintain that all this merely happened to assume its present shape and form. Did you ever hear of a scoffer who, gazing at masterpieces of art, Rembrandt canvases or Michelangelo statues, would maintain that

God, True and Triune

these paintings and sculptures made themselves? Yet when confronted by nature's incomparably greater glory, men otherwise famous for their keen intellects declare, that the wonderland of this world sprang into existence without divine direction.

Think also of the startling design in the architecture of the globe: land, water, air, in their good proportion and relation; the miracle of the calendar, with day and night, summer and winter, moisture and dryness; the ninety-six known elements found in the quantities and combinations required to meet the needs of the race, with perverted man, not God, splitting the atom for mass murder and devilish destruction; the number of babies almost equally divided between boys and girls, and often, after severe loss of men in war, a slight preponderance of male infants! Picture the innumerable marvels of planning and system evident not only in the mighty forces of nature around us, but in a blade of grass, a swallow of water, a breath of air, a ray of sunlight! Then ask yourself how, in an age when unbelievers demand scientific proof for every Bible statement, almost in the same breath they claim there is no God, no Designer for this stupendous universe of order, no Architect for the magnificent aggregate of nature's symmetry and system. It takes only seven separate pieces to make a pair of wooden-handled pruning shears. No infidel dare assert that these pieces created themselves, that the steel and the lumber automatically shaped themselves; yet some people do maintain that the tree which the shears prune and which in its beauty and growth represents a long series of divine miracles actually is the result of accident. No atheist would stultify himself by declaring that the Panama Canal is the product of mere chance; but many of them do say that the mighty Mississippi, many times larger and more marvelous than the Central American waterway, created itself, without divine supervision. What infidel, beholding a swift streamliner, would say: "This train, the Diesel locomotives and the coaches, built itself. No designer, no blueprints, no factories were required to form and fix its thousand parts; no workmen, no craftsmen and laborers were employed to put them together. They just jumped into their places"? "No one," you answer, "would be silly enough to utter such nonsensical dribble." Yet men with many university degrees are guilty of far worse folly. They actually claim that no God made the sunlight which speeds five and a half million times more rapidly than the fastest train; no God made the wind which has greater power than all the Diesel engines in the world; no God made you, who in your own body count mightier miracles of divine power than in the most advanced locomotive. The Bible warns atheists that *"His eternal power and Godhead" "are clearly seen,"* and pointedly Scripture tells all unbelievers that *"they are without excuse."* The Almighty has given them the proof of His existence; but they reject it.

Scripture registers another charge against scoffers who ridicule the Creator's existence. It says, *"They are corrupt; they have done abominable works; there is none that doeth good."* This connection between atheism and immorality is clearly seen in any place or age, in any individual life or family dominated by the denial of the Almighty. The lowest of criminals, the worst of cheats, the most vicious of murderers, the most notorious of liars, the most perverted of sex criminals have been atheists. The bloodiest wars, the widest massacres, the most screaming cruelties men have ever known, were started by atheists. Where in this or any other country is there a single self-confessed denier of God who in private life, home life, public life, gives his fellow men a high example of a noble life? I challenge you to name only one within our borders or beyond, today or in any past generation. Even atheists admit this. Recently a listener in New York wrote: "I have just heard your Sunday evening broadcast. Ordinarily I would not have listened for any length of time, holding the atheist viewpoint as I do. But something compelled me to listen. I cannot remember ever having believed in God, but it was not until I was fourteen that I applied the word 'atheist' to myself. For years I was practically alone in my disbelief. That was somewhat unsettling, because I continually came into contact with people I respected, yet who believed in God. Then when I came to New York to live, I began to associate with members of an atheist organization. I was rudely shocked by their ignorance and fanaticism. . . . At the present time I am just about as open-minded as an atheist can be. Go to work on me! . . . I am very appreciative of any steps you can take to help me." We submit this letter to you to enlist your prayers in behalf of this young man. An immortal soul is at stake, and your petition can invoke divine blessing. Do you remember that we asked your intercession for a Kansas doctor who was fighting the devil of drunkenness? Your prayers are being answered. He and his family now attend church regularly, and with the Spirit's help he is breaking the degrading habit. Keep on pleading until the victory is wholly his in Christ! Write us that you will pray for this New York agnostic, asking the Holy Ghost to open his eyes and show him that God lives and rules. Praise Heaven's grace, the Almighty has used the broadcast in bringing infidels to faith in the Savior! May He also lead this young man to the Lord! — We have read parts of his letter also to show you how even unbelievers themselves are disgusted by the practice of atheists.

Again, godlessness is to be condemned because of its utter inability to answer vital questions concerning the beginning of life and its end. This opposition to God cannot tell you even which came first, the hen or the egg, the oak or the acorn; just as it cannot tell what comes last after death and the decay of the grave. True, it speaks of total annihilation, claiming that man ends like the dumb brute; but infidels themselves do not believe this. Else why would so many of them on their deathbeds cringe in terror, scream in agony at the thought of eternity and its judgment?

We reject atheism also because those who dethrone the Almighty continually change their claims. Until recently opponents of creation claimed that it took many millions of years for the fire-filled earth which had called itself into existence to cool off. Now, however, a George Washington University physicist and two distinguished associates maintain that it took but an hour for the neutrons to decay into protons and electrons, thus forming the elements of the globe.

Besides, the setting aside of the Almighty is also based on serious mistakes. In 1919 excavators in Peru found a fossil which, it was claimed, showed that good cultivated corn existed there 100,000 years ago. Recently Dr. Roland W. Brown sawed off a piece of the so-called ear for further investigation. What did he discover? Revealing what has well been called "the greatest archaeological mistake of all time," he found not the 100,000-year-old produce of a primeval garden, but a modern, handmade, clay copy of an ear of corn which, he concludes, was probably a child's toy.

Can you entrust your eternal soul to a theory which repeatedly makes such errors and which continually changes? Why not build your hope for eternity on the Word that has never been disproved and on Him of whom it is written, *"Thou art the same,"* and who Himself said, *"I change not"*? Follow your reason, accept the verdict of great scientists — no outstanding scholar has ever been a real atheist — accept the facts of faith in Scripture, which in a myriad of mighty passages, like our text, conclusively prove that there is a God in control of the world and of all men, including you!

II

HE IS THE TRUE AND TRIUNE GOD

As we ask the Holy Spirit to bring you to this faith, we also plead that He will further bless you by showing you who the true God is and where you can find Him. Nature cannot teach you who the Lord of Lords is. Yesterday, on the West Coast, we came to a high hilltop, when suddenly the mighty Pacific flashed into view, revealing an unforgettable panaroma of verdure-clad mountains, miles of seashore, with six parallel lines of breakers, and a glorious curtain of azure sky. Almost involuntarily one of our party exclaimed, "And still some people say there is no God!" Yet all the marvels of creation, the most breath-taking scenic beauties — while they testify to our heavenly Father's power and love, will never give you His name nor describe His majestic Being. If you are searching for God in the sparkling radiance of spring, in the new-green forests, the freshly carpeted hills, the exquisite charm of budding blossoms, stop! They cannot identify the Almighty for you.

Again, human reason is unable to reveal His identity. A few months ago, on a train from Chicago to the East, I met a college graduate preparing for the ministry. In the course of our conversation I asked him how he had learned to know who God is. His answer named a number of modern books which, he said, were the source of his knowledge. When I told him that some of those volumes contained serious errors and inquired how he could trust such fallacies, he replied, "Well, I have formed my own ideas of God through these years at college and seminary." Once more I objected that merely human opinion is often notoriously false and unreliable. Then he asked, "Well, where do you get your concept of God?" "From the Bible, God's own book," I said. Can you imagine my surprise when he confessed, "I never thought of that"?

Too many people inside the church and outside make the same mistake. They never turn to Scripture, the only source of guidance, to find who the Almighty is. They never read passages of Holy Writ, like our text, to secure the facts concerning the Most High.

Here in the clear account of Christ's Baptism we meet God the Father, the *"Voice from heaven, saying, This is My beloved Son, in whom I am well pleased"*; Jesus Christ, thus acclaimed as Son; the Holy Spirit, whom the sacred writer beheld *"descending like a dove and lighting upon Him* [Christ]." In these three Persons, separate, yet marvelously united in one true Essence, is the Bible's unfailing answer to the superquestion, "Who is the true God?"

God, True and Triune 351

Before you begin to object: "I can't understand this. It is impossible to explain how three persons can be one," understand that I am not asking you with your puny mind to grasp the mystery which only heavenly wisdom will unfold. Yet I do urgently plead with you to trust the Almighty, to take God's Word at full face value. If every day you live you accept uncounted mysteries and marvels, though you cannot explain them, why should you hesitate to believe the mightiest of miracles? None of you will deny that you have a body, mind, soul, all in your one being. Why, then, deny the Trinity? If the rays of sunshine which help sustain your life have light and heat and energy; if the flowers of the field have color, form, and fragrance; if in uncounted instances you meet a trinity in unity here below, why should you reject the eternal Trinity above?

Don't think for a moment that we ask you to rest your belief on such frail and faulty comparisons with the Trinity! You can have only one real foundation for your faith: the Rock of God's Word! Scripture is clear and emphatic in teaching the Trinity; and our text, one of many which testify to its truth. The Old Testament exalts the Trinity. Turn to Isaiah 48:16, where Christ declares, *"The Lord God and His Spirit hath sent Me"*! Go back farther to the first chapter of the Bible, Genesis 1:26, and read the record preceding the creation of man, *"Let us make man in Our image, after Our likeness";* ask yourself who made the world with everything in it, including man, and learn that Holy Writ answers: First, God the Father, for it is written, *"The Lord God formed man,"* (Genesis 2:7); second, the Son, as we read, *"By Him* [Jesus Christ] *were all things created"* (Colossians 1:16); and third, by the Holy Spirit, since the inspired poet testifies, *"Thou sendest forth Thy Spirit, they are created"* (Psalm 104:30).

Even more impressively does the New Testament show the three Persons and the perfect Unity, here at the beginning of our Lord's public ministry, and later at the close, when Jesus directs that all nations be baptized *"in the name of the Father and of the Son and of the Holy Ghost"* (Matthew 28:19). It gives this testimony here in the Gospels, and again in the Epistles, when Peter calls the believers *"elect according to the foreknowledge of God the Father, through sanctification of the Spirit, unto obedience and sprinkling of the blood of Jesus Christ"* (I Peter 1:2). Therefore, on the strength of these and many other passages, we declare: You may not accept the Trinity and certainly you cannot understand it; but you will have to admit: the Bible does reveal and repeat that the true God is the Father, Son, and Holy Spirit, each a distinct Person, yet all divinely united as our one true God. Instead of questioning or contradicting this fundamental fact of our faith, why not believe the Trinity and trust its blessed comfort, love, power, and blessing? It gives you God the Father, enthroned in eternal glory and the majesty of His omnipotence; it gives you God the Son, who once descended to this earth as the Redeemer, Reconciler, and Rescuer of the race; it gives you God the Holy Spirit, who dwells within the hearts of believers, convicting them of sin, of righteousness, and of judgment. A Triune God, all-holy, all-knowing, all-powerful, can supply all your needs of soul and body, protect in life and death, answer the problems of sin or sorrow, dispel the grave's gloom, grant you the ressurection of the body, and finally bless you with Heaven's happiness by defeating hell's horror. Our

Trinity Sunday prayer, in which I urge you to join, asks: O Triune God, bring many souls in this mission of the air to Thee!

If some of you are now eager to worship Father, Son, and Spirit, yet, overcome by a sense of your sin and unworthiness, ask, "How can I, with the evil which stains my soul, mind, mouth, and hands, come before the all-holy God in His perfect purity?" I direct you once more to the scene of our text, the banks of the Jordan, and at Christ's Baptism show you how the Triune God can be yours. We are told that *"Jesus, when He was baptized, went up straightway out of the water."* He was to begin His public ministry of mercy without postponement or delay. Now His face was fixed toward Calvary, where, with agony too terrifying to be measured, He would give His own body and soul as the one means of removing your guilt, reconciling you with God and redeeming you from ruin. Here, then, at the start of Christ's soul-saving ministry, the voice from heaven proclaims, *"This is My beloved Son, in whom I am well pleased."*

Clearly, then, your heavenly Father was *"well pleased"* with Jesus' atoning self-sacrifice, for He wanted you rescued from the ravages of hell and reserved for the radiance of His eternal realm. So deep was His determination to deliver you from death and the devil that He showed you the deepest devotion, the loftiest love, the mightiest mercy that He Himself in His perfection and power could grant. Bow your heads and fold your hands reverently as you hear this: The Lord cherished your soul even more than His own Son's life, for, Saint John testifies, your heavenly *"Father sent the Son to be the Savior of the world"*; and Jesus, esteeming you more than His own lifeblood, willingly went the way of the cross to rescue your soul from the doom of damnation in the only way it could be saved — by serving as your Substitute in suffering the punishment and curse of your transgressions.

Compassion beyond all comparison! Christ's love for you is limitless; it yearns for your redemption and promises, *"Though your sins be as scarlet, they shall be as white as snow."* It is ceaseless, for though you may thanklessly turn your back on Him, He still continues to plead that you return to Him for the assurance, *"Him that cometh to Me I will in no wise cast out."* His devotion is changeless. You may have deserted Him and turned belief into blasphemy, but His pledge holds for you in your repentant faith, *"I will never leave thee nor forsake thee."* The Son of God's grace is priceless; no goodness in you deserves it, no offering you or anyone else can give will purchase it, but by the promise, *"Where sin abounded, grace did much more abound,"* your redemption is entirely Jesus' work, altogether His pure pardon, not the payment for any virtue you may falsely find in yourself. The Savior's mercy is boundless in its blessing, for it assures you of forgiven sin, peace with God, a prepared place in heaven, the resurrection of the body, and here on earth your Redeemer's abiding companionship, the new birth and the new life in the Holy Spirit, with its triumph over temptation, its comfort in sorrow, its radiant hope in the darkest moment.

Here, then, in this limitless, ceaseless, changeless, priceless, boundless love of the Lord you find the answer to the question, How can I come to the Triune God? Those who write me that your hands are stained by murder, those who hear this message behind penitentiary bars, or those who receive this record of redeeming love in homes which show the pinnacles of prosperity — all can approach the Mercy Seat through repentance and reliance on Christ's power to save. *"I am the Way,"* Jesus declares, and as *"the heavens were opened"* on the day of His Baptism, so they will be opened for you, both on the day your discipleship begins and on the day life's sorrows end for you. Then, with martyred Stephen, you can say, *"I see the heavens opened and the Son of Man standing on the right hand of God."*

However, learn this further truth: Our Savior is the only Way! He Himself tells us, *"No man cometh unto the Father but by Me."* There are thousands of false gods, but one alone, the Triune, who is true; there are thousands of creeds, but only one, the Gospel's, which saves. Therefore, as I emphasize in the word of unbreakable Scripture, *"There is none other name under heaven given among men whereby we must be saved,"* no other Deliverer than Christ, no other ransom than His blood, no other promise of pardon than His, I also plead with you personally: Come to the Triune Lord, through humble, contrite, trusting faith in the merciful Mediator! Then you will have the Almighty — and with Him the blessed assurance which enables you to exult, *"If God be for us, who can be against us?"* Why continue to fight a losing battle, with one punishment of divine wrath after another crushing you to the ground, when, as God's child, you can have peace of mind, divine help in every need, heavenly protection on all your ways, unfailing comfort in your sorrows, since the Lord, true and triune, is yours? The Holy Spirit grant that you who have rejected Jesus' grace will write, phone, or wire us: "Today I give myself to God. From this

Sunday on and forever, I am Christ's." Then we will be happy to show you more of your heavenly Father, your blessed Savior, your purifying Spirit.

Those of you who have found triumph over trouble by trusting the Triune God, defend your faith! In Hawaii, before the Gospel came, the natives worshiped the goddess Pele, who, it was believed, lived in the crater of the volcano, Kilauea. No woman was allowed to touch even the bottom of the mountain, for this contact, their superstition taught, would make the volcano erupt and destroy the island. After the missionaries began to win their converts, Kapiolani, wife of Hawaii's public orator and a devout disciple of our Lord, sought to break this bondage of fear. Despite the heathen priests' angry threats, she climbed to the edge of the crater and cried: "If I perish by the anger of Pele, then dread her power; but behold, I defy her wrath! I have broken her taboos; I live and am safe, for Jehovah, the Almighty, is my God. Oh, all ye people, behold how vain are the gods of Hawaii! Turn and serve the Lord!" On that day the power of paganism was destroyed in Hawaii. The Holy Spirit grant that you believers will be bold enough to denounce every false god with similar fearlessness, and champion the cause of the true God with like loyalty!

Only the Triune God can prevent the slaughter of another world war. He alone made America great and keeps it great. You need Him in your home, you need Him in your heart. What better benediction, then, can I leave with you than this blessing, which invokes the triumph of the Trinity on your life as it asks, *"The grace of the Lord Jesus Christ and the love of God and the communion of the Holy Ghost be with you all! Amen"?*

CHRIST'S PEACE FOR YOU!

"Peace I leave with you, My peace I give unto you; not as the world giveth, give I unto you. Let not your heart be troubled, neither let it be afraid." SAINT JOHN 14:27

LORD GOD ALMIGHTY: Show us today, as we commemorate the self-sacrifice of those who fell in the defense of our liberties, how shameful and destructive is the sin of ingratitude, the selfish forgetfulness of the pain endured by those whose death helped make and keep our country free! May the Holy Spirit fill us with the determination that their sacrifices have not been made in vain, and strengthen us to dedicate ourselves to promote that righteousness which alone exalts a nation! Keep our country, yes, our world, from war; and although in our sins and rebellion against Thy grace we have not deserved it, mercifully look down upon us for Jesus' sake! Since He died in our stead to pay the full penalty of our sins, we have no more guilt for which we can be punished. Bring the comfort of Christ's full, free forgiveness and the assurance of His never-failing companionship into many dreary, destitute souls! Show Thy lovingkindness to the thousands still in veterans' hospitals throughout the land! As we praise Thee once more this year for Thy bountiful blessings on our broadcast, the most abiding and abounding we have yet known, we beseech Thy continued benediction on this radio mission for one supreme purpose: that men everywhere may be saved by reliance on Thy Son as their everlasting Redeemer. Grant us this prayer, for we plead in His redeeming name! *Amen!*

ONE of the largest claims of inheritance ever to be brought before any court was made public just seventy years ago in Paris, when Thérèse Humbert announced that an American capitalist, R. H. Crawford, had bequeathed her his estate of $20,000,000. Immediately two men who said they were Crawford's nephews began a series of lawsuits against her. The court ordered that the securities of the estate be sealed in Mme. Humbert's bank vault and that she be prevented from using the fortune until a verdict was reached. The legal hearings dragged on for twenty-four years, during which time Thérèse Humbert borrowed $11,000,000 by signing notes "payable when the case is settled." Then, in 1922, someone discovered that there never had been an American millionaire by the name of R. H. Crawford, that the two alleged nephews were criminal accomplices. The police hurried to the vault, had it opened, but found it empty. Ten of the creditors committed suicide, totally deceived by a scheming woman who invented a fraudulent legacy and stole a fortune from her duped victims.

Today when I tell you that you can share in a true inheritance which makes Thérèse Humbert's fictitious $20,000,000 seem paltry, some of you will shake your heads and object that this promise is preposterous. Yet in all sincerity, emphasized by the fact that this is my last message for the present season and until — God grant it! — I return to the air in October, I insist: You, unnoticed and neglected, sorrowing and suffering, sin-laden and conscience-burdened, can be the heir to an inheritance more precious, more certain, more lasting, more blessed than any other legacy in our land. This is no fraud like that French falsehood, for the guarantee of this bequeathal is Bible truth, the sacred assurance of Holy Scripture. This inheritance offers not money, real estate, bonds, jewelry, but *"treasures in heaven, where neither moth nor rust doth corrupt,"* everlasting assets, which bankruptcy, inflation, depression, war, and disaster cannot remove. For this is the legacy of peace for you, peace with your heavenly Father, your fellow men and yourself, peace of soul, mind, conscience, peace in a world of war and wickedness, peace far above your understanding, for this life, for the hour of death, and for a blessed eternity with Jesus.

In His saving name I call out to you in our country, yes, to all who by short-wave may hear this message in distant continents:

CHRIST'S PEACE FOR YOU!

This wish of my last message during the present season is taken from the last words of our Lord to His disciples. This promise is a clause from our Savior's last will, as recorded in the Gospel of Saint John, chapter fourteen, verse twenty-seven, and preserved for all who are heirs of salvation in this plain but powerful pledge: *"Peace I leave with you, My peace I give unto you; not as the world giveth, give I unto you. Let not your heart be troubled, neither let it be afraid!"* The Holy Spirit grant that you will believe this blessed assurance, receive God's Son this day, and thus become *"heirs of salvation."*

I

THIS IS NOT POLITICAL PEACE
AS THE WORLD GIVES

See how certain this pledge of peace is by recalling that our Lord Himself spoke these words! Therefore, they are divine, infallible truth; for Jesus is our God, and therefore He cannot, He will not make a mistake. A professor at a tax-supported college in the Northwest breaks into the newspapers by declaring: "For twenty years I have been proclaiming a merely human Christ." How can a man find satisfaction in devoting his energies to contradict the Bible and overthrow the belief of his students? You parents do not have to stand by idly while teachers whose salaries you help pay step out of line to attack your faith. Ours is still a Government of, for, and by the people, in which Church and State are completely separated. No instructor at a public school, high or low, is legally permitted to belittle the Christian creed. Stand up for your rights and for your Redeemer! Speak up against anyone who assails your Savior's truth!

Note the time when Jesus gave this guarantee of peace! It was near the end of His life. A few hours later He would be nailed to Calvary's cross. This text, therefore, has the force of a last will and testament. Now if the courts of the land uphold a man's final words and wishes, certainly you should believe and follow the Savior's.

Keep in mind also the place where you find this peace pledge recorded — the pages of Scripture! An American marine dying at Guadalcanal whispered to his nurse that he wanted to make a will. He had only a few more minutes to live, so she handed him her pencil stub, and finding no paper, she told him to write his wishes on the starched cuff of her uniform. Painfully he scrawled this sentence: "I bequeath everything to mother," signed his name, and soon died. Later the nurse's cuff was sent back to our country, where the courts accepted this will as valid. How much more should we regard the Redeemer's promises, revealed in the sacred volume, as the unchangeable truth! It is often said, "No one can make a will which shrewd attorneys cannot break"; but a battery of distinguished lawyers cannot change one syllable in our Lord's legacy. Men have devoted their energies and their fortunes to discredit the Bible. Lewis Knapp, a Wisconsin pioneer, wrote 20,000 words of bitter assault on Holy Writ. To give his hatred of Christ both publicity and permanency, he planned to have his words cast in metal. At first the workmen in the foundry went on strike, refusing to handle the blasphemy which could call down God's wrath upon them. Finally, however, Knapp succeeded in having his attack on the Christian faith molded into eight metalic columns, which were to remain forever over his grave in the cemetery. What happened? For about thirty years after his death these tablets proclaimed his hatred of Jesus. Then his surviving relatives, opposed to his atheism, signed an agreement according to which these inscriptions were removed, broken into pieces, and then burned or thrown into the lake. Not one of the 20,000 words of wild unbelief remains; but not one of the Gospel's marvelous promises of mercy will ever pass away.

Learn also the definite certainty in this offer of peace! To be recognized by the courts of our country, a will must have witnesses who verify its truth; but the Savior's statement not only bears the Holy Spirit's witness, it also has Golgotha's guarantee that God's Son shed His lifeblood to give His testament proof and power.

Once more, consider this personal blessing, You can be Jesus' heir and inherit His peace! Often men make wills which leave the beneficiaries uncertain. Justice Oliver Wendell Holmes, called "the grand old man of jurisprudence," an attorney whose thirty years in the Supreme Court of the United States should have given him the training and experience required to write a perfect will, set aside more than a third of a million dollars in his estate and wrote, "I give, devise, and bequeath [it] to the United States of America." However he forgot to mention just what part, portion, unit, group, or institution of the United States he wished to remember. For years after his death a controversy raged as to whom or what Justice Holmes meant by this clause of his legacy. No such doubt remains in our text. When our Lord plainly and pointedly declares, *"Peace I leave with you,"* and in the rest of this verse three times repeats a similar assurance, He offers His grace and goodness first of all to His disciples who heard Him, and then to all of you who believe Him. *"The promise is unto you and to your children,"* the Bible states, and when in today's Scripture Christ proclaims, *"My peace I give unto you,"* realize that no matter how distressed and disturbed your past has been, however crushed your heart and crashed your hopes, whatever the unhappiness may be which haunts your home and burdens your soul, you, too, can find peace in the Savior if only you hear Him promise, *"Come unto Me, all ye that labor and are heavy laden, and I will give you rest,"* and trusting His matchless mercy, come to Him for divine calm and inner quiet!

Just what is our Lord's peace? Jesus Himself explains, first, *"Not as the world giveth, give I unto you."* He does not mean an outward harmony between nations, which the world has vainly sought to give but has regularly failed to bestow. His peace blesses the spirit and mind of His followers; it is the inner contentment of the redeemed.

This does not mean, of course, that Christ has nothing to do with banishing war and reducing the terror of savage struggles, which modern science seeks to increase. No, true faith is the strongest warrant of international amity we can ever have. How sorely we need such peace in our critical age! We have money, luxuries, creature comforts, power, inventions, colleges, culture, but no real peace. Indeed, ours, the richest and most advanced of the ages, has witnessed the worst bloodshed. World War I, a hell of hatred and massacre, was followed twenty-one years later by World War II, at least four times more savage and destructive. Yet before the heaviest wounds in this conflict have healed, General Omar N. Bradley, Chief of Staff, tells a Senate committee: "We are not so sure that there is no war ahead right away," although he was sure of this: "We are a little bit more afraid something will happen than we were three months ago." One of our highest military authorities thus openly admits that there is no guarantee of peace for the future. Indeed, atomic scientists publicly confess their profound fear. Dr. Harold C. Urey, one of the leaders who helped produce the first bomb, told a radio audience: "I am the apostle of doom. I am still a frightened man and I wish you to be frightened. The gravity of the present situation in the world is frightening beyond our ability to express. It is not possible to exaggerate this situation. . . . We have reached such a state of development in the arts of war that it is possible that another war will destroy this civilization." The same authority urged this nation to "forget all we know about atom bombs, destroy the plants which made them, and permit other countries to inspect the wreckage." Senator Brien McMahon asserts that both the United States and Russia have enough "radioactive materials above ground to destroy all human life." Equally gruesome is the devastation which will be produced by chemical or bacterial warfare. Northwestern University announces that its research department has discovered a poison so powerful that four ounces, dropped into the water supply of a city of 75,000 people, will kill every one of them. Far worse, one milliliter of parrot-fever virus, we are reliably informed, can fatally infect 20,000,000 people through the air they breathe. A scientist stationed at Lake Success, New York, reports the worst when he reveals: "Every nation — I repeat — every one has bacteriological weapons. I have seen some of them with my own eyes — one, just a bottle containing enough stuff to kill half the people of the world."

Despite these designs for genocide, drawn not by amateurs, but experts, voices are being raised to demand a third global struggle. Today is Memorial Day, when the nation should recall with gratitude the sufferings of those who in bloody battle helped give our country its liberties or who sacrificed themselves to preserve our freedoms. Three quarters of a million of our physically strongest men laid down their lives to defend our heritage of blessings; but do we remember them as we should? Last December 7 a reporter of the Hillsboro, Texas, *Evening Mirror* asked twenty-three people in this typical American community what that date meant to them. Thirteen citizens, more than one half of those questioned, answered, "Nothing." One man remembered that it was his wedding anniversary; another thought that Texas University had a football game scheduled; only five of the twenty-three recalled December 7 as the day of the Japanese attack on Pearl Harbor. America forgets too easily. Only a few years after the fighting in Europe was finished, people lose sight of the tragic fact that World War II cost the nations $1,352,000,000,000; that the United States paid, only for the direct expenses of its participation, $280,000,000,000, or $6,400 for each wage earner. No one has been able to compute accurately the number of lives, civilian and military, lost in that struggle; but some of the estimates run as high as 40,000,000. Today we dare not forget the third of a million American boys who paid the supreme price, nor the 24,000 veterans confined to mental hospitals, who, unless God is merciful and leads medical scientists to discover cures, will be doomed to suffer from unbalanced minds. May God forgive millions within our borders their shameful ingratitude toward those whose death made and kept our country free!

May all who love the Lord Jesus likewise take part in a spiritual offensive against a third world war and put into practice the high principles of their faith, which can restrict and retard the spread of atomic devastation! Let the believers serve as peace bringers in an age of bloodshed by following a program which includes: (1) daily prayers for the avoidance of conflict; (2) an annual day for national repentance; (3) a rededication by the churches to their chief and charter purpose, teaching and preaching the Gospel of a Savior slain to atone for all men's sins; (4) an energetic, mission-minded laity; (5) a new emphasis on Christ's Golden Rule and the blessings of brotherhood, which will remove Communism's reason for existence; (6) aggressive missionary policies in pagan and atheist lands; (7) a wide awakening among churchgoers to the privilege and blessings of a more generous stewardship; (8) the Scriptural education of our youth, designed to reduce crime; (9) the strengthening of the home, with a deeper appreciation for children, and a recoil from the ravages of divorce; (10) a new willingness on the part of Christian citizenry to follow God's Word, "*Seek the peace of the city,*" and to assume all the privileges and responsibilities of political life, especially the holding of public office; (11) the wartime drafting of money as well as men; (12) a department of peace at Washington, in compliance with divine directive, "*Seek peace and pursue it*"; (13) the removal of every penny of war profit; (14) increasing efforts on the part of the churches to maintain peace, with a constant re-emphasis on the truth that the Almighty would not permit David to build the holy Temple because his hands were stained with the blood of many battles.

No political program will adopt or endorse these fourteen points for the promotion of peace; instead, men will continue to rely on their own resources and seek to banish bloodshed themselves, disregarding the divine truth, "*Without Me ye can do nothing.*" In 1911 President William Howard Taft wrote with unbounded optimism: "The battle field as a place of settlement of disputes is gradually yielding to arbitral courts of justice. The interests of great masses are not being sacrificed, as in former times, to the selfishness, ambitions, and aggrandizement of sovereigns." Three short years later World War I began, and everything that as high an authority as President Taft had promised, cracked up completely. After that first global struggle the League of Nations was formed to prevent further strife; yet a few years ago on Lake Leman in Switzerland the marble halls of the League of Nations Building, which cost $15,000,000, were closed. This organization, which was to end war forever, is dead, a monument of man's failure to produce peace without the Almighty. Today the United Nations has been organized to create peace among all people; and as you pray that despite its difficulties it may survive, also ask our fathers' God to help us recognize that He is the Author of our liberty, the Founder of our freedom, the Preserver of our peace and prosperity. As we recall General MacArthur's words at the Japanese surrender: "Military alliance, balances of power, League of Nations, all in turn, failed. . . . We have had our last chance. . . . The problem basically is theological . . . it must be of the Spirit, if we are to save the flesh," the Holy Spirit help us understand that if we push Christ aside, we are invoking new and brutal disaster on ourselves.

Our strongest national defense, I repeat, is not international organization, military might, political party programs, but faith in the Lord Jesus and the God-pleasing walk of life which His Spirit creates. Only *"righteousness exalteth a nation,"* Scripture declares. Yet by transgressing divine ordinances, how seriously unbelievers and worldly, compromising church-members have endangered our national welfare. Today, when lust and unfaithfulness weaken the family foundation in this country as never before — recently a Los Angeles man, supported by public relief checks for more than a year, was divorced for the fifteenth time; in a critical time when newspapers report that 81 per cent of our homes have at least one drunkard; when an Iowa State College sociologist reports that the crimes committed in the United States last year were more numerous than before the war, showing that our country has not been brought closer to our heavenly Father by two sanguine struggles — a tragic fact confirmed by the increase of atheism and the spread of spiritual indifference within our borders — the cry re-echoes throughout the land: "America, repent! Return to God! Rely on Christ!"

In Congress recently a representative from New York arose to charge that the Statue of Liberty "is disgraced and demeaned by the inexcusable neglect and squalor about her on Bedloe Island." Yet how many in official Washington stand up to declare that our real American liberty is being savagely attacked by the godlessness in the hearts and lives of many citizens? On Memorial Day especially we should realize that if we continue to reject divine, redeeming love, we have no reason whatever to suppose that we can avoid a third world war with the multimillion toll in American lives and the trillion-dollar debt which experts predict will mark that struggle. If we fail to remember God, why should He remember us?

On the other hand, if this nation repents of its sins and thanklessness, remembers the Almighty, not only on Memorial Day, but everyday, it can be blessed with strengthening peace. Read the Old Testament records to find that when Israel humbled itself and trusted divine truth it had no war. If you say that this happened in ancient history, in a far-off land, recall this instance in our own century on this very continent! When Chile and Argentina were on the point of declaring a war over a boundary dispute, their devotion to Jesus prevailed. On Easter Day, 1900, both countries submitted the controversy to the king of England for arbitration, and both accepted his decision. Their armies were disbanded, arsenals turned into schools, war funds used to build good roads, and the very cannon which would have fired death and devastation across their boundaries were forged into a colossal bronze statue of the Savior, placed on the mountains three miles above sea level, between Chile and Argentina, there to display this immortal resolution: "Sooner shall these mountains crumble into dust than Argentinians and Chilians break the peace which, at the feet of Christ, the Redeemer, they have sworn to keep." Truly, the image of our Lord, pressed into human souls, brings the promise of peace and benediction, not the statue of a pagan goddess which symbolizes our liberties. If in the past, world leaders had been moved by God's Son rather than by selfish interests; if before hurrying to slaughter, they had hastened to prayer; if only one small per cent of the hundreds of billions devoted to kill men had been used to keep their souls alive in Jesus, many struggles could have been avoided, and millions, murdered in mass destruction, would still know the joy of life.

Similarly, the highest hope for restricting the ruins of international conflict, the strongest assurance against the massacre of atomic and chemical destruction, is Jesus. Britain's Air Chief Marshall, Sir Arthur Harris, correctly stated, "War will go on until there is a change in the human heart"; and the only way our hearts can be changed is through faith in Him who says, *"Behold, I make all things new."* Bring Christ to the Nations, and you bring them the love of peace! It is of the utmost importance that at a time when world powers are appropriating record military expenditures, we establish superpower broadcasting stations in Europe, Asia, and Africa, which day and night, in dozens of languages, will warn against sin as the cause of war and proclaim the peace that Scripture promises. Pray for a truly world-wide radio mission dedicated to one supreme purpose, the broadcasting of the saving, renewing Gospel!

We know, of course, that men will never completely accept the one Mediator between God and man. Indeed, we see leaders in control of human affairs today who boast that they blaspheme the Savior and sneer as they ridicule His grace. As long as this blatant unbelief continues — and the Bible plainly tells us that these last times will be marked by widespread rejection of the Redeemer — there can be no hope of lasting peace on earth. Atheism always promotes strife and slaughter. Therefore the Lord has warned us in this generation that as we approach *"the end of all things,"* we must be ready for *"wars and rumors of wars."* Despite this tragic truth, that sin will continue to provoke bloodshed, the faith of Christ firmly implanted in more hearts can help reduce the number of wars, restrict their atrocities, bring them to an earlier end, and work for the more humane treatment of prisoners and civilians. Don't make the mistake of concluding, "Well, if God's Word says we will have war until the end of time, doesn't that make every effort toward peace useless?" You know that you must die, but does this conviction make you lie down and complain, "What's the use of striving for the better things in life, since I must face death anyway?" Of course not! You try to get the best you can from the years the Lord gives you. Similarly, obeying the Apostle's admonition, *"Let us, therefore, follow after the things which make for peace,"* we should exalt Christ, convinced that as His Spirit changes the desires of men's hearts from hatred to love, from cruelty to compassion,

from the mania of murder to mercy, He can still give
us, repentant and reliant on His grace, a maximum of
peace and a minimum of miseries instead of the depressing reverse — drawn-out struggles separated by only
brief moments of quiet.

II

THIS IS SPIRITUAL PEACE, WHICH ONLY CHRIST CAN GIVE

Now, while Jesus never promised a warless age here
on earth, His legacy of love, *"Peace I leave with you,
My peace I give unto you,"* grants you the highest blessings of personal soul peace. When our Savior continues,
"Let not your heart be troubled, neither let it be afraid,"
He shows clearly that the calm and courage with which
He would enrich you starts where all permanent peace
must begin, in your heart and soul. You will never have
true joy in life unless fear and conflict have been banished from your soul. Men try, of course, to purchase
peace for themselves; but money usually creates heavier
conflict. They want to drink themselves into forgetfulness of their crime and their grief; but they awaken only
to deeper despair. People seek to think themselves into
happiness; but as David Strauss had to confess, "My
philosophy leaves me utterly forlorn," so today the list
of suicides contains too many names of college students
and teachers. Present-day leaders in human affairs seek
peace and power by ruthlessly mowing down their fellow men. What a shocking recoil this murder will bring!
Charles IX, the monster who ordered the massacre of at
least 100,000 Huguenots throughout France, in his last
hours told his physicians: "Asleep or awake, I see the
mangled forms of the Huguenots passing before me.
They drip with blood. They point at their open wounds.

Oh! that I had spared at least the little infants! . . . What blood! I know not where I am. Where will all this end? What shall I do? I am lost forever! I know it. Oh, I have done wrong. God forgive me!" No, for real, assured, lasting peace the heart must be quieted, the fears of the soul removed, the spirit strengthened.

Praise the Lord, that is exactly what our Savior did for us! He, the sinless Son of the Highest, went back to the root of evil in our lives and in our world, to our transgressions of the divine Will, to the sins that stain our souls, fill us with fright, and banish all joy. Therefore, if you and I are to have peace, our sins must be forgiven, canceled, and removed; not one of them can remain to haunt us with the horror of hell, to accuse us before the Almighty and our own conscience. You cannot have peace in your conscience when you are at war with your God; and you cannot have peace with your holy Father until all your unholiness has been wiped out of existence. That is why atheists and skeptics never know real joy.

Were it not for Christ, none of us could ever be blessed by peace. He not only loved us, He also *"gave Himself for us."* He not only hated sin, He even laid down His life to remove its ravages from our soul and body. He, the Son of God, yes, together with the Father and the Spirit, the Almighty Himself, is not only the Friend of sinners, but the Savior of sinners; not only the Redeemer of many men, but the Rescuer of the entire race.

As fifteen years ago, with fear and trembling, we began this mission of the air for one purpose, to proclaim Christ, the Son of God, as the only but all-sufficient

Mediator between Heaven and earth; as during this decade and a half, with Spirit-given assurance, we have been *"determined not to know anything among you, save Jesus Christ, and Him Crucified"*; so today, as I conclude my portion of this season's broadcasting, the mightiest and most blessed of all the fifteen years', in point of size, extent, number, mail, and especially souls won for the Savior, I repeat the message which has given the broadcast its power and blessing and which can enrich every one of you with its radiant peace: *"Jesus Christ, the same yesterday and today and forever,"* Son of God and Son of Man, loved you, despite your sins, with such depthless devotion that He chose the only way even He, the Lord, knew to deliver your soul from eternal death. In matchless mercy He *"took upon Him the form of a servant and was made in the likeness of men. And being found in a fashion as a man, He humbled Himself and became obedient unto death, even the death of the cross."* On bleak Calvary, forsaken by His own Father and rejected by those He had come to save, He was nailed to the coarse timbers of *"the accursed tree."* There, weighted by the world's woe, crushed by the burden of all men's guilt, He became your Substitute in suffering the pain and penalty, the death and damnation of your sins.

There, too, the atoning Redeemer purchased your peace at the highest price ever recorded. Shedding His own blood and sacrificing His own life, He rescued you from ruin, removed the guilt which separated you from your God, and did everything required to reconcile you with your heavenly Father. No wonder He calls this benediction *"My peace"*! He planned it, He perfected it, He paid for it, and, mercy of mercies! He has bequeathed it to you. Beholding Him, the Prince of Peace, crucified for your crimes and resurrected for your righteousness, you can join Saint Paul in the victory cry *"Being justified by faith, we have peace with God through our Lord Jesus Christ."* Thanks to His cleansing blood, your transgressions have all been taken away; as believers you have no sin, and therefore are God's own children, protected by His might, guided by His love, supplied by His riches, and sustained by His Spirit.

Again, with Jesus' peace pervading our souls, you can live lovingly in a world of strife, help your fellow men instead of hating them, obey the direction of Scripture, *"Follow peace with all men!"* and become the salt of the earth as you spread the glorious Gospel. If you have trouble and strife in your home, give the Savior the leadership in your family! Have Him take possession of the parents' and children's hearts; let Him be welcomed into your household in daily devotions, and you will see that His presence brings radiant peace within your walls, as it supplants selfishness with self-sacrifice. In the wild orgy of domestic debauch which now disgraces our country, make your home a place of peace by dedicating your dwelling to Jesus!

These wondrous words, *"Let not your heart be troubled, neither let it be afraid,"* seek to give you soul peace amid your fears. How urgently some of you need Christ's calm and quiet! You are worrying yourselves sick, terrorizing yourselves into nervous breakdowns, living narrow, cramped, dismal, darkened lives, when all the while the brightness of redeeming grace could flood your life with light and love. You may not have realized it this morning when you arose, but this Memorial Day can be a monumental day of peace for you. Not merely by accident or chance have many of you been led to tune in this program today; for the Holy Spirit does not operate haphazardly. Out on the Pacific coast I heard the remarkable story of a Portland, Oregon, child who, being sent to the first grade in September, mistook one of our Christian day schools for the public school where his parents had intended him to enroll. Because he liked our Bible stories and hymns, he stayed. When his parents investigated, they, too, became interested and were soon brought back to God. The lad so learned to love his Redeemer that he dedicated himself to the Lord. Today he is a chaplain at a Pacific Coast naval training station. Because of a mistake? Never! He was blessed by the same guidance which has brought you to hear the unbreakable promise today, *"Let not your heart be troubled, neither let it be afraid!"*

As you now behold the Crucified and hear this glorious Gospel guarantee, *"He is our Peace,"* I ask you, What robs you of your peace? The fear of your sins? As truly as Christ is your God and Savior, they have all been remitted and removed, atoned for by His self-sacrifice on the cross. The dread of death? The grave is not gruesome for those who believe His promise, *"I am the Resurrection and the Life; He that believeth in Me, though he were dead, yet shall he live."* Does painful sickness, long invalidism, wasting disease kill your joy? Believe that Jesus can always cure, if only it be His will; that no siege of suffering comes upon you, once you trust Him as your Deliverer, which is not designed for your good, directed to strengthen your faith, to rivet your affections more immovably on your precious Redeemer! Never lose sight of the triumphant truth that *"the sufferings of this present time are not worthy to be*

compared with the glory which shall be revealed in us"!
Once more I ask you, What makes you miserable and
morose? Loneliness, disappointment in love, the loss of
a dear one whom this Memorial Day recalls; lack of
home and lack of money, the unfairness and falsehoods
from which your suffer — any one of a hundred other
hardships which your own weakness or other men's
cruelties have imposed upon you? Pile up your gloom
and grief, but believe surely that Calvary's love is higher
than these woes and that you, too, can have the promise,
*"In all these things we are more than conquerors through
Him that loved us."* When you are truly Christ's, like
the Apostle you can declare, *"I . . . rejoice in my sufferings,"* since you know they come from divine love, not
anger; that *"all things work together for good to them
that love God"*; that *"whom the Lord loveth He chasteneth."* Here, then, in the confidence that Jesus is your
Savior, is Heaven's legacy of peace.

We can almost hear some of you say, "How can I
be sure that I will inherit this blessing, that I have been
named in Christ's last will and testament?" for the guarantee of this grace you need turn only to the marvelous
Gospel pledge, *"God so loved the world, that He gave
His only-begotten Son, that whosoever believeth in Him
should not perish, but have everlasting life,"* and in the
Lord's compassion for *"the world,"* and the all-embracing
scope of *"whosoever,"* find the record of your redemption
more definitely than if your own name were written
there. Even if in such passages of promises the Bible
actually contained your name, say, "Henry Smith," you
might feel that some other Henry Smith were meant; for
the Saint Louis directory alone lists thirty-four Henry
Smiths, and there must be hundreds throughout the

country; but the Bible's "WHOSOEVER *believeth in Him*" shall "*not perish*" does unquestionably include you.

If you continue to ask, "What must I do to become the beneficiary of the Savior's last will and testament?" We answer: "What must the heir of any estate do to receive his inheritance? Must he earn it, pay for it, buy it, give something in exchange for it? Never! A bequest is a gift, and the blessing of peace which Jesus has left us is among the most glorious gifts which even the resources of Heaven can bestow. Therefore, when our divine Redeemer tells us, "*My peace I* GIVE *unto you*," believe, because this promise is sealed in His blood, that this inheritance is yours freely and fully by pure grace. Simply take God's Son at His Word, trust Him triumphantly, and peace is yours.

Men often clutter their last wills with strange requirements. An Italian nobleman bequeathed to his widow an estate of about $50,000 with the stipulation that she pray for his soul all the days of her life. A Boston man wrote a will with the provision that his wife be cut off penniless unless she marry again within five years, for, he explained, he wanted someone else to find how hard it was to live with her. Another businessman in the East left his wife his property, but requested her not to enter matrimony again, since, he added, "I trust she will not again marry any man for fear of meeting with so evil a husband as I have been to her." However, our Lord's legacy of love is granted without condition or restriction — you need only believe that on the cross Christ paid the full price of your redemption, completely sealed your salvation, did everything His Father's holiness can require for your deliverance. Then His victory cry, *"It is finished!"* is the pledge that you have the guarantee of peace and pardon through trusting faith.

Of course, you can refuse this heavenly inheritance and sentence your soul to restlessness and ruin. *"There is no peace . . . unto the wicked,"* Scripture warns, and because the Holy Spirit may never give me the privilege of speaking to you again, I must tell you now: There is no peace for your soul except in Jesus. In that Savior's name we have now placed each of you before the choice of heaven or hell, of receiving or rejecting this legacy. Therefore we ask you pointedly and personally, as though we were now face to face with you: Which will it be for you, reliance on the Prince of Peace, and with Him the blessing of eternal joy, or the rejection of your Redeemer, and with that the curse of everlasting sorrow? As you answer, may the Holy Spirit so fill your soul with faith that you mark this Memorial Day by coming all the way to your divine Deliverer in contrite but confident faith!

Many of you are like the missing heirs for whom legal organizations are searching throughout the country. Riches and property await them, but they do not know it. Today on Memorial Day, when the Government seeks to express its gratitude to the men who fought for our cause, authorities in Washington are looking for Sergeant Frank Forbes; they want to give him a gold medal and more than $30,000 voted him by Congress for his willingness to endanger his life for others. However, the Government cannot find Forbes; and if he still lives, he is a rich man, although he does not realize it. To an immeasurably greater extent the Son of God has the wealth of heaven and the crown of glory for you, once you are His in trusting allegiance. We plead with you, accept

Christ's Peace for You! 379

your promised *"inheritance with the saints in light"!* Acclaim Christ your Savior now!

Because this is my farewell broadcast until the fall, when, if our heavenly Father wills, we begin our sixteenth season of Gospel broadcasting, we ask you to write us if we can do anything to help you receive Jesus as your Redeemer. At the same time we urge you, listen to the messengers of grace who take our place at the microphone! As a parting benediction I repeat for you the glorious promise of your divine Deliverer's last will and testament, *"Peace I leave with you, My peace I give unto you; not as the world giveth, give I unto you. Let not your heart be troubled, neither let it be afraid."* God be with you till we meet again — here in our radio mission, or there, in endless peace, at Jesus' feet! *Amen!*

AIR-WAVE TESTIMONY

In the following pages we give excerpts of letters from listeners, all personal references to us having been removed, to show how remarkably the Holy Spirit has helped us.

BROUGHT TO CHRIST

Conversion by the radio is a striking demonstration of divine grace. Here the preacher is separated from his hearers by many miles, sometimes by half the world. It is clear, then, that if souls are to be won for the Savior, the Holy Spirit must convert them to Christ. Every broadcast has clearly emphasized the full, free, and final salvation which Christ purchased for us with His death on Calvary's cross, and we have reason to believe that each appeal for repentance and reliance on Jesus was richly answered. Letters like these show, indeed, that as the rain and the snow come down from heaven to water the earth and make it *"bring forth and bud,"* so the broadcast Gospel has brought the new life of faith into many hearts:

Ohio — On behalf of my family I thank you and the blessed Word of God as heard on the Lutheran Hour radio program for bringing Christ to our family. We were lost and undone, but, thanks again to you and all concerned, we now know the truth and enjoy living in it. While lost and not knowing how to turn, I realize my family must have some sort of religion, as I have two children and must bring them up to know the truth. You recommended that I visit one of your Lutheran churches, which I did. I found it as you said — a light to the world, feeding the soul, and teaching Bible truth. I visited a Lutheran day school. Thank God and you as a servant of Him, my oldest child is in the first grade of Saint Paul's Lutheran School! The other child starts in September. It is inspiring to have them go to school, where they learn about God. I thank God and you as a humble servant because my wife and I joined the Gospel Center Lutheran Church.

Texas — All of us listen in each Sunday and enjoy your broadcast very much. Your program started me to go to church. We pray for you and your program. May God bless you!

Pennsylvania — We have enjoyed the Lutheran Hour messages for years. Through its powerful preaching we have become members of the Lutheran Church. Your sermons have always been an inspiration to us.

Iowa — Through your messages my husband will be baptized and confirmed on Palm Sunday. I am a happy wife, now that my husband will also be a Lutheran and a true believer in Christ. We hear your messages every Sunday after we come home from church services.

Texas — I was saved as a result of your broadcast some ten years ago. I never miss your sermons on the radio, and I am always waiting for them.

Connecticut — I am sending you a small donation, which was given to me by a merchant seaman. He enjoys the Lutheran Hour and is becoming a member of the Lutheran Church.

Nebraska — We enjoy your broadcasts. We are Lutherans. We have told some of our friends about them, and they are going to join the Church. May God bless the Lutheran Hour!

New Jersey — I listen with great interest each week to your transcribed broadcast. I am Jewish by birth and have had a relatively broad Jewish education compared to most Jews today. I would like to join the Lutheran Church, but I have not time to attend the Bible classes offered by the local church. Please enroll me in your Bible Correspondence Course!

Texas — A lady joined our church recently who was confirmed in the Lutheran Church but who had not attended regularly for years. Her husband is in the army. She mentioned the Lutheran Hour as instrumental in bringing her back to church. She comes every Sunday with her two youngest children. One girl is going to our Catechism class now. Another family, recently confirmed in Houston, told me that you had recommended our church to her when she wrote that she was moving here. They have joined. They had three small children and were pleased to find so many young couples with small infants, including my own four.

Illinois — Many are the half hours of feasting that I have enjoyed throughout the recent years on your wonderful messages, and many a time have I lifted a thankful heart to God for them. The Lord willing, I will soon be a member of the Lutheran Church, to which I'm looking forward with great anticipation and pride, as I consider how wonderfully and how fully the Lutherans teach the Bible, and the Bible only.

Florida — My wife and I are taking instruction in the Missouri Synod Lutheran Church here in Orlando. We shall complete this course by Christmas and plan on uniting with the Church at that time. We always dash home from church on Sundays so as not to miss your broadcasts. They have helped us immensely. At one time I felt that the man who stated he never has a disagreement or argument with his wife was a liar, but to my great joy I have found that where Christ abides in the home, there is never cause for dissension. We are truly happy and always remember your great work in our prayers.

Alabama — May God bless you in all your undertakings! Through your broadcast I was saved. I am enclosing a small amount to help spread the Gospel. I want to have part in helping win some souls.

Ohio — I know of a young matron who is now your regular listener but only a few months ago had no use for you, the Church, or God's Word. What a glorious change in that woman's life! Her one ambition now is to share the experience with her husband, who is a heavy drinker.

Oregon — Through the Lutheran Hour, my prayers, and God's help, I have won my husband to accept his Savior. I know the Word of God can do the same for two families who need Him. Thank you for any assistance you can give me!

Minnesota — We listen to your services and enjoy them so much. We love to hear the Word of God. It was through your programs that our only child was saved. He went home two years ago.

Washington — We listen to your broadcasts every Sunday. They may be partly credited with our conversion. May many more accept Christ through your wonderful work! Rest assured that our prayers are with you!

Missouri — I was converted while I was reading the tract you sent me in a letter.

Air-Wave Testimony 383

Michigan — Will you please send me my free miniature cross that you spoke about on your program? I am seventeen and was saved when I was seven. I have lived a happy life ever since and am glad that there are programs like yours on the radio. You see, my cousin and my father have both been saved through your program. I listen to it every Sunday.

Massachusetts — Some time ago I wrote to you concerning my mother and told you that our pastor was giving her instruction. I know you will rejoice with us that yesterday she was baptized and confirmed in Saint Matthew's Lutheran Church. We can truthfully say that the Lutheran Hour was responsible for it.

North Dakota — Some time ago I was called to the hospital to see a farmer who, while milking, had been kicked in the neck by a cow and who was paralyzed from the shoulders on down. His wife, a Catholic, told me that her husband regularly listened to the Lutheran Hour. He acknowledged Jesus as his Savior and requested Holy Communion. I asked him about his belief in the Sacrament, and he gave proper confession of faith. His religious background was Evangelical, although he had not attended church for years. You were his minister, he said. I gave him the Sacrament, visited him twice. He died two days later. His wife told me that he had always contributed to the support of the Lutheran Hour. The honorarium which she offered me I told her to send in to the Lutheran Hour.

Alabama — I am a regular listener of the Lutheran Hour. I live in a big apartment with about ten persons. I have asked them to listen with me, so they look forward to each Sunday. We all were in my apartment this morning, and I was just continuing praying that someone might accept Christ. So at the close of your sermon two young men were saved. You don't know how happy I was that someone did see the light and began to walk in it. I have started a Bible and prayer group in my apartment. We meet twice a week. If you have anything that you think might help us in our work, please send it to us!

Illinois — I enjoy your Lutheran Hour every Sunday. Although I've just started on my Bible Correspondence Course, I enjoy it very much and am learning new things about the Bible. Keep up the good work! Is it possible to direct me to texts and studies on the Lutheran doctrines? My husband is of the Lutheran faith, and I want to learn the faith and join the church before the Lord blesses us with a family. I will greatly appreciate any help you may give me.

Oregon — Please place on your mailing list immediately the name of Mrs. —! She is an ardent Lutheran Hour listener. Send her sermons and whatever else may be of spiritual and lasting soul value to this fine lady! Evidently the Lutheran Hour has brought her to Christ. She enclosed $9.73 which is her tithe money.

California — Here is the name of a new congregational membership secretary for our Lutheran Church. Met him yesterday — oh, for a thousand men like him! A fairly recent accession — brought to Christ through the Lutheran Hour while in service in some Pacific island!

Illinois — Four members of my houshold have accepted Christ the Savior, through listening to the Lutheran Hour.

Michigan — Three members of my household have come to faith in Jesus through your broadcast, and they are now members of our Lutheran Church.

North Dakota — I know of twelve to fourteen people, not members of our family, who have been won for faith in Jesus through the Lutheran Hour.

North Dakota — One member of our family has been brought to faith in Christ through your radio crusade. The messages are so emphatic and plain, and the speaker's pleading tone of voice make one want to accept Christ. All three in our family are now Lutheran.

California — There are thirteen in my acquaintanceship who have been brought to Christ as their Savior by means of your Gospel crusade. Several of these were formerly Jewish.

California — I know of a friend who was gained for membership in our Lutheran congregation through the work of Bringing Christ to the Nations.

Massachusetts — I have been gained for faith in Jesus through your radio mission. The family goes to church on Sunday, but I am elderly and can concentrate better by listening to the radio.

CLEANSED BY BAPTISMAL WASHING

In the Book of Acts the mighty missionary record of the Early Church, we read that those who came to faith after hearing the Gospel were immediately baptized. We praise God that in many instances our broadcast similarly has led

Air-Wave Testimony 385

many to follow the directive of the Apostle, *"Be baptized, every one of you, in the name of Jesus Christ for the remission of sins!"* How we thank the Lord for letters like these:

South Dakota — Several in our family were baptized through hearing your radio crusade for Christ.

Michigan — Three of us have been baptized after hearing the Lutheran Hour.

Ohio — Four of our household are baptized children of God since receiving your inspiring and wonderful messages.

Minnesota — Six in my household are now baptized since hearing your addresses.

Montana — Baptized in the name of the Triune God, one of us is a child of Jesus through hearing your messages.

Ohio — Our whole family has been baptized since hearing your messages.

Minnesota — My wife and children and I were all brought to Holy Baptism as a result of your radio addresses.

Arkansas — All three of us were baptized through your inspiring messages.

Michigan — My husband is now a baptized member of God's kingdom as a result of your radio broadcasts.

Colorado — My son was baptized in a Lutheran Church in Englewood after hearing your Gospel messages of truth.

ENROLLED IN THE CHRISTIAN DAY SCHOOL

Gratefully we acknowledge that the Christian ideal, a Bible education for our children, which has been put into practice by the day school system of my Church, is being widely recognized throughout Protestantism. Our broadcasts have invited parents to send their children to these schools with their Christ-centered programs. How they have accepted these invitations is expressed in such letters as these:

Michigan — Our children have been entered in the Christian day school since we began hearing your radio crusade for Christ.

Saskatchewan — Since tuning in your broadcasts, we are members of the parochial school here.

Kentucky — We heard your wonderful addresses and have sent our children to the parochial school.

Massachusetts — We have sent our children to receive religious training in our local Lutheran school after listening diligently to your broadcasts.

Arkansas — Now enrolled in our parish school, our children were brought to it as a result of our regular listening to the Lutheran Hour.

Kansas — My child is now enrolled in a school which teaches religion, thanks to the wonderful and faith-strengthening sermons delivered on your program of Bringing Christ to the Nations.

California — We have brought our children to a Christian day school as a result of hearing your weekly addresses.

North Carolina — We have enrolled our child in the parochial school here since we received great blessings through your sermons.

New York — Your preaching so inspired us that we sent our two children to receive religious training in our school.

Ontario — Three of our children are enrolled in a Christian day school since we began listening to the Lutheran Hour broadcasts.

BROUGHT BACK TO JESUS

One of the outstanding blessings of the radio is this, that it reaches many who have turned their backs on the church and refuse to attend its services. We praise God for the fact that the Holy Spirit has used the mission of the air in recalling many to repentance and faith. Read these excerpts and praise the Almighty's power!

Wisconsin — I almost dropped away from my church through my sinful life, but I thank God, you, and the Lutheran Hour for bringing me back to my Savior. Please pray for me that I will always keep on the narrow path! I don't know how to thank you for your wonderful sermons that brought me back to my Savior.

Kansas — We pray daily that God may keep you and all ministers who preach the Gospel of Jesus Christ on the air. My husband and I were saved nine years ago, but somehow I strayed away from the fold and have been as the man that Matthew 12:

Air-Wave Testimony

43-45 speaks about. Recently I've listened closely to you as you gave the Gospel, each word striking me, and I saw myself as a filthy sinner in need of a Savior. I have at last the peace that passeth all understanding, glory to His name! Our home is a bit of heaven on earth now. God bless you in your ministry!

Iowa — This morning your wonderful program came to me. I cannot tell you how much good it did me to receive it. I have been a backslider and have just come back to God. From now on I am always going to make it a point to be sure and hear your messages, because they are wonderful for us who really need help. May God bless you and keep you on the air for people like me to hear! I am back in God's arms, and I will never stray again. God bless you and keep you strong in His love!

Maryland — Your program helped me renew my pledge to become a follower of Christ. He spoke through you to me. I sincerely hope He spoke to many others also.

Indiana — Once more your radio message has come to us, and I can truly say it has been a great help in spiritual needs. At one time you helped me back to belief and back to my own church.

Nebraska — Once we were with Christ, but we have fallen away. We still believe and need prayer. The broadcast has brought back to memory the wonderful times and blessings I had while a true Christian and makes me want to go back to God's fold so I will be ready when He comes.

Iowa — Thank you for helping me find my way back to God! I could never stand the burden alone. My help cometh from the Lord. I enclose a check to help the radio mission.

Texas — Through the Lutheran Hour I came back to church. It makes me very happy, too. You had much influence over me in bringing me to the church. I am always your radio friend.

Ohio — Your broadcasts encourage me often. May God bless you and your helpers in all your work! I am a Lutheran, but I was seeking health and encouragement from Jesus in other churches. Your radio sermons brought me again to my childhood faith. I thank you with all my heart.

Iowa — Part of my tithe I send to your Lutheran Hour program, because through your messages I came back to the Lord, and I like to feel I may have even a small part in helping someone else come to Christ.

THE BIBLE CLASS OF THE AIR

The fifteenth season saw the beginning of the broadcast's Bible Correspondence Course, a series of thirty lessons, which present the doctrines of our Christian faith as taught in the Scriptures. No other feature of our work has grown more rapidly than this. Classes were formed in various prisons of our country, and members were enrolled in every State of the Union. At the end of the year, 30,000 listeners had enrolled, and by the grace of God many joined the church. The members of the Bible Correspondence Course write us appreciative lines like these:

Missouri — Since I have enrolled in your Bible Course, I have given my heart to God and am now enjoying the blessings of a Christian. I wish that earlier in my life I could have had an understanding of the Bible, which your lessons have given me. Thank you again for what your study has meant to me!

Minnesota — I have found the Bible Correspondence Course very interesting and instructive. Being a power-plant engineer, I studied many of the lessons amidst the purr and hum of electric generators. Much more powerful, however, is God's gracious and comforting Word. I thank you. May God bless you!

Ohio — The Bible lessons have helped me read the Bible. My courage would get very low, but this has been a lot of help.

Indiana — While studying your Bible lessons I was so drawn to my blessed Lord Jesus that I could not wait for the next lesson to arrive. I hunted and found a Lutheran Church. After attending several morning services, I joined an adult membership class and am to be confirmed soon.

Illinois — I had been a Christian Scientist until talking to the man who gave me the Bible Correspondence Course, and he has convinced me that there is only one true religion.

Minnesota — My knowledge has been increased, my memory has been refreshed in spiritual things, my joy and confidence in my blessed Redeemer's love has been renewed through the Bible Correspondence Course.

California — Being an invalid and living alone, I fill many lonely hours with the Bible Correspondence Course, which gives me renewed hope and much to think about. I shall miss these lessons very much. They have strengthened my faith.

Air-Wave Testimony 389

Wisconsin — The Bible course has taught me Christ, whom I knew not before.

New York — The Bible Correspondence Course has been a wonderful experience for me and has been a good refresher course in my Catechism, which I learned in 1934. This is a wonderful work. God bless you!

Illinois — I came to Jesus twelve years ago, and I have found Him again through your Bible Correspondence Course. It has brought me back to God and sent me convicted into His service, glorying in my afflictions, trials, and tribulations once more.

South Carolina — I can truthfully say that I have enjoyed every lesson and feel that I have been spiritually blessed by the study of this wonderfully prepared and simplified course. If and when I grow stronger physically, I may teach a Sunday school class again, and these lessons will help in that, too. The subject of every lesson appealed to me, and your notes of explanation helped me better to understand Bible readings and teachings.

Minnesota — The Bible Correspondence Course has encouraged my family and me to bear our cross with patience and use our talents for bringing in others.

Wisconsin — The Lutheran Hour Bible Correspondence Course has been a sacred pleasure. I always enjoyed doing the lessons; they have brought me to a closer understanding of our precious Bible truths, have helped me to memorize Bible passages again that were not as clear in my mind as they had once been, and thereby brought me closer to my Savior.

Ohio — I have enjoyed the course very much. It has helped me spiritually, revived and refreshed my early Christian training from my parents, and later from my pastor, who instructed and confirmed me sixty years ago.

New York — My heart has been strangely warmed in looking up some of the lessons, and a few things have been made plain to me. I thank and praise the Lord that I heard about this course on the radio.

Illinois — I am a member of the Lutheran Hour Bible Correspondence Course class. I am glad that I have the privilege to enroll and further my studies of the Word of God. I have attended an adult instruction class for six months, was confirmed recently, and became a communicant member of the Lutheran Church.

Ohio — The Lutheran Hour Bible Correspondence Course has made me realize both the blessings and the seriousness of my confirmation vows. It has renewed for me my instructions through adult eyes. It has also convinced me that Bible study is a necessity not only for youth, but as a companion throughout our entire life.

Washington, D. C. — I truly have enjoyed these lessons. I have been confined for ten days because of a heart attack. It has been a great pleasure to have these lessons to study.

Virginia — This is to express my gratitude and deepest thanks to you for your kindness and valuable support in forwarding me the Bible Correspondence Course, which I have completed. I am grateful to you for your efforts and feel confident that I have received valuable information from this course. It is a wonderful advantage to those who devote their attention to this great work and will inevitably be of great help to those who practice its teaching. It has broadened my ideas in numerous ways and tenders me much consolation and happiness, as I feel it will give me the pleasure and comfort of helping others who are less fortunate.

EARNEST PROTESTANTS SUPPORT THE BROADCAST

We find reason for rejoicing in the fact that members of all Protestant churches love the preaching of the Gospel and do not hesitate to step over denominational boundaries in testifying to their allegiance to Christ, in the face of increasing modernism. When letters like the following come to our desk, we feel more keenly than ever the necessity for working for true Christian unity:

Norfolk, England — For several months both my wife and I have become keen listeners to the radio mission. The first time we heard you preach it seemed rather by accident, but now I believe it was the Lord's doing. We never miss a service if at all possible. I am a Methodist lay preacher, twenty-eight years old, and I must say that although I have heard many an evangelist, I have never before heard a voice like yours. God has certainly raised up the right man to put him in the right place. I want to take this opportunity to thank you, for you have stirred me to the depths of my soul. The world today needs the challenge which it is now getting through the Lutheran Hour.

Washington — Having been a constant listener to your program for several years, I wish to express my gratitude to you.

Air-Wave Testimony 391

I am an ordained Baptist minister with several years of experience in pastoral and evangelistic ministry, and your sermons are very straight, to the heart, and inspiring. I am sorry at this time that I cannot enclose a liberal offering, since I am just out of the hospital after a major spinal operation. May God richly bless you in your untiring labor for souls for Christ! I remain a listener to your good ministry.

Arkansas — I am a Baptist, and the Lord is my Savior. I surely enjoyed the message this morning. Please send me a few pamphlets to read!

Michigan — Your Christ-centered messages are a welcome hour in our home every Sunday; they are as refreshing as a gentle rain. We hurry home from church every Sunday to receive your program featuring our blessed Redeemer. We have a lukewarm Laodicean church, where Christ's blood is mentioned only at Communion service. Please accept our check for $100.00; may it be used for the Christ we love and worship!

California — I belong to the Methodist Church and have been a member all my life. Sunday mornings I look forward with eager anticipation to your broadcast. It is my Sunday treat. I am so glad for your broadcasts, for they are wonderful in their widespread contact.

Georgia — Please send me information concerning your Correspondence Course mentioned in your broadcast! I am a Baptist pastor, but am very much interested in the work of other denominations. I enjoy your broadcasts so much. May God bless you as you minister in a mighty way!

Texas — I am a regular listener to your program and think it is a real blessing to anyone who listens to it. I know you are giving your all to Christ and spreading His Word far and near. We are Baptists, but we, too, are lovers of the plain Gospel, and this is what you preach.

Washington — I am a Christian Jew. We listen to your programs on Sundays and enjoy them very much. I am thankful there are Christians who stand up for the Lord.

South Carolina — I listen to and thoroughly enjoy the Lutheran Hour on Sunday mornings. You have given me great inspiration through your program. Thanks again for your wonderful work! I am the mother of two boys. They, my husband, and I listen to your program on Sunday morning before going to our own Baptist Sunday school.

Kansas — Accept the enclosed check for $25.00 as a token of appreciation from a Methodist family who greatly appreciates the excellent presentation of the Bible messages via the Lutheran Hour.

New York — Kindly enroll me in the Bible Course! I am an Episcopalian! My husband and I both enjoy your messages every Sunday evening.

Massachusetts — I teach Sunday school in the Greek Orthodox Church. My husband and I listen to your program every Sunday and enjoy it very much. Enclosed you will find a portion of our tithing money to use on your general radio work.

California — As a world-wide Presbyterian evangelist, I do not know of a better investment of the Lord's money than the Lutheran Hour. Enclosed please find a $25.00 check!

Maine — I belong to the Seventh Day Adventist Church. We all look forward to hearing you on Sunday over the air. Enclosed find one dollar! I only wish I had more.

California — I am not a member of the Lutheran Church, but as soon as I am able to, I am joining the church. My husband was baptized in the Lutheran faith, and we are both interested in the Lutheran teaching. I was reared a Methodist, but now have been helped very much by the sermons of the Lutheran Hour. God bless the wonderful work you are doing! May everyone that listens be brought to Christ as we were!

Wisconsin — May I say frankly and in all sincerity that several of your recent messages have combined to work a new courage in my ministry? Surely your fearlessness is needed today, and yet how often and to our shame do we evade or glance over sins that should be revealed in the white light of the glorious Gospel of Christ. I surely praise God, and without the least bit of professional jealousy or covetousness, for your ministry. May God raise up more like you in all of our denominations!

Bahamas — Although I am a member of the Seventh Day Adventist Church, your broadcast, Bringing Christ to the Nations, has helped me and brought me nearer to God. All of us here appreciate your broadcasts; they are a great blessing to us.

Ohio — We are faithful members of the Mennonite Church and are active in our young people's society. I love hearing your program on Sundays; you truly reach the hearts. God bless you in your great work!

Air-Wave Testimony

New York — I listen every Sunday to your program, Bringing Christ to the Nations, and I am wonderfully blessed. I think it is a marvelous thing that the precious Word of God can be brought into our homes. I belong to the Christian and Missionary Alliance Church, but as soon as I get home from church, I tune in your program.

Maine — I wish to inform you how much we appreciate your program. My husband is a Baptist minister and finds it refreshing to be able to hear you after giving his own sermon each Sunday. He has followed you for years and always speaks of you, whenever he can, as America's Number 1 program! Many is the time he has run into the house breathless in order to be on time for you. We are twelve miles north of Bangor; not too many speakers find their way this far north. You may like to know that there is a fair group among our friends who listen to you regularly and like your programs exceedingly well.

ROMAN CATHOLICS ACCLAIM THE GOSPEL

Among the most appreciative listeners to the broadcast are many Roman Catholics. Although there is a decisive difference between our message and that of the Catholic Church, it is a profound proof of the Holy Spirit's power that members of that Church not only tune in, but also write us grateful, Gospel-exalting statements like these, which are often accompanied by contributions for the spreading of the Gospel:

Wisconsin — I am a devoted listener to your radio program, and I would not miss it for anything in the world. Even though I am of the Catholic faith, I do hope and pray you are on the air more and more often. You see, I am a so-called shut-in since childhood with a heart illness, which does not permit me to live a life one would expect of a girl in her twenties.

Trinidad, B.W.I. — When I am out at times and your program is on the air, almost every radio is tuned to that station. I feel proud to hear it, although I am a Catholic.

New York — I am a Catholic and a regular listener to your program and receive rich blessing from it.

Kansas — Please accept this humble gift as a token of good will! I am a Catholic but accept and consider the Lutherans as brothers in Christ. "By their works you shall know them," and who dares deny your good works?

Ohio — I am a Catholic. I have been listening to your program on Sunday for years. I like it very much, and today it was especially lovely. People would have to have stone instead of hearts not to feel sorry for their sins and not to love our Lord for His suffering and mercy for us.

Massachusetts — Your sermon today was one of the most forceful I have ever heard. You hit the nail squarely on the head. While I am a Roman Catholic, I take great pleasure in giving credit where credit is due. I admire your sincerity and spirit. God bless you!

Florida — I regularly listen to the Sunday broadcast of several radio pastors. Please permit me to say in a few words that your broadcast of Bringing Christ to the Nations is the most magnificent and greatest of them all! I was a Catholic at one time, but after hearing your wonderful sermons over a period of time, I believe that the Lutheran services more completely relay the great truths of the Bible in a more understanding and complete manner than any I have ever heard before.

Washington — I think your Lutheran Hour is very beautiful, and I hear it often. As I am a Catholic, you have my deepest co-operation in prayer for world peace.

Alabama — I am a member of the Catholic Church, but have never been satisfied with my religion. I have talked to the Catholic priest and the Protestant ministers, but have never understood what being a Christian is. My mother has been listening to your sermons and thought possibly that you could tell me how I might be saved. I know what the Bible says about being saved, but for some reason cannot get to the point of knowing exactly or feeling the same emotions that people do who have been saved.

Minnesota — Your sermon on the Lutheran Hour today impressed me very much in regard to your honesty and charity. I am a Catholic, so doubtless we disagree on some matters. However, all of us can join in the prayer that all may be one.

"I WAS SICK, AND YE VISITED ME!"

One of the often forgotten hardships of illness and injury is the fact that those who are confined to sickrooms are prevented from attending church and are often without the guidance and comfort of pastors. Here the radio plays one of its most important roles. It brings the Gospel's cheering message to those who would not otherwise receive the assurance that *"all things work together for good to them that love God."* We praise the Almighty for permitting us to point many thousands of those suffering under physical weaknesses and handicaps to Him who can heal both body and soul.

Ohio — Your sermon Sunday was a keynote. I never heard anything to equal the truth as you told it. I am shut in during the winter months by incurable asthma. I certainly do enjoy your talks. Would to God that the world could see the truth of your sermon as I do! When we are in health, we do not see or heed the notice that the grim reaper is only a short way off.

New Jersey — Last Sunday I listened to you from a bed in the Presbyterian Hospital in Philadelphia, and all the men in our room enjoyed your message. May God bless you in your continued and faithful labors! We appreciate the Christian testimony that you raise so powerfully in these critical days.

Texas — Having been a bed patient in Harris County Tuberculosis Hospital for seven months, unable to attend church, I experience pleasure and blessing in receiving your messages by radio.

California — I am a shut-in, bedfast for five years. After I wrote, you sent me a pastor who gave me instructions in the Lutheran faith, so that for three years I have had the benefit of church and Communion, and friends of the same faith.

Ohio — Years ago I went on a missionary search in reverse to the usual meaning. I was searching for an agent of Christianity worthy of the meaning. After several years of attending church services of various denominations I sadly gave up, agreeing with the agnostic point of view. However, I did not serve the satanic force of spiritism. I did explore it in idle play, which is my sin, and I now constantly pray to our great Savior for forgiveness. If I could have heard sermons such as you are now delivering, I know that twelve years of wasted living could have been saved. Please have the local Lutheran minister come to see me, as I am not able to go and see him! I am not able to leave my bed, for I have been bedfast since May.

Washington, D. C. — I am a shut-in, confined to my bed most of the time, and your broadcast has been a great solace and comfort to me. I listen to it every Sunday on my radio.

Kentucky — I have been listening to your sermons for about four years. They help me live a better Christian life from day to day. I have been a cripple for a month and cannot go to church.

Pennsylvania — I have been and still am one of your regular Lutheran Hour listeners and have received much help and comfort from your broadcasts. I am a shut-in, have been for eleven years, and was in the hospital not long ago for nine weeks, five of which I did not know anyone or where I was, but, oh, how I did suffer! Now I am home again, only able to move about, and still suffer much. Now I am only waiting to go home, where I will not have to suffer any more pain, no more heartaches, and no more crying. Oh, that will be glory for me!

Indiana — I am not able to go to church because of a body ailment. I have had this for more than seven years and am in my seventy-eighth year, so if it were not for the Lutheran Hour, I would not get to hear any Lutheran sermons. I am very thankful for this.

Missouri — Our entire family, my husband, two little girls, and I, thank you for the Lutheran Hour. This winter my dear husband's health was so broken that he has been confined to his bed. Since we are not able to attend our own church services, we have enjoyed each of the messages we have received from you, and tonight our little girls returned from church in time to listen in with us. Thank God for men who so fearlessly and earnestly proclaim the Word of God to this sin-cursed, chaotic world! I have invited some of our friends to listen to your sermons.

Wisconsin — I have had arthritis for many years, so wasn't always able to get to my church. This year I suffered a heart ailment and haven't been able to get out since. The Lutheran Hour has meant much more to me now. I like your sermons and never miss them.

Virginia — I am a poor widow, confined to my room most of the time with rheumatism. I have a nice radio, which my church has given to me. I listen every Sunday morning for the Lutheran Hour. Your sermons are most inspiring and uplifting.

NO COLOR LINE IN OUR BROADCASTS

The Lutheran Hour consistently has protested against the injustices which Negroes in our country have to suffer, particularly against the prejudice which bars them from many of our churches. The Communists capitalize on this

Air-Wave Testimony

discrimination. We thank the Almighty that He has led many of our neighbors of another color to listen and to send us their reaction in letters like the following:

Kentucky — I have been a shut-in from a most peculiar stroke which seemingly settled in my spine. I heard your broadcast before I had this attack, but I had not followed the program as I have since my illness. I feel that I have been benefited greatly by your broadcast in mind, body, and soul. I am a Negro, thirty-five years old.

Ohio — For some time I have listened to the Christ-centered messages of the Lutheran Hour. I am a Negro. I have no church affiliation, but I do want to become a member of the Missouri Synod Lutheran Church. It was through the Gospel messages of the Lutheran Hour that I came to know the Redeemer as my Lord. I wish that every station under the sun were able to carry Bringing Christ to the Nations. God bless you and all who are affiliated with the Lutheran Hour ministry of the air!

Texas — I am a Negro. I listen to your sermon every Sunday, and I like it very much.

California — From firsthand experience in canvassing I can assure you that the vast majority of all Negroes are Lutheran Hour listeners, and that a number of them are taking the Lutheran Hour Bible Correspondence Course. They tell me they love the program, and I feel sure it is serving as an opening wedge for our work here.

New York — My wife and I are constant listeners to your broadcast and have tried to contribute in our meager way. We are returned missionaries from the island of St. Lucia, British West Indies, also have worked in South and Central America and, like all missionaries, are in need of funds to carry on God's work. We are colored people, but proud of our race. Not many doors are open to us to tell the story; our colored churches are poor, and our people also. Thank you again for the privilege of writing you! May God bless you in doing His work.

Virginia — It is with great pleasure that I send this small gift; wish it were many times more! I hear your Lutheran Hour sermon on Sundays and enjoy it. It is the pure, unadulterated Gospel, which you don't hear now from many pulpits. I am a colored woman and am glad to see from your booklet that many of my race are interested listeners.

New York — I have discovered and am watching a little group of Lutheran Hour listeners in the village of Yanceyville, North Carolina. They are of the colored race. There is not a Lutheran church within the county, and they seem to appreciate deeply the messages which you proclaim over the air. I have sent them a copy of the Lutheran Hour station log for their community, and I know they are making use of it.

LISTENERS BEHIND PENITENTIARY BARS

In recent years the Lutheran Hour has set itself the objective of following Christ's ideal expressed in the words: *"I was in prison, and ye visited Me,"* by reaching many thousands in our country's penal population. Uniformly the wardens have been happy to co-operate with us. Through the Holy Spirit's guidance we have been given a large group of reform-school and penitentiary listeners. That they have heard the Word with blessing may be seen in letters like these, which come to us from behind steel bars and granite walls:

Oklahoma — I hear your program at the state penitentiary. I enjoy your message each Sunday, and I would appreciate it very much if you would mail the Bible Correpsondence Course. Any literature that you have will be very much appreciated, as I would like to study it. I am sending you one dollar as a donation. I trust that you will pray for me.

Canada — This is a reply to your letter, in which you request that the inmate population of this institution be given the opportunity to listen to some of your programs. It has been decided to tune in the stations in Toronto and Stratford.

Virginia — Through listening to your Spirit-filled radio broadcasts I have been inspired to express my appreciation for such wonderful services. I really enjoy them. I am a prisoner of Virginia State Penitentiary, but I am a Christian, and even though I am eager to be released that I might be helpful to my family and to society, my seven years which I have spent here have been the happiest days of my life, for my Savior is here with me.

California — I was thrilled to hear your broadcast Sunday; it really opened a new life for me. Many men here in the San Quentin prison listen to your broadcast, and we all like it. It is one of the warden's favorite programs, and ours, too.

Air-Wave Testimony 399

Virginia — Thank you for your kind offer of regular Lutheran Hour transcriptions each week for use at the Reformatory. Our equipment for using professional broadcast recordings is on order, and the superintendent assured me that we would be able to use your transcriptions in the near future. The Lutheran Hour is an excellent program. The men will appreciate the opportunity of hearing your messages.

West Virginia — I was baptized in the Lutheran Church when I was a baby and confirmed when twelve. I didn't live up to it. If I had, I wouldn't be where I am now. I'm a prisoner of the West Virginia Penitentiary. Your radio programs have been a great help to me.

New York — It has been my pleasure to listen to your program many years, and I consider it the radio's outstanding Sunday program. I wish to mention a fact that may be of interest to you. In this penal institution, where I am incarcerated for a short time, we receive continuous radio programs, but the programs are selected in a master control room. The Sunday noon program has been the Lutheran Hour, selected by the officials as the most beneficial of the numerous programs on the air at that time. I know you feel the same as I that these officials must be complimented for this choice of radio program.

New York — I am now in prison, but thank God, walls cannot keep a man from accepting the Lord Jesus Christ as his Savior. Now that I have accepted Christ, I look around me, and I realize what the modern man really is.

COUNSEL AND COMFORT FOR THE PERPLEXED

Many listeners, beset by spiritual problems, often have no spiritual adviser to guide them. Each Sunday they are invited to present their problems and discuss them with us. Thousands during the fifteenth season have asked for counsel based on God's Word. Though their letters are treated with confidence, a few excerpts follow, from which personal identifications have been removed, to show the types of problems presented to the speaker for Scripture-grounded advice:

Minnesota — Please help me pray for my son to turn to Jesus at once before it is too late! Write to him, and help me bring him back to his Christian ways, from which he fell! May God give you the right words to write to him!

Oregon — I love my husband very much, also our two boys, but does the fact that his second wife is still alive mean that his marriage to me before God is classed as adultery? He was having his affair with his common-law wife when he let his second wife divorce him. Wouldn't this be classed as fornication? This has me worried; I never thought my marriage would have such a background. Why do men have to be like that? My husband says he loves me, but knowing all I do about him now makes me doubt his love at times. I try to be a good wife, but I was brought up by simple standards.

Wisconsin — I have broken every one of God's Commandments, and to make matters worse, I just can't find a way out of this turmoil of sin. I've searched the Scriptures and prayed constantly, but I haven't succeeded. My last hope is that probably your Bible Correspondence Course can help me. I don't believe I know how to pray, because I don't feel the solace one should after talking to God. I've thought of writing to you for months, but always hoped my life would be better. Please send me your Correspondence Course as soon as possible and any information that will help me lead a better life and be saved!

California — Although I've been a Christian three years now, I am going to a Christ-centered college and have heard many sermons on the subject. Can you please tell me how I can be sure of God's will and God's leading? I want so very much to be where He wants me, when He wants me, and above all, what He wants me to be. I know that God has the answer, and we must trust and obey, but will you help me become more certain about this? I'm willing to pay the price, whatever He may demand.

North Carolina — I would appreciate any help you could offer. For twenty-four years of my life I served the devil. After experiencing a Christian life, I am sorry I ever gave him a second of my time. I have been a drunkard and, of course, done other evil things, but now I am a Christian, praise God! My family has turned against me. My wife has threatened to lock me out when I go to church, but I can't turn back. I am a man of fifty-five. Please help me!

Nebraska — I listen to your sermons and enjoy them very much. I am not a Christian, but will you please pray that I may be saved before it is too late? It seems that I am bound by Satan and cannot be loosed. I can't seem to get rid of my sins. I want to trust the Lord. Please pray for me!

Air-Wave Testimony

Indiana — I desire to be a true child of God, but my trouble is that I cannot see my own sin and guilt. I do know that the Bible says all men are by nature sinful and eternally lost if not saved by Jesus. But if a person does not feel guilty, he does not desire the love and forgiveness of Jesus. I would like to get this straightened out so that I can serve God better and free my own conscience.

Wisconsin — Tell me what I can do to put my mind and soul at rest! I want to be saved and reassured that the Lord will cleanse me and that I will be with Him in eternity. Write to me and tell me how I can strengthen this weak faith of mine!

Washington — To get to the point immediately, my husband and I have a problem which still remains unsettled after two years of discussion. We expect our first child in December, and the big subject of Baptism is the one on which we cannot agree. I was baptized and confirmed in a Lutheran church in Iowa. We were also married in a Lutheran church. Naturally I want my child to be baptized, as I was. My husband sees no sense in baptizing infants.

Michigan — I am writing you for advice, for I know you will not tell me the wrong thing. Until I married, I was a Catholic. Although there were things that I did not believe in then, after I married, I left the church and have been in a Catholic church only two or three times since. I go to other church services, but not Sunday school. I am forty-four years old, have been married since 1920, and in all that time I thought nothing about the hereafter until about five or six months ago. I have prayed and read the Bible all that I possibly can each day. I feel much better, now that I can firmly believe that I am saved. If I should die, I have assurance, but it seems as if there is something else I should do or have. I can't think what it is. It would make me happy if you possibly can advise me.

Tennessee — In 1916 I was loading a 44 fire pistol. I dropped the cylinder on the concrete floor, and it went off, striking me in the face, and it was not removed. It is about an inch in my brain. It paralyzed my right side. I cannot make any headway. I want to do Christian work. Can you help me?

Minnesota — While listening to your radio program Sunday I was very much impressed when you spoke about adultery among our young people, which is so true; few will acknowledge this fact. My young son, who has spent three years in the service of our country, is one of these. I never thought it would happen to him. We gave him a world of advice; he was instructed in the Lutheran Church. He is fully aware of what his conduct as a Christian should be. When he was home on leave, I read a letter he had received from a girl, relating to their intimacy. I merely intended to find out what sort of company he was keeping; this letter certainly proved what you said about our young men. In the best way I know I talked with him about it, but he said as long as he was made to fight wars, no one had the right to tell him how to live. He seems bitter toward all things. If you could suggest any way of bringing him back to the right way of living, it would make me happy.

Colorado — I have to get advice from someone, and I hope you will be able to help. My husband is of Mexican descent and is of dark skin; I am Spanish and have light skin. We have two children. When we were married, we were happy and very much in love, but now that he is back from the army, he feels different about everything. We stay home, but he gets discouraged and says he is cheated out of life. It seems that he has started to lose faith in our marriage; he is tired of me and the life he has to live. We have both been trying to learn the Word of God, yet he wonders if there is any hope for those of dark skin. He feels that no matter how good they are or how much they keep the Lord's rules, there still seems to be no place in the world for them. What torture my husband has been through, though he is not really colored, and yet he is not white! It is just as a man without a country. Please help us!

Oklahoma — I am and have been a Government employee for the past years and have sacrificed my God-given rights until I look like a drunkard. I work six nights a week and four afternoons, and, of course, my Sunday comes in on the work schedule. My father was a minister, and I have always wanted to take up where he left off, but for the sake of physical living I am wasting my life. I want to take your Bible Correspondence Course. I need help in learning of the great Book. I was once a candidate for the ministry, but for the love of earthly living I have ignored it; now my life's ambition cannot be subdued. Please pray for me to acquire the power of knowledge and impart it to the people of hard hearts!

Kentucky — I hardly know how to begin my letter, yet I have some personal questions to ask you and some confessions to make, and somehow I feel as if you are the one I would like to confide in, as I enjoy hearing you on the radio. I ask you to pray to God about it and tell me just in plain truth what you think about it. I am in so much trouble and so condemned in the sight of God that I sometimes think of suicide as a way out, yet I know that would be the last chance I'd ever have.

Michigan — I should like very much to ask you a question which concerns many in these days of violence: What must I do to be saved? Many say that I must believe, others say I must be baptized, others say I must join a church, and still others say to be good, give to the poor, and give to the church. I have listened to you enough to know that you know God's Word. Thank you in advance for your kindness in helping me!

RADIO'S REMARKABLE PENETRATION

We cannot sufficiently thank God for the radio's startling reach. Through the remarkable facilities of the short wave the Lutheran Hour literally covers the globe. An officer of the United States Navy reported to us that he tuned in the Lutheran Hour while flying over the North Pole. However, the broadcast has a particular blessing for those who live in isolated places in our own country and Canada. Every Sunday many thousands beyond the reach of the Church hear the Gospel through our mission of the air, and we thank the Lord for letters like these:

Nebraska — I want to say how much we appreciate the broadcast of the Lutheran Hour on Sundays. We live nineteen miles from our church and cannot always attend services. We never miss tuning in the Lutheran Hour if we are home.

Ohio — I am a mother of four children and often do not get the opportunity to attend church services. I have become a constant listener of the Lutheran Hour. We are grateful for such programs of definite Christian teachings. My mother, a shut-in, is also grateful that she has the opportunity of hearing the Gospel through your voice. It has cleared many doubts in my mind and given me new energy for problems as a self-supporting mother of my family.

Colorado — We enjoy the Lutheran Hour very much. We live on the plains and have not been to a church service for a month, as a recent blizzard has clogged the roads with snow, so you can realize how welcome the radio ministry is to us.

Colorado — Synod has no congregation here, and I must drive fifty miles to go to services. When a man is seventy-seven years old, this is quite difficult. We like to listen to your programs very much. May God keep you in your work for a long time to come!

South Dakota — I am writing to let you know how much the Lutheran Hour means to us, as we live far from church and have poor roads, especially in winter. We get much comfort from your sermons.

North Dakota — The Lutheran Hour has certainly been a wonderful thing for us, since we were snowbound and completely isolated for nearly two months. We were so thankful to hear your inspiring sermons, not once, but three times every Sunday. Please accept our gift, so that others may get the blessing and inspiration we have had through your sermons!

ALASKA TUNES IN

The Lutheran Hour uses every station in Alaska to reach the multitudes, particularly in the remote and inaccessible districts, who have no opportunity otherwise to attend church regularly. How gratefully our messages are received is shown by letters like these:

Knik — I have just listened to your program, and I enjoyed the message very much. It will give me many blessings throughout my life every time I think of it.

Kasilof — Your program is enjoyed by many people in Alaska. May the Lord bless you and give you many souls for your efforts!

Juneau — I am enclosing a check for $200.00 for the Lutheran Hour. We have received it over our local station KINY, Juneau, for almost six years and sincerely hope it will continue. We greatly feel the need of the Lutheran Hour.

CHRIST FOR CANADA

By divine blessing we use nearly fifty stations in Canada and cover all of the provinces. The Canadian response is so stimulating that we have established two branch offices in the Dominion, one under the direction of the Rev. C. T. Wetzstein at Waterloo, Ontario, and the other for western Canada under the direction of the Rev. W. A. Raedeke at

Calgary, Alta. We are deeply and personally grateful to these two brothers for their help and leadership. Even in areas where our Church is almost entirely unknown, the plain Gospel of a Savior slain for the sins of an evil world has found many new friends. Their letters, as the following excerpts show, bespeak their gratitude for the Gospel:

NEWFOUNDLAND

Grand Falls — Having listened to your most inspiring program, I have been helped greatly, and having received spiritual strength for a closer walk with my blessed Redeemer, I pray the Lord to bless you now and make you a blessing to others, as you have been to me by my listening to your program.

Saint John's — I have just been listening to your sermon. Your inspiring sermons have helped me a lot, as I feel it has done for thousands. I am a lay agent of the United Church, and it is my job to teach and preach.

Saint John's — It was a great pleasure to hear your voice on Sunday afternoon. We listen in every Sunday; your inspiring sermons are a great help to anyone in this troubled world.

NOVA SCOTIA

Ingonish — We listen to your programs every Sunday. We think they are grand. Among all the services I hear, yours is the best. May God bless you and enable you to keep up the good work!

Half Island Cove — I have been greatly blessed by your programs and never miss one if I can help it. I was once far away from God and His love, but thanks to your programs, I have been drawn closer to God, my precious Savior! I have told my friends to tune in your programs.

Ingonish — I just finished listening to your wonderful sermons. I would not miss them for anything. I have found comfort in your messages. The only fault I find in them is that they are not long enough. May God bless you in your good work, and may it long continue!

NEW BRUNSWICK

Mill Cove — We are listeners of your service which we enjoy and from which we receive much help. We live too far out in the country to go to church services regularly.

College Bridge — We look forward with keen interest to hearing the Lutheran Hour each Sunday on the radio. You make the plan of salvation so clear; some ministers never speak of it in their sermons.

Seal Cove — We are sitting here in our home on this little island, where we hear your wonderful message. It stirs our hearts and fills us with a determination to do more for the Master in the years ahead. Our prayer is that the dear Lord will abundantly bless and strengthen you in this great ministry.

QUEBEC

Sorel — I am a French Canadian from Quebec. Last Sunday I heard the most beautiful sermon in my life. I am proud that your religion is as well observed in the other provinces, and I congratulate you.

Montreal — I am one of your listeners of the Lutheran Hour on Sunday mornings, from which I get a great amount of comfort. Your broadcast on Sunday made me go all the way in accepting the Lord Jesus Christ as my own personal Savior. I was baptized that same Sunday evening in a little church here in Montreal, and the past week has been the most comforting week of my life, as I have been filled with the peace of the dear Savior.

Verdun — We enjoy your messages over the air on Sunday mornings. It is a grand way of going out into the highways and byways to compel them to come in. We always remember your work in prayer, and God will answer. Enclosed is a small contribution. May He multiply its usefulness to you a hundredfold!

ONTARIO

Hornings Mills — Your sermons each Sunday are truly a blessing to us. I have found my way back to God through your messages and certainly will do all I can for my Lord in sending tracts to my friends and neighbors, and praying for the Lutheran Hour, too. May I have a poster to place on the house advertising your program?

Stirling — My wife and I, with six children, take great pleasure and comfort in uniting together with you for your service each Sunday at 3:30 when you proclaim a true Gospel.

Meaford — I was listening to your program on the radio, and I love it. I surely wish you could stay on longer. I am a bachelor

Air-Wave Testimony

of twenty-seven years and thought I would change my life, so on Sunday I sought Christ as my personal Savior and found for myself it is a loving life to live. I got down on my knees in front of my radio right after your program. Please send me your leaflets!

ALBERTA

Edmonton — There are three of us in this one room, and we listen to your programs on Sundays and like them very much. We find them helpful in cheering us up, as we have T. B. and spend months and even years in this hospital. We pray to the Lord to send you strength to bring the truth to the world that needs it.

Edmonton — I enjoy your broadcast very much. I work quite often on Sunday mornings, as I have done today. This gives me an opportunity to tune in your program and put it on our public address system so that the unsaved friends with whom I work can hear it. Keep up the good work, and may God richly bless you all!

Edmonton — Owing to my type of work here at the hospital, I find it difficult to attend church services regularly. I have therefore become an ardent listener to the Lutheran Hour. It is very gratifying to see the number of patients who tune in regularly. They find great comfort in your messages.

MANITOBA

Plumas — At our last meeting we set aside ten dollars as a gift to the Lutheran Hour. Your broadcast is well received in our community, and we realize that the cost of continuing such work is high. We hope that this token of appreciation will help continue to bring your messages to us. The prayers of our entire society are with you.

Portage la Prairie — For the past few Sundays we have been listening to the Lutheran Hour. My parents suggested that I enroll as one of your correspondence pupils. I am fourteen years old and want to learn more of the Bible.

Winnipeg — I listen regularly to your broadcast on Sunday mornings and enjoy it very much. If you have any literature you could send me for unsaved ones, I would like to have it. I find myself inadequate in speaking to my own dear ones and others and would like to have literature to help me say what is in my heart. I had never really known the way of salvation until I listened to your broadcast.

SASKATCHEWAN

Hubbard — For some time my husband and I have been steady listeners to your Sunday broadcast. Your sermons have been of great interest and help to us. We live on a farm and during the winter months are rarely able to go to church, so we depend on our radio for our Sunday worship. We would greatly appreciate it if you could send us the lessons you offer.

McNutt — I am dumb and can't talk, but went to a school and can read and write a little. I hear your broadcasts every week. They are wonderful, and I surely like them.

Carrot River — Thanks for the wonderful and inspiring messages! Three of our family have been influenced to accept Christ by your messages. They have joined a Lutheran Church.

BRITISH COLUMBIA

Vancouver — It is certainly encouraging to hear the Gospel go forth, and the manner in which you so capably proclaim it is a real blessing. Please accept this contribution for your radio work, and may God bless your ministry even more abundantly!

New Westminster — Enclosed is a small gift for your use in the service of the Master. It is good to note that, in this age of compromises, there are a few men and women who, like your speaker, are in obedience to their God, speaking the truth in love regarding salvation, and showing the people their transgressions. Some of your addresses have gone to loved ones in England and have been favorably received.

Willow River — We are always glad to listen in to the Lutheran Hour, as we are getting old and long to hear the trumpet call. We loved the sermon preached today.

REPLIES FROM THE WEST INDIES AND CENTRAL AMERICA

In few places on the globe are our messages more eagerly welcomed than in the territory north of Panama to the Rio Grande and in the many islands of the Caribbean. People of various countries, creeds, and colors are united in praising God for our Gospel. All friends of missions will join us in thanking the Holy Spirit for letters like these and the coverage they represent:

BAHAMAS

Spanish Wells — I have listened to your programs several times and was listening today. I am fourteen years old and am still at school.

Nassau — I thought I would like to drop you a few lines to let you know how much we enjoy your fine sermons. We listen every Sunday; our family gathers around the radio to hear you, for we find your service a great help to us.

Nassau — I have listened to the Lutheran Hour for quite a long time and have been benefited spiritually by your sermons. I would like to interest more of my friends.

BERMUDA

Pembroke — I have been listening to your Sunday broadcasts, and I have really enjoyed them. They bring comfort and joy to my soul.

Warwick — I am a regular listener to your broadcast and have been blessed by it. Will you please continue to pray for me?

Pembroke East — I am a convert of eighteen years and am desirous of winning souls for Christ in my small way. You have my earnest prayers that God will open the way for your broadcasting stations and that you will win more souls for Him.

BRITISH HONDURAS

Belize — May I take this opportunity to thank you most sincerely for the uplifting messages of Bringing Christ to the Nations? They have been a great inspiration and brought rich spiritual blessings into my heart and life.

Belize — Greetings to you in the name of the Lord Jesus Christ, our Savior. I appreciate very much the booklets "Pray Without Ceasing" and the sermons. I gave them to many people to help them find or feel God near to them and hoped that they may allow Him to enter into their hearts. Oh, what a blessed day that was when I accepted the Lord Jesus as my personal Savior! I have no radio now, but I go around to different people whom I know and ask them to tune in this very refreshing station, which heralds Jesus Christ's blessing around the world in so many different languages that all may know that wonderful Savior who died that we might be saved from the brink of hell.

Punta Gorda — Each Sunday your Spanish messages come into our little home clearly and with blessing. How I thank God for the fact that He has permitted us to hear the Gospel regularly over the air lanes!

BARBADOS

Bridgetown — I gave my heart to God last Sunday, and it is all through the inspiration of your words. May God bless you, that at the end you may say as Paul, *"I have fought a good fight; I have finished my course; I have kept the faith. Henceforth there is laid up for me a crown of righteousness, which the Lord, the righteous Judge, shall give me at that day, and not to me only, but unto all them also that love His appearing."*

Bridgetown — It is some time now that I have been listening to your broadcast. I can't begin to tell you how much I appreciate the sermons and also the beautiful singing. I am learning the tunes and am very much interested. It is such a joy to know that one can hear such lovely messages over the radio so many miles away. I do hope God will truly bless my husband to make him listen in. I am eager for him to know something about God. Do pray for him!

St. Michael — Having accepted Christ in our youth, we enjoy your teachings very much each Sunday, and we are hoping that we will grow stronger by your wonderful preaching.

JAMAICA

Kingston — I am a constant radio listener on your station, and I have found your Sunday afternoon spiritual program very interesting.

Morant Bay — I am delighted with your Sunday afternoon broadcasts. Please continue your good work! I shall always be listening in.

Kingston — For several weeks now I have listened to Bringing Christ to the Nations. I have enjoyed the broadcasts and feel sure that they are doing a deal of good.

LEEWARD ISLANDS

Montserrat — I take this opportunity of expressing my thankfulness and appreciation of the services broadcast by you on Sundays. Really, I've been spiritually moved, and I trust that God will strengthen you preachers and help you to continue in this most wonderful work.

Sandy Point, St. Kitts — Your sermons have done much for me. I was led to see more of Christ's promises for fallen humanity and the realization of the nearness of the end when He shall come to claim His own. My desire is to be among the redeemed of all ages.

Basseterre, St. Kitts — I am keenly interested in your Lutheran Hour broadcast. Your sermons are most inspiring. You need not wonder if I will continue to tune in regularly. We really have to be very grateful to you for your sermons, which are so very helpful.

TRINIDAD

Port-of-Spain — I must first sincerely thank you for your inspiring and very helpful, Biblical messages which you have given us.

Arima — Thank you for your very timely messages from the Gospel pages, which are always sources of spiritual encouragement to both my little family and myself! I want you to know we are grateful for them and sincerely trust that the Gospel truth will continue to triumph in all the world. Be assured of our best interest!

Port-of-Spain — Since I have installed a radio system in my home, I have listened attentively each Sunday to your interesting and inspiring sermons, and believe me, I have benefited greatly by them.

WINDWARD ISLANDS

St. Georges — I can assure you that it did me a lot of good when I was on my sickbed, for I was able to read more carefully and concentrate and digest your messages!

Castries — Our entire family always listens to your inspiring sermons, and we are always reminded of our Creator, to whom we owe our hearing. I hope He will bless you always to continue your work.

St. Georges — I believe that God has blessed your broadcast and trust and pray that souls may be won for His honor and glory. I tune in every Sunday for your broadcast over Station ZBM, Bermuda, and I enjoy listening.

CANAL ZONE

Cristobal — For several weeks now we have heard your wonderful radio program, Bringing Christ to the Nations, over our local radio station. We both enjoy, and get a great deal of benefit from, your weekly message. You have my sincere wishes and fervent prayers that more and more people will tune in your program.

Cristobal — I have been listening to the broadcasts, and they are a real blessing and strength to my soul. I am telling the people about your services.

Cristobal — Last Sunday I accidentally tuned in the Spanish Lutheran Hour, and the message really touched my heart. Please send me that message and more literature!

COSTA RICA

Alajuela — One of my neighbors asked me to listen to the Lutheran Hour. At first I was reluctant, but I listened anyhow. Allow me to congratulate you upon such soul-stirring messages! I had never before heard anything like them. I shall keep on listening.

Puntarenas — My family and I receive great spiritual strengthening through the messages of Bringing Christ to the Nations, as they come into our home each week over the radio. May God bless your mission of the air!

San Jose — I cannot begin to tell you how greatly all of us are blessed through your Scripture-based Gospel appeals. I know that many here listen in regularly each week.

CUBA

Placetas — Every Sunday I tune in the Lutheran Hour. I have now accepted Christ in my heart. Your words tell us to follow Jesus' example. I admire your preaching, because it is Christ-centered.

Santiago de Cuba — Permit me to assure you that the Lutheran Hour is doing a wonderful work in Cuba! May God bless the wonderful work you are doing. It is the Word that the world needs most!

Pedro Betancourt — I am very much pleased to listen to the stirring messages delivered on Sunday afternoons. I would like to be enrolled as a member of the Bible Correspondence Course.

DOMINICAN REPUBLIC

Ciudad Trujillo — Your voice is very clear, your preaching is unexcelled. I shall keep on listening to your messages. They are a comfort to me in every hour of tribulation.

Air-Wave Testimony

San Pedro — I am a constant listener to Bringing Christ to the Nations and find the broadcast very interesting.

Ciudad Trujillo — If you could just see us once, on a Wednesday evening, after the day's work is done, crowding around the radio a few minutes before 6:30 P. M. — in order not to miss a word — you will understand why we all feel so thankful to you for the heart-warming gift of the Lutheran Hour, which is at present our only spoken spiritual link with Lutheran fellowship. The messages themselves are so impressive by their plain language and earnest sincerity that we are sure the seed of the Word will lastingly benefit the hearts of thousands of listeners in this and many countries.

GUATEMALA

Guatemala City — Permit me to congratulate you on those messages of good will that come to fill a great need in the souls that are weary and heavy laden by the sufferings of life! The programs of the Spanish Lutheran Hour to which I have listened have been of great comfort to me whenever I think of them in the moments of moral sufferings. I believe that the comfort they impart is not only for me but for the millions and millions of listeners all over the world.

Guatemala City — It has been of great comfort to us who believe in Jesus Christ to listen to your sermons based on Holy Scripture. I listen to them every Sunday.

Guatemala City — I feel that it is an honor to write to you, even though I am a Roman Catholic in every respect. My family also belongs to this Church, but I listen with true devotion to the messages of the Lutheran Hour and have found in them spiritual uplifting for us and our home.

HAITI

Port-au-Prince — I would like to send you these few lines to tell you that our whole family listens to your marvelous Gospel addresses every week. They certainly are a blessing to us, and we thank you for making it possible to hear them.

Port-au-Prince — We enjoy your program and hope that it will continue to remain on the air.

Jacmel — Thanks in our Lord's name for the wonderful sermon of last Sunday afternoon! We hope and pray that your message may be a blessing to all your listeners. Please enroll me in your Bible Course!

HONDURAS

Tegucigalpa — Every Sunday a group here listens to your program. It means tremendously much that we are able to hear the Gospel over the airlanes. It brings rich spiritual blessing into our hearts.

Trujillo — Tonight as I listened to the Lutheran Hour program, I thought I would write and let you know how much I enjoyed it.

Tegucigalpa — I have enjoyed your programs very much. I love the Lord Jesus and like to see His Word distributed in every home.

MEXICO

Ciudad Anahuac — Your preaching came to fill my heart with joy and courage, especially after having heard the sermon about freedom from fear. I shall be listening every Sunday and want to be ready to do God's will. Please send me some Christian literature!

Ciudad Anahuac — There is no doubt in my mind that your messages are the means of salvation for many souls. You preach the true and full Gospel of Christ Crucified. Please send me some of your literature!

Ciudad Anahuac — It is a joy for me to listen to your Christian messages. Since I live quite a way from town, I am not able to attend the church of my choice. Your program, therefore, constitutes my church. Please send me your written messages in Spanish!

NICARAGUA

Bluefields — We are sending you a check for the Lutheran Hour. We truly hope that this broadcast will be able to continue preaching the Gospel.

Managua — Being a Christian of Nicaragua, I assiduously tune in your blessed radio messages, enjoying your well-prepared and glorious religious programs in English as well as in Spanish. I am very happy in my Savior to state that every time I tune in your Spanish broadcasts, I open up the volume key so that all the people living around my house may hear the Gospel message. Your broadcasts are eagerly heard by many people here.

Granada — What blessings flow into my heart each week through your Gospel crusade! May the Almighty give you many souls through your powerful Gospel appeals as proclaimed over the radio!

PUERTO RICO

San German — I consider it a great loss when I am not able to listen to your sermons. They are real spiritual food for my soul and the means of strengthening my faith in the Savior. May the Lord give you wisdom to continue preaching the Gospel of Christ, so that the Lutheran Hour may be a blessing to the nations in general and to individuals in particular! Please send me some more literature and sermons!

San Juan — I listen to the Lutheran Hour with all my family, and I call the attention of all my friends and acquaintances to the zealous work that you are doing. Believe me that I pray for you and ask God to increase the effectiveness of your mission for the good of all!

San Juan — I have been listening to your programs, Bringing Christ to the Nations, and I like them, though I am a Roman Catholic. Will you please send me a copy of your free booklets?

EL SALVADOR

San Salvador — I am a Roman Catholic, but have found in the messages of the Lutheran Hour truths that are profoundly educational, moral, and spiritual. Your Spanish orator is outstanding.

La Palma — A group gathers in our home each Lord's Day to hear your messages in the Spanish language. We count it a privilege to be numbered among your regular listeners.

Santa Rosa — How we thank God for granting us the grace to hear His Word each Sunday over your programs of Bringing Christ to the Nations! Your messages are a stream of living water in a desert land, as they lead us to Christ, the Savior of our souls.

VIRGIN ISLANDS

St. Croix — I listen to Bringing Christ to the Nations on Sunday morning and enjoy it very much. I think it is a wonderful work and wish you every success in its continuance. The addresses are inspiring and helpful.

Saint Croix — I am writing these few lines to let you know how much we appreciate your fine broadcasts.

St. Thomas — Thank you for copies of Lutheran Hour sermons and literature describing the program. May the blessings of God rest on you and your work!

SOUTH AMERICA SENDS ITS THANKS

The broadcast is one of the strongest ties that binds masses in South America with us in North America. We praise God that He has opened the door for our broadcast in every South American country. So large has the work in this field become that we have opened two offices to expedite the mail, one for the Portuguese programs, under the direction of Pastor Rudolph Hasse, in Rio de Janeiro, and the other for the Spanish broadcasts, under the direction of Pastor A. L. Muniz, in Buenos Aires. These brothers in Christ have worked hard and efficiently. All of us should remember them gratefully in our prayers.

We wish that we had pages with which to describe the work in each South American country. Limited as we are, however, we print only three letters from each of the South American nations:

ARGENTINA

Salta — I am a militant Catholic, but I listen to your program each Sunday.

Anatuva — The glorious message of salvation you broadcast over Radio Libertad has reached even this remote place of the country. My family and I eagerly wait each Sunday for the Lutheran Hour sermons.

La Plata — The powerful transmitter in Buenos Aires brings us your Gospel messages each week. Our whole family is given new spiritual strength through the Word of God, as proclaimed on your wonderful programs.

BOLIVIA

La Paz — We are missionaries of the Interdenominational Missionary Board of Union Bible Seminary, Westfield, Indiana, and enjoy the English broadcasts that come over the short-wave station of HCJB, Quito, Ecuador. We have been here six years and have several churches as well as a Bible School and printing plant. We shall appreciate your prayers for the work of the Lord in Bolivia.

Sta. Cruz — Last Sunday we had the opportunity of listening to the message of the Spanish Lutheran Hour. We are in a camp of young students at this place, and we feel that your Gospel embraces the truth of God's Word. For this reason we would like to accept the Gospel as you preach it. Your message is truly spiritual food for us, and we hope it will be such for thousands of others. Please accept our sincere congratulations on the wonderful work you are doing in the interest of humanity!

La Paz — Last Sunday I listened to your wonderful message on the Lutheran Hour. My sincere congratulations, and may God bless you in your work!

BRAZIL

Minas Gerais — I listen to the Lutheran Hour. Many persons who come to my home admire your programs more and more. We regret that the programs come only once a week. We are doing everything possible to make them known among the people.

Joacaba — Kind regards from the southern harvest field! We have heard, with growing blessing, most of your Gospel broadcasts, and they are deeply inspiring to our souls.

Parana — It is with the greatest enthusiasm that I address these lines to the Lutheran Hour. I have been listening to your program with the greatest attention and devotion. It is truly a Bible message, based on the beautiful teachings of Jesus. Since I am sick and unable to attend church, I believe your messages are God-sent.

BRITISH GUIANA

Demerara — I usually tune in every week to listen to your broadcast, and every one I hear gives me a new spirit. I pray that God will continue to shower His blessing on your broadcast. I have arranged with a preacher here that each Sunday he must read one of your addresses to the people, and last Sunday we started. I am proud to tell you that more than 2,000 people were present to listen to the address. We had to use a loud speaker.

Demerara — I do hope that the Lutheran Hour is getting on nicely with God's help. When I tune in a Lutheran Hour broadcast over Station ZFY, British Guiana, I wish that it never had an end, because I enjoy it very much. The sermon is very touching, and the hymns are beautiful. This wonderful service, which has enlightened me very much, shows that the Holy Spirit is really working through the Lutheran Hour.

Georgetown — I was listening to your broadcast for quite some time and wanted to write you before now, but owing to my illness I could not manage. I appreciate very much the way in which you preach the Gospel, and I hope that God will keep you safe to proceed with this broadcast.

CHILE

Vina del Mar — I am addressing you because I am a regular listener of your Sunday conferences. If it is not much trouble to you, I will be pleased to receive the needed literature for my personal knowledge of our Lord and to my spiritual betterment.

Santiago — Every Sunday I listen to your beautiful and wonderful program, Christ for all the Nations. It is very pleasing both to me and my whole family.

Parral — My most sincere congratulations on your very interesting message! We hear it every Sunday and shall continue to tune in regularly. I wish you more and more success.

COLOMBIA

Barranquilla — I am writing to ask you for copies of your sermon "A Clean Heart," which you offered over the radio. This message impressed me very much. My daughters and I listen to you with much interest and devotion.

Barranquilla — These lines are being written to ask you for the literature that you offer in your program, Bringing Christ to the Nations. Will you also send me the picture of Christ?

Barranquilla — It is indeed with deep pleasure that I endeavor to inform you that I listen to Bringing Christ to the Nations every Sunday. I listen attentively to the sermons. They are really Bible-centered.

DUTCH GUIANA

Paramaribo — We are still constant listeners to the program and derive rich spiritual blessing from your messages.

Coronie — Here on the northern coast of South America we hear your messages clearly each week. What a blessing we receive! May God grant you many more years of effective testimony to the Gospel of our Lord Jesus Christ!

Paramaribo — Though our country is small, you have a large number of faithful listeners here in Dutch Guiana. May the Almighty give you the health and strength to carry on in His name to proclaim the Gospel for the saving of precious souls!

ECUADOR

Quito — This morning I listened to the Lutheran Hour, and God's words were powerful and loving. I am glad that you proclaim Christ's Gospel and nothing less, and I shall always pray that God will bless your work and that many will give their hearts to Christ Jesus. This program gives me strength to "nail my colors to the mast," and I praise God for this special blessing.

Guayaquil — Your program comes to our home through HCJB. It is very clear. I cannot describe to you how much your words mean to me. Every time I listen my soul feels inspired.

Quito — Five years ago the Lord led me to listen to the Lutheran Hour. Through that blessing I came to the knowledge of my Savior, and I was saved. I am now able to understand the things that I could not understand before. I feel that I am a Lutheran at heart. Please send me some more literature regarding the teachings of the Lutheran Church!

PARAGUAY

Asuncion — Every Sunday I listen to the Lutheran Hour; I receive great comfort from your messages and the hymns. May God bless this work of faith which you are doing!

Villarrica — May our heavenly Father give your great mission of the air many more listeners and stations throughout the world! You are doing a blessed work in the Savior's name.

Encarnacion — Your messages in the Spanish language serve to build my faith through the Word of God. I look forward to next Sunday's message with great eagerness.

PERU

Arequipa — We shall never be able to tell you what overflowing benedictions God has showered on us through your radio programs. May our heavenly Father continue to bestow upon you His mighty blessing!

Chorrillos — My emotion was beyond description when today I turned on my radio and was able to listen to the message of the Lutheran Hour. We rarely get a chance to listen to the real Word of God due to the religious intolerance prevalent in this country. I pray the Lord that He may keep you on the air, so that many people may hear the true Word of God for the salvation of their souls. His Word shall never return void, according to His promise.

Lima — Your sermons are so wonderful, inspirational, and so spiritually educational that we use them for our daily family devotions. Please send them to us as they are published. God bless you!

URUGUAY

Montevideo — As a faithful listener to your program, I congratulate you upon the way in which your messages reach the hearts of your hearers and dispose even the unbelievers to accept the Word that is spoken. I already had a Bible, but I had never given it the importance that it really possesses. Now, thanks to your messages, I have learned that God, the Creator of all, and Jesus Christ, His Son, are supreme above all, and that in the Son we have redemption from sin.

Pueblo Solis — I want to tell you that my family and I are eager listeners to the Lutheran Hour and that we are in entire conformity with your teachings. We pray God that He may bless many others through these fitting, timely messages.

Ombues de Lavalle — For a long time my household has followed your program with deep interest. We wish you success in your work for Christ, in order that the Lutheran Hour may go forward and be the means of healing souls that are troubled and bowed down. May you bring many to a knowledge of their Savior and their salvation!

VENEZUELA

Merida, Edo. Menda — I want to say I especially like the Lutheran Hour.

Caracas — The powerful transmitter of Station HCJB in Quito, Ecuador, beams the Gospel of the Lord Jesus Christ into our home each week. We are blessed greatly through your messages on Bringing Christ to the Nations.

Maracaibo — I cannot tell you how eagerly we receive and appreciate your Gospel broadcasts. As they come into our home each week, we find the presence of the Holy Spirit and His direction of our lives.

INCREASED COVERAGE IN WAR-WRECKED EUROPE

Striking proof of the Gospel's power to save and sustain comes to us from our European broadcasts. We praise God that during the fifteenth season our audiences, tuned to Radio Luxembourg, Radio Normandie, and Radio Monte Carlo, constantly grew. The fact that in some European countries the radio is under government control prevented us from securing local coverage. Pray that every barrier against broadcasting in the various European countries may be removed! Pray also that the Lord may lead us to establish a superpower radio station in an appropriate place in Europe where daily the Gospel may be broadcast in two dozen different languages! During the fifteenth season our European broadcasts used English, French, and Italian, but preliminary efforts were made to secure other languages. We wish that our readers could have spent a day at our London Office (established during the fifteenth season), which is under the direction of the Reverend E. George Pearce. They would thank God, as we do, for the Spirit's blessing on our broadcast throughout the countries represented by these letters:

AUSTRIA

Dornbirn — I have been brought closer to Christ through your radio ministry.

Innsbruck — How I thank God for granting me the opportunity of hearing the Gospel over the air each week! Our local station carries your messages, to my spiritual blessing.

Landeck — Eagerly we receive and look forward to your weekly broadcasts. Please send me some of your sermon copies!

BELGIUM

Carleroi — This morning for the first time I heard your program on the wireless, and I was so impressed that I am writing to your station right away.

Antwerp — The powerful transmitter of Radio Luxembourg brings us your powerful messages each week. I know that many here are listening in each week.

Brussels — Your messages of Christ Crucified carry the Gospel we need for war-torn Europe. They will serve mightily in bringing about a spiritual rebirth in our nation.

DENMARK

Copenhagen — A group gathers in my home each week to hear challenging Gospel sermons.

Aalborg — With hearts filled with gratitude to God we write you these few lines to tell you how deeply we appreciate your weekly Gospel proclamations.

Odense — I know that several here listen in each week to your programs of Bringing Christ to the Nations. Please continue to bring the Gospel into our homes in this way!

ENGLAND

Cheshire — Tonight when my husband was seeing what he could pick up on the short wave of our radio, he found your service. We were immensely impressed by your sermon.

London — I am writing to let you know what comfort and joy I get from your messages. After hearing you, I feel I cannot love my Savior enough. Sometimes life seems hard and disappointing, but now I know I have a Savior to guide and help me in all things. I have been thinking about being baptized; after your broadcast about Baptism I feel that I want to confess Christ in that special way.

Paighton — It is with great pleasure that I write and thank you for the messages broadcast each week. They are a source of comfort and help, and I pray God will mightily bless your work. I have received rich blessing from you. It is really wonderful to hear over the air someone reaching man's soul. Often when I have felt low and have listened, I have been lifted up, and I thank God for you. Our pastor advertises your program.

FRANCE

Blaton — Your broadcasts are the true symbol of Christian love, charity, and happiness in our lives. This happiness you gave to my wife and my children in your broadcast coming from faraway Saint Louis. We are very thankful for your sermons, and we listen to them eagerly. It is our only joy and the only food for our souls, which we so badly need today. I hope that you will bring many souls to our God. May God grant that your broadcasts will bring the same joy to listeners of many countries!

Drome — Being a widow, I often feel very lonesome. In those moments my radio is my most agreeable and most desired companion. I love to listen every Sunday to the Lutheran Hour, and I am looking forward the whole day to 6:30 P. M. Your messages are always very clear and beneficial.

Lyons — I am at present in the hospital and very ill. The loss of three of my children made me lose my faith in God, but I have regained that faith as a result of listening to your broadcasts.

GERMANY

Hamburg — I am still critically ill in a hospital, but your broadcast gave me new courage and a desire to continue living. You have shown me new goals in my life. May God bless you for your wonderful work!

Neustadt — I listen regularly to Bringing Christ to the Nations. I want to use your series of sermons for our Christian young people's meeting. I beg you to send us copies of the sermons regularly.

Westphalia — Each Saturday a group of five members of the Brotherhood listens to your program. The aim of this congregation is to reunite all Christians.

HOLLAND

Doesburg — I cannot thank you enough for your wonderful message broadcast from Radio Luxembourg. We will pray for you. May the Lord bless you!

Breda — Today, as usual, I switched on my radio to hear your message. For a long time I have been listening to your broadcasts, and today I decided to drop you a few lines. I have never before heard such truths going out of the mouth of the pastor who spoke! I am a Roman Catholic, but soon now I would like to study the Word of God.

Doesburg — Thanks for your broadcast! It was the first time I tuned in Radio Luxembourg. Being a teacher, I must teach every Saturday morning. But now the schools are closed by the coal shortage. I happened to be very depressed that morning by many difficulties, and then I heard you speaking. My joy came back. Many thanks to you, unknown pastor! I am a youth leader here in Doesburg, and I try to show the young people (boys and girls of eighteen years) the way to salvation. So I ask you if you can help me by sending some literature for distribution.

IRELAND

Bangor Down — Only the past few Saturdays I have had the privilege of hearing your radio service, because on other Saturdays I worked. Your program encourages us to pray, and we shall, indeed, also pray for you in this effort to bring Christ to the nations.

Bangor Down — I am very much interested in your broadcast and look forward to it every Saturday evening.

Athlone — Just by the merest chance I turned on Radio Luxembourg this morning and heard for the first time what I considered to be the real Gospel preached as I have not heard it preached for years. It can and will do a lot of good for the Savior's world.

NORWAY

Langesund — We have been listening to Bringing Christ to the Nations over Radio Luxembourg. We derive rich spiritual blessing from these broadcasts.

Lillehammer — We listen to your services and glorious preaching from Luxembourg. We enjoy your wonderful singing, too. God bless you! We are praying for you.

Lillehammer — We thank you from the bottom of our hearts. God bless you for your work in the Lord by bringing His Gospel to the very ends of the earth!

POLAND

Zlakow Borowy — All those who haven't radios are coming to our house to hear your broacasts just as they would in church. All of them are very much satisfied, and we are eagerly awaiting the day when we will be able to listen to your broadcasts daily.

Makow — Nowadays people haven't much faith because materialism and degradation have taken the place of Christ. Your broadcasts are appealing to our hearts, and many of our people are returning to God and are showing their charity toward their neighbors. I believe and sincerely hope that through your broadcasts we will return to the ways of our fathers, who had a deep faith. Thank you very much for preserving our faith and saving us from eternal destruction!

Czaekowy — Every Friday we listen to your broadcast and invite all of our neighbors who are without a radio to listen and pray together with you. We thank you all very much for your wonderful sermons. May God grant that some day you will be able to broadcast every day.

SCOTLAND

Glasgow — I was delighted to receive a copy of the *Lutheran Hour News* today; reading through it I found it interesting indeed. It is truly amazing, the scope which this wonderful broadcast covers. I trust and pray that your ministry will continue to be blessed.

Shetland — First of all let me say how much I enjoy listening to your services over Radio Luxembourg! I must admit I was a onetime Christian, but am sorry to say I have slowly drifted from the straight and narrow path. I still enjoy listening to services or Christian talks on the radio or elsewhere. I was brought up by a good Christian father and mother. I am twenty-one years old. The happiest years of my life were when I was serving my Lord and Master, Jesus Christ.

Edinburgh — Last Saturday evening we listened to the broadcast from Radio Luxembourg and greatly enjoyed the message and singing. It is only the last few Saturdays that we have been able to listen, for we are usually engaged on the week ends in Gospel work, and I think I am right in saying that when giving your address you mentioned that we could write to you for literature.

NORTH WALES

Holyhead — Just a few lines to let you know how much I enjoyed listening to the religious broadcast over your short-wave station. I shall be looking forward to your next broadcast, when I will be listening again and hope to enjoy it as much as I enjoyed your last service.

Holyhead — Many thanks for the calendar and literature which arrived safely! I would like to tell you how greatly impressed I am with your powerful sermons. My wife has also received many a blessing through listening with me to these wonderful broadcasts. My parents, living not far away from me, are also regular listeners to your program.

Holyhead — I listened to your service on the radio Sunday. It was a real spiritual treat, and considering the distance of more than 3,000 miles, I received the broadcast very well. Thank you once again for such a powerful, heart-stirring rendition of the Gospel!

SOUTH WALES

Glamorgan — Perhaps the messages you send over the radio may one day strike a chord in someone's heart and bring about the revival which the world so much needs. May God bless your mission, and may you have strength and courage to go on with the worthy cause which you have chosen to serve!

Rhondda — I am very much interested in your great work. I pray that God will bless you all and will give you strength to carry on this work, which has brought blessing and enjoyment to many. I am a young girl of fifteen and a Salvationist. Please send me some of your leaflets, so that I can follow your work!

Rhondda — There is a dynamic power in your organization of Bringing Christ to the Nations, and your persistency in this noble effort is bound to be crowned with success, because its structure is built upon a foundation which is indestructible, which endures for time and for eternity.

CHANNEL ISLANDS

Guernsey — I am writing to tell you that three weeks ago my son happened to tune in Luxembourg, and it was with great joy that I heard the Gospel message coming over the air. I praised God for it. Though I am a Christian, I am thrilled to know the message is reaching so many in this way. May God bless you and all those who are taking part in this work! I have been much blessed and will endeavor to get others to listen.

Guernsey — I rejoice to think that messages like those are being sent out on the radio, and I pray that the Gospel of the grace of God shall find its way into many hearts. Only recently we heard about these broadcasts. We in our turn will tell others to tune in, and we pray that God's kingdom may spread abroad and also in our own little Channel Islands. We are longing for a revival. We wish you God's blessing on all your efforts.

Millbrook — I was deeply convinced after hearing your two broadcasts over Radio Luxembourg on last Saturday. I would appreciate any literature you can send me, including your radio addresses. God prosper your work on the need for Christ today, and I pray that you and all your helpers may be abundantly blessed!

GREECE

Athens — I had a great spiritual pleasure listening to your broadcast this afternoon. Your speech inspired by God will have, I am sure, the desired effect upon every soul. In a life so highly industrialized as ours, a broadcast like yours is an oasis in the desert, and I wish we had more messages like yours. I think the world then would be better.

Athens — I heard and enjoyed your yesterday's broadcast from the Athens radio station. I ardently hope that your work may prove to be an inspiration to the performers and organizers of our Greek religious broadcasts.

Izmir — I was very glad and somehow proud when I heard your program by the radio yesterday. Just when Christianity seems to be taken for granted, your program by radio is like a piece of bread after years of hunger. The name you have chosen for the program is wonderful.

ITALY

Sanremo — I heard your voice for the first time two Sundays ago and was deeply touched. I am sorry not to have a radio, but hear it when I am at my sister's in Bordighera. Your message has indeed done me good. The world has great need of the voice of Christ, which alone can bring the happiness which is sought for elsewhere.

Chiett — I am writing you and asking if it is at all possible for you to send a free copy of your Lutheran Hour address? I am an Italian Methodist pastor, ruined by the war, on the way to reconstruction of the missionary camp, house and family. I hope that you will help me by letting me have your literature, which will bring me new strength and inspiration. May God bless you and your work and give me strength to imitate you in my fields!

Genoa — I am a regular listener of Bringing Christ to the Nations in Italian, French, and English. I can assure you it does me good to hear your messages.

SPAIN

Madrid — The Spanish program Bringing Christ to the Nations, is magnificent, for both its religious contents and its presentation. I take this opportunity to congratulate you and the Lutheran Hour.

Cadiz — The Gospel broadcasts, which I have the pleasure to enjoy through Tangier, in my humble opinion constitute a very much wanted spiritual bread for my country and, perhaps, the only means to introduce the Gospel in many houses by a public way, for, as you will certainly know, we Protestants have to face many difficulties in Spain to preach God's Word. At the same time I take advantage of this opportunity to say to you that Spain is in great want of more Gospel broadcasts. Can you not find a means of increasing your broadcasts for my country?

Madrid — I was fortunate last Sunday to tune in Bringing Christ to the Nations. I was very much pleased. I shall always try to listen to it.

SWITZERLAND

Leysin — I enjoy the Bringing-Christ-to-the-Nations service on a Sunday morning, and it really makes me rejoice for the rest of the day.

La Chaux de Fonds — I was listening to your message over Radio Luxembourg at 2:45 P. M. This message found me in a state of despondency, but when it was over, I was restored spiritually and had acquired hope and courage again. In spite of my age I hope to travel through part of this world as a living witness, because three times already I was near dying, and now I feel myself a victor in the liberation. I thank you very much that you take care of the salvation of souls.

Bern — Praise God for giving me a safe journey to Switzerland and for helping my mother, who was very ill and who is now much better! Thanks for your prayers, and God bless you! Enclosed find my offering of $10.00 for the Lord's work!

TO DARK AFRICA

Despite opposition from Mohammedans our African broadcasts in English, Spanish, French, and Afrikaans move on. Radio Internationale in Tangier, North Africa, helps us cover the countries that border on the Mediterranean in the north, while Radio Mozambique in Lourenco Marques, Portuguese East Africa, and Radio Angola in West Africa cover thickly populated South Africa. The mail response from this area is so large that a branch office has been opened in Johannesburg under the direction of G. J. McHarry. Here are a few typical responses from our African listeners, which show us that the broadcast Word, heard thousands of miles away from the speaker, does not return void:

BASUTOLAND

Wepener — I know that each week many in this community hear Bringing Christ to the Nations. Our family is blessed through your fervent Gospel appeals. I hope that God will give you many more opportunities for service to Him.

Morija — May the grace of God rest upon you as you proclaim the Gospel in His name! We receive a blessing for our souls through the Word of God as proclaimed on the air.

Air-Wave Testimony

Maseru — The continent of Africa needs Gospel messages such as those proclaimed over your wonderful radio mission. Please continue to beam the Gospel into our land!

BECHUANALAND PROTECTORATE

Vryburg — May I express my deep appreciation for your fine message of Bringing Christ to the Nations? My entire family and I have listened with great benefit. Thank God for your message!

Serowe — I am writing to tell you how much I enjoy your broadcasts from Lourenco Marques. Though English speaking, with little knowledge of Afrikaans, I listen to your sermons on Wednesdays and on Thursdays. I shall continue to pray for God's blessing in this wonderful work you are doing.

Lobatse — By short wave we hear your messages each week. We thank God for them and invite others to listen in.

CAPE OF GOOD HOPE

Port Elizabeth — We have just been listening to the Lutheran Hour program from the Lourenco Marques station and would like to mention that both my wife and I have been really encouraged by tonight's message. Furthermore, we both agree that it has been a lovely ending to a quietly spent wedding anniversary.

King William's Town — I had just returned after a long and tiresome day in my mission field, when I tuned in the Lutheran Hour. Thank you for the fearless, loving, and earnest preaching of the Gospel which comes from your station! May the Lord bless you and extend the scope of your witness!

Cape Town — I have just enjoyed your broadcast over the radio for the first time. I was hoping to find something of a deeper nature than the usual programs. What a joy and surprise it was to hear the message of the Gospel!

NATAL

Pietermaritzburg — By accident one day I heard your sermon over the Lourenco Marques station, and ever since I earnestly looked forward to Thursday night. Words cannot adequately convey the religious fervor created in the minds of those who earnestly listen to your mighty and wonderful talks about our Lord. You do indeed bring Christ to the nations.

Creighton — You have simply no idea what the service you send out each week over the radio does for me. It is of great value, I am sure, not only to me but hundreds of other listeners, and has brought blessing to many homes. It is wonderful how the precious Savior has given the means of transmitting his message so many hundreds of miles. We do appreciate the singing, too, which is always beautiful.

South Coast — We belong to the German Lutheran Church at Kirchdorf (Wartburg), Natal, and because it is 110 miles from here, we can't always go, so we tune in your broadcasts. Your literature is very good. My mother-in-law would like very much to read it, but she can't read English, so if you have any in the German language, we would appreciate it very much. I gave these you sent to my father, and he was pleased. We wish you good results with your broadcast and hope that it will soon come to all nations.

NORTHERN RHODESIA

Nkala — Last Sunday I had the great pleasure of tuning in Bringing Christ to the Nations. Will you please send me further information regarding your program? I shall listen each week.

Choma — Tucked away in Central Africa, I have just again listened to your inspiring message. It brought fresh courage and strength to me as we push forward for Christ among sin, superstition, and darkness. Here we have over a hundred youths whom we are endeavoring to train for Christ.

Lusaka — Your radio mission numbers many faithful listeners here in Northern Rhodesia. Please continue to send us your Gospel appeals by means of the radio!

ORANGE FREE STATE

Ladybrand — I find the reading matter you sent very interesting. My prayers will go with you from now onward on the great work you are doing for our great Master.

Petrussteyn — I listen to your program often. It is an inspiration to us.

Ladybrand — I have spoken to lots of people here about your broadcast, and they have promised to listen. I wish you every success.

SOUTHERN RHODESIA

Nyamandhlorre — We have just listened to your weekly broadcast and were greatly blessed. We are living in a remote part of Africa and are not able to get in for services very often; so we always look forward to your broadcast. We assure you that you have our prayers.

Bueanayo — I have often enjoyed your Bringing Christ to the Nations from Lourenco Marques, Portuguese South Africa, and pray God to bless your every effort in the widened field for His glory and the saving of souls. I can use your printed matter for distribution.

Bulawayo — I have just finished listening to your broadcast. I have enjoyed it very much. I am a member of the Baptist Church in Bulawayo.

TRANSVAAL

Germiston — My husband and I listen each Sunday evening to your inspiring messages, as they bring us great joy, to think we can hear the Gospel preached from many miles away. We have accepted Christ as our personal Savior.

Johannesburg — It is really marvelous how through your services we receive so many blessings. No matter how tired I may be at the end of the day, I feel like a different person after I have listened to your message. May God grant that we always have this message sent to us!

Klerksdorn — I must say it is a pleasure when it is time to tune in your messages. To me, each message could be half an hour longer.

WIDESPREAD AUSTRALIAN COVERAGE

The Australian Lutheran Hour marched on during the fifteenth season. Some forty-eight stations were used to cover this vast territory. No other religious broadcast "down under" used so many outlets. We are grateful to our brothers in the faith, the Evangelical Lutheran Church of Australia, for their efficient direction of the broadcast through their representative, the Reverend Clarence Zweck, in charge of our branch office at Adelaide. We regret once more that we can present only a small sampling of letters from the entire continent, which is territorially almost as large as the whole United States; but these excerpts will give our readers a picture of the gratitude and the blessing expressed in many thousands of Australian letters:

NEW SOUTH WALES

Menindie — I am taking the pleasure of thanking you for the comfort I receive through your Lutheran Hour every Sunday afternoon. It gives me great comfort and strength to battle on through the week's toil. I am working here and have no church near by to attend, so you see it helps me on my way.

Sydney — I cannot explain the spiritual blessing I get from the Lutheran Hour, and I know the session really does advocate Jesus Christ as Lord and Savior. This session strengthens me more in my faith in one-half hour than most churches in our district would strengthen me in ten years.

Wallsend — Although I am very busy in the Baptist ministry of the Gospel, I seek to tune in your splendid session wherever practicable. It certainly makes my heart rejoice to hear the Gospel preached in such a sure and clear manner.

QUEENSLAND

Gympie — I have not long ago finished hearing your wonderful message for our Savior Jesus Christ, and I am pleased to be a listener to such a faithful disciple as you. I am a young local preacher in the Methodist Church and a firm believer in Jesus Christ as my Savior and Lord. Will you please send me copies of addresses that you have?

Yandina — I wasn't a Christian, but through your service I became a follower of Christ. May your services and talks inspire many others who have grown cold and indifferent to God's claims upon them!

Bundaberg — We never miss your Sunday evening broadcast, which we think is just wonderful and should be the means of bringing quite a few poor souls to Christ, for this is very necessary. We trust that your broadcast, with God's help, may continue for a long time. May God add His blessings to such a wonderful broadcast!

SOUTH AUSTRALIA

Klemzig — I listened to your address a few minutes ago and decided to write immediately. Although I do not belong to the Lutheran Church, I hear your broadcast for spiritual comfort and guidance, as there is no church of my denomination near by, and my children are too small to travel far. However, since hearing you speak, we have picked up the threads of Christianity again, and our eldest, only three years old, knows that God watches over her.

Taplan — We have listened regularly to your soul-stirring broadcasts on the air each Sunday. This radio program of Bringing Christ to the Nations is eagerly awaited by all the members of the family. I am enclosing a donation, which I hope will help keep this glorious message on the air.

Prospect — I have two little girls, who are never tired of hearing the story of Jesus or anything in any way about Him. They have both been very sick in the past few months, and at times my nerves almost reached the breaking point; but each Sunday afternoon I find time to listen to your sermon, and it makes me feel much better in body and mind.

TASMANIA

Wynyard — We always when possible listen to your sermon. My husband says it is the best program on the air. Only heaven will reveal the good you have done. May God use you still for His glory to the salvation of sinners and the uplift of saints!

Invermay — Please send some more sermons; the others I have read and passed on to neighbors! The sermons helped me, and I know those to whom I have given them will benefit through reading them. We pray continually that God will bless your services for Him more and more.

Forth — My husband and I both listen to your broadcasts regularly and find great help. It seems incredible that so much wisdom and understanding can be passed on to listeners in such a short time. We are both churchgoers, and so are our families, but never do the services give the help the Lutheran Hour does. I hope that many will be brought to Christ through the broadcasts.

VICTORIA

Geelong — Thank you for the sermons which you so ably deliver over the various stations to which I listen! I am an eighty-five-year-old listener, who has heard the preaching of God's Word during his whole life. Now that my faith and hope need to be greater than before because of my age, I find your words the most inspiring I have ever heard.

Kaniva — I have just been listening to your broadcast, and I feel now I would like to write and thank you for the wonderful uplift and brightness it brings into my life. I have listened to it before, and it always seems to bring new hope and new thoughts to me. I wish it were broadcast more often.

Mitcham — This afternoon my husband and I were having afternoon tea, and my husband turned on the wireless. To our astonishment we heard you preaching the Gospel and thoroughly enjoyed every minute of it. I am a member of the Church of Christ; my husband is Presbyterian. We live far from any church building, and being no longer young, we do not often have an opportunity to listen to a Gospel service.

WESTERN AUSTRALIA

Subiaco — On behalf of my husband and myself, thank you for the helpful and uplifting service which comes over the air each Sunday from your church. We listen in each Sunday, as do many of our friends. The splendid inspiring addresses mean much to us; we would not miss a sentence. My husband is not a Christian, but I pray always that something in these deeply spiritual addresses may help him give up the things that now hinder him, and I believe it will be so.

Fremantle — Enclosed is a donation for the Lutheran Hour. Living 180 miles from the station, I found this radio message is a blessing. We have services only every six weeks, and this radio sermon now keeps us over the remaining Sundays. The Gospel session is a blessing to the far-scattered population in this state, where Sunday is mostly spent in sports.

Victoria Park — We have been listening for about eighteen months now and never like to miss your sessions. It is easily the best religious service we get.

CHINA REPORTS

It was our privilege during the fifteenth season to establish a branch office at Shanghai under the direction of Missionary R. J. Mueller. We broadcast in English and Chinese over the superpower station XORA in Shanghai. Among China's 450,000,000 the Holy Spirit has used our broadcast to bless many, and we praise His name for letters like these:

Shanghai — I feel sure that a good number of other people in these parts, like myself, have been both enlightened and uplifted by these messages. I personally enjoy them and often purposely keep any visitors who may be in my home at the time for the Lutheran Hour broadcast. Many of them have been greatly impressed by your speaker's forceful manner of delivery and evident sincerity. The messages do not mince words and are different from the usual sermons heard in our church.

Szechwan — Last Sunday evening we were overjoyed to tune in part of your program. We did enjoy your inspiring and timely message and prayed that God would richly bless you in your good work. Religious programs over the air are difficult to get here, so yours are especially welcome. This comes from a group of evacuee missionaries from North China.

Nyandaw, Maymyo, Burma — I have had the privilege of listening to your Gospel service. May I take this opportunity of thanking you for this Christian message broadcast every Sunday through XGOY. What a source of help and inspiration it has been!

The Reverend R. J. Mueller, Lutheran missionary at Shanghai, China, wrote that one Sunday afternoon, shortly after the conclusion of the Lutheran Hour program, there was a knock at his door. An official of the governmental highway department came in, declared that he had heard the Lutheran Hour broadcasts in Chinese, and asked for instructions in the Christian religion. A few moments later three Chinese young ladies, students at Saint John's University in Shanghai, also appeared at Missionary Mueller's door with a similar request for Christian instruction. All four were instructed and baptized, and the young ladies were later actively helpful in sending out copies of Lutheran Hour addresses and in following up the contacts made possible through the radio mail.

THE PACIFIC ISLANDS HEAR OF CHRIST'S LOVE

It would require a large missionary force to reach only those who hear our broadcast on the islands of the Pacific. During the fifteenth season we secured new outlets in the Philippines and were thus able to work hand in hand with the missionary forces of our Church that began our work in the archipelago. At the outset of the war the powerful transmitter of Station KZRM in Manila was dynamited by its owners so that it would not fall into enemy hands. Yet God's grace gave us seven stations in place of the one that had been lost, to cover the Philippines and the Far East as never before. The powerful superstation in the Fijis helped us bring the Gospel to multitudes. In Hawaii, Stations KIPA in Hilo, KULA and KHON in Honolulu, KTOH in Lihue, Kauai, and KMVI in Wailuku, Mauai, helped us cover these islands with the Gospel. New Zealand, where the radio is under government control and, therefore, closed to religious broadcasts, was regularly supplied from Station HCJB, short wave, Quito, Ecuador. We praise God for using the marvel of the radio in testifying to the Savior's love and in bringing replies like these from many remote places of the Pacific:

FIJI ISLANDS

Suva — I have suddenly taken great interest in your program and will never miss an hour on Sundays.

Suva — I have been listening to your broadcast every Sunday and am very much interested in it.

Suva — I listened to your sermon this evening from my sickbed. It certainly filled my heart with joy and has brought tears to my eyes. The sermon was interesting. I cannot describe in words how much it all meant to me.

HAWAII

Wahiawa — We hear the Lutheran Hour over the Lihue, Kauai, station. Although we are not Lutherans, we appreciate your messages and believe that they are what our nation needs. Therefore we are sending this small contribution to help you continue your great work of broadcasting the Gospel. May God bless your messages to the revival of Christians and the salvation of sinners!

Pearl Harbor — How happy I am that the Lutheran Hour is being broadcast in the Hawaiian Islands! I wish you much success in this undertaking.

Honolulu — It is indeed a pleasure to be able to listen to the Lutheran Hour. I would appreciate a copy of your sermon, also some tracts that I could distribute to help advertise the Lutheran Hour. May the Lord continue to bless your work!

NEW ZEALAND

Auckland — I have just had the pleasure of listening to one of the most inspiring sermons I have heard, delivered by your speaker. The reception here was extremely good and came through KJE8, San Francisco.

Halcombe — It is not often now that I am fortunate enough to be at home or near a wireless on a Thursday afternoon to hear your God-sent Lutheran Hour, because my duties in the post office do not allow me this privilege. Nevertheless, owing to illness, I was home and heard your wonderful sermon today. The reception out here in New Zealand is perfect.

Saint Hilda — Thank you very much for your messages! They have been helpful. It is just lately we have been able to tune in, so that there are still many more helpful messages to hear, and we are beginning to look forward to 3:00 o'clock.

PHILIPPINE ISLANDS

Dumaguete — I am writing this letter of appreciation for the things that I have received recently. They have given us inspiration. You cannot imagine how grateful we are to God and to your broadcast especially this time, when this turbulent world is hanging in the balance. Please accept our congratulations for the achievements of your broadcast!

Manila — I have been a constant listener of your radio broadcast in the Philippines for several months now. It has been my long-felt desire to know more of the truths regarding religious faith, but I have never been fortunate enough to acquire the real knowledge and clear understanding thereof. Since you are offering a Bible course by correspondence, I would like, therefore, to take advantage of the opportunity, trusting that I will be enlightened spiritually by studying the course with your help and guidance.

Manila — Let me extend to you my sincere and heartfelt thanks for your interest and determination in Bringing Christ to the Nations. I am trying my best to transmit your messages personally to my friends here in the university. I know how great are the responsibilities confronting you in the radio mission for the Redeemer. I feel it is my duty to take advantage of the opportunity and also to help in Bringing Christ to the Nations. As for my own opinion, the program is an incomparable blessing to humanity.

FINANCING THE WORLD'S LARGEST BROADCAST

Many in the Lutheran Hour audience do not realize that the broadcast pays for every moment on the air at full station rates. Broadcasting regulations forbid us to mention this or to invite interested listeners to contribute. While we regard this restriction as both unfair and unwarranted, we are happy to acknowledge the Almighty's blessing and the Holy Spirit's guidance in opening the hearts of millions throughout the country to send us the funds required to keep the broadcast on the air. During the fifteenth season our mission of the air cost $1,261,000.00. Listeners contributed $1,256,000.00. We thank the Lord and every contributor for this blessing.

Because the increase of our foreign broadcasting will constantly require larger sums for Bringing Christ to the Nations, we once more call attention to these various methods by which individuals and organizations can help us meet our budget:

1. Personal contributions, deductible from Federal and State income taxes, or congregational gifts can be sent directly to the Lutheran Hour, 3558 South Jefferson Avenue, Saint Louis 18, Missouri.

2. The Acres-for-Christ movement enables farmers to dedicate a portion of their land to the Lord and to give its proceeds to our broadcast.

3. Sponsorship of a foreign broadcasting station (for amounts that range annually from $150 upward) offers a most economical and effective way for individuals or societies to support the Gospel.

4. Memorial-wreath cards, attractively colored folders, available at our office, record the contributions to the broadcast made in memory of a deceased relative or friend.

5. Congregational support. The number of churches which regularly and annually contribute to our cause is growing. Our Saint Louis headquarters office offers Lutheran Hour collection envelopes, together with broadcast literature and other helps, for churches which put the Lutheran Hour

on their budget. Special programs, slide lectures, and rally programs are also offered by headquarters.

6. Special thankofferings. Birthdays, weddings, and anniversaries have frequently become the occasion for thankofferings thoughtfully designated for the Lutheran Hour, dedicated to maintain and support the broadcast.

7. Lutheran Hour annuities. Those who wish to insure their financial support for their old age will be happy to follow this plan, which guarantees a fixed rate of income during one's entire lifetime. Our headquarters will gladly send particulars.

8. Bequests for the broadcast. Friends are beginning to remember the Lutheran Hour in their will. They recognize that our method of spreading the Gospel is one of the most direct, inexpensive, and speedy methods for Gospel preaching. Dr. Eugene R. Bertermann, Director of the Lutheran Hour, 3558 South Jefferson Avenue, Saint Louis 18, Missouri, will gladly send legally acceptable forms for making bequests for the broadcast.

The following letters show the spirit of self-sacrifice and generous stewardship which, under God, combined to see us through fifteen years of increasingly more widespread Gospel broadcasting:

Minnesota — I am sending you a gift of $40.00 to help do my bit in bringing the message of our dear Jesus to the nations. I listen to your Lutheran Hour program, and I just can't say in words how richly I am blessed from it. My sincere prayer is that God will bless and guide you in your wonderful work.

Ohio — This contribution is made for two eleven-year-old Gospel Center boys, who collected 1,060 pounds of waste newspaper and sold it to make up this contribution.

New Hampshire — I am asking your prayers for myself and family. I am sending you the last dollar I have and pray God will bless it by bringing some soul to Him by its use.

Minnesota — Enclosed is a check for $100.00 for your radio work. This is in memory of our dear little granddaughter, who was one year and ten months old when she passed away. She was spastic and could neither walk nor talk, but was so very sweet!

Illinois — Enclosed is a collection taken at our reunion for the Lutheran Hour.

New York — I am sending you one dollar, and I will try and send you a dollar at the first of every month. I have two dollars for my own needs, and if I send half to the Lord, I am well pleased. I listen to the Gospel over the radio every Sunday.

North Dakota — Heaven alone will reveal the good you are doing in Bringing Christ to the Nations. My prayer is that God will keep you well and strong to carry on your work. I thank God for inspiring you to preach the true Gospel. Enclosed is $100.00 as a gift to carry on for saving souls. I am so happy Christ has redeemed me!

Illinois — We are enclosing a check for $25.00 for our Easter gift to help bring Christ to the nations. We listen to the broadcast every Sunday. We find great enjoyment in reading the *Lutheran Hour News* and learning how many people of other churches write in and how the broadcast helps in other countries.

Nebraska — In loving memory of my husband I am sending a contribution to help bring Christ to many people. The broadcast has indeed helped to comfort me in my extreme sorrow. The ways of the Lord are mysterious; may they some day be revealed to us!

Montana — I received the tiny cross several weeks ago. I am sending a contribution, for I want to help you in the blessed work you are doing in preaching the Christ and His love for sinners. I can't really spare it, if I were depending on money for my sustenance. I depend on our omnipotent God. I have proved His love and His mercy over and over again. I know that He will still care for my every need. It is truly blessed to hear you preach Christ. God bless you richly in this work! Please pray for me, for I need constant help in my work of ministry among the needy!

Ohio — I wish to say a few words with the sincere purpose of commending you for the wonderful sermons our family hears on your broadcast. These sermons are truly God's Word and are not the product of man's deductions. They are not contaminated, but are the pure and clear teachings God intended. Many teachers would better themselves by following your example. It is with joy that we forward the enclosed gift. We know that it will be used to strengthen your great work and to bring God's Word in the true form to even more and more people.

Air-Wave Testimony 441

Michigan — I read that you need help to keep the Lutheran Hour on the air. A few days ago I, my children, and other friends celebrated my ninetieth birthday. In thankfulness for that rare occasion I am sending you a check. If you have material that I can use to make the Lutheran Hour better known to neighbors and friends, I will use it and spread it around for the good of our Church.

Wisconsin — Enclosed you will find my contribution to the Lutheran Hour! I am sorry I am unable to send you more. I know my gift isn't large, but hope it will help toward the great expense of Bringing Christ to the Nations. You are doing a wonderful job, and may God bless you in your work! I am sure your broadcast has helped thousands as it has helped me.

Washington — Because I received a salary bonus, it gives me an opportunity to make this offering to you for the Lord's work. I wish it were more, but there are too many other ministering agencies to whom a similar offering is going. I pray that the Lord will multiply this little seed into a bountiful harvest through your work.

Michigan — Enclosed is a tithe for the last two months. As during the past year, I hope to be able to send you a monthly tithe for the radio fund. It is my prayer that God may bestow His richest blessings upon all who are in any way connected with the program, and that He will give you the spiritual and physical strength to continue to bring Christ to the nations.

New York — Once again it is my pleasure to express to the Lutheran Hour my sincere thanks and appreciation for your wonderful work and for the great benefit I derive therefrom. Enclosed is my check, which I send in memory of my mother, who passed into life eternal last spring. I am happy to tell you that she always listened to your messages and died in the Lord Jesus.

New York — Please find a check donated by the ladies' aid society of our dissolved Saint Paul's Evangelical and Reformed Church, to be used toward your splendid radio work!

WITH DEEP GRATITUDE

To avoid all possibility of misunderstanding, we restate the foundation fact with which this foreword began: "All broadcast blessings come from God." How gratefully, then, we personally acknowledge His help and the demonstration that His divine strength has used our human weakness! How thankfully, too, Christians all over the world should behold the demonstration of His almighty power and recognize that the Lord can use small numbers for mighty purposes. Without Christ we can do nothing. Without the Holy Spirit's blessings our efforts would have been in vain. Above everything we deserved, the Almighty has used the broadcast for marvelous purposes. To Him be all glory and honor!

However, even the Lord uses human agencies in building His kingdom, and we give our thanks to these groups and individuals who have consistently and unselfishly helped us:

The Lutheran Laymen's League, sponsors of the broadcast, and especially these men, members of the operating committee in Saint Louis: Oscar P. Brauer, William H. Lahrmann, Alfred T. Leimbach, John Fleischli, T. G. Eggers, and Dr. Eugene R. Bertermann.

The many thousands of friends who throughout the country worked, gave, prayed, and testified for the broadcast. Without their intercessions and their material help, as blessed by God, our broadcast could not have reached the remarkable blessings it has recorded. God richly bless them!

The pastors and teachers throughout the country who spoke for the broadcast, prayed for it, and unselfishly helped in guiding and instructing those who were brought to the faith.

The Radio Director, Dr. Eugene R. Bertermann. Without his self-effacing help by day and night it would have been impossible for me to maintain the many contacts required for the successful operation of the broadcast. No task was too difficult for him if only he could help speed the course of the Gospel.

The Lutheran Hour announcers, the Reverend Elmer J. Knoernschild for the network programs and Professor Louis J. Menking for the transcription programs, and more than a dozen others who serve in the foreign language broadcasts.

The choruses which have helped beautify the programs. Particularly do we pay our tribute to the Concordia Seminary students in the Lutheran Hour Chorus and their director, Bernhard Kurzweg, who unselfishly gave much of their time to furnish their widely acclaimed musical background to the broadcasts. At the conclusion of the fifteenth season this chorus made an extended tour throughout the eastern half of the United States, singing to approximately fourteen thousand people in many audiences. The Saint Louis Lutheran Hour Chorus, under the direction of E. W. Schroeter, also rendered helpful and consecrated service in supplying the musical background for the Lutheran Hour programs, particularly during the summer and the holiday seasons. As a matter of record, the Saint Louis Lutheran Hour Chorus sang over a larger number of broadcasts than any other single musical organization. With deep appreciation we also acknowledge the local choruses featured in programs which originated outside Saint Louis. None of those who thus praised the Lord in song accepted salaries for their services.

The summer speakers, the Reverend Professor Oswald Hoffmann, the Reverend Lawrence Acker, the Reverend Oliver R. Harms, the Reverend Edwin Pieplow, and the Reverend Doctor John W. Behnken. All these broadcast the glorious Gospel. May our merciful Savior always remember them!

The Lutheran Hour Office. About a hundred workers, under the direction of Wilbur H. Wiese, office manager, enthusiastically discharged the tremendous tasks placed upon them by this broadcast. We thank them sincerely and in the Savior's name.

The Mutual Broadcasting Company, the World Broadcasting Company, the Gotham Advertising Company, and the Pan American Broadcasting Company, all played a prominent and co-operative part in bringing the broadcast to its present wide scope.

My personal staff of advisers and assistants: Dr. William Arndt, who read each message before broadcasting and before printing; Miss Harriet E. Schwenk, in charge of my office, who helped prepare the manuscript for the press and generously served in many other ways; Mrs. Bernhard Keiser and Miss Lucille Biehl, who generously contributed their time without compensation.

Especially my dear wife, who, whether in Saint Louis or on the arduous traveling to broadcast outside the city, gladly took dictation in connection with the messages and helped in ways too numerous to mention.

As this volume makes its appearance in a day of growing unbelief and increasing atheism, we beseech the God who has unfailingly helped us in the past to bless each page in the lives of doubters or unbelievers and to use the printed page for the same purpose as He has mercifully employed each broadcast, to lead souls to His Son, our blessed and all-sufficient Savior, whom to know is life eternal!

WALTER ARTHUR MAIER

"Adorn the doctrine of God our Savior in all things."
TITUS 2:10